D1475126

ROYALTY AND DIPLOMACY
IN EUROPE, 1890–1914

This book examines the diplomatic role of royal families in the era before the outbreak of the First World War. It argues that previous historians have neglected for political reasons the important political and diplomatic role of monarchs during the period. In so doing, it opens up an alternative approach that places monarchs at the centre of diplomatic developments in the last years of peace before 1914.

Particular attention is given to the Prusso-German, Russian and British monarchies. The Prusso-German and Russian monarchies played a central role in their countries' diplomacy and foreign policy, primarily as a result of their control over diplomatic and political appointments. However, the book also argues that the British monarchy played a much more influential role in British diplomacy than has been accepted hitherto by historians.

Individual themes examined include relations between the Prussian and Russian monarchies in the era of Kaiser Wilhelm II and Tsar Nicholas II, the political significance of the ill-feeling between Willhelm II and his uncle King Edward VII, the role of Edward VII in British diplomacy, and the impact of royal visits on Anglo-German relations before 1914. The book argues that royal influence in diplomacy remained a political reality in early twentieth-century Europe. The analysis is supported by a wealth of archival evidence, much of which has never before been brought to light.

RODERICK R. MCLEAN was educated at the Universities of Edinburgh and Sussex, and subsequently taught at Edinburgh and the University of Glasgow. He is now employed by the Scottish Executive.

NEW STUDIES IN EUROPEAN HISTORY

Edited by
PETER BALDWIN
University of California, Los Angeles
CHRISTOPHER CLARK
St Catharine's College, Cambridge
JAMES B. COLLINS
Georgetown University
MIA RODRÍGUEZ-SALGADO
London School of Economics and Political Science
LYNDAL ROPER
Royal Holloway, University of London

This is a new series of scholarly monographs in early modern and modern European history. Its aim is to publish outstanding works of research, addressed to important themes across a wide geographical range, from southern and central Europe, to Scandinavia and Russia, and from the time of the Renaissance to the Second World War. As it develops the series will comprise focused works of wide contextual range and intellectual ambition.

ROYALTY AND DIPLOMACY IN EUROPE
1890–1914

RODERICK R. MCLEAN

CAMBRIDGE
UNIVERSITY PRESS

PUBLISHED BY THE PRESS SYNDICATE OF THE UNIVERSITY OF CAMBRIDGE
The Pitt Building, Trumpington Street, Cambridge, United Kingdom

CAMBRIDGE UNIVERSITY PRESS
The Edinburgh Building, Cambridge, CB2 2RU, UK   http://www.cup.cam.ac.uk
40 West 20th Street, New York, NY 10011–4211, USA   http://www.cup.org
10 Stamford Road, Oakleigh, Melbourne 3166, Australia
Ruiz de Alarcón 13, 28014 Madrid, Spain

First published 2001

Printed in the United Kingdom at the University Press, Cambridge

Typeset in Baskerville 11/12.5pt [VN]

A catalogue record for this book is available from the British Library

Library of Congress Cataloguing in Publication data
McLean, Roderick R., 1969–
Royalty and diplomacy in Europe, 1890–1914 / Roderick R. McLean.
p.   cm.
Includes bibliographical references.
ISBN 0 521 59200 3
1. Great Britain – Foreign relations – Germany.   2. Great Britain –
Foreign relations – 1901–1910.   3. Great Britain – Foreign relations – 1910–1936.
4. Germany – Foreign relations – Great Britain.   5. Germany – Foreign
relations – 1888–1918.   6. Germany – Foreign relations – Russia.   7. Russia–
Foreign relations – Germany.   8. Europe – Kings and rulers.   I. Title.
DA47.2.M27 2000
327.41043–dc21   00-023691

ISBN 0 521 59200 3 hardback

To my parents and to Frédérique

Contents

List of illustrations		*page* viii
Acknowledgements		ix
List of abbreviations		xi
	Introduction	1
1	The Kaiser and the Tsar: German–Russian dynastic relations, 1888–1914	15
2	Uncle and nephew: Edward VII, Wilhelm II and the Anglo-German dynastic antagonism before 1914	73
3	King Edward VII and British diplomacy, 1901–1910	141
4	The limits of dynastic diplomacy: royal visits and Anglo-German relations, 1906–1914	186
5	Conclusion	211
	Bibliography	215
	Index	231

Illustrations

Between pages 140 and 141

1 Victoria, Kaiserin Friedrich of Germany, March 1891
2 Queen Victoria, 1893
3 Group, Coburg, April 1894, at the time of the wedding of Princess Victoria Melita of Saxe-Coburg-Gotha and Ernest Louis, Grand Duke of Hesse
4 Queen Victoria's funeral procession, Windsor, February 1901
5 Kaiser Wilhelm II, 1901
6 King Edward VII, *c.* 1902
7 Queen Alexandra, *c.* 1903
8 King Edward VII and Tsar Nicholas II on board the imperial yacht *Standart*, Reval, June 1908
9 Royal party at Windsor, during the Kaiser's visit in November 1907
10 Tsar Nicholas II, signed and dated 'Cowes, Aug. 1909'
11 Group, Barton Manor, 4 August 1909
12 Nine sovereigns at Windsor for the funeral of King Edward VII, 20 May 1910
13 King George V, 1912
14 Kaiserin Augusta Victoria, 1913
15 King George V and Tsar Nicholas II in Berlin, May 1913, for the wedding of Princess Victoria Louise of Prussia and Ernest Augustus, Duke of Brunswick

I would like to record my thanks to Her Majesty The Queen for granting me permission to publish the photographs, all of which come from the Royal Archives, Windsor Castle.

Acknowledgements

I wish to acknowledge the assistance and encouragement which various institutions and individuals have given me during the years that I have been working on this project. First, I would like to express my thanks to Her Majesty The Queen for permission to consult material held at the Royal Archives relating to her great-grandfather, King Edward VII. I also wish to acknowledge the help of Lady Sheila de Bellaigue, the Registrar of the Royal Archives, and her staff, for their hospitality during my research trips to Windsor. Thanks are due to the following archives and individuals for permission to quote from private papers held by them: the Syndics of Cambridge University Library in respect of the Hardinge Papers, Lord Esher, in respect of the Esher Papers, the Trustees of the Broadlands Archives in respect of the Broadlands Archives, the Public Records Office, London, in respect of the Grey, Lascelles and Lansdowne Papers, and the Trustees of the National Library of Scotland in respect of the Elibank, Haldane and Rosebery Papers.

In Germany, I owe a particular debt to H.R.H. the late Princess Margaret of Hesse, for granting me permission to consult the correspondence of Grand Duke Ernst Ludwig of Hesse, and to Professor Franz of the Hessisches Staatsarchiv in Darmstadt. However, I also wish to thank the staff of the following archives: the Geheimes Staatsarchiv, Berlin, the Geheimes Staatsarchiv, Merseburg, and the Politisches Archiv des Auswärtigen Amtes in Bonn. In addition, I wish to acknowledge the assistance of the staff of the various libraries in which I have worked: the Sussex University Library, the British Library, the German Historical Institute, London, and the National Library of Scotland in Edinburgh.

For the financial support which sustained me as a research student, I thank the Scottish Education Department for granting me a three-year bursary, and for extra funds to support my research expenses while in Germany.

I would like to thank the examiners of the D. Phil. thesis on which much of this book is based, Ms Beryl Williams, of Sussex University, and Dr Christopher Clark, of St Catharine's College, Cambridge. However, I owe my greatest academic debt to two individuals. I would like to thank Mr Terry Cole of Edinburgh University, who first awakened my interest in the role of monarchs in European diplomacy. Above all, however, I would like to thank my supervisor at Sussex, Professor John Röhl, for encouraging my research at every stage and for his extremely useful advice. On a more personal level, I wish to thank my family for their support during the many years that it has taken to bring this project to completion. This book is dedicated to my parents and to my partner, Frédérique, who have shown remarkable patience in the face of my obsession with long-dead European dynasts.

Abbreviations

BD	*British Documents on the Origins of the War, 1898–1914*, ed. G. P. Gooch and Harold Temperley, 11 vols. (London, 1926–38)
BKW	*Briefe Kaiser Wilhelms II. an den Zaren 1894–1914*, ed. W. Goetz (Berlin, 1920)
DDF	*Documents diplomatiques français, 1871–1914*, Ministère des Affaires Etrangères, 32 vols. (Paris, 1929–62)
DdR	Chlodwig Fürst zu Hohenlohe-Schillingsfürst, *Denkwürdigkeiten der Reichskanzlerzeit*, ed. Alexander von Müller (Berlin, 1931)
EK	*Philipp Eulenburgs politische Korrespondenz*, ed. John C. G. Röhl, 3 vols. (Boppard am Rhein, 1975–83)
ESHR	Esher Papers, Churchill College, Cambridge
GP	*Die grosse Politik der europäischen Kabinette, 1871–1914*, ed. Johannes Lepsius et al., 40 vols. (Berlin, 1922–7)
GStA Berlin (BPH)	Geheimes Staatsarchiv Preussischer Kulturbesitz, Berlin (Brandenburg-Preussisches Hausarchiv)
GStA Merseburg (HA)	Geheimes Staatsarchiv Preussischer Kulturbesitz, Merseburg (Haus Archiv)
HNP	*Botschafter Paul Graf von Hatzfeldt: nachgelassene Papiere 1838–1901*, ed. Gerhard Ebel, 2 vols. (Boppard am Rhein, 1976–7)
HP	*The Holstein Papers*, ed. Norman Rich and M. H. Fisher, 4 vols. (Cambridge, 1955–63)
HStA Darmstadt	Hessisches Staatsarchiv, Darmstadt

LQV	*The Letters of Queen Victoria*, ed. George E. Buckle, 3rd series, 3 vols. (London, 1930–2)
ÖUA	*Österreich-Ungarns Aussenpolitik von der Bosnischen Krise 1908 bis zum Kriegsausbruch 1914*, ed. Ludwig Bittner and Hans Uebersberger, 8 vols. (Vienna, 1930)
PA Bonn	Politisches Archiv des Auswärtigen Amtes, Bonn
PRO FO	Public Records Office, London, Foreign Office
RA	Royal Archives, Windsor Castle

Introduction

On the eve of the outbreak of the First World War in 1914, all the major powers of Europe, except France, were monarchical states. The extent of the power of the monarch over individual areas of state policy varied from country to country. In Russia, the power of the Tsar was unlimited until 1905, in theory if not in practice, whereas in Britain, two centuries of political evolution, dating back to the conflict between crown and parliament in the seventeenth century, had by the end of the nineteenth century created a situation in which the power of the monarchy had been greatly eroded. Between these two extremes, politically and geographically, lay the German empire, a state where a national parliament existed, but where the right to appoint government ministers, together with considerable powers regarding foreign and military policy, continued to be the prerogative of the Emperor.

The statements made above ought to be uncontroversial. Indeed, a standard textbook states that in Europe before 1914 'the monarchs were justified in considering themselves the most important persons in the ... political arena.'[1] However, if one examines the historiography, a very different impression emerges. Monarchs are either almost completely ignored,[2] or else they are treated as decorative irrelevances, whose high-profile visits abroad were insignificant politically,[3] and whose advisers had the dominant voice in decision-making and the conduct of foreign policy.[4]

The central aim of the present study is to seek to redress this imbalance in academic research through an examination of the diplomatic

---

[1] Felix Gilbert and David C. Large, *The End of the European Era, 1890 to the Present* (London and New York, 1991), p. 20.

[2] Hans-Ulrich Wehler, *The German Empire, 1871–1918*, English translation (Leamington Spa, 1985).

[3] G. W. Monger, *The End of Isolation. British Foreign Policy, 1900–1907* (London, 1963); Zara S. Steiner, *The Foreign Office and Foreign Policy, 1898–1914* (Cambridge, 1969).

[4] W. L. Langer, *The Diplomacy of Imperialism, 1890–1902*, 2nd edition (New York, 1965); A. J. P. Taylor, *The Struggle for Mastery in Europe, 1848–1918* (Oxford, 1954).

role of monarchs in the years preceding the outbreak of war in 1914. Previous attempts to study international relations in this era have not been wholly convincing because they have failed to take into account the fact that in addition to socio-economic factors, and diplomatic decision-making at the governmental level, a further component has to be taken into consideration. In Europe before the First World War, the political views and prejudices of monarchs, together with the changing relationships between the dynasties themselves, could, in certain circumstances, have a bearing on relations between different states and on the future of Europe as a whole. To write the history of a continent in which monarchy was the prevalent form of government without reference to the monarchs themselves represents a distortion of the past.

In general two historiographical 'schools' have dominated the study of international relations, in turn, since 1945. Until the 1960s, history writing was dominated by a genre which can be characterised as the 'bureaucratic' school. Historians of this type sought to analyse foreign policy and diplomacy from the perspective of governments and diplomats. They paid only limited attention to the domestic pressures which inevitably influenced the contexts in which decisions were made, and played down the importance of 'anachronistic' individuals and institutions, such as monarchs and royal courts, in the conduct of diplomacy.[5]

Since the 1960s, historians have turned their attention towards the social and economic pressures which influenced the formation and conduct of foreign policy, placing much emphasis on the processes of modernization within European society. Thus, considerable attention has been given to issues such as industrialization, the creation of a mass society, and the rise of democratic and revolutionary forces on the European continent. As a consequence, declining elements within European society, such as artisans, peasants, aristocrats and monarchs, have become increasingly marginalised in academic history. A concern that contemporary scholarship was in danger of predating Europe's transition to modernity led the American historian, Arno J. Mayer, to write a book in which he sought to emphasise the continued vitality of certain pre-industrial elements in Europe before 1914. In doing so, he put forward a powerful case for a change in the direction of historical research.[6] Mayer's attempt to stress 'the persistence of the old' contrasted sharply with a more orthodox view of turn of the century Europe set out shortly afterwards by Norman Stone. Stone concentrated on the

---

[5] Taylor, *Struggle for Mastery in Europe*, xx-xxxiv, p. 428.
[6] Arno J. Mayer, *The Persistence of the Old Régime: Europe to the Great War* (London, 1981), pp. 5–11.

forces of modernization which began to change the social, economic and, to a lesser extent, political structure of Europe before 1914. His analysis of economic and social change was simultaneously wide-ranging and penetrating. However, the political role of monarchs was rarely addressed, and when it did receive a mention, it was usually in dismissive terms.[7]

An analysis of modern historical scholarship as it has been applied to the history of individual countries supplies some of the clues as to the relative neglect of monarchy as an institution, and monarchs as individuals, by historians. The example of the historiography of Wilhelmine Germany is instructive in this regard. The tragic history of Germany in the twentieth century has contributed towards certain peculiarities in the approach of German historians to their own country's past.[8] In the 1920s, German historians sought to dispel the stigma of war guilt which had been attached to their country by the victors in the Treaty of Versailles.[9] In Klaus Hildebrand's view, the problem with this genre of research was that political interests took precedence over empirical knowledge.[10] Even the great collection of documents on German diplomacy before 1914, *Die grosse Politik der europäischen Kabinette*,[11] the most important bequest of the historians of the 1920s to those of today, was, as Hildebrand and Barbara Vogel have pointed out, selectively edited in order to remove material deemed damaging to the cause of German rehabilitation into the international community.[12] Two of Germany's leading historians in the inter-war years, Hans Delbrück and Erich Brandenburg, even went so far as to blame Russia and France for the outbreak of the First World War,[13] as did retired diplomats in their memoirs.[14]

---

[7] Norman Stone, *Europe Transformed, 1878–1919* (London, 1983), pp. 205–6.

[8] Klaus Hildebrand, *Deutsche Aussenpolitik, 1871–1914* (Munich, 1990); Richard J. Evans, 'Wilhelmine Germany and the Historians', in *Society and Politics in Wilhelmine Germany*, ed. Richard J. Evans (London, 1978), pp. 12–28; David Blackbourn, *Populists and Patricians: Essays in Modern German History* (Oxford, 1987), pp. 11–24; James Retallack, 'Wilhelmine Germany', in *Modern Germany Reconsidered, 1870–1945*, ed. Gordon Martel (London, 1992), pp. 33–40.

[9] Cf. Holger Herwig, 'Clio Deceived. Patriotic Self-Censorship in Germany after the Great War', *International Security* 12, 2 (1987), 5–44.

[10] Hildebrand, *Deutsche Aussenpolitik*, p. 54.

[11] Johannes Lepsius et al. (eds.), *Die grosse Politik der europäischen Kabinette, 1871–1914. Sammlung der diplomatischen Akten des auswärtigen Amtes*, 40 vols. (Berlin, 1922–27).

[12] Hildebrand, *Deutsche Aussenpolitik*, pp. 54–7; Barbara Vogel, *Deutsche Russlandpolitik, 1900–1906: Das Scheitern der deutschen Weltpolitik unter Bülow 1900–1906* (Düsseldorf, 1973), pp. 8, 173.

[13] Hildebrand, *Deutsche Aussenpolitik*, p. 66.

[14] Freiherr von Schoen, *The Memoirs of an Ambassador. A Contribution to the Political History of Modern Times*, English translation (London, 1922), pp. 215–50.

After the defeat of the Nazi dictatorship, and the division of Germany which resulted from this, historians in West Germany sought to emphasise that Hitler's régime had been an aberration, out of keeping with the development of Germany in previous generations towards a civilised, modern society. As in the 1920s, the political motives for this approach were obvious. By arguing that German traditions were embodied by 'great men', such as Luther and Frederick the Great, and by worthy bureaucrats, such as Bethmann Hollweg, they sought to play down German guilt and responsibility for the Nazi régime and the Holocaust. As John Röhl has pointed out,[15] the political motives of the historians also had the effect of marginalising Germany's last monarch, Kaiser Wilhelm II, from scholarly discussion of the period of German history which bears his name. The last Kaiser, whose style of government was characterised by a tendency to make belligerent speeches, and whose neurotic personality led Edward VII's close friend Lord Esher to conclude that he had inherited the madness of King George III,[16] was passed over in embarrassed silence by historians who were more interested in discontinuity than continuity between the Second *Reich* and the Third *Reich*.

The publication of a major book on Germany's war aims in the First World War by Professor Fritz Fischer, in 1961,[17] shattered the comfortable assumptions of the conservative, nationalist historians with regard to their country's recent past. Fischer argued that Germany pursued an expansionist policy during the Great War, which prefigured the aims of the Nazis in the Second World War. He followed this argument up in a later work, in which he argued that the German leadership had systematically planned, as early as December 1912, to unleash a European war in the summer of 1914.[18]

The 'Fischer controversy' had two major consequences which concern the historian of foreign policy and monarchy. First, although Fischer and his colleagues were not hostile to the discussion of the role of personalities, his conservative opponents sought to deflect attention from the disturbing continuities, which Fischer had discovered in early twentieth-century German history, by contrasting the good qualities of

---

[15] John C. G. Röhl, 'Introduction', in *Kaiser Wilhelm II: New Interpretations*, ed. John C. G. Röhl and Nicolaus Sombart, (Cambridge, 1982), pp. 2–3.

[16] Lord Esher, journal entry, 21 November 1908, Esher Papers, Churchill College, Cambridge, ESHR 2/11.

[17] Fritz Fischer, *Griff nach der Weltmacht* (Düsseldorf, 1961); English translation: *Germany's Aims in the First World War* (London, 1967).

[18] Fritz Fischer, *Krieg der Illusionen. Die deutsche Politik von 1911 bis 1914* (Düsseldorf, 1969), pp. 231–5; English translation: *War of Illusions: German Policies from 1911–1914* (London, 1975).

Bethmann Hollweg with those of the evil Hitler. The abuse of the role of personalities by Fischer's opponents caused the generation of historians which emerged in the 1960s to shy away from explanations which gave weight to the behaviour of individuals in favour of approaches which stressed impersonal factors.

In the aftermath of the Fischer controversy, a new school of historians came to dominate historical scholarship of the German empire within West Germany. Taking on board much of Fischer's evidence concerning continuities in German history, they sought to analyse the structure of German society in the Wilhelmine era in order to understand the reasons for the rise of the Nazis in the 1930s. The technical German name for this type of historiography is *Gesellschaftsgeschichte* or the 'history of society'. Its leading practitioner is Professor Hans-Ulrich Wehler, whose history of the *Kaiserreich* has become standard reading for students of the period.[19] The model of interpretation favoured by Wehler was referred to by one of his opponents as representing the 'new orthodoxy' in the study of imperial Germany,[20] whereas another critic of Wehler's warned that *Gesellschaftsgeschichte* risked stifling debate on the history of the *Kaiserreich*.[21]

As sceptics were quick to point out, many of the theoretical and ideological standpoints which characterised *Gesellschaftsgeschichte* were flawed. One British historian noted that the revisionist historians who emerged in West Germany in the 1960s 'retained much of the framework favoured by their conservative opponents but turned the moral judgements upside down'.[22] Thus, the attention given previously by historians to foreign policy was replaced by the doctrine of 'the primacy of domestic politics' – a belief that the foreign policy of Bismarckian and Wilhelmine Germany was part of a manipulative strategy on the part of the country's pre-industrial élites, who wished to deflect the attention of the masses away from aspirations for democracy or social revolution.[23] The sociologist Max Weber was one of the key intellectual influences on the practitioners of *Gesellschaftsgeschichte*. Weber's own conviction that the faulty political structure of imperial Germany, rather than the unstable personality of Wilhelm II, was the root cause of the empire's political malaise,[24] helps to explain why Wehler almost completely ignored the

---

[19] Wehler, *German Empire*.   [20] Röhl, 'Introduction', p. 5.
[21] T. Nipperdey, 'Wehlers Kaiserreich. Eine kritische Auseinandersetzung', *Geschichte und Gesellschaft* 1 (1975), 539–40.
[22] Blackbourn, *Populists*, p. 14.   [23] Wehler, *German Empire*, p. 177.
[24] Max Weber to Friedrich Naumann, 12 November 1908, M. Rainer Lepsius and Wolfgang J. Mommsen (eds.), *Max Weber. Briefe, 1906–1908* (Tübingen, 1990), p. 694.

role of the Kaiser in his analysis of the *Kaiserreich*. A Weberian influence on the system of government, rather than the personalities of the political actors, was complimented in *Gesellschaftsgeschichte* by a historically determinist view of the development of German society, clearly derived from Karl Marx.

By the end of the 1980s, *Gesellschaftsgeschichte* was reckoned even in Germany, 'to have failed as a theoretical model and methodological concept', and it was criticised by Lothar Gall for the 'banality of the argumentation, the "relativity" of the perspective and the "dependence and historicity" of its approach'.[25] The credibility of the Marxist theories of *Gesellschaftsgeschichte*, and the belief of its practitioners that the course of history could be determined, was dealt a fatal blow by the collapse of the GDR in 1989, which none of them had predicted. In addition, they had always stressed that structures rather than personalities were the crucial factors in the historical process, yet the collapse of the Honecker régime was made possible by the decision of the Soviet leader, Mikhail Gorbachev, not to intervene. Thus the events of 1989–90 proved in an emphatic manner that individuals can, in certain circumstances, leave a profound mark on the course of history. It was a development with which the revisionist historians had difficulty coming to terms.[26]

However, Wehler's thesis had come under sustained attack long before the late 1980s. His characterisation of the *Reich*'s constitution under Bismarck as a 'Bonapartist dictatorship based on plebiscitary support and operating within the framework of a semi-absolutist, pseudo-constitutional military monarchy'[27] was derided by Otto Pflanze as a distortion of the historical reality. Pflanze observed that, although Wehler was hostile to a discussion of the role of individuals in history, paradoxically, he seemed to attribute the powers of a Machiavellian genius to Bismarck. Pflanze was also concerned by Wehler's tendency to give theoretical models, drawn from Marx and Weber, precedence in his work over empirical evidence.[28]

Wehler's analysis of Wilhelmine Germany has similarly been the

---

[25] Gregor Schöllgen (ed.), *Escape into War? The Foreign Policy of Imperial Germany*, English translation (Oxford, 1990), p. 5; Lothar Gall, 'Deutsche Gesellschaftsgeschichte', *Historische Zeitschrift* 248 (1989), 365–74.

[26] Jürgen Kocha, 'Überraschung und Erklärung. Was die Umbrüche von 1989/90 für die Gesellschaftsgeschichte bedeuten könnten', in *Was ist Gesellschaftsgeschichte?*, ed. Manfred Hettling (Munich, 1991), pp. 11–21.

[27] Wehler, *German Empire*, p. 60.

[28] Otto Pflanze, 'Bismarcks Herrschaftstecknik als Problem der gegenwärtigen Historiographie', *Historiche Zeitschrift* 234 (1982), 561–99.

subject of attack from historians. Wehler asserted that after Bismarck's dismissal, there was 'a permanent crisis of the state behind its façade of high-handed leadership'. He dismissed the idea that Wilhelm II was the dominant political figure in Berlin, preferring the view that power had been exercised by 'the traditional oligarchies in conjunction with the anonymous forces of an authoritarian polycracy'.[29] John Röhl, in particular, has made perceptive criticisms of Wehler's characterisation of the power structure of the Second *Reich*. In his view, there is no evidence to support Wehler's claim that there was a permanent political crisis after 1890. Röhl also took Wehler to task for denying the significance of Wilhelm II, when the last Kaiser's contemporaries were convinced of his central importance in German politics. In addition, both Röhl and Geoff Eley have pointed out that Wehler's theory of power had a comforting aspect, which, by placing all the blame on an unnamed élite, absolved the vast majority of the German people from blame for the disastrous course of German history between 1871 and 1945, when the historical reality was more complex and disturbing.[30] In addition, Wehler's stress on 'the primacy of domestic politics' was understandably criticised by diplomatic historians. Klaus Hildebrand, in particular, castigated Wehler for seeking to substitute *Gesellschaftsgeschichte* for the history of foreign policy. He pointed out that *Gesellschaftsgeschichte*, which set out to understand the dynamics of industrial society, failed to recognise that many of the concepts used to describe international rivalry, such as 'hegemony' and the 'balance of power', were in existence long before the industrial age, and were not changed fundamentally by its consequences.[31]

The relative ascendancy of *Gesellschaftsgeschichte*, and its opposition to the discussion of the role of personalities in politics, together with the dominant preference of historiography in general for social and economic approaches, contributed to the neglect of the role of courts and monarchs by German historians down to the 1980s. However, research on the *Kaiserreich* by British and American scholars has contributed,

[29] Wehler, *German Empire*, pp. 62–4.
[30] Röhl, 'Introduction', p. 19; John C. G. Röhl, *Kaiser, Hof und Staat: Wilhelm II. und die deutsche Politik* (Munich, 1987), pp. 119–20; English translation: *The Kaiser and his Court: Wilhelm II and the Government of Germany* (Cambridge, 1994); Geoff Eley, 'Recent Works in Modern German History', *Historical Journal* 23, 2 (1980), 463–79.
[31] Klaus Hildebrand, 'Geschichte oder "Gesellschaftsgeschichte"? Die Notwendigkeit einer politischen Geschichtsschreibung von den internationalen Beziehungen', *Historische Zeitschrift* 223 (1976), 328–57; Hildebrand, *Deutsche Aussenpolitik*, pp. 99–106.

recently, to a greater level of academic interest in the role of Kaiser Wilhelm II in German politics. This research is above all associated with the work of John Röhl.

In a path-breaking analysis, published in 1967, Röhl reopened the controversy as to whether there was a monarchical 'personal régime' in Wilhelmine Germany.[32] He asserted that such a régime had existed, and backed up his thesis with the aid of many primary sources which had never been examined by historians before. He claimed that by 1897, through his control over bureaucratic appointments, and under the guidance of his confidant, Philipp Eulenburg, Wilhelm II had managed to create a government committed to putting his wishes into practice. The Kaiser's power was, in turn, bolstered by his personal military, naval and civil cabinets, which became instruments of monarchical authority. He countered the argument that Wilhelm could not have ruled personally by placing emphasis on the imperative of the executive to act in line with the monarch's wishes.[33] The reception of Röhl's book by the practitioners of *Gesellschaftsgeschichte* was predictably unfavour-able,[34] but it is more generally considered to have contained a 'pioneer-ing' thesis, which 'set a new standard of archival scholarship for work on Wilhelmine political history'.[35]

Since the 1960s, Röhl has refined his argument in the light of new discoveries, and in response to his critics. He has introduced the concept of 'negative personal rule' to refer to the measures which government officials did not initiate because they appreciated that the Kaiser and his courtiers would oppose them.[36] In addition, he has placed emphasis on the 'kingship mechanism', whereby all government officials were forced to court the favour of the Kaiser if they wished to reach the heights of power and influence.[37] His edition of the correspondence of Philipp Eulenburg revealed much new information about the high politics of Wilhelmine Germany,[38] as did the work of one of the historians inspired by Röhl, Isabel Hull, on Wilhelm II's entourage.[39] Even previously

---

[32] John C. G. Röhl, *Germany without Bismarck: The Crisis of Government in the Second Reich, 1890–1900* (London, 1967).

[33] *Ibid.*, p. 279.

[34] Wehler, *German Empire*, p. 274, note 34.

[35] Geoff Eley, 'The View from the Throne: The Personal Rule of Kaiser Wilhelm II', *Historical Journal* 28, 2 (1985), 471.

[36] Röhl, 'Introduction', p. 15.

[37] Röhl, *Kaiser, Hof und Staat*, pp. 116–40.

[38] John C. G. Röhl (ed.), *Philipp Eulenburgs politische Korrespondenz*, 3 vols. (Boppard am Rhein, 1976–83).

[39] Isabel V. Hull, *The Entourage of Kaiser Wilhelm II, 1888–1918* (Cambridge, 1982).

sceptical historians, such as Wolfgang Mommsen, have found it impossible to ignore the results of this research.[40]

However, debate over the reality of 'personal rule' has continued. Geoff Eley stressed the practical limits on Wilhelm II's authority, and claimed that there was a reduction in his political involvement after 1900,[41] as did Volker Berghahn in a recent textbook.[42] Hull, in a convincing rebuttal to Eley's argument, emphasised that he had failed to come to terms fully with the significance of Röhl's stress on the 'kingship mechanism' and 'negative personal rule'. She noted that Eley had concentrated his argument on domestic politics, whereas foreign and military policy were the spheres where the Kaiser's personal powers were most evident. Hull observed that there was much evidence, even after 1900, that Wilhelm II had played a key role in these areas. In addition, she refuted Eley's contention that Bernhard von Bülow, the Chancellor from 1900–1909, was able to pursue his own policies, independent of the Kaiser,[43] as did a recent major study of Bülow's chancellorship.[44] New research on the German monarchy has not been restricted solely to the issue of 'personal rule'. Prior to the 1980s, no academic historian had written a biography of Wilhelm II based on primary sources. However, in the last few years, several have appeared, most notably by Lamar Cecil and John Röhl.[45] One historian has even established that Wilhelm II's role during the First World War was more significant than his image as a 'shadow emperor' during this period would suggest.[46] Thus, the absence of studies of the Kaiser himself, which represented a shaming gap in the historiography of the period of German history associated with him, is now being rectified.

However, although the German monarchy may now be taken seriously

---

[40] Wolfgang J. Mommsen, 'Kaiser Wilhelm II and German Politics', *Journal of Contemporary History* 25 (1990), 289–316.

[41] Eley, 'The View from the Throne', 469–85.

[42] Volker R. Berghahn, *Imperial Germany, 1871–1914: Economy, Society, Culture and Politics* (Oxford, 1994), p. 195.

[43] Isabel V. Hull, 'Persönliches Regiment', in *Der Ort Kaiser Wilhelms II. in der deutschen Geschichte*, ed. John C. G. Röhl, (Munich, 1991), pp. 3–23.

[44] Katharine A. Lerman, *The Chancellor as Courtier: Bernhard von Bülow and the Governance of Germany, 1900–1909* (Cambridge, 1990).

[45] Lamar J. R. Cecil, *Wilhelm II*, 2 vols. (Chapel Hill, NC, and London, 1989–96); John C. G. Röhl, *Wilhelm II.: Die Jugend des Kaisers, 1859–1888* (Munich, 1993); English translation: *Young Wilhelm. The Kaiser's Early Life, 1859–1888* (Cambridge, 1998); Thomas Kohut, *Wilhelm II and the Germans: A Study in Leadership* (Oxford and New York, 1991); Willibald Gutsche, *Wilhelm II.: Der letzte Kaiser des deutschen Reiches* (Berlin, 1991); Willibald Gutsche, *Ein Kaiser im Exil: Der letzte deutsche Kaiser Wilhelm II. in Holland* (Marburg, 1991).

[46] Holger Afflerbach, 'Wilhelm II as Supreme Warlord in the First World War', *War in History* 5 (1998), 427–49.

by historians concerned with German politics and diplomacy, this cannot be said with confidence for the history of other major European monarchies. Russian history of the pre-1917 era has been dominated by explaining the Russian Revolution. Western historians have tended to ask whether liberal democracy could have triumphed in imperial Russia, whereas Soviet historians were inclined to view the history of the last years of tsarism as a prelude to the 'inevitable' triumph of communism. This situation meant that hardly anyone sought to examine the tsarist régime on its own terms, as a form of government, which was outdated by the early twentieth century, but one which had evolved out of Russian traditions, and may perhaps have been the only real alternative to communism in a country which lacked strong liberal forces.

As a consequence, Nicholas II, the last Tsar, has generally been portrayed in a negative light by the academic community. Western historians have derided him for his weakness, commitment to reactionary policies, and for upholding an anachronistic system of government. Biographies of Nicholas II have generally concentrated on his tragic family history, and have devoted very little attention to his political role.[47] Indeed, the first genuine political biography of Nicholas II, by Dominic Lieven, only appeared in 1993,[48] although a work of more restricted scope had been published in 1990.[49]

It is in Lieven's work that the first signs of a new approach to the study of the Russian monarchy can be discerned. In his magisterial study of the state council under Nicholas II, published in 1989,[50] he lamented the absence of a serious political biography of Nicholas II. Lieven compared the situation unfavourably to that of the Prusso-German monarchy, and suggested that an approach, similar to that adopted by Röhl towards the history of the *Kaiserreich*, was now necessary for Russia as well.[51] His own biography of the last Tsar combined the methodology adopted by Röhl and Hull in their studies of the court of Wilhelm II with an older approach, that of the Russian nationalist historian S. S. Oldenbourg.[52] Oldenbourg examined the reign of Nicholas II from a conservative

[47] Robert K. Massie, *Nicholas and Alexandra* (London, 1968); Marc Ferro, *Nicholas II: The Last of the Tsars*, English translation (London, 1991); Edvard Radzinsky, *The Last Tsar: The Life and Death of Nicholas II*, English translation (London, 1992).
[48] Dominic C. B. Lieven, *Nicholas II: Emperor of all the Russias* (London, 1993).
[49] Andrew M. Verner, *The Crisis of the Russian Autocracy: Nicholas II and the 1905 Revolution* (Princeton, 1990).
[50] Dominic C. B. Lieven, *Russia's Rulers under the Old Regime* (London and New Haven, 1989).
[51] *Ibid.*, pp. 278–89.
[52] S. S. Oldenbourg, *The Last Tsar: Nicholas II, His Reign and His Russia*, 4 vols., English translation (Gulf Breeze, FL, 1975–77).

perspective, depicting Nicholas II as a strong ruler committed to his empire and its people. The translation of Oldenbourg's biography of Nicholas into English, in the 1970s, was motivated by a concern that, in addition to the western and Soviet perspectives on Russian history, a third perspective, that of the defenders of the old régime, also deserved to be publicised. The editor of the English translation made a powerful case for an end to the neglect of Nicholas II and his court by contemporary historians.[53] Lieven's biography represented a fresh attempt to view Nicholas II as a serious political figure. It is to be hoped that it will lead to further scholarly studies of the last Tsar and his reign.

Until recently, the situation with regard to scholarly interest in the British monarchy was even bleaker. Study of the subject has been hampered by a tendency, identified by David Cannadine, for historians and royal biographers 'to plough their separate furroughs'.[54] The restricted nature of access to the Royal Archives, and the need for the Queen's approval prior to publication, protects the royal family, to a great extent, from historical criticism. There have been many biographies of Edward VII, the British monarch with whom this study is principally concerned. These have, in the main, been of a high standard.[55] Despite this, professional historians have tended to treat him dismissively when they come to analyse British foreign policy during his reign.[56] The exaggerated claims made for the King's importance by his less judicious biographers have not helped in this regard.[57] However there are signs that the neglect of the British monarchy by professional historians may now be coming to an end. Cannadine himself has produced a number of essays on monarchy in the nineteenth and twentieth centuries,[58] and the respected constitutional expert Vernon

---

[53] Patrick J. Rollins, 'Searching for the Last Tsar', introduction to Oldenbourg, *Last Tsar*, 1, xiv–xxxi.

[54] David Cannadine, *The Pleasures of the Past* (London, 1989), p. 24.

[55] Sir Sidney Lee, *King Edward VII: A Biography*, 2 vols. (London, 1925–7); Sir Philip Magnus, *King Edward the Seventh* (London, 1964); Keith Middlemas, *The Life and Times of Edward VII* (London, 1972); Giles St Aubyn, *Edward VII: Prince and King* (London, 1979).

[56] Paul M. Kennedy, *The Rise of the Anglo-German Antagonism, 1860–1914* (London, 1980), pp. 400–3.

[57] Gordon Brook-Shepherd, *Uncle of Europe: The Social and Diplomatic Life of King Edward VII* (London, 1975).

[58] David Cannadine, 'The Context, Performance and Meaning of Ritual: The British Monarchy and the "Invention of Tradition", c. 1820–1977', in *The Invention of Tradition*, ed. E. Hobsbawm and T. Ranger (Cambridge, 1983), pp. 101–62; David Cannadine, 'The Last Hanoverian Sovereign? The Victorian Monarchy in Historical Perspective, 1688–1988', in *The First Modern Society. Essays in English History in Honour of Lawrence Stone*, ed. A. L. Beier, David Cannadine and James M. Rosenheim (Cambridge, 1989), pp. 127–66; David Cannadine, 'Kaiser Wilhelm II and the British Monarchy', in *History and Biography. Essays in Honour of Derek Beales*, ed. T. C. W. Blanning and David Cannadine (Cambridge, 1996), pp. 188–202.

Bogdanor has also published a study on the political role of the monarchy.[59] Scholarly interest in the history of Europe's other royal courts has been sporadic, but interesting studies exist on the role of Archduke Franz Ferdinand in Austro-Hungarian politics before 1914[60] and on the Belgian monarchy since 1830.[61]

The present study examines the significance of dynastic factors in European diplomacy in the last decade of the nineteenth century and first years of the twentieth. This is done by analysing the importance of the political and personal relationships between monarchs, and by looking at various events where monarchical involvement can be seen to be at work in the diplomatic sphere. Thus, the first chapter addresses Wilhelm II's attempts to encourage Nicholas II to abandon the Franco-Russian alliance in favour of co-operation with Berlin, and stresses the key importance of both monarchs in German-Russian relations before the First World War. They were able to determine the foreign policies of their empires to a considerable extent, notably as a result of the control that they exercised over ministerial and ambassadorial appointments. However, due attention is also given to structures and to the pressures that rendered dynastic links less efficacious as the conflagration of 1914 approached. The conflicting ambitions of Germany and Russia in the Balkans reduced the value of diplomatic exchanges between the two emperors, notably after the Bosnian crisis of 1908/9. Similarly, the mutual antagonism that developed between German and Russian public opinion in the early years of the twentieth century also reduced the scope for co-operation between the two powers. By 1914, appeals to the monarchical principle were no longer sufficient to prevent Germany and Russia from going to war on opposing sides.

The second chapter looks at the turbulent relationship between Edward VII and his nephew, Wilhelm II. This is a subject which has not been fully scrutinised since the 1930s.[62] Yet the antagonism which existed between them was of more than personal significance, for it came to have a profoundly negative political impact on Anglo-German relations, particularly after the accession of Edward VII in 1901.

[59] Vernon Bogdanor, *The Monarchy and the Constitution* (Oxford, 1995).
[60] Samuel R. Williamson, 'Influence, Power and the Policy Process: The Case of Franz Ferdinand, 1906–1914', *Historical Journal* 17, 2 (1974), 417–34.
[61] Jean Stengers, *L'action du roi en Belgique depuis 1830. Pouvoir et influence* (Brussels, 1992).
[62] E. F. Benson, *The Kaiser and his English Relations* (London, 1936).

Wilhelm II's love–hate relationship with the British royal family influenced his entire attitude towards Britain politically, most notably by stimulating his desire to create a large battlefleet to rival the Royal Navy. His paranoid conviction that his uncle Edward VII was orchestrating Germany's diplomatic encirclement caused Wilhelm to refuse political compromise with Britain, most notably on the issue of naval armaments. Edward VII, in contrast to the Kaiser, was able to influence his country's foreign policy but not to determine it. However the King's suspicion that Wilhelm II harboured malevolent intentions towards Britain eventually led him to give his support to the policy of *entente* with France and Russia that was pursued by both Conservative and Liberal governments during his reign, to further the careers of diplomats who were convinced that Germany wished to obtain the mastery of Europe, and to support a robust British naval and military policy. The antagonism between the Kaiser and the King thus provides a good example of the way in which palace politics could actually contribute towards a deterioration in bilateral relations between states.

The third chapter examines Edward VII's involvement in British diplomacy, and seeks to find a middle path between the professional historians, who dismiss him as a decorative non-entity, and the royal biographers, who occasionally exaggerate his significance. The evidence indicates that the King played a significant role in the establishment and maintenance of Britain's *ententes* with France and Russia. He manifested his influence most notably by cultivating French and Russians diplomats and foreign ministers, together with a number of French presidents and Tsar Nicholas II. The King's influence has traditionally been played down by historians, yet the judgement of contemporaries was that his role in Anglo-French and Anglo-Russian relations was a significant and sometimes vital one. The chapter also gives due regard to the limits on the King's diplomatic influence that emanated from the gradual diminution in the power of the British monarchy in the late nineteenth and early twentieth centuries, Edward VII's own fraught relationships with a succession of prime ministers, and his inclination towards a life of pleasure rather than desk work. However, the evidence still suggests that Edward VII's diplomatic influence was much greater than many historians have been prepared to concede.

Finally, attention is focused on royal visits before 1914 and their impact on Anglo-German relations. Royal visits represented the public face of royal diplomacy before the Great War, yet they are rarely

examined for their own sake.[63] In the context of Anglo-German relations, royal visits reveal the limits of dynastic diplomacy. Even in the era
after the accession of King George V in May 1910, when relations
between the British and Prussian courts again became cordial after the
period of antagonism of Edward VII's reign, there was no more than a
superficial political *rapprochement* between the British and German governments. Cordial dynastic relations had a beneficial influence on
Anglo-German relations, but this influence was circumscribed by factors
such as the attitude of public opinion, the views of politicians and
military leaders, and most crucially by the conflicting vital interests of the
two states. The German leadership was determined to achieve supremacy in Europe, whereas the British government believed that the survival
of Britain and her empire depended on preventing this. Exchanges of
royal visits could do nothing to alter these entrenched positions.

The topic is a vast one, and thus the approach taken is selective.
Certain issues, such as the diplomatic role of minor royalty, are mentioned only in passing. Equally it has not been possible to give detailed
consideration to the diplomatic role of the Habsburg monarchy. However, all the chapters illustrate the general theme: that monarchs remained important figures in European diplomacy in the first decade of
the twentieth century and that dynastic factors must be taken into
account when historians examine international relations during the
period. In some cases, such as the role of Kaiser Wilhelm II in Germany's relations with Britain, royal influence could have decisive consequences. The Kaiser's decision to build a navy to challenge that of
Britain, and his refusal to contemplate an arms limitation agreement
with London, ensured that the British would enter the war in 1914 on the
side of Germany's enemies. More often, royal influence served to modify
existing trends, for example in the way in which the ties of monarchical
and conservative solidarity between the Kaiser and the Tsar slowed the
pace of German–Russian estrangement, or to accelerate their pace, as in
the case of Edward VII's role in the formation and consolidation of
Britain's *ententes* with France and Russia. However, despite the impression given by traditional diplomatic history, monarchs were rarely
sidelined completely, as will become evident as we now turn to a detailed
examination of royal diplomacy before the Great War.

---

[63] Two exceptions are: Jonathan Steinberg, 'The Kaiser and the British: The State Visit to
Windsor, November 1907', in *Kaiser Wilhelm II: New Interpretations*, ed. John C. G. Röhl and
Nicolaus Sombart (Cambridge, 1982), pp. 121–41; Jean Stengers, 'Guillaume II et le Roi Albert à
Potsdam en novembre 1913', *Bulletin de la classe des lettres et des sciences morales et politiques de l'Academie
Royale de Belgique*, 6th series, IV, 7 12 (1993), 227–53.

CHAPTER I

The Kaiser and the Tsar: German–Russian dynastic relations, 1888–1914

In the closing stages of the July crisis of 1914, Kaiser Wilhelm II appealed to Tsar Nicholas II not to intervene on the side of Serbia. In doing so, he drew attention to the need for all monarchs to show solidarity against those who had been responsible for the murder of the Austrian Archduke Franz Ferdinand and his wife.[1] This plea to the Tsar ultimately failed to fulfil its object, of preventing Russia from entering the war,[2] and Wilhelm blamed Nicholas II's 'frivolity and weakness'[3] for precipitating the escalation of a Balkan dispute between Austria and Serbia into a European conflict. The inability of the Kaiser to persuade the Tsar to join him in defending the monarchical principle against Serbia underlined the failure of the *Russlandpolitik* pursued by Germany since Nicholas II's accession in 1894, a policy which had been over-reliant on the maintenance of good dynastic relations as a means of solidifying the ties between the *Kaiserreich* and the Tsarist empire. The central aim of the strategy had been, at least until 1906, the re-establishment of the alliance between the two countries, which had come to an end in 1890 after Wilhelm II's refusal, on the advice of the chancellor, General Leo von Caprivi, and the German foreign office, to renew the Reinsurance Treaty with Russia. A close study of the development of the relationship between the Kaiser and the Tsar helps to explain, first, the failure to resurrect an alliance between the two powers and, second-ly, the growing antagonism between the two emperors in the years immediately preceding the outbreak of the First World War, which

---

[1] Wilhelm II's comments on Theobald von Bethmann Hollweg to Wilhelm II, 29 July 1914, GStA Merseburg, HA Rep. 53 J Lit. B Nr 7.

[2] Dominic C. B. Lieven, *Russia and the Origins of the First World War* (London, 1983), pp.141–51; D. W. Spring, 'Russia and the Coming of War', in *The Coming of the First World War*, ed. R. J. W. Evans and Hartmut Pogge von Strandmann (Oxford, 1988), pp. 57–86; Keith Neilson, 'Russia', in *Decisions for War, 1914*, ed. Keith M. Wilson (London, 1995), pp. 97–120.

[3] Wilhelm II's comment on Pourtalès to Bethmann Hollweg, 29 July 1914. Imanuel Geiss (ed.), *July 1914. The Outbreak of the First World War. Selected Documents*, English translation (London, 1967), no.135, p. 294.

meant that when the decisive moment came, in July 1914, good-will between them had been exhausted, and neither monarch was prepared to prevent a conflict which was to result in the collapse of both their thrones, the ignominious flight into exile of the Kaiser, and the murder of the Tsar and his family by the Bolsheviks.

The accession of Nicholas II, at the young age of twenty-six, in 1894 represented both a challenge and an opportunity for those in Berlin who wished to see a renewal of close ties between Germany and Russia. The young Tsar had had a sheltered upbringing, a rather narrow education, and had been given little chance to participate in affairs of state prior to his accession.[4] Alexander III, Nicholas's father, was largely responsible for this situation. Sergei Witte, who served both Alexander and Nicholas as minister of finance, recalled that when he suggested appointing the Tsarevitch as chairman of a government committee, in 1891, the Tsar replied, 'He is nothing but a boy, whose judgements are childish.'[5] Alexander showed his contempt for his son on one occasion by pelting him with bread-balls, and he was inclined to depict Nicholas as a 'girlie', with a puerile personality and ideas, entirely unfit for the duties that were awaiting him.[6] Such behaviour was not designed to inspire confidence and it is hardly surprising that when his father died, Nicholas despaired of his own ability to assume the responsibilities of emperor.[7] Yet the new Tsar also had many fine qualities. He was not unintelligent, speaking five languages with varying degrees of fluency, and even Witte, no admirer of Nicholas II, conceded that he had a quick mind and learned easily.[8] He also had a courteous nature, being described by one relative as 'exasperatingly polite', a characteristic which was often mistaken for deviousness, not least by Wilhelm II.[9]

Despite the new Tsar's youth and inexperience in affairs of state, the German chargé d'affaires in St Petersburg, Count Rex, reported that the members of Nicholas's entourage were convinced that he had a

[4] Dominic C. B. Lieven, *Nicholas II, Emperor of all the Russias* (London, 1993), pp. 22–43; Marc Ferro, *Nicholas II, the Last of the Tsars*, English translation (London, 1991), pp.7–28; Andrew M. Verner, *The Crisis of the Russian Autocracy: Nicholas II and the 1905 Revolution* (Princeton, 1990), pp. 7–44.

[5] Sidney Harcave (ed.), *The Memoirs of Count Witte*, English translation (New York and London, 1990), p. 125; cf. Ian Vorres, *The Last Grand-Duchess: Her Imperial Highness Grand Duchess Olga Alexandrovna, 1882–1960* (London, 1964), p. 67.

[6] Richard Pipes, *The Russian Revolution, 1899–1919* (London, 1990), p. 58.

[7] Grand Duke Alexander of Russia, *Once a Grand Duke* (New York, 1932), p. 169.

[8] Harcave, *Witte*, p. 126.

[9] Grand Duke Alexander, *Once a Grand Duke*, pp. 178–80; note by Wilhelm II, 28 March 1927 GStA Berlin BPH 53/165.

strong will, and that his mild manner disguised a firmness of purpose. Rex suggested that any improvement in relations between Russia and Germany would have to be achieved gradually, and at the dynastic level.[10] The Kaiser appeared to agree that a cautious policy would be the best one to adopt with the new Tsar, but was nevertheless hopeful of an improvement in Germany's relations with Russia.[11]

The desire, shared by the Kaiser and his chancellor, Chlodwig Prince zu Hohenlohe-Schillingsfürst, to make Nicholas II's accession the occasion for a new beginning in Russo-German relations could not obscure the fact that formidable obstacles stood in the way of this aim. The reign of Alexander III had seen a rapid deterioration in relations between the two countries, and by 1894 those hostile to Germany predominated at the Russian court, in the Russian army and among the Romanov family.[12] During the 1880s, clashes of interest between the Tsarist empire and Germany's other ally, Austria, in the Balkans, and the rise of a new virulent strain of Russian nationalism, had made it increasingly difficult for Bismarck to preserve the diplomatic link with St Petersburg.[13] Wilhelm II's accession as Kaiser in 1888 had played a role in speeding up the disintegration of the alliance.

Wilhelm had first been sent on a mission to Alexander III in May 1884. On that occasion, his manner had pleased the Tsar, and earned the approval of Bismarck.[14] The visit made a profound effect on Wilhelm. He came to see Alexander III as a role model, and, after the latter's death, he declared to Witte that the Tsar had been 'truly an autocrat and an emperor'.[15] On his return to Germany, Wilhelm initiated a secret correspondence with the Tsar, in which he tried to incite Alexander against England, the British royal family and even against his own parents, Crown Prince Friedrich Wilhelm and Crown Princess Victoria of Prussia. These letters, written without the knowledge of Bismarck, came close to provoking a war between Britain and

[10] Note by Graf Rex, December 1894 *GP*, IX, no. 2308, pp. 337–9.

[11] Hohenlohe, journal entry, 14 December 1894, Karl Alexander von Müller (ed.), *Fürst Chlodwig zu Hohenlohe-Schillingsfürst, Denkwürdigkeiten der Reichskanzlerzeit* (Stuttgart and Berlin, 1931), p. 24.

[12] Note by Graf Rex, December 1894, *GP*, IX, no. 2308, pp. 337–41.

[13] George F. Kennan, *The Decline of Bismarck's European Order: Franco-Russian Relations, 1875–1890* (Princeton, 1979); A. J. P. Taylor, *The Struggle for Mastery in Europe, 1848–1918* (London, 1954), pp. 255–324.

[14] Otto Fürst von Bismarck to Prince Wilhelm of Prussia, 23 May 1884, GStA Berlin BPH 53/133.

[15] Abraham Yarmolinsky (ed.), *The Memoirs of Count Witte*, English translation (Garden City, NY, 1921), pp. 402–3; cf. John C. G. Röhl, *Wilhelm II.: Die Jugend des Kaisers, 1859–1888* (Munich, 1993), pp. 432–9.

Russia,[16] but the Tsar initially welcomed them, seeing Wilhelm as a political ally in Berlin.[17] However, the Tsar's favourable opinion of Wilhelm seems to have been undermined during a visit paid by the latter to Russia in 1886, and by the time of Alexander III's own visit to Germany, the following year, there was a noticeable frostiness to the meeting between them.[18] Even before this encounter, Wilhelm had turned against the Tsar and become a supporter of the 'preventive war' strategy, advocated by General Alfred Count von Waldersee as a means of crushing Russia before she had a chance to attack the *Kaiserreich*.[19]

Thus, by the time of Wilhelm's accession, in 1888, his relationship with Alexander III, which had started so promisingly, had become one characterised by growing personal and political alienation. Alexander III did not have the feelings of respect for the new Kaiser which he had had for the latter's grandfather, Kaiser Wilhelm I. Therefore his attachment to the alliance with Germany became weaker, and he became more willing to contemplate a break with Berlin.[20] The Tsar seems to have been irritated by the arrogant behaviour which Wilhelm displayed during a visit to St Petersburg in 1888,[21] and by the time of his own return visit to Berlin, in October 1889, Alexander's growing distaste for Wilhelm II and Germany was noted by several observers.[22] The Tsar's suspicion of German foreign policy played a role in his behaviour. He believed that the Kaiser had formed an alliance with England, while visiting Queen Victoria the previous summer, and he also suspected that the Germans were planning to sign a treaty with Turkey directed against Russia.[23] The Kaiser's domestic policies were also arousing Alexander III's suspicion. Wilhelm's attempts to conciliate the working classes were disapproved of by the reactionary Tsar and had become, by February 1890, according to a German diplomat 'a new factor impeding

---

[16] Röhl, *Jugend des Kaisers*, pp. 440–5; Lamar J. R. Cecil, 'William II and his Russian "Colleagues"', in *German Nationalism and the European Response, 1890–1945*, ed. Carol Fink et al., (Norman, OK, and London, 1985), pp. 105–6.

[17] Alexander III to Prince Wilhelm of Prussia, 7/19 May 1885, GStA Merseburg HA Rep. 53 J Lit. R Nr 6.

[18] Röhl, *Jugend des Kaisers*, pp. 580–4, 739–42; Mathilde Gräfin von Keller, *Vierzig Jahre im Dienst der Kaiserin: Ein Kulturbild aus den Jahren 1881–1921* (Leipzig, 1935), diary entry, 18 November 1887, p. 65.

[19] Röhl, *Jugend des Kaisers*, ch. 22; Cecil, 'William II', p. 107.

[20] Kennan, *Bismarck's European Order*, pp. 367–72.

[21] *Ibid.*, pp. 370–71; Cecil, 'William II', p. 106.

[22] Kennan, *Bismarck's European Order*, p. 398; Keller, *Vierzig Jahre*, diary entry, 15 October 1889, p. 105; memorandum by Ludwig Raschdau, Germany's relationship with Russia, 15 July 1890, GStA Merseburg HA Rep. 53 E 1: Russland 1, pp. 57–9.

[23] Cecil, 'William II', p. 109.

the re-establishment of really intimate relations between Russia and ourselves'.[24]

The dismissal of Bismarck as chancellor in March 1890 had a damaging effect on relations between Russia and Germany, for it was followed by the decision of the German government not to renew the Reinsurance Treaty, which the chancellor had made with Russia in 1887. There was a general feeling in the *Wilhelmstrasse* that the treaty had failed to prevent a deterioration in relations between the two empires, and that it was in conflict with Germany's treaty obligations towards Austria.[25] The cancellation of the treaty met with conflicting reactions in St Petersburg. The Russian foreign minister, N. K. Giers, bemoaned its passing and pointed out the advantages which it had possessed, notably in allowing the Tsar to ignore the loud, anti-German, voices of the slavophiles and chauvinistic generals, and in ensuring that Russia would remain neutral in the event of a Franco-German war.[26] Alexander III, while accepting the Kaiser's assurances that Bismarck's dismissal and the end of the alliance would make no differences to German–Russian relations,[27] was far from saddened by the German government's decision as his own attitude towards the Reinsurance Treaty had been lukewarm from the first.[28]

The Kaiser believed that the end of the alliance was free from political dangers. Attachment to the monarchical principle would prevent Alexander III from seeking an understanding with the French republic and, in any case, Russia was too weak internally to contemplate an attack on Germany.[29] The Tsar, however, did not trust Wilhelm and the removal of Bismarck had increased his animosity towards Germany, for he was also suspicious of the new chancellor, General Leo von Caprivi. Alexander avoided Berlin when travelling back from Denmark in the summer of 1890, and later in the same year he treated Wilhelm rudely during a visit which the latter paid to Russia. In the following year, the renewal of the Triple Alliance between Germany, Austria and Italy caused Alexander considerable alarm and he initiated moves towards a rapprochement with France. This resulted in a visit by a

[24] Friedrich von Pourtalès to Friedrich von Holstein, 22 February 1890, *HP*, III, p. 327.
[25] Memorandum by Raschdau, 15 July 1890. GStA Merseburg HA Rep. 53 E I: Russland I, p.60. Cecil, 'William II', pp. 109–10; Kennan, *Bismarck's European Order*, pp. 398–410.
[26] Schweinitz to Caprivi, 3 April 1890, *GP*, VII, no. 1370, pp. 11–15.
[27] Schweinitz to Wilhelm II, 3 April 1890, *ibid.*, no. 1371, pp. 15–17.
[28] Kennan, *Bismarck's European Order*, p. 409.
[29] Wilhelm II's comments on Münster to Caprivi, 4 January 1891, *GP*, VII, no. 1492, pp. 195–6; Cecil, 'William II', p 110.

French naval squadron to Kronstadt, near St Petersburg, in July 1891, which awakened fears in Berlin that Alexander would give in to pressure from his people for an alliance with the French republic.[30] The personal relationship between the two Emperors had by this stage deteriorated irreparably.[31] In consequence of this, and the growing tension in German–Russian relations, the Tsar took the initiative in opening negotiations with Paris. These were to culminate in the signing of the Franco-Russian alliance in January 1894.[32]

Thus, in foreign policy terms, Nicholas II was bequeathed a pro-French and anti-German legacy by his father. The new Tsar was at pains to reassure the French that he wished to preserve Russia's alliance with Paris.[33] Nicholas's commitment to France never wavered, and it was to be the major obstacle to all attempts made by the Kaiser to bring about a *rapprochement* with St Petersburg. It was reinforced by many of his relatives, the most influential being, at least in the first years of his reign, his mother, the Dowager Empress Marie Feodorovna. She had been born as Princess Dagmar of Denmark and had married Alexander III in 1866. The marriage had clear political overtones. She was the daughter of King Christian IX and Queen Louise, both of whom had strong grievances against Prussia, which had seized the formerly Danish possessions of Schleswig and Holstein in 1864.[34] Marie Feodorovna had inherited her mother's vehement anti-Prussian feelings, and although her influence over Alexander III had been limited, she had encouraged her husband's suspicions of Germany.[35] The outbreak of war in 1914 allowed her to expose her contempt for the Germans more openly. 'I have hated Germany for 50 years,' she declared, 'but now I hate it more than ever'.[36]

[30] Cecil, 'William II', pp. 111–13; Alfred von Bülow to Caprivi, 30 July 1891 and Schweinitz to Caprivi, 5 August 1891, *GP*, VII, nos. 1502 and 1504, pp. 207–10, 211–15; report by the military attaché in Vienna Lieutenant-Colonel von Deines, 4 November 1891, *GP*, VII, no. 1511, pp. 225–6.

[31] Herbette to Ribot, 10 December 1891 *DDF*, 1st series, IX, no. 101, pp. 158–9.

[32] Cf. George F. Kennan, *The Fateful Alliance. France, Russia and the Coming of the First World War* (Princeton, 1984).

[33] General de Boisdeffre to Hanotaux, 17 November 1894, *DDF*, 1st, series, IX, no. 284, p. 427; Nicholas II to M. Casimir-Périer, President of the French Republic, 11 November 1894, *ibid.*, no. 277, p. 417.

[34] Cf. Theo Aronson, *A Family of Kings: The Descendants of Christian IX of Denmark* (London, 1976); Roderick R. McLean, 'Monarchy and Diplomacy in Europe, 1900–1910', DPhil. dissertation, University of Sussex (1996), pp. 149–50.

[35] Kennan, *Bismarck's European Order*, pp. 62–3; Viktor A. Wroblewski, 'Lambsdorff über Deutschland und seine Zukunft', *Berliner Monatshefte* 14, 5 (1936), 362.

[36] Rantzau to the German foreign office, 19 August 1914. PA Bonn Russland Nr 82 Nr 1 Bd 63; Jagow to Wilhelm II, 2 August 1914 and Jagow to the German foreign office, 2 August 1914, *ibid.*

Her opinions would not have been a matter of political concern in Berlin had it not been for the influence which she exercised over her son, the new Tsar. Nicholas had been very close to his mother as a child, and this continued into adulthood.[37] Whenever they were apart, mother and son corresponded frequently. Marie's letters often mentioned her dislike of Germany, and she also encouraged her son to view Wilhelm II with a jaundiced eye. Her own hatred of the Kaiser reached pathological proportions and Nicholas's tone was usually apologetic when he informed her of the arrangements for meetings between himself and Wilhelm.[38] Nicholas consulted her frequently during the first years of his reign over matters of foreign policy and over government and diplomatic appointments. She used this influence to ensure that her son appointed a succession of foreign ministers who were determined to preserve the alliance with France, and who shared her opposition to closer ties with Berlin.[39] Marie Feodorovna's influence over her son waned gradually after 1900 as she spent more and more time in Denmark, and also due to disagreements between her and Nicholas over domestic policy, particularly during the years of revolution between 1904 and 1906.[40] However, even after 1905, her influence was occasionally brought to bear on her son. She was an enthusiastic supporter of the Anglo-Russian *rapprochement*, which culminated in the signing of an agreement between the two countries, in 1907, and, as late as 1913, German diplomats continued to fear that she was active in the sphere of international relations to the detriment of the interests of the *Reich*.[41]

[37] Richard Wortman, 'The Russian Empress as Mother', in *The Family in Imperial Russia*, ed. David L. Ransel (Urbana, Chicago and London, 1978), pp. 67–74; Lieven, *Nicholas II*, pp. 27–8, 32, 44; Verner, *Crisis*, pp. 7–44.

[38] Edward J. Bing (ed.), *The Letters of Tsar Nicholas and Empress Marie*, English translation (London, 1937). Examples of her dislike of Germany and the Kaiser can be found in her letters to her son of 8 August 1897, 21 November 1897, 31 March 1903, 26 October 1906, 25 March 1909, 5 November 1910. Nicholas's letters often paid deference to his mother's views, which he shared, at least in part. See letters of 2 October 1896, 23 July 1897, 1 August 1897, 16 January 1901, 26 March 1903, 18/19 March 1909, 21 October 1910, 31 October 1910. (The letters are dated according to the Julian calendar, twelve days behind the Gregorian calendar in the nineteenth century, and thirteen days behind in the twentieth century.)

[39] Harcave, *Witte*, pp. 212, 262; Vorres, *Grand-Duchess*, pp. 72, 79; A. A Mossolov, *At the Court of the Last Tsar*, English translation (London, 1935), pp. 66–7; Baroness Sophie Buxhoeveden, *The Life and Tragedy of Alexandra Feodorovna* (London, 1928), p. 49; Gustav Graf von Lambsdorff, *Die Militärbevollmächtigten Kaiser Wilhelms II. am Zarenhofe, 1904–1914* (Berlin, 1937), pp. 58–9.

[40] Harcave, *Witte*, p. 374; Verner, *Crisis*, pp. 104–52; Lieven, *Nicholas II*, pp. 134–5, 147–8; for specific examples see Alvensleben to Bülow, 17 March 1905, PA Bonn Russland Nr 82 Nr 1 Bd 53; Bülow to Wilhelm II, 10 April 1905, GStA Merseburg HA Rep. 53 J Lit. B Nr 16a Bd III; Prince Heinrich of Prussia to Wilhelm II, 11 April 1905. GStA Merseburg HA Rep 52 V 1 Nr 13; Sir Charles Hardinge to Lord Knollys, 15 March 1905, RA W 45/143.

[41] Lieven, *Russia and the Origins*, p. 70; Lieven, 'Pro-Germans and Russian Foreign Policy, 1890–1914', *International History Review* 2, 1 (1980), 42; Seeger (ed.), *The Memoirs of Alexander Iswolsky*, p. 22;

The Kaiser and German diplomats had to take into account other relatives of Nicholas II when trying to improve relations with St Petersburg, not least among them were the Tsar's uncles, the four grand dukes,[42] upon whom he relied for advice in the first decade of his reign.[43] Grand Duke Sergei was the uncle whose views had the greatest influence with Nicholas II on political questions. He was a political reactionary who, paradoxically, was a strong supporter of the Franco-Russian alliance. Sergei and Wilhelm II hated each other for a mixture of personal and political reasons.[44] The Kaiser viewed him as Nicholas's 'evil demon' and as Germany's 'most determined enemy'.[45] Sergei's death, at the hands of revolutionaries, in 1905, came as a real relief to Wilhelm, as it removed one influential enemy of a German–Russian *rapprochement* from the political scene.[46]

Sergei's eldest surviving brother, the Grand Duke Vladimir, was considered in Berlin to be the most pro-German of the Tsar's uncles. He was married to the Grand Duchess Maria Pavlovna, who had been born a Mecklenburg princess. She was often consulted by Nicholas on German attitudes, as she was felt to be well acquainted with the views of the Berlin court.[47] Grand Duke Vladimir often acted as the intermediary between Wilhelm and Nicholas. However, his main interests were concentrated on the arts rather than on politics,[48] and by 1900 the Kaiser had lost faith in Vladimir's commitment to improved relations with Berlin, and his ability to persuade the Tsar to adopt such a course.[49]

David M. McDonald, *United Government and Foreign Policy in Russia 1900–1914* (Cambridge, MA., 1992), p. 158; Marie Feodorovna to Nicholas II, 25 March and 30 March 1909, *Letters of Tsar Nicholas*, pp. 241–4; Sir Charles Hardinge to Queen Alexandra, 4 June 1904, Hardinge Papers, University Library, Cambridge, vol. 6; Bernhard Fürst von Bülow, *Memoirs*, 4 vols., English translation (London, 1931), II, p. 63; Captain Paul von Hintze to Wilhelm II, 28 January 1909, PA Bonn Russland Nr 82 Nr 1 geheim. Bd 3; Hintze to Wilhelm II, 21 February 1910, Lambsdorff, *Militärbevollmächtigten*, pp. 366–7; Rantzau to Bethmann Hollweg, 6 February 1913, PA Bonn Russland Nr 82 Nr 1 Bd 62.

[42] Vladimir Alexandrovitch, 1847–1909, Alexei Alexandrovitch, 1850–1908, Sergei Alexandrovitch, 1857–1905, Pavel (Paul) Alexandrovitch, 1860–1919.
[43] Grand Duke Alexander, *Grand Duke*, pp. 136, 173.
[44] Röhl, *Jugend des Kaisers*, pp. 339–50; Eckhart G. Franz (ed.), *Ernst Ludwig, Grossherzog von Hessen und bei Rhein, Erinnertes* (Darmstadt, 1983), p. 97; General Karl von Villaume to Wilhelm II, 22 February 1891, PA Bonn Russland Nr 82 Nr 1 geheim. Bd 1; Holstein to Eulenburg, 1 April 1892, *EK*, II, no. 638, p. 839; note by Graf Rex, December 1894, *GP*, XI, no. 2308, p. 339.
[45] Wilhelm II to Hohenlohe, 20 October 1896. *GP*, XI, no. 2868, p. 370.
[46] Wilhelm II's comments on Radolin to Bülow, 18 February 1905; Wilhelm II's comments on Alvensleben to Bülow, 22 February 1905; Schoen to Bülow, 24 February 1905, PA Bonn Russland Nr 82 Nr 1 Bd 53.
[47] Mossolov, *Last Tsar*, p. 68.   [48] Grand Duke Alexander, *Grand Duke*, pp. 137–8.
[49] See below.

The Tsar's wife, Alexandra Feodorovna, and her brother, Grand Duke Ernst Ludwig of Hesse, also needed to be taken into consideration in Wilhelm's dealings with Nicholas. The Kaiser's failure to establish a satisfactory relationship with either of them represented the squandering of a favourable opportunity to exploit dynastic ties for Germany's political benefit, for both were his first cousins. The Tsarina, although a German by birth, was English in culture and upbringing, as was her brother, the Grand Duke. She disliked Wilhelm, and this situation was made worse by the ill-feeling which existed between the Tsarina and the Kaiserin, who could not forgive Alexandra for having converted to Russian Orthodoxy. There was no rapport between Wilhelm and the Grand Duke of Hesse, whom he distrusted as a political liberal, who was more English than German. The Kaiser's dislike of Ernst Ludwig meant that he turned down all the latter's offers to act as a mediator with St Petersburg, and thus closed off one particular avenue to a *rapprochement* with Nicholas II.[50]

Two other obstacles blocked the path to a *rapprochement* between Germany and Russia. They were the attitudes of a succession of Russian foreign ministers and diplomats, and the stance taken by Russian public opinion. All of the five foreign ministers who served Nicholas II between 1895 and 1914, Lobanov, Muraviev, Lamsdorf, Isvolsky and Sazonov, wished to maintain St Petersburg's links with Paris. Wilhelm II failed to establish a satisfactory relationship with any of them, and proved unable to persuade Nicholas to appoint a pro-German to this key post. In addition, the majority of Russia's ambassadors favoured the maintenance of Russia's existing foreign policy. Public opinion was less important in Russia than in any other country in Europe. Nicholas II was contemptuous of it and, living for the most part in isolation at Tsarskoe Selo, outside St Petersburg, he did not allow it to influence his decisions.[51] Russian public opinion was, in the main, anti-German and

---

[50] Sigurd von Ilsemann, *Der Kaiser in Holland: Aufzeichnungen des letzten Flügeladjutanten Kaiser Wilhelms II.*, 2 vols. (Munich, 1967–8), ii, pp. 50–1; Prietz to the Prussian foreign ministry, 29 May 1919, PA Bonn Hessen Nr 56 Nr 1 geheim. Bd 2; Mossolov, *Last Tsar*, pp. 31, 34–5; note by Eulenburg, 12/13 October 1895, *EK*, iii, no. 1145, p. 1568; Bülow, *Memoirs*, i, pp. 300–1; Maurice Paléologue, *Guillaume II et Nicolas II* (Paris, 1935), pp. 77–9; W. H-H. Waters, *Potsdam and Doorn* (London, 1935), p. 194; Wilhelm II's comments on Hohenlohe to Bülow, 3 January 1901, PA Bonn Hessen Nr 56 Nr 1 geheim Bd 1; Wilhelm II to Grand Duke Ernst Ludwig of Hesse, 11 November 1901, *ibid.*; Bülow to Wilhelm II, 15 July 1904, *GP*, xix; no. 6043, p. 200; Sir Rennell Rodd to Hardinge, 12 May 1908, Hardinge Papers, vol. 12. Roderick R. McLean, 'Kaiser Wilhelm II and his Hessian Cousins: Intra-State Relations in the German Empire and International Dynastic Politics, 1890–1918', *German History* 19 (forthcoming).

[51] Lieven, *Russia*, pp. 54–5.

favourable towards France, and despite the Tsar's lack of willingness to allow it to influence his political actions, it did serve as a constraining factor on the adoption of a pro-German foreign policy, particularly in the years after 1905, when the régime had been weakened by revolution.[52]

Many factors, therefore, militated against the resurrection of intimate relations between Germany and Russia. In foreign policy terms, Nicholas had been bequeathed an alliance with France by his father, and in the dynastic and political spheres the obstacles to an understanding between the two empires were formidable. The indifferent political relations between the two countries paradoxically accentuated the importance of the relationship between the two emperors, for an appeal to the traditional friendship between the Romanovs and Hohenzollerns was seen in Berlin as a mechanism which could reduce the warmth of Russia's ties with the French republic.[53] The importance accorded to Wilhelm II's relationship with Nicholas II by the German government was put most clearly by Bernhard Prince von Bülow in 1905. He stated: 'Many years' experiences tells us that much less can be achieved with Russian diplomats, than through direct contact between His Majesty and the Tsar.'[54] This tendency to see the dynastic relationship as the decisive political link between Berlin and Petersburg was reinforced by the attitudes of Russian diplomats, notably the Ambassador to Germany between 1895 and 1912, Count von Osten-Sacken, who told a French diplomat on one occasion that in the *Kaiserreich*, 'everything depends on the always changing and personal whim of the Emperor'.[55]

The Tsar's own utterances and behaviour in the first months after his accession did not provide much support for the Kaiser's view that Alexander III's death would open a new, more favourable era for Germany's *Russlandpolitik*. Nicholas rejected the Kaiser's suggestion that they revive the traditional practice of appointing military plenipotentiaries to each other's suites, on the grounds that 'it would provoke all kinds of gossip'.[56] This initial set-back did not deter Wilhelm from initiating a

[52] Lieven, 'Pro-Germans', 41.
[53] Barbara Vogel, *Deutsche Russlandpolitik, 1900–1906: Das Scheitern der deutschen Weltpolitik unter Bülow 1900–1906* (Düsseldorf, 1973), p. 44.
[54] Bülow to the German foreign office, 12 August 1905, PA Bonn Deutschland Nr 131 Nr 4 Bd 5.
[55] Barrère to Hanotaux, 30 September 1896, *DDF*, 1st series, XII, no. 464, p. 763.
[56] Nicholas II to Wilhelm II, November 1894, *DdR*, p. 9; Lambsdorff, *Militärbevollmächtigten*, pp. 94–5.

regular, secret, correspondence with Nicholas which continued, with various ebbs and flows, until the outbreak of the First World War.[57] Four main themes recurred in these letters, whose contents were often of an incendiary political character. The Kaiser cast himself in the role of Nicholas's experienced colleague and protector, he stressed the need for all monarchs to defend the 'monarchical principle' and political conservatism, attacked the 'regicidal' French republic (and also Britain) and encouraged the Tsar to believe that Russia's mission lay in the Far East as the European bulwark against the 'yellow peril'.[58] Like the letters which Wilhelm had written to Alexander III in the mid-1880s, of which Bismarck had been unaware, his correspondence with Nicholas II was conducted without the knowledge of the chancellor, Prince zu Hohenlohe.[59] Although Hohenlohe's successor, Bülow, was privy to the contents of the letters in later years, they were never read by German diplomats at St Petersburg.[60]

The central aims of the correspondence in the 1890s were, first, to weaken, and if possible, destroy the Franco-Russian alliance and, secondly, to encourage the Tsar to proceed with Russian expansion in Siberia and the Far East as a way of redirecting the orientation of Russian policy away from the Balkans, where her interests were liable to collide with those of Austria. Wilhelm remained convinced that the alliance between the Tsarist empire and the France could not survive, for it was going against nature for a monarchy to co-operate politically with a republic. He made his views plain to the Russian foreign minister, Prince Lobanov-Rostovsky, when the latter visited Berlin in the autumn of 1895. Wilhelm told Lobanov that the Franco-Russian alliance risked legitimising republicanism at the expense of the monarchical principle, and thus could pose a danger to all the kingdoms and empires in Europe. The Kaiser informed the Russian foreign minister that his own preferred option for the reorganisation of the international system involved the resurrection of the *Dreikaiserbund* (Three Emperors' League) between Germany, Russia and Austria, together with the isolation and eventual subjugation of France. His words were unfortunate, for Lobanov, a strong supporter of the diplomatic status quo,

---

[57] Goetz (ed.), *Briefe Kaiser Wilhelms II.*; N. F. Grant (ed.), *The Kaiser's Letters to the Tsar* (London, 1920).

[58] Cf. Wilhelm II to Nicholas II, 8 November 1894, 7 February 1895, 26 April 1895, 10 July 1895 and 26 September 1895, *BKW*, pp. 287–96.

[59] Note by Eulenburg, 5 July 1895, *EK*, III, no. 1116, pp. 1512–14.

[60] Peter Winzen, *Bülows Weltmachtkonzept. Untersuchungen zur Frühphase seiner Aussenpolitik, 1897–1901* (Boppard am Rhein, 1977), pp. 141–2, 409–10; Vogel, *Deutsche Russlandpolitik*, p. 55; Freiherr von Schoen, *The Memoirs of an Ambassador*, English translation (London, 1922), p. 44.

communicated details of the Kaiser's remarks to M. Hanotaux, his French counterpart.[61]

Wilhelm's attempts to encourage Russian expansion in the Far East,[62] which were to continue until the outbreak of the Russo-Japanese War, and beyond, made a mockery of his agreement with Hohenlohe that Nicholas should be handled in a reserved and discreet manner.[63] On 5 July 1895, Philipp Count zu Eulenburg, the German ambassador to Vienna, and the Kaiser's closest confidant,[64] noted that the Kaiser had told the Tsar's uncle, Grand Duke Alexei, during a visit to Kiel, that he was prepared to guarantee Russia's western frontier while the Tsar confronted the 'yellow peril' in the Far East. Wilhelm had already raised this suggestion with Nicholas in a letter on 26 April, and he repeated his pledge in a further letter to Nicholas on 10 July 1895. This was kept secret from Hohenlohe.[65] Thus, a matter with serious security implications was being decided behind the back of the chancellor, in a blatant assertion of the monarch's right to decide on matters of foreign and military policy. Eulenburg trusted neither Nicholas, nor the Grand Duke Alexei, and feared that the Kaiser's guarantee could lead to a serious political crisis.[66]

Despite the controversial character of their contents, Nicholas was initially appreciative of Wilhelm's letters. When Hohenlohe visited St Petersburg in September 1895, he formed a favourable impression of the young Tsar. Nicholas told the chancellor that he would have no objections if Germany were to acquire a naval coaling station in the Far East, and he also spoke out vociferously about the perfidious nature of England's imperial policies. For his part, Hohenlohe found the Tsar to be thoroughly versed in all aspects of government. Nicholas told the chancellor to inform Wilhelm that he should continue the practice of writing to him on matters of importance.[67] The Kaiser responded by writing an appreciative letter to Nicholas after Hohenlohe's return and by presenting him with an engraving depicting their joint mission of

[61] Prince Lobanov to Hanotaux, 12/24 October 1895, *DDF*, 1st series, XII, no. 182, pp. 261–3.
[62] Note by the under-secretary in the German foreign office, Freiherr von Rotenhan, 30 July 1895, *GP*, IX, no. 2318, pp. 358–60.
[63] See above.
[64] John C. G. Röhl, *Kaiser, Hof und Staat: Wilhelm II. und die deutsche Politik* (Munich, 1987), pp. 35–77; Isabel V. Hull, *The Entourage of Kaiser Wilhelm II, 1888–1918* (Cambridge, 1982).
[65] Note by Eulenburg, 5 July 1895, *EK*, III, no. 1116, pp. 1513–14; Wilhelm II to Nicholas II, 26 April 1895 and 10 July 1895, *BKW*, pp. 290–4.
[66] Note by Eulenburg, 13 July 1895, *EK*, III, no. 1117, pp. 1514–15.
[67] Hohenlohe to Wilhelm II, 12 September 1895, *GP*, IX, no. 2319, pp. 360–1.

'resisting the inroads of Buddhism, heathenism and barbarism for the Defence of the Cross'.[68]

Technically, until 1905, Nicholas II's power as Tsar was unlimited. Thus a foreign policy based on the promotion of friendly relations between the two Emperors appeared to be the best way to ensure that Russia would not pursue an anti-German political course. However, in reality, Nicholas's power was circumscribed by a number of factors. The first was his lack of experience of government which meant that in the early years of his reign he often needed to turn to his relatives and ministers for advice. Secondly, unlike Wilhelm II, he had no court party to rely upon, nor a preconceived view of how he would direct the conduct of government.[69] This flaw was accentuated, at least initially, by the Tsar's lack of confidence in his own judgement and ability.[70] The third factor which reduced the practical ability of Nicholas II to exercise his autocratic powers was the absence of the civil, military and naval cabinets which underpinned the authority of Wilhelm II in Germany.[71] In contrast, Nicholas did not even have a private secretary,[72] and, as a consequence, much of his time was spent in dealing with trivialities, which in other circumstances he could have delegated to a secretariat.[73]

The imbalance between the Tsar's theoretical omnipotence and the practical limitations upon his power was recognised by several observers at the time. In February 1895, Friedrich von Holstein warned the Kaiser's adviser, Philipp Eulenburg, not to champion the cause of monarchical absolutism. In doing so, he noted that Wilhelm II was becoming much more of an autocrat than Nicholas II.[74] Bülow also eventually came to the same conclusion. In 1902, prior to the meeting between the Kaiser and the Tsar at Reval, he warned Wilhelm not to alienate Lamsdorf, the then Russian foreign minister, by drawing attention to the limitations upon the Tsar's practical authority. The Tsar was

---

[68] Wilhelm II to Nicholas II, 26 September 1895, *BKW*, pp. 294–6.
[69] Lieven, *Nicholas II*, pp. 68–101; Mossolov, *Last Tsar*, p. 126.
[70] Nicholas II to Grand Duke Vladimir, 26 November 1896. Theodore von Laue, *Sergei Witte and the Industrialization of Russia* (New York, 1969), p. 123.
[71] Dominic C. B. Lieven, *Russia's Rulers under the Old Régime* (London and New Haven, 1989), pp. 279–89; John C. G. Röhl, *Germany without Bismarck: The Crisis of Government in the Second Reich* (London, 1967); Röhl, *Kaiser, Hof und Staat*, pp.77–140; Isabel V. Hull, *The Entourage of Kaiser Wilhelm II*; Isabel V. Hull, 'Persönliches Regiment', in *Der Ort Kaiser Wilhelms II. in der deutschen Geschichte*, ed. John C. G. Röhl (Munich, 1991), pp. 3–23.
[72] Mossolov, *Last Tsar*, p. 12   [73] Verner, *Crisis*, pp. 51–2.
[74] Holstein to Eulenburg, 17 February 1895, *EK*, III, no. 1089, pp. 1470–2.

not a monarch like his German counterpart and was likely to adopt an anti-German policy if his foreign minister were to suggest such a course.[75] Even the Duke of York, the future King George V, and the cousin of both Wilhelm and Nicholas, told a German diplomat on one occasion that, although an autocrat, Nicholas II had less practical power than the Kaiser. The Tsar appeared to be unable to control his ministers, and whereas the German Emperor could always rely on the loyalty of the army, this was no longer the case in Russia. The Duke concluded that of the three monarchical systems, in Britain, Russia and Germany (respectively parliamentary monarchy, autocracy and constitutional monarchy), the German one was that which accorded most power to the sovereign.[76] None of this, however, altered the basic political fact in both Germany and Russia, namely that the monarch controlled all important governmental appointments, and that a minister could only stay in office if he retained the ruler's confidence. Thus no minister could seek to implement policies with which the Emperor disagreed and expect to remain in office.[77] In such a context, the Kaiser's personal appeals to the Tsar remained the most promising way to bring about a *rapprochement* between the two empires, although they should have been allied to other diplomatic strategies.

Before Nicholas's accession, Wilhelm had already identified the influence of Marie Feodorovna over her son as a major reason for the Tsarevitch's somewhat diffident character. Thus, when Nicholas visited Vienna in the autumn of 1892, and the German ambassador described him as shy and awkward, the Kaiser's blamed this on Marie Feodorovna's debilitating influence.[78] After Nicholas became Tsar, the Kaiser believed that if the power of the Dowager Empress over her son could be broken, this would open the way for a *rapprochement* between St Petersburg and Berlin. In the early years of the new Tsar's reign, Wilhelm and German diplomats constantly monitored the behaviour of

[75] Bülow to Wilhelm II, 22 July 1902, *GP*, xviii(i), pp. 60–1.
[76] Metternich to Bülow, 23 February 1900, PA Bonn Russland Nr 82 Nr 1 Bd 42.
[77] Cf. Röhl, *Kaiser, Hof und Staat*, pp. 116–40; Lieven, *Russia's Rulers*, pp. 280–2; S. S. Oldenbourg, *The Last Tsar: Nicholas II, His Reign and His Russia*, 4 vols., English translation (Gulf Breeze, FL, 1975–7), ii, p. 163; Verner, *Crisis*, pp. 53 8; McDonald, *United Government*, p. 212; Hintze to Wilhelm II, 28 January 1909, PA Bonn Russland Nr 82 Nr 1 Bd 3; Seeger, *Iswolsky*, p. 141; Katharine A. Lerman, *The Chancellor as Courtier: Bernhard von Bülow and the Governance of Germany, 1900–1909* (Cambridge, 1990); Gerd Fesser, *Reichskanzler Bernhard von Bülow* (Berlin, 1991).
[78] Wilhelm II's comment on Prince Heinrich VII, Reuss to Caprivi, 15 November 1892, *GP*, vii, no. 1638, note 4, p. 412.

both Nicholas and the Dowager Empress for signs of a break between them. Their mood turned to one of increasing frustration as it became clear that no such event was likely to occur, and as each new ministerial and ambassadorial appointment exhibited the continuing influence of Marie Feodorovna.

On 24 November 1894, the German ambassador in St Petersburg, Werder, wrote to Hohenlohe in pessimistic terms about the possibility that Nicholas would assert his own authority at the expense of his relationship with his mother. He believed that Nicholas was more likely to turn to his mother for advice on political questions.[79] It did not take long for her influence to make its mark, for in February 1895 Prince Lobanov-Rostovsky, the candidate favoured by the Dowager Empress and the French ambassador, was chosen as the new foreign minister, in place of the deceased N. K. Giers. The Kaiser, however, refused to be discouraged, and declared that a decisive break between the Tsar and the Dowager Empress would soon occur.[80]

In the months that followed, German diplomats believed that the Dowager Empress was strengthening her influence over the Tsar, and expressed scepticism as to the likelihood that Nicholas would soon alter his views towards Germany.[81] The Kaiser tried to counteract the growing influence of Lobanov and the Dowager Empress by appealing directly to Nicholas. To this end, he sent his aide de camp, Colonel Helmuth von Moltke, on a mission to St Petersburg in October 1895. Wilhelm was particularly alarmed by the international situation at this time because of the French decision to increase the strength of their forces on Germany's western frontier to coincide with a visit by Lobanov to Paris.[82] When Nicholas received Moltke he went out of his way to assure him that he had instructed his foreign minister to influence the French in a peaceable direction, and that if he had been aware that the French would seek to make political capital out of the visit, he would never have permitted Lobanov to go to Paris. Nicholas's comments on Russia's relations with Germany were similarly reassuring. He felt that

---

[79] Werder to Hohenlohe, 24 November 1894, PA Bonn Russland Nr 82 Nr 1 geheim. Bd 1; cf. note by Graf Rex, December 1894, *GP*, IX, no. 2308, pp. 338–9.

[80] Werder to Hohenlohe, 15 February 1895, *ibid.*, no. 2310, pp. 324–6. Wilhelm's comment, p. 326, note 5.

[81] Cf. Eulenburg to Holstein, 11 January 1895. *HP*, III, no. 434, p. 489; note by Eulenburg, 28 July 1895, *EK*, III, no. 1119, pp. 1516–17; Radolin to Eulenburg, 23 September and 2 October 1895, *ibid.*, nos. 1128, 1143, pp. 1536–9, 1561–4; Radolin to Hohenlohe, 14 July 1895, *GP*, IX, no. 2317, pp. 357–8.

[82] Wilhelm II to Nicholas II, 26 September 1895, *BKW*, pp. 295–6.

war between the two countries would only bring misery to both.[83] The Kaiser was satisfied with the outcome of Moltke's mission and heartened by the latter's conclusion that agreement could always be reached with the Tsar by appealing to the monarchical principle. However, he continued to believe that Nicholas was ill-informed about the political situation, a conviction strengthened by what he saw as the Tsar's naive view that Russia would be able to restrain the chauvinists in Paris.[84] Hugo Prince von Radolin, the German ambassador at St Peters-burg, took a similarly circumspect view. He felt that, despite his good intentions, Nicholas might not be able to resist the anti-German tendencies of his ministers, sentiments which were echoed by the influential director of the political section of the German foreign office Friedrich von Holstein.[85]

By November 1895 Wilhelm too was becoming frustrated at the lack of political concessions from Nicholas, and he made his feelings clear during a visit to Berlin by the Tsar's uncle, the Grand Duke Vladimir. Holstein informed Radolin:

> H.M. is beginning to be quite angry with the Tsar because of the repeated cool rebuffs. I don't know the details, but can pretty well construct the matter from the general picture. H.M. would like to restore the Holy Alliance, but Lobanov, who runs the Tsar, won't desert France.[86]

The Kaiser failed to hold his tongue on another occasion, when, out of anger against the Russians, he appeared to offer the British military attaché German support to force open the Dardanelles. A few weeks earlier Wilhelm had promised Nicholas II aid to achieve the same objective.[87] He had thus placed himself in the invidious position of having offered the Straits to two powers simultaneously. Holstein feared the damage which the remarks would cause if the British communicated them to St Petersburg, and even Eulenburg believed that the Kaiser's behaviour was exposing the dangers of personal decision-making in the sphere of foreign policy.[88]

---

[83] Helmuth von Moltke, report on a farewell audience with the Emperor of Russia, 3 October 1895, GStA Berlin BPH 53/116; Moltke, *Erinnerungen*, pp. 198–203; cf. Marschall to Hohenlohe, 1 October 1895, *DdR*, pp. 110–11.

[84] Note by Eulenburg, 12/13 October 1895, *EK*, III, no. 1145, pp. 1567–71; Eulenburg to Hohenlohe, 1 October 1895, *DdR*, pp. 111–12.

[85] Radolin to Eulenburg, 2/3 October 1895, *EK*, no. 1143, pp. 1561–5; Holstein to Eulenburg, 2 November 1895, *ibid.*, no. 1152, pp. 1583–4.

[86] Holstein to Radolin, 16 November 1895, *HP*, III, no. 501, p. 562.

[87] Note by Hohenlohe, 13 November 1895, *DdR*, pp. 120–2.

[88] Holstein to Eulenburg, 21 December 1895 and Eulenburg to Holstein, 31 December 1895, *ibid.*, nos. 515 and 517, pp. 576–85.

The Kruger telegram affair of January 1896 put a stop to any ideas which the Kaiser might have had of coming to an arrangement with Britain.[89] Thus, during 1896, Wilhelm continued to place his faith in his ability to persuade the Tsar of the merits of co-operation with Germany. The experiences of the previous year had failed to remove the wishful thinking which had motivated his *Russlandpolitik* since Nicholas's accession. The only people who stood in the way of a Russo-German understanding were the Dowager Empress and the foreign minister. The Tsar, by contrast, despite the evidence of his own pro-French sympathies, could be relied upon.[90] However, the reports being sent by German diplomats back to Berlin did not make encouraging reading from the Kaiser's viewpoint. Both Lobanov and the Dowager Empress continued to dominate the Tsar, and their opinions remained unconducive to an understanding with Germany.[91] None of this seemed to undermine the Kaiser's naive faith that the political constellation at St Petersburg would soon alter in Germany's favour. He shared his views with the newly appointed British ambassador, Sir Frank Lascelles, who subsequently communicated them to Count Hatzfeldt, the German ambassador in London. Lascelles 'told me . . .,' Hatzfeldt informed Holstein, 'that H.M. claims to know from a good source, that Lobanov will not remain in office any more. The young Emperor will now come into the foreground to a greater extent and enunciate his own foreign policy.'[92]

Wilhelm turned out to be correct. However the grim reaper rather than the Tsar was responsible for the Russian foreign minister's political demise. Lobanov's death in August 1896, shortly before a visit by the Tsar to Breslau, seemed to provide the Kaiser with an excellent opportunity to convince Nicholas of his good faith and to encourage him to appoint a pro-German foreign minister. The meeting between the two emperors appeared to go well,[93] and Hohenlohe's report on his audience with Nicholas II was also more than satisfactory from a German perspective. The Tsar had spoken of his desire to open up Siberia to Russian colonisation, to carry through the completion of the

---

[89] See ch. 2.

[90] Marschall, diary entry, 11 June 1896, Walther P. Fuchs (ed.), *Grossherzog Friedrich I. von Baden und die Reichspolitik 1871–1907*, 4 vols. (Stuttgart, 1968–80), III, p. 526.

[91] Radolin to Hohenlohe, 18 April 1896, *GP*, XI, no. 2847, pp. 340–42; cf. Marschall to Münster, 19 May 1896, *ibid.*, no. 2851, p. 346.

[92] Hatzfeldt to Holstein, 4 June 1896, *HNP*, II, no. 683, pp. 1086–7.

[93] Wilhelm II to the German foreign office, 9 September 1896, *GP*, XI, no. 2861, p. 360.

Trans-Siberian railway, and to confront the Japanese in the Far East once the line to the Pacific was finished.[94] All of which conformed with the Kaiser's wish to see Russian expansionism directed away from Europe.

Despite the visit's superficial success, events over the subsequent month were to prove that it had been counter-productive, for it encouraged Nicholas's doubts about Wilhelm's character and sincerity. The Tsar had been growing tired of the Kaiser's patronising manner towards him.[95] However, Nicholas's mother played the decisive part in transforming the Tsar's doubts about the Kaiser into a profound distaste. For after the visit to Breslau, the Tsar and Tsarina travelled to Copenhagen. In the anti-German atmosphere of the Danish royal palace at Bernstorff, Marie Feodorovna managed to regain influence over her son. According to a well-informed Danish source, who passed on information to Alfred von Kiderlen-Wächter, the German minister in Copenhagen, Nicholas had intially spoken favourably about his meeting with the Kaiser at Breslau. However, the Dowager Empress had responded by pouring scorn and derision upon her son, and, in so doing, had destroyed the excellent impression made on the Tsar by his visit to Germany.[96] Statements which the Tsar made to the British prime minister, Lord Salisbury, during a subsequent visit to Balmoral, and to the French foreign minister, M. Hanotaux, whilst in Paris confirmed that his visit to Denmark had resulted in a marked increase in his hostility towards the Kaiser. Nicholas was at pains to assure the French foreign minister that under no circumstances would he give in to Wilhelm's overtures to abandon the alliance with Paris in favour of a return to co-operation with Berlin.[97]

The suspicion that the summit between Nicholas and Wilhelm at Breslau had been counter-productive was reinforced by a disastrous subsequent exchange of visits between the two monarchs at Darmstadt and Wiesbaden. The Tsar, who was staying with his brother-in-law, the Grand Duke of Hesse, had initially declined to meet Wilhelm for a second time, and made no secret of his distaste for the Kaiser, during their discussions, by behaving in an off-hand manner. Wilhelm was

[94] Note by Hohenlohe, 10 September 1896, _ibid_, no. 2862, pp. 361–2.
[95] Radolin to Hatzfeldt, 15 September 1896, _HNP_, II, no. 689, p. 1093; Soulange-Boudin to Hanotaux, 16 September 1896, _DDF_, 1st series, XII, no. 454, pp. 748–51; Schelking, _Recollections_, p. 129.
[96] Kiderlen-Wächter to Hohenlohe, 16 September 1896, PA Bonn Dänemark 32 Nr 1; Schelking, _Recollections_, p. 129.
[97] Margaret M. Jefferson, 'Lord Salisbury's Conversations with the Tsar at Balmoral, 27 and 29 September 1896', _Slavonic and East European Review_ 39, 22 (1960), 220; note by Hanotaux, 12 October 1896, _DDF_, 1st series, XII, no. 472, p. 781.

greatly shaken by the change in the Tsar's attitude towards him, which he blamed on the Grand Duke Sergei, who was also present at Darmstadt, and on the influence of the Dowager Empress upon her son.[98] When Eulenburg raised the matter of the visit, two weeks after it had occurred, the Kaiser turned pale. Eulenburg recorded: 'H.M. said very little to me about it. I sensed how much it tormented him. "An Emperor under the rule of his mother," he said, with a certain bitter contempt.'[99]

Two events following closely on the disastrous summit between the two emperors indicated that Nicholas now wished to distance himself from the Kaiser, thus demonstrating that the personal contact upon which Wilhelm placed so much importance in his dealings with the Tsar had proved itself to be an ineffectual mechanism for bringing about an improvement in Russo-German relations. Soon after his return from Germany, Nicholas decided that he wished to discontinue his correspondence with Wilhelm. He had grown uneasy with the letters' contents and his doubts had been strengthened when he learned that the Kaiser had written them without Hohenlohe's knowledge. The Tsar's hapless Uncle Micha, the Grand Duke Vladimir, again acted as the intermediary between Nicholas and Wilhelm. The Kaiser ignored the Tsar's desire to break off the correspondence and proceeded to continue writing to Nicholas for a further eighteen years.[100]

The Tsar's choice of Muraviev as his new foreign minister was a more serious set-back still for the Kaiser. Wilhelm had vetoed Muraviev's appointment two years previously as Russian ambassador to Berlin, so the new foreign minister had no reason to be favourably disposed towards him.[101] In addition, as a former minister in Copenhagen, Muraviev's rise to high office had been aided by the patronage of Marie Feodorovna.[102] Holstein believed that Wilhelm II's own disastrous interventions in the sphere of foreign policy had resulted in Muraviev's appointment. The Kaiser's policy of courting Russia and England in turn, at one point seeming to offer the Dardanelles to both powers, had simply resulted in the alienation of both Nicholas II and Queen Victoria, to the detriment of Germany's international interests.[103] Additionally, the issue of the Germanophobe influence of the Dowager Empress

[98] Wilhelm II to Hohenlohe, 20 October 1896, *GP*, XI, no. 2868, pp. 369–70.
[99] Note by Eulenburg, 8 November 1896, *EK*, III, no. 1272, p. 1751.
[100] Holstein to Hatzfeldt, 27/28 November 1896, *HNP*, II, no. 692, p. 1098; Rudolf Vierhaus (ed.), *Das Tagebuch der Baronin von Spitzemberg* (Göttingen, 1960), diary entry, 18 November 1896, p. 348; Wilhelm II to Nicholas II, 12 November 1896, *BKW*, pp. 303–4.
[101] Holstein to Radolin, 10 January 1897, *HP*, IV, no. 592, p. 1.
[102] Eulenburg to Holstein, 13 January 1897, *ibid.*, no. 593, pp. 2–3; cf. Holstein to Hatzfeldt, 15 January 1897, *HNP*, II, no. 697, p. 1112, note 5.
[103] Holstein to Hatzfeldt, 15 January 1897, *HNP*, II, no. 697, pp. 1122–5.

had still not been addressed. The disconcerting nature of her views continued to matter because of the hold she exercised over her son. Radolin lamented to Hohenlohe that Marie Feodorovna's power had reached levels never seen during the reign of Alexander III.[104]

Despite these political set-backs during the winter of 1896/97, Wilhelm II remained determined to continue to pursue the aim of an understanding with Russia. However the visit which the Kaiser paid to St Petersburg in August 1897 exposed the limits of the Tsar's desire for good relations with Germany, and it also served to confirm Nicholas's distaste for his German counterpart.[105] The chargé d'affaires of the French embassy in Berlin, Soulange-Boudin, noted the gulf between the myth of intimacy with the Tsar and the Russians, which the Kaiser and the German government wished to promote, and the reality of continuing distrust between the two emperors and governments.[106] The Tsar's growing animosity towards Wilhelm had been confirmed before the Kaiser's arrival in St Petersburg. Nicholas informed his mother that he would have to make the Kaiser an honorary admiral in the Russian navy as an act of courtesy prior to the visit. 'C'est à vomir!', he wrote.[107] Despite this, the political discussions during the Kaiser's visit seemed to go well. Wilhelm appeared to get Nicholas's permission to establish a German naval base at Kiaochow on the Chinese coast, though the conversation between them on this issue was hypothetical in nature,[108] and Nicholas told the German foreign minister, Bernhard von Bülow, that he believed that Russia's relations with Germany were too important to be damaged by economic differences caused by the attempts of German landowners to get the government to raise the tariffs on Russian agricultural imports. Bülow, in turn, was heartened by the anti-English views of Nicholas and his ministers, and believed that enthusiasm in St Petersburg for the alliance with France was declining.[109]

As in the previous year, these hopes were misplaced. The French ambassador to Berlin noted that in spite of the claims of the *Wilhelmstrasse* that the visit had been a success beyond expectations, there was

---

[104] Radolin to Hohenlohe, 17 January 1897, *DdR*, pp. 292–4.
[105] Paléologue, *Guillaume II et Nicolas II*, pp. 15–16.
[106] Soulange-Boudin to Hanotaux, 8 August 1897, *DDF*, 1st series, XIII, pp. 487–9.
[107] Nicholas II to Marie Feodorovna, 23 July 1897, *Letters of Tsar Nicholas*, p. 128.
[108] Bülow to the German Foreign Office, 11 August 1897; note by Bülow, 17 August 1897, *GP*, XIV(i), nos. 3679–80, pp. 58–60.
[109] Bülow to the German foreign office, 10 August 1897, *GP*, XIII, no. 3438, pp. 75–6; cf. Radolin to the German foreign office, 12 August 1897, *ibid.*, nos. 3439, p. 77; Bülow to Eulenburg, 20 August 1897, *ibid.*, no. 3444, pp. 81–2; Radolin to the German foreign office, 18 August 1897, *ibid.*, no. 3443, pp. 79–81.

evidence to the contrary. He pointed to the reserved nature of the Tsar's toast, in contrast to warmth of that of his guest.[110] Nicholas was greatly relieved by Wilhelm's departure, and although he described the Kaiser as 'cheerful, calm and courteous' during the visit, he made no secret of his dislike of the Kaiserin. 'She tried to be charming and looked very ugly in rich clothes chosen without taste', he wrote to his mother.[111] In any case, a visit paid by President Faure of France to St Petersburg, soon after Wilhelm's departure, served to destroy the meagre benefits which the Kaiser's state visit had brought to German–Russian relations.[112]

The German seizure of the Chinese port of Kiaochow as a naval base in November 1897 caused more serious damage to German–Russian relations and to the relationship between Wilhelm and Nicholas. The Tsar believed that Russia, which had used the bay of Kiaochow as an anchorage for its Pacific fleet, had first claim on the port and that the Kaiser had tricked him over Germany's plans, both during his visit to St Petersburg, and in a telegram shortly before the seizure of the port.[113] The ill-feeling between the Kaiser and the Tsar had already been heightened before the seizure of Kiaochow by Wilhelm's tactless complaint to a Russian diplomat about Nicholas's failure to pay a visit to Berlin on his way to Darmstadt, where the Tsar spent the autumn of 1897 as the guest of the Grand Duke of Hesse.[114] Radolin had no doubt that the Kiaochow incident had caused enormous damage to Russo-German relations, not least at the dynastic level. The Tsar would continue to bear a grudge against Germany and would be unlikely to trust the Kaiser in future.[115] This proved to be the case, for Nicholas again avoided Berlin when travelling to Darmstadt in the autumn of 1898, and at his next meeting with the Kaiser, he refused to discuss political questions with him alone, for fear of being tricked for a second time.[116]

---

[110] Marquis de Noailles to M. Méline, 20 August 1897, *DDF*, 1st series, XIII, no. 303, pp. 508–9.

[111] Nicholas II to Marie Feodorovna, 1/14 August 1897, *Letters of Tsar Nicholas*, pp. 128–31.

[112] Cf. Radolin to Hohenlohe, 20 August 1897. *DdR*, p. 377; Radolin to Hohenlohe, 28 August 1897. *GP*, XIII, no. 3447, p. 85.

[113] *GP*, XIV(i), nos. 3679–711, pp. 58–98; Lord Onslow, minute, undated, *BD*, III, p. 382; Oldenbourg, *The Last Tsar*, I, pp. 124–5; Ian Nish, *The Origins of the Russo-Japanese War* (London, 1985), pp. 38–47.

[114] Schelking, *Recollections*, p. 130.

[115] Letter by Radolin, 28 December 1897, *HP*, IV, no. 639, pp. 60–1; cf. Cecil Spring-Rice to Sir Frank Lascelles, 27 September 1904, PRO FO 800/12.

[116] Onslow, minute, undated, *BD*, III, p. 382; Maurice Paléologue, *The Turning Point. Three Critical Years, 1904–1906*, English translation (London, 1935), diary entry, 16 February 1904, p. 36.

In the late 1890s, German diplomats and the Kaiser were becoming increasingly aware of the weakness of the Russian monarchy. In June 1898, Heinrich von Tschirschky und Bögendorff, the chargé at the German embassy in St Petersburg, reported that the standing of the monarchy in the eyes of the Russian people had declined in the three and a half years since Nicholas's accession. The Tsar's own failure to assert his authority was a major factor in this. Nicholas was referred to more and more often in official circles by the contemptuous nickname 'the Colonel', and his reign was increasingly seen as one of transition, perhaps to a republic.[117] The Kaiser also seems to have doubted the Russian empire's capacity for survival, writing on a diplomatic report in the summer of 1899: 'In any case it is still very questionable which [empire] will collapse first, Habsburg or Romanov.'[118]

Despite this, the maintenance of good relations with Russia remained a priority for the *Reichsleitung*. The German *Weltpolitik* initiated in 1897 with the appointments of Admiral von Tirpitz, as state secretary of the imperial navy office, and of Bülow, as state secretary of the German foreign office, had an anti-English orientation, and was based on the belief that an understanding between Russia and England was impossible. Germany thus pursued a pro-Russian policy in the years that followed, which was cloaked under the myth that the *Reich* stood equidistant, in political terms, between St Petersburg and London.[119] The classic exposition of the policy was made in Bülow's letter to Wilhelm II of 19 August 1898. Germany should bide her time, awaiting the Anglo-Russian war, which Bülow believed would eventually occur. She should also maintain good relations with both of these powers so that when the time came, she would be able to choose between them.[120] A few months later, Wilhelm II's brother Prince Heinrich proposed a diplomatic alternative to that outlined by Bülow. The Prince believed that Germany's interests in the Far East, and elsewhere, would be best served by an alliance with both England and Russia. The Kaiser described his brother's views as 'naive' and 'utopian', and wrote in relation to the possibility of an Anglo-German-Russian combination: 'Squaring the circle would be easier than this!'[121] The options were thus limited to a

[117] Tschirschky to Hohenlohe, 16 June 1898, PA Bonn Russland Nr 82 Nr 1 geheim. Bd 1.
[118] Wilhelm II's comment on Derenthall to Hohenlohe, 21 June 1899, *GP*, XIII, no. 3539, p. 216.
[119] Paul M. Kennedy, *The Rise of the Anglo-German Antagonism, 1860–1914* (London, 1980); Peter Winzen, *Bülows Weltmachtkonzept*; Vogel, *Deutsche Russlandpolitik*; Volker R. Berghahn, *Der Tirpitz-Plan. Genesis und Verfall einer innenpolitischen Krisenstrategie unter Wilhelm II.* (Düsseldorf, 1971).
[120] Bülow to Wilhelm II, 19 August 1898, GStA Merseburg HA Rep. 53 J Lit.B Nr 16a Bd 1.
[121] Prince Heinrich to Wilhelm II, with comments by Wilhelm, 4 February 1899. GStA Merseburg HA Rep. 52 V1 Nr 13.

choice between the two powers, and this meant in reality that Germany had no alternative but to seek closer relations with Russia.[122]

The key problem was that this policy depended heavily on the maintenance of a warm and trusting relationship between the two Emperors, and by 1899 this was patently lacking. What Nicholas perceived as the Kaiser's duplicitousness over the seizure of Kiachow had been compounded in the winter of 1898/9 by Wilhelm's attempts to exploit the Fashoda crisis in the Sudan between Britain and France, first to embroil both Russia and France in a war with Britain, and then to use the crisis as a pretext to detach Russia from France.[123] In June 1899, the Russian envoy in Stuttgart told his Prussian counterpart that the ill-feeling between the Kaiser and the Tsar was an obstacle to an improvement in relations between the two countries. Wilhelm's statements were often presented in St Petersburg in an unfavourable light, and had made a bad impression on Nicholas.[124] The Tsar's own behaviour also contributed to the deterioration in his relationship with the Kaiser. He took a perverse pleasure in wounding Wilhelm's *amour propre*, for example by giving the Kaiser the honorary colonelcy in a Russian guards regiment which had occupied Berlin during the Seven Years War.[125] In addition, Nicholas's repeated failure to visit Berlin or Potsdam, despite frequent trips to Darmstadt since his accession, understandably gave the Kaiser the impression that the Tsar wished to avoid him. When the Tsar visited Hesse in the autumn of 1899, he again refused to travel to Potsdam for an interview with Wilhelm, on the grounds that he was in mourning for his recently deceased brother, Grand Duke George. On this occasion, having lost patience with Nicholas, Wilhelm vowed that he would not accept the Tsar's refusal, thus provoking a minor diplomatic crisis.[126] Considerable pressure was exerted by the Germans on the Russians to get the Tsar to agree to a meeting with the Kaiser at Potsdam, and grave warnings were given as to the likely consequences for German–Russian relations if Nicholas were to refuse.[127]

---

[122] Winzen, *Bülows Weltmachtkonzept*, p. 81.

[123] Roderick R. McLean, 'The Kaiser's Diplomacy and the Reconquest of the Sudan', in *Sudan. The Reconquest Reappraised*, ed. Edward M. Spiers, (London, 1998), pp. 149, 151–7.

[124] Derenthall to Hohenlohe, 21 June 1899, *GP*, xiii, no. 3539, pp. 213–16; Radolin to Holstein, 30 June 1899, *HP*, iv, no. 695, pp. 136–7.

[125] Schelking, *Recollections*, pp. 135–6.

[126] Bülow to Wihelm II, 16 September 1899, with footnote, *GP*, xiii, no. 3540, pp. 216–18; Princess Heinrich to Wilhelm II, 11 September 1899, GStA Merseburg HA Rep. 52 Vi Nr 23.

[127] Radolin to Holstein, 29 September 1899, *HP*, iv, no. 708, pp. 157–8; Bülow to Wilhelm II, 6 August 1899, GStA Merseburg HA Rep. 53 J Lit B Nr 16a Bd 1; Richthofen to Radolin, 19 September 1899, Bülow to the German foreign office, 21 September 1899, Radolin to the German foreign office, 22 September 1899, *GP* xiii, nos. 3541–3, pp. 218–23.

Having given in to German pressure, Nicholas reluctantly agreed to visit Potsdam on 8 November 1899. The signing of an agreement between Britain and Germany on Samoa, on the day of the Tsar's visit, served as a warning to Nicholas of the dangers which might follow if Russia were to alienate the *Reich*.[128] In the course of the political discussions, Nicholas stressed his desire for close co-operation between Russia and Germany, and his wish to maintain peace. However, he also made clear that Russia's interests in the Near East must be respected, indicating that Germany's growing political and economic influence in Turkey was causing him disquiet.[129] The Tsar's views on this subject were echoed by Muraviev.[130] Despite these warnings, Bülow, in a letter to Radolin, stressed that nothing stood in the way of the maintenance of friendly relations between Germany and Russia.[131]

However such optimism could not disguise the reality. Since Nicholas II's accession, there had been no fundamental improvement in German–Russian relations. The seizure of Kiaochow had destroyed the Tsar's faith in the Kaiser. Similarly meetings between the two emperors had encouraged Nicholas's personal antipathy towards Wilhelm. In addition, the Kaiser's attitude towards the Tsar and the Russians was one of increasing resentment. He had offered Nicholas support for Russian expansion in the Far East and had assiduously pursued the latter's friendship. In return, the Tsar had grown wary of Wilhelm, tried, whenever possible, to avoid meeting him, and seemed, on every occasion, to give in to pressure, on political issues, from the grand dukes, the Dowager Empress and his foreign minister. Nicholas showed no sign of wishing to abandon France in favour of an alliance with Berlin, preferring to keep Germany and her ruler at arm's length. The Kaiser's frustration at the difficulty of reaching agreement with the Russians was made clear in a note which he added to a report of a conversation between Radolin and Witte, in which the Russian finance minister stressed his support for a continental league. Wilhelm wrote: 'I have indeed already been prepared for it, but at the last moment a firm will and purposeful action has always been missing in Russia.'[132]

Relations between Germany and Russia actually deteriorated in the eighteen months after the Tsar's visit to Potsdam. The involvement of

---

[128] Bülow to Wilhelm II, 8 November 1899, GStA Merseburg HA Rep. 53 J Lit. B Nr 16a Bd 1.
[129] Note by Bülow, 8 November 1899, *GP*, XIII, no. 3547, pp. 227–9
[130] Note by Bülow, 8 November 1899, *ibid.*, no. 3548, pp. 229–30.
[131] Bülow to Radolin, 13 November 1899, *ibid.*, no. 3549, pp. 230–1.
[132] Wilhelm II's comment on Radolin to Hohenlohe, 2 April 1899, *GP*, XIII, no. 3537, pp. 209–11, note 12.

both German and Russian troops in the international expedition to crush the Boxer Rebellion in China, in 1900, ended in recrimination, not least between the two Emperors. The Kaiser believed that the Russians were pursuing their own selfish political agenda, seeking to defend their interests in Manchuria, whereas the Tsar was said to be angered by the appointment of Field Marshall von Waldersee as head of the expedition, believing that Wilhelm had foisted the appointment upon the other countries without adequate consultation.[133] The Kaiser's ill-humour towards the Tsar was not restricted to politics. It also extended to a mockery of the latter's attachment to religious mysticism, which he sarcastically compared to that of Philip II of Spain.[134]

Bülow's letters to the Kaiser in the summer of 1900 acknowledged Wilhelm's irritation with Nicholas. Nevertheless, he continued to stress the importance of maintaining good relations with Russia, so as to secure the safety of Germany's eastern frontier. In his letter to the Kaiser of 6 August, Bülow noted the difficulty of reaching agreement with the Russians, particularly as no one knew who truly ruled in St Petersburg. However, in the same letter, he emphasised that co-operation with the English was not an alternative to working with the Russians. The former were unreliable, and in any case, Germany's historic mission was to succeed the British Empire as the leading world power.[135] In a further letter, on 22 August, Bülow warned the Kaiser that if Germany alienated the Tsar over the China Expedition, the Russians might seek an agreement with England over their mutual interests in China. Thus, caution remained the best policy.[136]

The Kaiser, however, continued to complain about Nicholas, and not always discreetly. While in England for Queen Victoria's funeral, Wilhelm complained to his uncle, Edward VII, that the Russians seemed to want to withdraw from China before the Chinese government had made adequate concessions.[137] In conversation with the British foreign

---

[133] Holstein to Hatzfeldt, 26 July 1900, *HNP*, no. 824, pp. 1331–4; Holstein to Hatzfeldt, 23 August 1900, Radolin to Holstein, 31 August 1900, and Hatzfeldt to Holstein, 29 September 1900, *HP*, IV, nos. 741, 745, 750, pp. 195–7, 201, 207; Hohenlohe to Prince Alexander Hohenlohe, 26 September 1900, and Prince Alexander to Hohenlohe, 30 September 1900. *DdR*, pp. 586–7; Nish, *Russo-Japanese War*, pp. 64–94.

[134] Wilhelm II's comment on Hohenau to Hohenlohe, 15 June 1900, PA Bonn Russland Nr 82 Nr 1 Bd 42; cf. Wilhelm II's comments on Alvensleben to Bülow, 8 August 1903, *ibid.*, Bd 49.

[135] Bülow to Wilhelm II, 6 August 1900, GStA Merseburg HA Rep. 53 J Lit. B Nr 16a Bd II.

[136] Bülow to Wilhelm II, 22 August 1900, *ibid.*

[137] Metternich to Bülow, 22 January 1901, *HP*, IV, no. 765, pp. 217–18; Eckardstein to the German foreign office, 29 January 1901, *GP*, XVII, no. 4986, pp. 23–4.

secretary, Lord Lansdowne, the Kaiser declared, 'The signs of the time mean that the future will belong to either the Slavic or the Germanic race',[138] which suggested he now saw Russia as a probable enemy in a future racial war. Lansdowne, in a retrospective note on the conversation, recorded that Wilhelm had described Nicholas II as only 'fit to live in a country house and rear turnips'.[139] The Kaiser had also turned against the Tsar's uncle, Grand Duke Vladimir, formerly seen as the most pro-German of the Romanovs, who he believed was gradually becoming aware of the sins which he had committed against Germany over the previous ten years.[140]

Wilhelm's Russophobe sentiments and his antagonism towards the Tsar and the Russian royal family caused Bülow alarm, for the chancellor believed that everything had to be done to avoid alienating Nicholas II and his court. He outlined the policy which he wished to be adopted towards Russia in a letter to the Kaiser's uncle, Grand Duke Friedrich of Baden. 'We must not run after the Russians; however we must avoid in particular anything that would anger the Russian Court and the Russian Emperor unnecessarily.'[141] When the Grand Duke met Wilhelm, he tried to convince his nephew that the Tsar's good-will was a prerequisite for friendly relations between the two empires. However, the Kaiser remained hostile to Russia and critical of Nicholas.[142]

In the summer of 1901, arrangements were made for a meeting between the Kaiser and the Tsar at the German port of Danzig.[143] However Wilhelm's attitude towards Nicholas and the Russians remained one of increasing frustration and resentment. The Kaiser was irritated by the long delays before Nicholas replied to his letters. Bülow, rather than giving the obvious reason, that the Tsar had tired of the correspondence, somewhat unconvincingly attributed it to Russian inefficiency.[144] Further alarm had been caused in Berlin by the news that following his visit to Danzig, Nicholas would attend the French army manoeuvres at Compiègne. The Kaiser even suggested to Bülow that in

---

[138] Wilhelm II to Bülow, 29 January 1901, *GP*, XVII, no. 4987, pp. 24–9.
[139] Lansdowne, notes on a conversation with the Kaiser, Sandringham 1901. Lansdowne Papers, PRO FO 800/130.
[140] Wilhelm II's comments on Pourtalès to Bülow, 11 February 1901, PA Bonn Russland Nr 82 Nr 1 Bd 43.
[141] Bülow to Grand Duke of Baden, 26 April 1901, *Grossherzog Friedrich*, IV, no. 2173, p. 307.
[142] Grand Duke of Baden to Bülow, 18 May 1901, *ibid.*, no. 2190, p. 324; cf. Wilhelm II's comments on Schlözer to Hohenlohe, 5 September 1900. PA Bonn Russland Nr 82 Nr 1 Bd 43 and on Hatzfeldt to the German foreign office, 29 April 1901, *ibid.*, Bd. 44.
[143] Wilhelm II to Nicholas II, 22 August 1901, *BKW*, pp. 320–1.
[144] Bülow to Wilhelm II, 22 August 1901, *GP*, XVIII(i), no. 5391, p. 19.

the light of the military character of the Tsar's visit to France, measures should be taken to reinforce Germany's frontiers.[145] Bülow and the Kaiser both believed that Russia's need for a loan from France explained the Tsar's visit, and the fact that the French had requested it served to confirm this.[146]

Despite German displeasure at Nicholas's decision to follow his visit to Danzig with one to France, the meeting between the two emperors at the German port in September 1901 marked the start of an improvement in dynastic relations between St Petersburg and Berlin which was to last for several years. By the time of the Danzig visit, the Kaiser's advisers had become resigned to the fact that Wilhelm would talk openly to Nicholas no matter what the advice given.[147] The Tsar's visit was judged a resounding success, with Bülow being particularly heartened to learn that on leaving Nicholas had said to a German admiral, 'I hope that we will always fight shoulder to shoulder.'[148] During the political discussions, Nicholas, as in 1899, showed himself to be distrustful of the English, and in particular of the British prime minister, Lord Salisbury. Both Nicholas and Lamsdorf made clear that, in principle, they supported the aim of a continental league, which had long been the Kaiser's obsession, although the Tsar stressed that he regarded this as an objective for the future.[149] One encouraging sign was that Nicholas had also found Wilhelm more agreeable than usual, describing him as 'in good spirits, calm, and very amiable.'[150] Even the Russian press, traditionally hostile to Germany, had reported favourably on the meeting. One of the St Petersburg newspapers had maintained that only co-operation between the two emperors could maintain peace in Europe. The Kaiser noted, with approval, 'So it is and will be if God wishes it.'[151]

The success of the Danzig meeting was not the only indication that relations between the two emperors, and between Germany and Russia, were improving. The Tsar's reception in France appeared, from the German perspective, to be much less cordial than that which he had

---

[145] Wilhelm II's comment on Mühlberg to Wilhelm II, 20 August 1901, PA Bonn Russland Nr 82 Nr 1 Bd 44; Wilhelm II to Bülow, 20 August 1901, *GP*, xviii(i), no. 5388, pp. 14–16.

[146] Wilhelm II to Bülow, 20 August 1901, *GP*, xviii(i), no. 5388, pp. 14–15; Bülow to Wilhelm II, 21 August 1901, PA Bonn Russland Nr 82 Nr 1. Bd 44; Wilhelm II's comment on Bülow to Wilhelm II, 22 August 1901, *ibid.*; Spring, 'Russia', p. 568.

[147] Holstein to Bülow, 10 August 1901, *GP*, xviii(i), p. 24.

[148] Bülow to the German foreign office, 14 September 1901, *GP*, xviii(i), no. 5394, p. 29.

[149] Note by Bülow, 14 September 1901, *ibid.*, no. 5395, pp. 29–31.

[150] Nicholas II to Marie Feodorovna, 2/15 September 1901, *Letters of Tsar Nicholas*, pp. 150–2.

[151] Wilhelm II's comment on Pückler to Bülow, 16 September 1901, *GP*, xviii(i), no. 5396, p. 32.

received on his last visit there in 1896. The French newspaper *La libre parole* caught the general mood of disappointment. It criticised Nicholas for failing to visit Paris, and for not mentioning the legitimacy of French claims to Alsace in any of his speeches. The Kaiser saw this example of awakening French disenchantment with the Russians as an encouraging sign that the days of the Dual Alliance were numbered. He noted with regard to the change in French attitudes:

Finally the meaning of the alliance is beginning to be understood in France! After only 10 years! We have known it for a long time! The Emperor of Russia ratified the treaty at Metz by ambassador, at Compiègne he did it personally, what more could I want??![152]

Prince Heinrich spent October 1901 as the guest of the Tsar at Spala, the latter's hunting lodge in Poland. The impressions which he brought back of his brother-in-law's character and political opinions gave encouragement to German hopes that Nicholas would play a more assertive role in the interests of warmer relations with Berlin. The Tsar had stressed his determination to maintain the autocratic system, and also his hostility towards England. In contrast, Nicholas was now more favourably disposed towards Wilhelm personally than had previously been the case, confirming the benefit of the meeting between them at Danzig. In foreign policy terms, the Tsar's chief interest remained the construction of the Siberian railway, but he was also convinced that Germany and Russia should always co-operate. The Prince concluded, according to a note made by Bülow, 'One must be friendly towards the Tsar, dare not make him mistrustful, but must leave him in peace.'[153]

Heinrich's stay at Spala was followed by other exchanges of visits between the two royal families, designed to promote good-will between Germany and Russia and to reinforce dynastic ties. In the summer of 1902, the Tsar's younger brother, the Grand Duke Michael, visited Kiel, an event which was exploited for propaganda purposes by the German government as an indication of the warmth of the *Reich*'s relations with St Petersburg.[154] Subsequently, the Kaiser's eldest son, Crown Prince Wilhelm, visited Russia, and, as with the visit of the Grand Duke Michael to Germany, it was depicted in the German press as a manifestation of the intimacy of the ties between the Hohenzollerns and

[152] Wilhelm II's comment on *La libre parole*, 22 September 1901, PA Bonn Russland Nr 82 Nr 1 Bd 45.
[153] Note by Bülow, 4 November 1901, *GP*, xviii(i), no. 5399, pp. 34–5.
[154] Bülow to the German foreign office, 1 July 1902, PA Bonn Russland Nr 82 Nr 1 Bd 46.

Romanovs.[155] A further hopeful signal came in February 1902, when the Austrian ambassador in Petersburg, Baron Aehrenthal, told his German counterpart, Count Alvensleben, that the Russian monarch was beginning to have doubts about his country's close relationship with the French republic. The Tsar was now showing a noticeable inclination to consider a return to Russia's traditional policy of co-operation with Germany and Austria. For Wilhelm, this information offered great encouragement, and he was not prepared to let Austrian suspicions of Russia stand in the way of a *rapprochement* with the latter power, the aim he had pursued for most of the previous decade. 'Whether Austria shows itself indifferent or not is wholly irrelevant for the course of world history! It is our ally and will go along with whatever I agree with the Tsar!! The two of us make history and determine fates!'[156]

During an audience given by the Kaiser, in April 1902, the Russian naval attaché Paulis confirmed that the Tsar had become favourably inclined towards Germany and Wilhelm personally. Nicholas wished to meet the Kaiser again during 1902. Wilhelm had responded by reiterating his offer to guard Russia's western frontier, thus allowing the Tsar the freedom to move against the Japanese in Asia.[157] Bülow remained convinced, in the light of the conversation, that the friendship between the two emperors remained the best guarantee of good relations between Germany and Russia.[158] However, in his conversation with Wilhelm, the Russian naval attaché had made clear that Lamsdorf was not favourably disposed towards Germany and continued to influence Nicholas against the *Reich*.[159]

At the same time, the Kaiser remained suspicious of the Russian foreign minister and unwilling to take any step which might conciliate him. This represented a major flaw in Germany's *Russlandpolitik*, for in practical terms, while Lamsdorf remained in office, he also needed to be persuaded of the merits of co-operation with Berlin. The Kaiser was due to visit the Tsar at Reval in August 1902. In July of the same year, it became evident that Lamsdorf did not plan to attend the meeting between the two emperors. Both Holstein and Bülow saw the Russian

---

[155]　Wilhelm II to Nicholas II, 14 January 1903, *BKW*, pp. 329–30; Nicholas II to Wilhelm II, 10/23 January 1903, GStA Merseburg HA Rep. 53 J Lit. R Nr. 16; Noailles to Delcassé, 3 January 1903, *DDF*, 2nd series, III, no. 3, pp. 3–4.

[156]　Wilhelm II's comment on Alvensleben to Bülow, 18 February 1902, *GP*, XVIII(ii), no. 5900, p. 824.

[157]　Note by Richthofen, 3 April 1902, *GP*, XVIII(i), no. 5408, pp. 47–50.

[158]　Bülow to Wilhelm II, 5 April 1902, *ibid.*, no. 5409, p. 50.

[159]　Note by Richthofen, 3 April 1902, *ibid.*, no. 5408, p. 48.

foreign minister's presence as crucial if Germany's enemies were not to present Lamsdorf's absence as a political setback for the *Reich*. The chancellor wished the Kaiser to encourage Lamsdorf to attend, perhaps by offering him the Order of the Black Eagle.[160] Wilhelm initially refused to make any concessions to ensure the presence of Lamsdorf at Reval. His reasons for doing so indicated his capacity for wishful thinking and his tendency to let personal feelings interfere with his attitude towards political issues. Wilhelm accused the Russian foreign minister of having intrigued constantly against him, and of trying to convince the Tsar that he could not be trusted. In any case, Wilhelm claimed, Lamsdorf no longer possessed Nicholas's favour and was likely to be replaced soon.[161] In fact, he retained the post of foreign minister for another four years. It fell to Bülow to remind the Kaiser that Nicholas II did not make policy alone and that it would be dangerous to alienate his foreign minister. The chancellor did not share Wilhelm's belief that Nicholas would soon dismiss Lamsdorf and wished to ensure that the latter would not seek to poison the Tsar against Germany. The argument worked and after pressure from the St Petersburg embassy, Lamsdorf agreed to come to Reval.[162]

During the visit, the Tsar assured Bülow of his continuing sympathy for Wilhelm and of his faith in the sincerity of the Kaiser's commitment to peace. In addition, Nicholas had not hidden his growing anger with Japan and his opposition to her claims in Korea.[163] Nevertheless, the meeting seems to have been less successful than the encounter between the two emperors at Danzig the previous year. One of Nicholas's courtiers recalled that every interview which the Tsar had with the German Emperor 'got on his nerves'. The meeting at Reval was no exception, Nicholas reportedly declaring to the members of his suite as Wilhelm sailed away at the end of the visit, 'He's raving mad!'[164] The Reval summit also failed to stimulate pro-German feelings in Lamsdorf. The French ambassador to Russia, the Marquis de Montebello, reported that the Russian foreign minister viewed such visits with repugnance and found Wilhelm II distasteful on a personal level.[165]

[160] Richthofen to Tschirschky, 9 July 1902, *ibid.*, no. 5411, pp. 52–3.
[161] Wilhelm II's note on Bülow to Wilhelm II, 11 July 1902, *ibid.*, no. 5413, enclosure I, pp. 56–7.
[162] Bülow to Wilhelm II, 22 July 1902, *ibid.*, no. 5413, enclosure IV, pp. 60–1; Bülow to the German foreign office, 28 July 1902, Alvensleben to the German foreign office, 30 July 1902, *ibid.*, nos. 5414–15, p. 62.
[163] Bülow to Metternich, 8 August 1902, *ibid.*, no. 5416, pp. 63–6.
[164] Mossolov, *Last Tsar*, pp. 202–3.
[165] Marquis de Montebello to Delcassé, 15 August 1902, *DDF*, 2nd series, II, no. 375, p. 450.

By late 1902, there were signs of escalating tension between Japan and Russia in the Far East, where both powers had conflicting territorial ambitions, notably in Korea.[166] In March 1900, the Tsar's brother-in-law, Grand Duke Alexander Mikhailovitch, had informed the German naval attaché that a war between Russia and Japan could not be avoided in the long run. However, he was of the view that a conflict should be delayed until 1905, because the Russian Pacific fleet would not be strong enough to defeat the Japanese at sea before that date.[167] Despite this Russian preference to postpone a confrontation with Japan, Wilhelm II sought, in the aftermath of his visit to Reval, to renew his attempts to encourage the Tsar to take strong action in North East Asia. On 1 November 1902, the Kaiser wrote to Nicholas advocating co-operation between Russia and Germany, and warning that 'certain symptoms in the East seem to show that Japan is becoming a rather restless customer'. He pointed to signs that the Japanese were gaining influence over the Chinese army, and also drew Nicholas's attention to the combined naval strength of the Japanese and the English, with whom the former power had made an alliance in 1902, in eastern waters.[168]

The Tsar and his family spent the autumn of 1903 in Hesse, as the guests of Grand Duke Ernst Ludwig. During Nicholas's stay, a meeting was arranged between him and Wilhelm at Wiesbaden, at the initiative of Prince Heinrich. Before the visit, Russian diplomats had gone out of their way to assure the French that it would be bereft of political significance, and no way indicated a waning attachment on the Tsar's part to the Dual Alliance.[169] Nonetheless, during their meeting Wilhelm and Nicholas discussed most issues of international politics. It is clear that the Kaiser failed in his efforts to turn the Tsar against the French. Wilhelm pointed to the atheistic nature of the French Republic, and its origins as a regicidal state. The Tsar responded by stressing the benefits of Russia's restraining influence on Paris. Similarly, Wilhelm was not altogether successful in his attempts to encourage Nicholas against the Japanese, for the Tsar still wished, if at all possible, to maintain peace, and was worried by the possibility of English intervention against Russia, should war break out between her and Japan. Wilhelm tried to

---

[166] MacDonald, *United Government*, pp. 24–30; Nish, *Russo-Japanese War*, pp. 138–51.
[167] Schiemalmow to Radolin, 7 March 1900, PA Bonn Russland Nr 82 Nr 1 Bd 42.
[168] Wilhelm II to Nicholas II, 1 November 1902, PA Bonn Russland Nr 82 Nr 1. geheim. Bd 1; *BKW*, pp. 326–8.
[169] Note by Delcassé, 28 October 1903, Prinet to Delcassé, 29 October 1903, *DDF*, 2nd series, IV, nos. 45, 48, pp. 68, 71.

persuade Nicholas that British intervention was unlikely, as the Anglo-Japanese Treaty stipulated that each power would only intervene in a conflict in the case of one of them being attacked by two powers. Despite these minor differences of opinion, Bülow's memorandum recorded that the two emperors were in complete agreement on political matters.[170] After the interview between the two monarchs, Wilhelm wrote a letter to Nicholas in which he tried to convince the Tsar that the 'Crimean Combination' of England and France was reviving against Russian interests in the Balkans.[171] Nicholas reciprocated Wilhelm's hostility towards England,[172] but the Kaiser's attacks on France at Wiesbaden and afterwards had made no impression on the Russian Emperor. Nicholas remained determined to preserve St Petersburg's alliance with Paris.[173]

In the years after the turn of the century, Nicholas II became an increasingly assertive ruler, particularly in the sphere of foreign policy, where his chief interest lay in the affairs of the Far East. In 1901 he had rejected a proposal from Witte to settle Russia's disagreements with Japan in the region by granting the latter power a free hand in Korea.[174] From the autumn of 1902 onwards, Nicholas took a more active role in Far Eastern policy, and his interventions contributed to an escalation of tensions with Japan. He began to pursue a policy in the region independent of his ministers, going behind the backs of Witte, and the minister of war, Kuropatkin, both of whom had become convinced by January 1903 that Russia should sign a treaty with Japan, even if its terms were unfavourable, in order to safeguard Russia's control of Manchuria.[175] Instead, Nicholas gave his support to a group of unofficial advisers and courtiers, led by his brother-in-law, Grand Duke Alexander Mikhailovitch, and the aristocrat A. A. Bezobrazov, who favoured a much more belligerent policy towards Japan. They had both invested money in a timber concession on the Yalu River in Northern Korea, which inflamed Japanese suspicions that Russia planned to take control of Korea. In May 1903, the Tsar appointed Bezobrazov as a state secre-

[170] Note by Bülow, 7 November 1903, *GP*, xviii(i), no. 5421, pp. 68–76; Romberg to Bülow, 7 November 1903, *ibid.*, no. 5423, pp. 76–8; Prinet to Delcassé, 6 November 1903 and Boutiron to Delcassé, 7 November 1903, *DDF*, 2nd, series iv, nos. 62, 68, pp. 85–7, 92–4.
[171] Wilhelm II to Nicholas II, 19 November 1903, *BKW*, pp. 330–1.
[172] Nicholas II to Wilhelm II, 7/20 December 1903, GStA Merseburg HA Rep. 53 J Lit. R Nr 17.
[173] Delcassé to France's diplomatic representatives abroad, 12 November 1903, *DDF*, 2nd series, iv, pp. 106–8.
[174] MacDonald, *United Government*, p. 24.   [175] *Ibid.*, pp. 28–30.

tary, a rank of high authority, with special responsibility for Far Eastern affairs, and in July of the same year he appointed another hard-liner, Admiral Alexseev, as viceroy of the Far East, a move which aggravated the tension between Russia and Japan.[176] Simultaneously, the Tsarist régime faced the possibility of an upsurge in domestic unrest. The former foreign editor of *The Times*, Sir Donald Mackenzie Wallace, informed King Edward VII's private secretary, Lord Knollys, of the prospects facing Russia in a perceptive report in November 1903. Wallace was convinced that Nicholas had 'not the slightest intention of limiting His autocratic power, or otherwise changing materially the existing form of Government'. This left a stark choice as reform in Russia could only come about either at the initiative of the Tsar or through revolution. Wallace feared that the necessary preconditions of poverty and discontent, in both rural and urban areas, existed for a renewal of revolutionary activity.[177]

The outbreak of war between Russia and Japan in February 1904 underlined the disastrous consequences of the Tsar's interventions in the sphere of foreign policy, and the upsurge in domestic unrest which occurred during the war confirmed the accuracy of Wallace's prediction. Nicholas II bore a large share of the blame for the outbreak of the war, for which Russia was insufficiently prepared. It was Nicholas who had seemed to pursue two policies at once, playing off his ministers against his unofficial advisers. He had shown himself to be indecisive during the negotiations with the Japanese, never seeming to know whether he wanted peace or war.[178] In addition, the Tsar's long absence in Hesse in the autumn of 1903 had impeded the Russian government's attempts to reach a compromise with Japan, for he was the arbiter of policy and had not delegated responsibility.[179] Nicholas seems to have exhibited an extraordinary naivity, believing that through force of will he could prevent the outbreak of the war, and he only became genuinely concerned about the possibility of conflict on the eve of the Japanese attack on Port Arthur, which initiated hostilities.[180]

Wilhelm II, as has been seen, had encouraged the Tsar's ambitions in

---

[176] *Ibid.*, pp. 31–64; Lieven, *Nicholas II*, pp. 96–100; Nish, *Russo-Japanese War*, pp. 138–76; Alexander Savinskii, 'Guillaume II et la Russie; ses dépêches à Nicolas II, 1903–1905', *Revue des Deux Mondes* (December 1922), 765–9; Moulin to André, 30 September 1903, *DDF*, 2nd series, III, no. 448, pp. 593–5.

[177] Mackenzie Wallace to Knollys, 10 November 1903, RA W 43/149.

[178] Moulin to André, 20 February 1904, *DDF*, 2nd series, IV, no. 301, pp. 397–402.

[179] Nish, *Russo-Japanese War*, p. 189.

[180] MacDonald, *United Government*, pp. 63–75; Lieven, *Nicholas II*, pp. 100–1.

the Far East since the time of the latter's accession in 1894. His behaviour in the weeks preceding the outbreak of the Russo-Japanese War indicated that he was eager to see the conflict occur, and he was angered by Nicholas's vacillation. In his letters to Nicholas in December 1903 and January 1904, Wilhelm sought to incite the Tsar against the Japanese. On 4 December 1903, he warned Nicholas about 'the growing influence of Japan with the Chinese Army', and on 3 January 1904, he declared that 'it is evident to every unbiassed mind that Korea must and will be Russian'.[181] The Kaiser, in his letters, appeared to show sympathy with Nicholas's desire for a solution through mediation,[182] but in his comments on diplomatic reports, and in conversation with Bülow, the Kaiser made no secret of his desire to see a war between Russia and Japan. Wilhelm believed that Nicholas was 'damaging the monarchical principle through his shilly-shallying' and that the 'yellow race' would be at the gates of Moscow within twenty years if the Tsar failed to take a stand against Japan.[183]

After the outbreak of war, with the sinking of the Russian Pacific fleet by the Japanese at Port Arthur, on 8 February 1904, Wilhelm offered his loyal support to Nicholas.[184] The war had many advantages for Germany. It removed the threat of a Russian attack on the *Reich*'s eastern frontier and relieved Germany's international position, which had been undermined by the signs of a *rapprochement* between Britain and France, apparent since Edward VII's highly successful visit to Paris in May 1903. In addition, by bringing Russia into conflict with Britain's ally, Japan, the Kaiser hoped that the war would lead the Tsar to question the wisdom of maintaining his own alliance with Britain's new partner, France.[185] Throughout the war, the Kaiser posed as the Tsar's mentor and steadfast ally against the 'yellow peril'. Wilhelm was rewarded, at least in the early stages of the conflict, with the Tsar's complete trust,[186] and he made no secret of his desire to exploit Nicholas's faith as a

---

[181] Wilhelm II to Nicholas II, 4 December 1903 and 3 January 1904. *BKW*, pp. 332–5; Maurice Paléologue, *Turning Point*, diary entry, 19 January 1904, p. 20.

[182] Wilhelm II to Nicholas II, 9 January 1904, *BKW*, pp. 335–6; Paléologue, *Turning Point*, diary entry, 24 January 1904, p. 23; Nicholas II to Wilhelm II, 11/24 January 1904. *GP*, XIX(i), no. 5952, pp. 52–3.

[183] Bülow, *Memoirs*, II, pp. 60–1; Wilhelm II's marginalia on Graf von Arco to the German foreign office, 13 January 1904, *GP*, XIX(i), no. 5937, pp. 27–8; Wilhelm II's comments on Bülow's note, 14 February 1904, *ibid.*, pp. 62–3; Radziwill, *Briefe*, 20 February 1904, pp. 248–9.

[184] Wilhelm II to Nicholas II, 11 February 1904, *BKW*, pp. 337–8.

[185] Friedrich von Holstein to Ida von Stulpnägel, 21 January 1904. Helmuth Rogge (ed.), *Friedrich von Holstein: Lebensbekenntnis* (Berlin, 1932), pp. 227–8.

[186] Radolin to Bülow, 28 February 1904, PA Bonn Deutschland Nr 131 Bd 23.

mechanism for resurrecting an alliance between Russia and Germany.[187] The *Reich* accorded considerable help to Russia during the war, most notably by providing the coal for the Russian Baltic fleet sent to reinforce Russia's naval strength in the Pacific, though this aid was, to some extent, offset by the signing of a commercial treaty between the two powers on terms which were highly unfavourable to Russian goods.[188]

The revival of the practice of appointing military plenipotentiaries to their respective personal suites served as an important symbolic indication of the warmth of the relationship between the Kaiser and the Tsar, and the extent to which it had improved since 1900. The plenipotentiaries were responsible solely to their respective sovereigns, and therefore took precedence over military attachés, who were also responsible to the minister of war.[189] The appointment of plenipotentiaries caused considerable disquiet to Russia's French allies, who interpreted it as a sign of growing intimacy between the Russian and Prussian courts, and evidence of the Kaiser's renewed determination to destroy the Dual Alliance.[190] However, the French fears as to the dangers involved in the exchange of plenipotentiaries were to some extent misplaced. On a political level, the re-establishment of the practice did not lead to the benefits which Wilhelm had expected. The Kaiser's appointee, Major General von Lambsdorff, complained that he had received no special treatment from the Tsar since his arrival in Russia, and that Nicholas kept him at arm's length. Wilhelm noted that Lambsdorff's Russian counterpart, Colonel Schebeko, also exhibited a remarkable reticence.[191] This was characteristic of a pattern which was to develop. Wilhelm treated the Russian plenipotentiary as Nicholas's representative, and spoke openly to him. In contrast, with the notable exception of one of Lambsdorff's successors, Captain Paul von Hintze, the Tsar had minimal contact with the Kaiser's representative.[192]

---

[187] Bihourd to Delcassé, 26 March 1904, *DDF*, 2nd series, IV, no. 366, pp. 506–7.

[188] Lamar Cecil, 'Coal for the Fleet that Had to Die', *American Historical Review* 69, 4 (1964), 990–1005; Jonathan Steinberg, 'Germany and the Russo-Japanese War', *American Historical Review* 75, 7 (1970), 1975–7; Vogel, *Deutsche Russlandpolitik*, pp. 25, 55; Schelking, *Recollections*, p. 142; Bernard F. Oppel, 'The Waning of a Traditional Alliance: Russia and Germany after the Portsmouth Peace Conference', *Central European History* 5 (1972), 318–29.

[189] Lambsdorff, *Militärbevollmächtigten*, p. 94; Wilhelm II to Nicholas II, 6 June 1904, *BKW*, pp. 340–2.

[190] Boutiron to Delcassé, 26 October 1904, *DDF*, 2nd series, V, no. 394, pp. 470–2.

[191] The Kaiser's comment on Major General von Lambsdorff to Wilhelm II, 19 September 1904, Lambsdorff, *Militärbevollmächtigten*, p. 232.

[192] *Ibid.*, pp. 39–40, 103–5.

Throughout the Russo-Japanese War, and during the revolutionary upheavals in Russia during 1905, the Kaiser continued to write frequently to the Tsar. He offered him advice on matters of both foreign and domestic politics and also persisted in his attempts to persuade Nicholas of the iniquity of the French and the English.[193] In addition, he did not hide his views from foreign and German diplomats, being particularly critical of the Tsar's seeming indecisiveness in the face of the Russian revolution.[194] His support for Nicholas II was based on the belief that only a monarchical Russia could be relied on by Germany, whereas if the revolutionaries were to triumph, Russia would become the *Reich*'s implacable foe. In an astonishing comment on a diplomatic despatch in November 1905, he accused Lord Lansdowne, the British foreign secretary, of actively seeking the triumph of the revolution, because the English realised that Nicholas would never agree to an alliance with London.[195] The Kaiser's support for the embattled Tsarist régime was appreciated not just by Nicholas, but also by the members of his entourage. Count Fredericksz, the Tsar's minister of the court, told Hintze, the German naval attaché, in November 1905: 'The sympathy of Kaiser Wilhelm needs no words: we feel it!'[196]

Two attempts were made by the Kaiser and Bülow to exploit this solidarity between Russia and Germany as a means of bringing about an alliance between the two powers. The first project for an alliance foundered in December 1904 due to the Tsar's reluctance to sign an agreement without the participation of the French, and due to German fears that an alliance with Russia could leave the *Reich* open to an English attack. The second round of alliance negotiations, in the summer of 1905, resulted in the signing of a treaty between the Kaiser and the Tsar at Björkö. The treaty failed to come into effect. This was partly due to French objections and the doubts of Russian diplomats. However, the major factor was Nicholas II's own lack of willingness to enter into any arrangement with Berlin, which conflicted with Russia's obli-

---

[193] Wilhelm II to Nicholas II, 6 February 1905, 21 February 1905, 22 August 1905, *BKW*, pp. 358–69, 376–7.

[194] Bihourd to Delcassé, 18 March 1905, *DDF*, 2nd series, VI, no. 158, pp. 203–5; Wilhelm II's comments on Alvensleben to Bülow, 17 March 1905, PA Bonn Russland Nr 82 Nr 1 Bd 53; Wilhelm II's comments on Miquel to Bülow, 15 November 1905, PA Bonn Russland Nr 61 geheim. Bd 5; Wilhelm II's comment on Miquel to Bülow, 20 November 1905, PA Bonn Russland Nr 82 Nr 1 Bd 54; Wilhelm II's comment on Alvensleben to Bülow, 23 December 1905, *ibid.*

[195] Wilhelm II's comment on Metternich to Bülow, 1 November 1905, PA Bonn England Nr 78 geheim. Bd 8.

[196] Hintze to Wilhelm II, 3 November 1905, PA Bonn Russland Nr 82 Nr 1 Bd 54.

gations to France. The support given by Russia to France at the Algeciras conference, to settle the Moroccan crisis, in the spring of 1906, finally ended German hopes of a revival of the traditional alliance with St Petersburg.[197]

Wilhelm II's saw Nicholas II's conduct over Björkö as duplicitous, and was greatly angered by the Tsar's steadfast commitment to France. He made his frustration clear in a conversation with the Russian finance minister, Kokovtsov, in January 1906. Wilhelm lectured Kokovtsov on his familiar theme of the need for the Hohenzollern and Romanov monarchies to stand together, and asked rhetorically: 'Is it not downright folly that, instead of this, and over the head of monarchist Germany, monarchist Russia seeks for the support of republican France and always acts with her against her natural and historic ally?'[198] Wilhelm accused Nicholas of having gone back on all that he had said and written to him,[199] and seemed to exhibit an almost fatalistic resignation with regard to the possibility of a *rapprochement* between Russia and England: 'That makes no difference! and cannot be prevented!' The Kaiser was in no mind to make further efforts to conciliate the Russians. 'We have pursued [them]! without effect!', he wrote, 'Now the Russians ought to pursue [us] for once!'[200]

Nevertheless, Bülow appreciated that Russia under a monarchical régime had been, in general, a good neighbour to Germany, and that a liberal, democratic Russia would soon become the *Reich*'s enemy. Therefore, the chancellor hoped that the Tsarist autocracy would withstand the revolutionary upheavals which still threatened to engulf it. In a letter to the Kaiser in June 1906, he pointed to the fact that the structure of the Russian autocracy had many features of Germanic origin, and noted that many of the high officials of the régime were Baltic Germans. In contrast, the 'real' Russia was Asiatic at its core and most unlikely to be friendly towards conservative Germany. The sympathy which many in France and England had with the revolutionaries was evidence of this.[201]

The Russian autocracy, of course, withstood the unrest of 1905 to

[197] Cf. McLean, 'Monarchy', ch. 4.
[198] H. H. Fisher (ed.), *Out of My Past: The Memoirs of Count Kokovtsov*, English translation (Oxford and Stanford, 1935), p. 98.
[199] Wilhelm II's comments on Radolin to Bülow, 14 April 1906, PA Bonn England Nr 81 Nr 1 Bd 16.
[200] Wilhelm II's comments on Wedel to Bülow, 30 April 1906, *GP*, xxv(i), no. 8506.
[201] Bülow to Wilhelm II, 17 June 1906, GStA Merseburg HA Rep. 53 J Lit. B Nr 16a Bd III.

1906, and thus some of Bülow's fears were misplaced. Indeed, in the years that followed, Nicholas II's continuing gratitude towards the Kaiser for the support he had given him against the Japanese and the revolutionaries counterbalanced, to some extent, the *rapprochement* between Russia and Britain and helped to prevent an irremediable deterioration in relations between the Tsarist empire and the *Kaiserreich*. In November 1906, the Tsar expressed warm feelings for the Kaiser at an audience which he gave to the German ambassador and stressed the need for solidarity between the Russian and German monarchies in defence of their mutual interests.[202] In his annual report on Russia, submitted in January 1907, the British ambassador at St Petersburg, Sir Arthur Nicolson, presented a surprisingly favourable picture of the relations between the German and Russian courts and governments. He noted that these were 'at the present time intimate and cordial. I should be inclined to go further and state that German influence is to-day predominant both at the Court and in Government circles.' Nicolson observed further that Germany enjoyed a privileged diplomatic position in the Russian capital and that the Russians remained eager 'to keep on good terms with the powerful western neighbour whose military strength is so superior to their own'.[203]

Yet the residual sympathy of the Tsar and his courtiers for Wilhelm II and Germany was of only limited value politically. For the years after the Russo-Japanese War saw Nicholas II turn away from the active part which he had taken in the formation of foreign policy before 1905 and retreat into the role of 'legal' sovereign, his confidence having been diminished by the defeat in the Far East and by the revolution.[204] During this period, the court became less significant as a centre of diplomacy. Sir Donald Mackenzie Wallace observed, when on a visit to Russia in the autumn of 1906, that Nicholas now lived in seclusion at his palace of Peterhof 'as if he were a private person with no special interest in the course of events'.[205] A letter written by Nicolson, in February 1908, also reveals the transformation in the balance of power between the Tsar and his foreign minister which occurred during these years. The British ambassador regretted the fact that Admiral Touchard had been appointed as French ambassador, believing that

[202] Schoen to Bülow, 15 November 1906, *GP*, xxii, no. 7368, pp. 47–9.
[203] Sir Arthur Nicolson, Annual Report for Russia 1906 (extract), *BD*, iv, no. 243, pp. 256–8.
[204] McDonald, *United Government*, p. 106.
[205] Mackenzie Wallace to Knollys, 25 October 1906, RA W 50/29.

new circumstances made it more appropriate to have civilian diplomats at St Petersburg:

In former days when Ambassadors were in close and frequent relations with the Emperor, a General or an Admiral were most suitable Representatives, . . . But nowadays when the Court lives in seclusion, and Ambassadorial intercourse is rare and formal, it is with the Foreign Minister that all business has, in reality, to be exclusively conducted: and for this a military or a naval man is not specially adapted.[206]

Russia's foreign minister between 1906 and 1910, Alexander Isvolsky, had risen through the ranks of the diplomatic service due to the patronage of the Dowager Empress Marie Feodorovna, whom he got to know well while serving as Russian minister in Copenhagen.[207] However, he had been widely seen as a future foreign minister before his appointment and at various stages both Edward VII[208] and the Kaiser had recommended Isvolsky to the Tsar.[209] Isvolsky was politically liberal and was one of the chief advocates of a *rapprochement* between Russia and Britain. However, he also wished, as far as possible, to maintain cordial relations with Germany, an aim which was compromised by Russia's increasing dependence on France in the years after 1906. The latter power used its financial influence over the Tsarist government in order to thwart the preservation of close ties between St Petersburg and Berlin.[210]

During the first year of Isvolsky's tenure as foreign minister, his most conspicuous success was the negotiation of an agreement with Britain, signed in August 1907, to overcome the differences between the two powers in Central Asia. By the spring of 1907, these negotiations were arousing considerable suspicion in Berlin. Wilhelm II castigated the Tsar for agreeing to the policy of *rapprochement* with England, and poured scorn on Nicholas's attempts to reassure the German ambassador that the negotiations would be limited solely to colonial issues: 'The Emperor is not false but weak! Weakness is not falseness, but it takes its place, and it fills its functions!'[211]

The alteration in the general direction of Russian foreign policy after 1906 troubled the Kaiser as much as the Anglo-Russian negotiations.

[206] Sir Arthur Nicolson to Sir Charles Hardinge, 22 February 1908, Hardinge Papers, vol. 12.
[207] Seeger, *Iswolsky*, p. 22; McDonald, *United Government*, p. 158.
[208] Edward VII to Nicholas II, 12 May 1904, RA W 44/95.
[209] Wilhelm II to Nicholas II, 2 January 1905, *BKW*, pp. 355–8.
[210] McDonald, *United Government*, pp. 103, 110–11; Lieven, *Russia and the Origins*, pp. 29–33; Oppel, 'Traditional Alliance', 327–29; Spring, 'Russia', 584–9; Neilson, 'Russia', pp. 107–8.
[211] Wilhelm II's comment on Schoen to Bülow, 16 March 1907, *GP*, xxiii(i), no. 7877, p. 161.

The Tsarist régime saw its chief concern as being to safeguard its position as a Great Power in Europe, and had abandoned the aim of dominance in the Far East, which had ended so disastrously with the defeat at the hands of the Japanese. Russia's renewed interest in Europe, and the Balkans in particular, caused the Kaiser anxiety as Russia's ambitions had been in conflict with those of Germany and Austria in the region since the 1870s, and because he believed that the Tsarist empire's historic role should be that of defending Europe against the 'yellow races'. He expressed opinions of this nature in a conversation with the French chargé d'affaires at Berlin, Raymond Lecomte, in March 1907. Wilhelm told Lecomte that he was convinced that the Anglo-Russian negotiations involved a secret agreement whereby the two powers would divide the Straits, linking the Black Sea and the Aegean, between them. The real threat to Europe, the Kaiser declared, came from the Japanese. 'If I were the Emperor of Russia,' he informed Lecomte, 'I would have already begun to fortify the Urals.'[212] This was a theme to which he was to return in subsequent years, but neither the Tsar nor his advisers were to be lulled into returning to a policy which had proved so calamitous in the past.[213]

A meeting between the Kaiser and the Tsar at Swinemünde in August 1907 provided an opportunity to heal some of the damage caused to the relationship between the two emperors by the events of 1905/6. However, the presence of Isvolsky and Bülow served to limit the political importance of the visit as both of these statesmen were determined to avoid a repeat of the events which had occurred at Björkö two years previously, Bülow because he no longer believed a German–Russian alliance to be a realistic objective, in view of Russia's dependence on the French financial markets, and Isvolsky, as he did not see such an alliance as a desirable option. Although the Swinemünde meeting passed off to the satisfaction of both monarchs, it achieved nothing politically. In particular, though the Kaiser continued to believe in the traditional friendship between the Romanovs and Hohenzollerns, he retained a deep distrust of Isvolsky and was convinced that his interview with Nicholas had done nothing to prevent the process of

[212] Note by M. Lecomte, March 1907, *DDF*, 2nd series, x, pp. 705–6.
[213] Cf. Jules Cambon to Pichon, 17 February 1909, *DDF*, 2nd series, xii, no. 22, pp. 30–1; memorandum by Colonel Trench, 21 February 1910, *BD*, vi, no. 149, pp. 234–37; note by Aehrenthal, 22–5 February 1910, *ÖUA*, ii, no. 2024, pp. 724–5; Sergei Sazonov, *Fateful Years 1909–1916*, English translation (London, 1928), pp. 46–7; Sazonov to Nicholas II (undated), René Marchand (ed.), *Un livre noir. Diplomatie d'avant-guerre d'après les documents des archives russes, novembre 1910 –juillet 1914*, French translation, 2 vols. (Paris, 1922–3), ii, p. 337.

German encirclement.[214] Wilhelm's grounds for pessimism were confirmed by the signing of the Anglo-Russian agreement and by rumours that Isvolsky and Count Alexander Benckendorff, the Russian ambassador to London, saw it as a first step towards a general political agreement between Britain and Russia.[215]

The Anglo-Russian convention had been coupled with a dynastic *rapprochement* between the Russian and British royal families which culminated in a highly successful visit paid by Edward VII and Queen Alexandra to Reval in June 1908. This provoked a hysterical reaction in Berlin, not least from Wilhelm II, who saw the meeting as a portent of war and a sign that the long feared encirclement of Germany had been achieved.[216] Sir Charles Hardinge, the permanent under-secretary of the British foreign office, and a close friend of King Edward VII, did not fail to gloat at the German reaction.[217] In a perceptive letter to the Comte de Salis, the chargé of the British embassy at Berlin, Hardinge exposed the true reasons for Wilhelm II's anger:

It is, I think, a ridiculous pretension on the part of the Germans that the Emperor alone should have a monopoly amongst reigning Sovereigns of paying official visits to Russia. It has been his aim, and was a cardinal principle of the Bismarckian tradition of keeping Russia away from other Powers, but I am glad to think that we now have a policy which no Foreign Minister in London ever had during the days of Bismarck, and it was this which rendered Bismarck's task comparatively easy.[218]

In November 1908, Nicolson was able to report that Anglo-Russian relations 'could' not 'be better'.[219] By this stage, the British had come to regard Nicholas II as a reliable ally.[220]

Wilhelm II, however, failed to appreciate that the policy of *rapprochement* with England could not have been pursued without the Tsar's approval. He continued to see Nicholas as the captive of his liberal foreign minister, and to await the moment when the Tsar would reassert his authority in the interests of an improvement in Russia's relations with Berlin. The events of 1905/6 had strengthened the Kaiser's view that the Russian autocracy would be overthrown by the revolutionaries sooner rather than later. In January 1908, Count Pourtalès, the German

[214] Note by Tschirschky, 7 August 1907, *GP*, xxii, no. 7378, pp. 67–8; Moltke, *Erinnerungen*, p. 348; Wilhelm II's comments on Miquel to Bülow, 27 September 1907, *GP*, xxv(i), no. 8537, pp. 45–7.
[215] Stumm to Bülow, 22 August 1907, *GP*, xxv(i), no. 8533, pp. 37–40.   [216] Cf. ch. 3.
[217] Hardinge to O'Beirne, 24 June 1908, Hardinge Papers, vol. 13.
[218] Hardinge to the Comte de Salis, 24 June 1908, Hardinge Papers, vol. 13; cf. Hardinge to O'Beirne, 24 June 1908, *ibid.*
[219] Nicolson to Hardinge, 4 November 1908, Hardinge Papers, vol. 12.
[220] Hardinge to Nicolson, 11 November 1908, Hardinge Papers, vol. 13.

ambassador to Russia, reported that preparations were beginning in St Petersburg for the Romanov tercentenary in 1913. Wilhelm commented, cynically, 'if they are still there!!'[221] His initial reaction when he learned of the possibility of Edward VII visiting Russia was that it was part of an English inspired plot to strengthen the power of the Russian parliament against Nicholas II.[222]

By 1908, Nicholas II had recovered much of the confidence which he had lost as a result of the events of 1905. When Nicholas's brother-in-law, the Grand Duke of Hesse, visited Russia in the spring of 1908, he found the Tsar 'far brighter and resoluter' than he had long seen him.[223] At this time the Kaiser was able to gain perceptive and accurate intelligence as to the Tsar's moods and opinions through the reports of Captain Paul von Hintze. Hintze had served in St Petersburg as naval attaché since 1903, and in 1908 he was named by the Kaiser as the new military plenipotentiary attached to Nicholas II's personal suite. Hintze's appointment revived the importance of the post, as he was the only plenipotentiary in whom the Tsar had confidence and to whom he talked openly.[224]

The privileged status which Hintze enjoyed during his period as a military plenipotentiary owed much to the close links which he had established with the Russian court during his five years as naval attaché.[225] Hintze's contacts with the Tsar were viewed with suspicion by British diplomats both during and after this time. In December 1905, Cecil Spring-Rice, the chargé at the British embassy in St Petersburg, noted that Hintze 'seems to see a good deal of the Emperor',[226] and in January 1908, Sir Arthur Nicolson voiced suspicions as to the real role played by Hintze who, he informed Hardinge, 'is constantly running backwards and forwards between St. Petersburg and Berlin'. He described Hintze as 'an active and intelligent man whose duties are, I imagine, more diplomatic than naval'.[227]

[221] Wilhelm II's comment on Pourtalès to Bülow, 3 January 1908, PA Bonn Russland Nr 82 Nr 1 Bd 56.
[222] Wilhelm II's comment on Tschirschky to the German foreign office, 25 February 1908, PA Bonn England Nr 81 Nr 1 Bd 18.
[223] Grand Duke Ernst Ludwig of Hesse to Princess Victoria of Battenberg, 27 April 1908. HStA Darmstadt Abt. D 24 35/4.
[224] Lambsdorff, *Militärbevollmächtigten*, pp. 39–40, pp. 53–7, 158–9, 167–9.
[225] Steinberg, 'Germany', 1969–70.
[226] Cecil Spring-Rice to Lord Knollys, 6 December 1905, RA W 47/354.
[227] Nicolson to Hardinge, 29 January 1908, Hardinge Papers, vol. 12; cf. Nicolson to Hardinge, 22 February 1908, *ibid.*

A report which Hintze sent to the Kaiser on 12 December 1908 indicated the extent to which Nicholas II had recovered his self-confidence and faith in his ability to exercise his autocratic powers. The Tsar stressed his determination to keep the reins of government in his own hands. 'I myself decide', he informed the German plenipotentiary. 'There can be no other system with half-developed nations; a crowd wants a firm and strong hand over it.' At the end of the audience, Nicholas told Hintze: 'Report to His Majesty, that He may put full confidence in me, and that I am the master here.'[228] In a further letter to Wilhelm, in January 1909, Hintze sought to analyse the likely political repercussions of the Tsar's reacquired assertiveness. He asked, rhetorically, whether Nicholas would now stamp his will on all issues of foreign and domestic policy. His answer made depressing reading. 'I think not. His Majesty is indeed highly intelligent and extremely diligent, but he is also highly impressionable and very unworldly. He will as before come under the influence of the last one who has his ear.' The Tsar would continue to do as his ministers wished, particularly in important matters. 'His Majesty Emperor Nicholas II certainly wants to rule himself; he is actually wholly in the hands of his current minister.' Despite this, Hintze concluded that the Tsar remained the key figure in Russian politics because a minister could only continue to remain in office if he enjoyed Nicholas's confidence. It was still therefore important to treat him with respect and to pay consideration to his basic political principles.[229]

In the years after 1906, the turn of Russian foreign policy back towards Europe and the growth of Pan-Slavism had both helped to prevent the maintenance of close relations between Russia and Germany.[230] In such a context, the continuing residual warmth of the dynastic relationship between the Kaiser and the Tsar had helped to prevent a rapid deterioration in the relations between the two empires. However, the international crisis caused by Austria's annexation of Bosnia-Herzegovina in the autumn of 1908, ending with the German ultimatum to Russia in March 1909, underlined the political gulf which now existed between Russia and Germany and also exposed the hollowness of the continuing expressions of friendship between the two emperors.[231] Nicholas II's persisting tendency to believe in the Kaiser's

---

[228] Hintze to Wilhelm II, 12 December 1908, Lambsdorff, *Militärbevollmächtigten*, p. 319.
[229] Hintze to Wilhelm II, 28 January 1909, PA Bonn Russland Nr 82 Nr 1 geheim. Bd 3; Lambsdorff, *Militärbevollmächtigten*, pp. 322–4.
[230] Lieven, 'Pro-Germans', 41.
[231] Lieven, *Russia and the Origins*, pp. 33–7; McDonald, *United Government*, pp. 127–51; Samuel R. Williamson, *Austria-Hungary and the Origins of the First World War* (London, 1991); F. R. Bridge,

good faith, which was still evident during the initial phase of the Bosnian crisis,[232] did not correspond to the feelings of his officials, the majority of whom blamed the Germans as well as the Austrians for their country's diplomatic humiliation. The British ambassador detected a subtle change in Russian policy in the Balkans, which was likely to have profoundly negative repercussions, not only for Russia's relations with Austria, but also for those with Germany. The Bosnian crisis had put an end to the clandestine co-operation between Austria and Russia, which had been a feature of Balkan politics since the 1880s:

> The policy of 'squaring' Austria for the benefit of Russian predominance over the Balkan Slavs has given way to a policy of resisting the encroachments of Austria on Slav interests; and of checking her alleged aspirations to having a leading voice in Balkan affairs. So far as can be seen, there is also a desire to be done with the old Pan Slavism, which was in reality Pan Russianism, and to come into sympathetic touch and relations with all slav peoples in order to resist Germanism.[233]

If the trend of official thinking in St Petersburg was towards a new 'anti-Germanism', the attitudes of the Kaiser and Bülow indicated that in Berlin too, the idea of co-operation with Russia had lost much of its attraction, and that the latter power was now seen as a potential enemy. An exchange of letters between the Tsar and the Kaiser at the end of 1908 indicated that Wilhelm was no longer willing to be as accommodating towards the Russians as in the past. On 28 December, the Tsar appealed to the Kaiser to use his influence with the Austrians to prevent the dispute between Austria and Serbia over Bosnia from developing into a European conflagration.[234] In his reply, the Kaiser expressed frustration at the turn of Russia away from Germany since 1906. He refused to put any further pressure on the Austrians and reminded Nicholas that the Serbians had assassinated their monarch six years previously, thus warning the Tsar that by backing them, he was betraying the monarchical principle.[235] The Kaiser's attitude mirrored the belief of Baroness Spitzemberg, an astute observer of the official world in Berlin during these years, that Nicholas II's expressions of friendship

'Izvolsky, Aehrenthal, and the End of the Austro-Russian Entente, 1906–8', *Mitteilungen des Österreichischen Staatsarchivs* 29 (1976), 315–62; Imanuel Geiss, *German Foreign Policy, 1871–1914* (London, 1976), pp. 106–18; Bülow to Pourtalès, 21 March 1909, *GP*, xxvi(i), no. 9640.

[232] Cf. Hintze to Wilhelm II, 12 December 1908. Lambsdorff, *Militärbevollmächtigten*, p. 318.
[233] Nicolson to Hardinge, 2 December 1908, Hardinge Papers, vol. 12.
[234] Nicholas II to Wilhelm II, 15/28 December 1908, *GP*, xxvi(i), no. 9187, pp. 387–8.
[235] Wilhelm II to Nicholas II, 5 January 1909, *ibid.*, no. 9188, pp. 388–91; *BKW*, pp. 395–8.

were of little worth politically.[236] In a letter to the Kaiser on 11 January, Bülow took this disenchantment with the Tsar and the Russians a stage further and, in comments which prefigured the German attitude in July 1914, identified the Tsarist empire as the enemy. He believed that it should be Germany's aim to convince the Austrians that the Russians and their English and French allies could do nothing to force Vienna to back down over the annexation of Bosnia. In the event of the outbreak of a general war, both Germany and Austria would proceed with all force against the Russians.[237] The German ultimatum to Russia in March 1909, demanding that the latter power accept the Austrian annexation, was the natural product of this thinking.

The ultimatum ended forever any prospect of the revival of the Three Emperors' League,[238] though, as has been seen, official thinking in both St Petersburg and Berlin was tending towards this conclusion beforehand. Nicholas II had no alternative but to accept Austria's annexation of Bosnia, as he was aware that Russia was not in a position to oppose it militarily.[239] The ultimatum had destroyed the Tsar's trust in Germany. He commented that 'the method of Germany's actions . . . has been brutal and we won't forget it'.[240] Wilhelm II was, however, slow to appreciate the new political realities in the light of the acrimonious end to the Bosnian crisis. His optimism as to the prospects of a *rapprochement* with Russia in the aftermath of the dispute was stimulated by a report sent by Hintze at the end of March 1909, which hinted that Nicholas II wished to see cordial relations restored with Germany.[241] To this end, a meeting was arranged, at the Kaiser's initiative, at Björkö in June 1909. Although this contributed to an improvement in the personal relationship between Wilhelm and Nicholas, it was of limited value politically. Wilhelm II's virulent hatred of Isvolsky remained an obstacle to improved relations between the two empires, both before and after the visit, and Russia's lingering resentment towards Austria prevented a return of the traditional friendship between St Petersburg and Berlin.[242]

The change in Nicholas II's own views was the most important reason

---

[236] Vierhaus, *Spitzemberg*, diary entry, 1 January 1909, pp. 497–8.
[237] Bülow to Wilhelm II, 11 January 1909, GStA Merseburg HA Rep. 53 J Lit. B Nr 16a Bd IV.
[238] Geiss, *German Foreign Policy*, p. 117.
[239] Lieven, *Nicholas II*, pp. 193–4; McDonald, *United Government*, pp. 150–1.
[240] Nicholas II to Marie Feodorovna, 18/19 March 1909, *Letters of Tsar Nicholas*, pp. 240–1; cf. Marie Feodorovna to Nicholas II, 25 March 1909, *ibid.*, pp. 241–2.
[241] Hintze to Wilhelm II, 27 March 1909, Lambsdorff, *Militärbevollmächtigten*, pp. 336–9.
[242] Note by Schoen, 18 June 1909, *GP*, XXVI(ii), no. 9552, pp. 823–8; Bethmann Hollweg to Wilhelm II, 15 September 1909, *ibid.*, no. 9568, pp. 852–5.

for the limited success of the Kaiser's attempt to resurrect close ties between Germany and Russia. German attempts to persuade Russia to abandon the French and the English had been fruitless before the events of 1908/9, and they were even more so afterwards, for the Tsar no longer believed German expressions of good-will and was determined that Russia would never again be humiliated, as in March 1909. Nicholas had decreed 'that in no case would there be any change in the foreign policy of Russia in her relations towards France and England',[243] and took a keen interest in the reconstruction of Russia's armed forces, which had been weakened so disastrously by the war with Japan. He gave the French ambassador assurances as to the moral and military reconstruction of the Russian army, and was clearly preparing for a situation where Russia and France would face Germany and Austria in a future war.[244]

The poor state of the relations between the Kaiser and the Tsar, as between Germany and Russia, manifested itself in the falling away of the correspondence between the two emperors. At the end of 1909, both Hintze and Count Pourtalès, the German ambassador to Russia, doubted whether there was any point in Wilhelm writing to Nicholas to pass on New Year's greetings. In a letter to Theobald von Bethmann Hollweg, who had replaced Bülow as chancellor in July 1909, Pourtalès noted that, in recent years, the Tsar had either not answered the Kaiser's letters at all, or had taken a long time to answer them. Although the ambassador concluded that Wilhelm should write to Nicholas, he observed that the content could not be anything other than 'banal' given the poor state of relations between the two governments.[245] Bethmann's assessment of Russo-German relations was equally pessimistic. The chancellor believed that Wilhelm II had played the major role in keeping relations between the two empires tolerable since the signing of the Franco-Russian alliance. By contrast, the Russians had played no part in the cultivation of these relations, and 'Official Russia' had done little to restrain the anti-German tone of the press in that country. He noted that although Nicholas II continued to give expression to his personal sympathy for Germany, he did not have the necessary strength

[243] Hardinge to Edward VII, 7 April 1909, RA W 55/16; cf. Touchard to Pichon, 7 May 1909, *DDF*, 2nd series, XII, no. 182, p. 228.

[244] Touchard to Pichon, 9 June 1909, *ibid.*, no. 214, pp. 292.

[245] Pourtalès to Bethmann Hollweg, 27 December 1909, PA Bonn Russland Nr 82 Nr 1 geheim. Bd 3; cf. Hintze to Wilhelm II, 27 December 1909, *ibid.*; Szögyény to Berchtold, 12 March 1914, *ÖUA*, VII, no. 9470, p. 966.

of will to overrule his advisers. In any case, the Tsar's assurances of friendship had done nothing to change the course of Russian foreign policy, which had tended more and more towards *rapprochement* with England.[246]

Nonetheless, Wilhelm did not wholly share the bleak views of his advisers with regard to Germany's relations with Russia. He had received a friendly New Year's card from Nicholas, suggesting that they meet during 1910, which had confounded Hintze's prediction that the Tsar would not write to him.[247] In addition, Wilhelm had a further reason for optimism. Prince Heinrich visited Russia in January 1910 and secured a promise from the Tsar to remove four army corps from Russia's western frontier. Wilhelm believed that Nicholas's decision had been motivated, in part, by his fear of a renewed Japanese military build-up in the Far East,[248] but he was also inclined to see it as a sign that the policy of seeking to improve the *Reich*'s relations with Russia through dynastic channels was beginning to work.[249]

Hintze's reports in January 1910, however, continued to question Nicholas II's ability to assert himself in the political sphere. On 6 January, for example, he pointed to the emptiness of the Tsar's attachment to good relations with Germany, and noted that the ritualistic evocation of the traditional friendship between the two empires was part of a game for the Russians, which did not represent reality. He believed that Nicholas II would continue to submit to Isvolsky's views on foreign affairs and would only assert himself if there was a danger of war.[250] In the face of such pessimism, it is little wonder that when he held discussions with the Austrian foreign minister, Count Aehrenthal, at Berlin later in the same month, the Kaiser's judgement of Nicholas had again become a negative one. He told Aehrenthal of his belief that a new war would soon break out between Russia and Japan, a development which would be of benefit to Germany by turning Russian attention

---

[246] Bethmann Hollweg to Wilhelm II, 2 January 1910, PA Bonn Russland Nr 82 Nr 1 geheim. Bd 3, *GP*, xxvi(ii), no. 9571, pp. 859–63.
[247] Wilhelm II's comment on Hintze to Wilhelm II, 27 December 1909. PA Bonn Russland Nr 82 Nr 1 geheim. Bd 3.
[248] Wilhelm II to General Helmuth von Moltke, 10 January 1910, GStA Merseburg HA Rep. 53 J Lit. M Nr 11.
[249] Wilhelm II's comment on Bethmann Hollweg to Wilhelm II, 2 January 1910. PA Bonn Russland Nr 82 Nr 1 geheim. Bd 3; cf. Wilhelm II to Nicholas II, 11 January 1910, *BKW*, pp. 404–5.
[250] Hintze to Wilhelm II, 6 January 1910, PA Bonn Russland Nr 82 Nr 1 Bd 59; cf. Hintze to Wilhelm II, 28 January and 21 February 1910. Lambsdorff, *Militärbevollmächtigten*, pp. 362–5, 366–7.

away from Europe. He believed that the Tsar shared his fears about the renewal of Japanese aggression in the Far East, but would do nothing about it. Echoing Hintze's view of the Russian Emperor, Wilhelm informed his guest that even when he fully understood a situation, Nicholas seemed to be incapable of taking decisive action.[251]

Relations between Germany and Russia remained strained. In September 1910, Tschirschky, the German ambassador in Vienna, told his French counterpart, M. Crozier, that he believed the causes of the breach were so profound that a meeting between the two emperors would change nothing.[252] However, the months thereafter saw a perceptible improvement in relations between the two empires. In the autumn of 1910, Nicholas II and his family spent three months on a private visit to Hesse.[253] During his stay in Germany, Nicholas had the chance to remove two sources of friction with the *Reich*. First, he managed, through the mediation of his brother-in-law, the Grand Duke of Hesse, to secure the Kaiser's agreement to replace Hintze as military plenipotentiary. The latter had been accused of spying, and although Nicholas valued Hintze, he had no choice but to seek his removal from St Petersburg.[254] The Chief of the Kaiser's naval cabinet, Admiral Georg Alexander von Müller, tried to persuade Wilhelm that the post of military plenipotentiary should be abolished, on the grounds that it had become 'without purpose' in political terms, but to no avail.[255] The second action which removed a source of tension between the two powers was the Tsar's decision to replace Alexander Isvolsky as foreign minister, in September 1910. The Kaiser and Bethmann had both been convinced that no improvement in Russo-German relations could occur while Isvolsky remained at this key post. His replacement, Sergei Sazonov, was more acceptable to the Germans.[256]

During his prolonged stay in Germany, Nicholas decided, with his

---

[251] Note by Aehrenthal, 22–5 February 1910, *ÖUA*, II, no. 2024, p. 725.

[252] Crozier to Pichon, 13 September 1910, *DDF*, 2nd series, XII, no. 568, p. 899.

[253] Grand Duke Ernst Ludwig to Princess Victoria of Battenberg, 29 June 1910, HStA Darmstadt Abt. D24 35/4; Manfred Knodt, *Ernst Ludwig: Grossherzog von Hessen und bei Rhein* (Darmstadt, 1978), pp. 139–49.

[254] Plessen to Bethmann Hollweg, 17 September 1910, *GP*, XVII(ii), no. 9957, pp. 554–5; Lambsdorff, *Militärbevollmächtigten*, pp. 164–5, 180–94; Wilhelm II to Nicholas II, undated (autumn 1910?), *BKW*, p. 405.

[255] W. Görlitz (ed.), *Der Kaiser ... Aufzeichnungen des Chefs des Marinekabinetts Admiral Georg Alexander von Müller* (Göttingen, 1965), p. 80; cf. Zedlitz, *Twelve Years*, diary entry, 13 January 1909, pp. 241–4; Wilhelm II to Nicholas II, 24 December 1910, *BKW*, pp. 406–7; Nicholas II to Wilhelm II, 3/16 January 1911, PA Bonn Russland Nr 82 Nr 1 Bd 60.

[256] McDonald, *United Government*, p. 158.

new foreign minister, to pay a visit to the Kaiser at Potsdam, in November 1910. A pragmatic desire to improve Russia's relations with the *Reich* motivated this decision.[257] Sazonov was anxious to reassure the French ambassador to Russia, M. Louis, about the form which the meeting between the two emperors would take. Sazonov expected that the traditional friendship between the Romanovs and Hohenzollerns would be raised during the meeting, but he described this as a 'sentimental game' and observed 'The times have changed.' His own discussions with Bethmann and Alfred von Kiderlen-Wächter, the state secretary of the German foreign office, would focus principally on the affairs of the Near East, where German economic penetration was causing the Russians increasing concern.[258]

The German aims for the meeting between the two emperors at Potsdam were set out in a memorandum by Kiderlen on 30 October 1910. He believed that dynastic ties and an attachment to conservative principles still bound Germany and Russia together. However, he appreciated Russian concern about Germany's close relations with Austria. Kiderlen took the view that an agreement with Russia could be reached if Germany were to guarantee not to support an aggressive Austrian policy in the Balkans and assure the Tsar and his foreign minister that the Berlin–Baghdad railway was a purely economic undertaking, and not designed to turn the Ottoman empire into a German colony. In return for these concessions, he hoped that the Germans would be able to end the situation where Russia co-operated automatically with France and Britain.[259] Sazonov assured Bethmann of Russia's peaceable intentions and desire to maintain the political status quo. The chancellor himself believed that there was every possibility that good relations between Germany and Russia could be restored, but that there was no longer any prospect of an alliance between them. Sazonov informed Bethmann that the Tsar intended to speak freely and openly about political matters with the Kaiser. The experience of the previous fifteen years had left Wilhelm cynical in the face of such statements. 'I have expected that from year to year,' he wrote, 'but it has never occurred!'[260]

Wilhelm was to be pleasantly surprised, for Nicholas spoke frankly

---

[257] Nicholas II to Marie Feodorovna, 21 October/3 November 1910, *Letters of Tsar Nicholas*, p. 258.
[258] Louis to Pichon, 26 October 1910, *DDF*, 2nd series, XII, no. 602, pp. 963–5.
[259] Note by Kiderlen, 30 October 1910. *GP*, XXVII(ii), no. 10151, pp. 832–4.
[260] Bethmann Hollweg to Wilhelm II, 1 November 1910, *ibid.*, no. 10152, pp. 835–8. Wilhelm II's comment, note 2, p. 837.

with him on international political issues, and made clear his commitment to preserve the status quo in the Balkans, and to improve Russia's relations, not only with Berlin, but also with Vienna. Sazonov also pleased the Kaiser with his attitude, and Wilhelm was content to hear that the new Russian foreign minister intended to restore Petersburg's relations with Berlin to their position before the Bosnian Crisis.[261] On a political level too, the meeting between the two emperors at Potsdam was a resounding success. An agreement was concluded, in principle, between the two powers, on a basis similar to that proposed by Kiderlen. Germany promised not to support aggressive Austrian actions in the Balkans and renounced all rights to build railways and establish telegraph services in the Russian zone of Persia. In return, the Russians guaranteed to withdraw opposition to the Berlin–Baghdad railway and agreed to construct a branch line to Tehran.[262] As one historian has pointed out, the Potsdam agreements initiated a period of *détente* between the two empires and in the eighteen months thereafter, 'Russo-German relations improved considerably, becoming much warmer than Berlin's links with London and Paris.'[263]

Nicholas II had been satisfied by his visit to Potsdam.[264] However, there can be no doubt that his desire to improve Russia's relations with Germany was motivated by his country's need for a period of tranquility, rather than by a sentimental attachment to the old dynastic ties between the Romanovs and Hohenzollerns. After his return to Russia, in conversation with a French politician, Monsieur Doumer, Nicholas defended his decision to visit the Kaiser by emphasising Russia's need for good relations with all powers in the interests of peace. Yet the Tsar made no secret of his personal distaste for Wilhelm II, nor of the fact that the visit had been a strain.[265] The Tsar took a similar line during an audience with the French ambassador, M. Louis, in March 1911, and assured him that Russia had no intention of abandoning the Dual Alliance, describing his commitment to it as 'unwavering', a fact which was known in Berlin, as in Paris.[266]

---

[261] Sazonov, *Fateful Years*, p. 27.
[262] *GP*, xxvii(ii), nos. 10154–62, pp. 839–54; Sazonov, *Fateful Years*, pp. 27–35; Sazonov to Nicholas II, 4 November 1910, *Livre noir*, ii, pp. 331–4.
[263] Lieven, *Russia and the Origins*, p. 38; cf. Spring, 'Russia', p. 584.
[264] Nicholas II to Marie Feodorovna, 31 October/13 November 1910, *Letters of Tsar Nicholas*, pp. 259–60.
[265] Louis to Pichon, 5 January 1911, *DDF*, 2nd series, xiii, no. 111, p. 200.
[266] Louis to Cruppi, 4 March 1911, *ibid.*, no. 173, pp. 313–14.

Despite the evident lack of personal sympathy between Wilhelm and Nicholas, the period of *détente* between Russia and Germany, initiated by the Potsdam agreements persisted until the summer of 1912. In July of that year the Kaiser met the Tsar at Baltic Port, near St. Petersburg. It was to be the last political summit between the two monarchs before the outbreak of the Great War. The growing tension between the Balkan states and the Ottoman empire formed the background to the discussions between the Kaiser and the Tsar. Nicholas was gratified by Wilhelm's assurance that 'he would not permit the Balkan complications to become a world conflagration'.[267] In addition, as a sign of his own good faith, the Tsar agreed to award the contract for two Russian destroyers to a German shipyard.[268] However, as after his visit to Potsdam two years before, Nicholas was clearly relieved when his meeting with Wilhelm was over, telling Count Kokovtsov, who had succeeded the assassinated Stolypin as Russian premier in September 1911, 'Thank heaven! Now one does not have to watch one's every word lest it be misconstrued in a way one had not even dreamed.'[269]

Nicholas did not come away from the meeting with full confidence in the Kaiser's guarantee to prevent a general war. He told Kokovtsov, 'we must get ready', and noted the great advances which were being made in the reconstruction of Russia's naval and land forces.[270] The Tsar had grown wary of the sudden initiatives that Wilhelm occasionally sprang upon him, as an exchange of letters between the two emperors, in the autumn of 1912, regarding the construction of railways across their mutual frontier, made clear. On 3 October, the Kaiser wrote to Nicholas, stressing the economic benefits that new railways could bring to the people on both sides of the border, and requesting the Tsar's support for joint action.[271] Nicholas answered in a guarded fashion, no doubt because, with war raging in south east Europe between the Balkan League and Turkey, and the risk of a general European conflict, he feared that the railways, which the Kaiser proposed, might be used for military purposes rather than for economic ones. He had passed details of the scheme onto Kokovtsov, not wishing to make the decision without prior consultation, signifying that caution was now the dominant factor in his dealings with the Kaiser.[272]

[267] Fisher, *Kokovtsov*, p. 323.   [268] Spring, 'Russia', p. 583.
[269] Fisher, *Kokovtsov*, p. 320; cf. Sazonov to Nicholas II (undated), *Livre noir*, pp. 335–8.
[270] Fisher, *Kokovtsov*, p. 323.
[271] Wilhelm II to Nicholas II, 3 October 1912, *BKW*, pp. 411–12.
[272] Nicholas II to Wilhelm II, 23 October/5 November 1912, GStA Berlin BPH 53/247.

The war, which broke out on 8 October 1912, between the states of the Balkan League and Turkey put strains on Russo-German relations. This was because the gains made by Serbia against the Turks raised fears in Vienna, not least that Serbia, Austria's principal enemy in the region, would become too strong and, by gaining a port on the Adriatic, break Austria's stranglehold over the Serbian economy. Germany as Austria's ally risked becoming involved, for if the *Reich* were to fail to act in support of her ally, she would find herself completely isolated in Europe. Similarly, Russia, as the traditional protector of the Balkan Slavs, was not willing to stand back and let Serbia be crushed by Austria.

The attitudes of Wilhelm II and Nicholas II during this crisis were radically different. The Kaiser, after receiving news from London that the English would intervene on the side of France and Russia in the event of a general conflict, convened a 'war council' on 8 December 1912, at which it was decided to postpone a general conflict, but to prepare German public opinion for a war against Russia in the near future.[273] In a conversation with Alfred de Claparède, the Swiss ambassador to Berlin, just two days after the war council, the Kaiser's hostility towards Russia was clearly in evidence and he told his interlocutor of his belief in the inevitability of 'a racial war, the war of Slavdom against Germandom', in one or two years' time. Germany and Austria would not tolerate a strong Serbia, and if diplomacy could not prevent this, then force would.[274] In contrast, Nicholas II's behaviour during the international crisis in the closing months of 1912 indicated that he preserved some residual faith in the Kaiser's commitment to peace. In November 1912, the Tsar refused his war minister's request for a partial mobilisation of the Russian army against Germany as well as Austria, believing, somewhat naively, that Russia's quarrel was with Vienna alone and not with Berlin. The mobilisation order against Austria was later cancelled, when it became clear that a negotiated solution to the Balkan disputes was possible.[275]

[273] Fritz Fischer, *Krieg der Illusionen. Die deutsche Politik von 1911 bis 1914* (Düsseldorf, 1969), pp. 231–5; John C. G. Röhl, 'Admiral von Müller and the Approach of War 1912–1914', *Historical Journal* 12, 4 (1969), 651–89; John C. G. Röhl, 'An der Schwelle zum Weltkrieg: Eine Dokumentation über den "Kriegsrat" vom 8. Dezember 1912', *Militärgeschichtliche Mitteilungen* 21 (1977), 77–134; Bernd F. Schulte, *Vor dem Kriegsausbruch 1914. Deutschland, die Türkei und der Balkan* (Düsseldorf, 1980), pp. 77–80, 86–93.
[274] De Claparède's Report, 10 December 1912, Terence F. Cole, 'German Decision-Making on the Eve of the First World War: The Records of the Swiss Embassy in Berlin', in *Der Ort Kaiser Wilhelms II. in der deutschen Geschichte*, ed. John C. G. Röhl (Munich, 1991), pp. 62–3.
[275] McDonald, *United Government*, pp. 181–6.

The appointment of a German officer, Colonel Liman von Sanders, to command the Turkish garrison at Constantinople, in the autumn of 1913, caused a further crisis in Russo-German relations, for it stimulated Russian fears that the Germans were attempting to gain control over the Straits, through which 37 per cent of Russia's exports and 75 per cent of her grain exports passed.[276] In the face of Russian objections, the Germans yielded, although their concession was disguised by Liman von Sanders's appointment as a German general of cavalry and a Turkish Marshall, in January 1914.[277] After the German climbdown, Nicholas II told the *Reich*'s ambassador, Count Pourtalès, 'Now I have only friendly smiles for Germany.' The Kaiser made clear his anger at being forced into a humiliating retreat by the Tsar, 'That is quite enough!', he wrote, 'That is all we ever get from him!'[278]

Nicholas's words to Pourtalès did not reflect his true attitude. The Liman von Sanders affair had destroyed the residual trust which the Tsar had placed in the Kaiser and the German government. Afterwards, both he, and his foreign minister, Sazonov, realised that no understanding was possible with Berlin on the politically sensitive issue of their mutual interests in the Near East.[279] Wilhelm II's actions and those which his advisers had sanctioned, with his approval, had now turned the Tsar into an enemy. Shortly after the resolution of the Liman von Sanders crisis, the Tsar gave an audience to Théophile Delcassé, the former French foreign minister. In the course of the discussion, Nicholas's resolve to resist Germany, should the need arise, was evident. He told Delcassé that the Liman von Sanders affair had represented a threat to Russia's vital interests, for the free passage of goods through the Dardanelles was essential for her commerce. He assured Delcassé that he had never had any intention of abandoning the Dual Alliance and returning to a policy based on the Three Emperors' League, despite Wilhelm II's attempts to persuade him to change sides. In contrast, Nicholas had become convinced of the need for ever closer co-operation between St Petersburg, Paris and London. The Tsar spoke to Delcassé of the prospect of 'the perhaps inevitable and imminent collision between German ambitions and Russian interest'. Nicholas vowed, with regard to the possibility of war with Germany, 'We will not let them

---

[276] Lieven, *Russia and the Origins*, p. 45–6; cf. Kokovtsov to Nicholas II, 19 November 1913, *Livre noir*, II, pp. 411–12.

[277] Oldenbourg, *Last Tsar*, III, p. 133; McDonald, *United Government*, pp. 190–5.

[278] Wilhelm II's comment on Pourtalès to Bethmann Hollweg, 14 January 1914. Oldenbourg, *Last Tsar*, III, p. 134.

[279] McDonald, *United Government*, pp. 195–6.

tread on our toes and, this time, it will not be like the war in the Far East: the national mood will support us.'[280]

In the winter of 1914, two prominent Russian statesmen, P. N. Durnovo, a former interior minister, and Count Witte both advocated the merits of co-operation with Berlin. Durnovo favoured abandoning the Triple *Entente* in the process, whereas Witte wished to see a revival of the project of a continental league, excluding Britain, but including France. Durnovo, in particular, feared that a war with the *Kaiserreich* could fatally undermine the Russian monarchy by leading to a revolution.[281] Nicholas II and Sazonov dismissed such views out of hand. Sazonov told the British ambassador that such a change of course was now 'unthinkable'.[282] The Tsar echoed his foreign minister's views in conversation with Sir George Buchanan, the British ambassador. He tried to convince the ambassador of the merits of a defensive alliance between Britain and Russia, in order to deter German aggression, and he also stressed his anxiety about German designs on the Straits, the issue which had formed the substance of his conversation with Delcassé in January 1914. Despite these concerns, Nicholas emphasised that he 'wished to live on good terms with Germany'.[283] The Tsar's desire to see peace maintained led him, to some extent, into wishful thinking. He told his sister, the Grand Duchess Olga, in 1914 that the Kaiser was, 'a bore and an exhibitionist, but he would never start a war'.[284] However, when the decisive crisis came in July 1914, Nicholas II was determined to resist Germany, avenge the humiliation of the Bosnian crisis, and maintain Russia's status as a Great Power. In a context where Russia's vital interests were deemed to be at stake, Wilhelm II's attempt to persuade the Tsar to join him in defending the monarchical principle against Serbia was an inadequate mechanism for preventing the escalation of an Austro-Serbian dispute into a general war. The time had long past when such appeals could be effective.

Writing in 1917, Philipp Eulenburg blamed the German government's failure to renew the Reinsurance Treaty in 1890 for the subsequent

---

[280] Delcassé to Doumergue, 29 January 1914, *DDF*, 3rd series, IX, no. 189, pp. 234–5.
[281] Lieven, *Russia's Rulers*, pp. 228–30; Lieven, 'Pro-Germans', pp. 43–6; McDonald, *United Government*, pp. 200–1; Pourtalès to Bethmann Hollweg, 31 March 1914, PA Bonn Deutschland Nr 131 Nr 4 geheim. Bd 6.
[282] Buchanan to Grey, 31 March 1914, *BD*, X(ii), no. 536, p. 778.
[283] Buchanan to Grey, 3 April 1914, *ibid.*, no. 537, pp. 780–2; cf. Isvolsky to Sazonov, 5/18 March 1914, *Livre noir*, II, pp. 249–50.
[284] Vorres, *Grand-Duchess*, p. 131.

estrangement between Berlin and St Petersburg.[285] Although relations between the two powers had been deteriorating steadily throughout the 1880s, Eulenburg's view was correct in so far as the failure to renew the treaty removed the guarantee that Russia would not seek an accommodation with France.[286] In the two decades after the formation of the Franco-Russian alliance in 1894, Wilhelm II's aim and that of German *Russlandpolitik* was to destroy or neutralise the damage caused to the *Reich*'s international position by the *rapprochement* between St Petersburg and Paris, principally by appealing to Nicholas II to abandon the atheistic French Republic and return to the traditional conservative, monarchist path embodied by the Three Emperors' League.

The present study has revealed several factors which explain why this objective was never achieved. Wilhelm failed to create a relationship of real trust with Nicholas. He tricked him over the German acquisition of Kiaochow in 1897, drove him towards a disastrous war against Japan, and gave his blessing to the ultimatum which brought about Russia's humiliation in the Bosnian crisis. The personal incompatibility between the two emperors rendered Wilhelm's efforts to convince the Tsar of the advantages of co-operation with Berlin ineffective. Nicholas seems to have found the Kaiser less congenial at each meeting and came to resent Wilhelm's pestering letters and patronising manner.[287] In any case, German policy towards Russia was incomplete as too much emphasis was placed on the maintenance of good relations between the two emperors, and not enough of an attempt was made to persuade a succession of Russian foreign ministers of the value of Germany as an ally. Wilhelm II's suspicion of most of those whom Nicholas appointed to the post did not help in this regard.

A fourth factor which reduced the chances of a Russo-German *rapprochement* was the fact that, during the twenty years before the outbreak of the First World War, the pro-Germans were a small and diminishing minority among the Russian élite. Russian nationalism and public opinion were adopting an increasingly virulent anti-German character. Although the Tsar was less prone to consult public opinion than other rulers, this transformation in the attitudes of educated society inevitably had a bearing on Russian foreign policy, particularly after

---

[285] Note by Eulenburg, February 1917, *EK*, III, no. 1563, p. 2230.
[286] Kennan, *Bismarck's European Order*, pp. 398–421.
[287] Zedlitz, *Twelve Years*, diary entry, 13 March 1906, pp. 161–2; Hugo Graf Lerchenfeld Köfering, *Kaiser Wilhelm II. als Persönlichkeit und Herrscher, eine Rückschau*, ed. Dieter Albrecht (Regensburg, 1985), p. 24.

1906 when the régime, weakened by defeat against Japan, and by internal unrest, would have risked its survival if it had embarked upon an unpopular foreign policy. Wilhelm II himself seems to have recognised this, albeit belatedly. He told the Austrian foreign minister, Count Berchtold, in October 1913 that there could be no return to the Three Emperors' League because Russia had changed since the time of Alexander III. One now had to deal, he observed, with 'another Russia which is hostile towards us, working towards our destruction, and in which elements other than the Emperor govern'.[288]

The fifth factor which explains the Kaiser's inability to resurrect the alliance between Berlin and St Petersburg was the influence exercised by the French over Russian foreign policy. This has often been exaggerated by historians. However, the French were able to exploit their financial muscle over Russia to ensure in the years after 1906 that Russia's relations with Germany did not regain the warmth which they had possessed before and during the Russo-Japanese War. Russia's alliance with France, although never a partnership of equals, did have the advantage of possessing a semblance of interdependence, for both powers had a mutual interest in preventing a German hegemony on the European continent. By contrast, the enormous economic and military power of Imperial Germany meant that an alliance with Berlin risked reducing Russia to the level of a German satellite state. Russia's humiliation by Germany in the Bosnian crisis provided a foretaste of what this would involve.[289]

By far the most important reason for the failure of Germany to detach Russia from the Dual Alliance, and the Triple *Entente*, was the attitude taken by Nicholas II himself. He remained the key political actor in imperial Russia, a fact obscured, but not altered, by his retreat into the background in the years immediately after the Russo-Japanese War.[290] As Hintze noted, in his report to the Kaiser on 28 January 1909,[291] the Tsar's confidence remained vital if a Russian minister wished to remain in office. If a minister lost Nicholas's confidence, then he would fall from power. No minister, therefore, could carry out a foreign policy which conflicted with the Tsar's basic convictions. Nicholas II was, throughout his reign, determined to maintain the Franco-Russian alliance. He saw

---

[288] Note by Berchtold, 28 October 1913, *ÖUA*, VII, no. 8934, p. 515; cf. Szögyény to Berchtold, 12 March 1914, *ibid.*, VII, no. 9470, p. 966.
[289] Cf. Spring, 'Russia', pp. 564–92; Lieven, 'Pro-Germans', pp. 51–4.
[290] Lieven, *Russia and the Origins*, pp. 50–61; McDonald, *United Government*, p. 212.
[291] Hintze to Wilhelm II, 28 January 1909, PA Bonn Russland Nr 82 Nr 1 geheim. Bd 3.

it as a sacred inheritance from his father, Alexander III, and the cornerstone of Russian foreign policy, a sentiment which was readily encouraged by Nicholas's Germanophobe mother, Marie Feodorovna, who had considerable influence over her son during the early years of his reign. Numerous attempts by the Kaiser could not change this, for Nicholas had a strong will when his fundamental beliefs were at stake. He appreciated that his country's alliance with France gave her a greater degree of freedom than she would have had in a political arrangement with Berlin. In this regard, it is significant that when Wilhelm came closest to achieving an alliance with Russia, at Björkö in July 1905, Nicholas II later turned against the idea when it became clear that the French would never agree to join such a combination. For despite the Tsar's genuine desire for good relations with Germany and his undoubted attachment to the monarchical principle, he believed that St Petersburg's relationship with Paris had to take precedence over her ties with Berlin.

Despite Nicholas II's enduring commitment to the Dual Alliance, the relationship between the Kaiser and the Tsar did serve a useful function, both in terms of Russo-German relations and general international stability. Until at least 1908, both monarchs remained convinced that neither would undertake a hostile act against the other. The residual trust between the two emperors to some extent counter-balanced the trend in Russian foreign policy after 1906 towards *rapprochement* with England, and Wilhelm II's distrust of Alexander Isvolsky, the Russian foreign minister, whom he saw as the chief architect of this policy. On a political level, as Bülow pointed out in 1906,[292] the preservation of the Russian monarchy remained in German interests. A republican or revolutionary Russia, which did not share the attachment to conservatism and monarchism of the Romanovs, would have been much less likely than the Tsarist régime to preserve cordial relations with Berlin.

However, the meeting between the Tsar and Edward VII at Reval in June 1908 led Wilhelm II to believe that, despite the Tsar's attachment to the traditional friendship between the two dynasties, Russia had become Germany's enemy. Likewise, the Bosnian crisis, indicated to Nicholas II that the Germans were prepared to humiliate Russia, rather than risk abandoning Austria-Hungary. However, the fact that the Kaiser attempted to keep Russia out of the war in July 1914 by appealing to the Tsar's sense of monarchical solidarity indicated that he had not

---

[292] Bülow to Wilhelm II, 17 June 1906, GStA Merseburg HA Rep. 53 J Lit. B Nr 16a Bd III.

lost all faith in his ability to win Nicholas's support through an appeal to their common dynastic interests. The appeal was in vain because, by 1914, the vital interests of Germany and Russia were no longer in harmony, particularly in south east Europe. The turn of Russia's foreign interests away from the Far East and back towards the Balkans, after 1906, had brought her into increasing conflict with Austrian and German ambitions in the region. German conduct over Bosnia in 1909, and the Liman von Sanders affair in 1913, meant that Nicholas II's patience with Berlin, and with the Kaiser, had been exhausted by 1914. The fact that Russia and Germany went to war on opposing sides in 1914 indicated that the defence of the 'monarchical principle' was no longer an adequate basis for co-operation between two Empires whose political and strategic interests had diverged so sharply.

CHAPTER 2

Uncle and nephew: Edward VII, Wilhelm II and the Anglo-German dynastic antagonism before 1914

Looking back at the reasons for the outbreak of the First World War from the perspective of Germany's defeat, Philipp Eulenburg isolated two factors as being of particular significance. These were the Anglo-German naval arms race, stimulated by Wilhelm II's desire for a battle fleet to rival that of Britain, and the unbridgeable conflict between the latter and his uncle, King Edward VII.[1] Eulenburg charged the King with having sponsored a policy of encirclement, aimed at cutting his nephew down to size and bringing about a reduction in the strength of the German navy.[2] The quarrel which developed between the Kaiser and the King undermined the previously good dynastic relationship between London and Berlin, and thus removed one of the ties which, in the nineteenth century, had bound Britain and Germany together. The purpose of what follows is to examine the origins and development of the ill-feeling between uncle and nephew, and to assess the political repercussions of this for the wider Anglo-German relationship, beginning with an analysis of Wilhelm II's complex attitude towards his English relatives and Britain.

The marriage between Princess Victoria of Great Britain and Prince Friedrich Wilhelm of Prussia was conceived by the bride's father, Prince Albert, as a means of bringing Prussia and Britain closer together and as a way of furthering the promotion of liberal constitutionalism within Germany.[3] Sadly, the Crown Princess, as Victoria became in 1861, three years after her marriage, failed to fulfil the grandiose plans which her father had conceived for her. She remained deeply attached to her English homeland and was seen in Berlin as favouring British political

---

[1] Note by Eulenburg, 28 February 1919, *EK*, III, no. 1578, pp. 2256–7.
[2] Eulenburg to Professor Kurt Breysig, 27 April 1919, *ibid.*, no. 1582, p. 2277.
[3] Andrew Sinclair, *The Other Victoria: The Princess Royal and the Great Game of Europe* (London, 1981), pp. 8–9.

interests ahead of those of Prussia.[4] In particular, she was viewed with suspicion by Bismarck, who considered her to be little better than an English spy and who referred to her contemptuously as 'die Engländerin'.[5] The dominance which she exercised over her husband, the Crown Prince was also resented in Prussia and contributed to her unpopularity.[6]

Isolated in the political sphere, the Crown Princess sought to ensure that through their upbringing and education her children would develop into liberal Anglophiles. In the case of her eldest child, the future Kaiser Wilhelm II, this aim failed utterly. Wilhelm came to admire various aspects of English culture, notably the life of the English aristocracy,[7] and spoke English as a second mother tongue. At certain times his attachment to aspects of Englishness was ironic in the extreme. For instance, when arriving in Holland in 1918, fleeing a war in which the English had played a large role in Germany's defeat, his first request to his host, Count Bentinck, was for 'a cup of tea, good, hot English tea.'[8] However, this love of certain facets of English culture did not extend to an admiration for that country's political institutions.

The recent research which has been carried out on the Kaiser's early life has shown that from the late 1870s onwards, during Wilhelm's period as a student at the University of Bonn and as a young guards officer at Potsdam, he came to reject the liberal political agenda of his parents, the Crown Prince and Princess, and to associate with the conservatism embodied by his grandfather, Kaiser Wilhelm I, and the chancellor, Otto Fürst von Bismarck.[9] Wilhelm's suspicion of England increased throughout the 1880s, as additional Anglophobic voices were added to his circle. In 1881, he married Dona of Schleswig

---

[4] *HP*, I, p. 169; Holstein, diary entry, 16 April 1885, *ibid.*, II, p. 190; the Crown Princess to Queen Victoria, 11 December 1880, Roger Fulford (ed.), *Beloved Mama. Private Correspondence of Queen Victoria and the German Crown Princess 1878–1885* (London, 1981), pp. 93–4.

[5] Sinclair, *The Other Victoria*, p. 2. On Bismarck's suspicion of the Crown Princess, see: Patricia A. Kollander, 'Politics for the Defence? Bismarck, Battenberg, and the Origins of the *Cartel* of 1887', *German History* 13, I, (1995), 28–46; Patricia A. Kollander, 'The Liberalism of Frederick III', PhD dissertation, Brown University (1992). See also the many recent studies of the early life of Wilhelm II, in particular: John C. G. Röhl, *Wilhelm II.: Die Jugend des Kaisers, 1859–1888* (Munich, 1993); Lamar Cecil, *Wilhelm II: Prince and Emperor, 1859–1900* (Chapel Hill and London, 1989); Thomas A. Kohut, *Wilhelm II and the Germans: A Study in Leadership* (Oxford and New York, 1991).

[6] Lamar J. R. Cecil, 'History as Family Chronicle: Kaiser Wilhelm II and the Dynastic Roots of the Anglo-German Antagonism', in *Kaiser Wilhelm II: New Interpretations*, ed. John C. G. Röhl and Nicolaus Sombart (Cambridge, 1982), pp. 92–3; Holstein, diary entry, 6 May 1885, *HP*, II, p. 195.

[7] Ludwig Raschdau, *In Weimar als preussischer Gesandter: Ein Buch der Erinnerungen an deutsche Fürstenhöfe 1894–1897* (Berlin, 1939), diary entry, 14 December 1895, p. 40.

[8] Sir John W. Wheeler-Bennett, *Three Episodes in the Life of Kaiser Wilhelm II* (Cambridge, 1956), p. 19.

[9] Röhl, *Jugend des Kaisers*, pp. 379–431; Cecil, *Wilhelm II*, ch. 3.

Holstein, who was distrustful of the English and disapproved of them both morally and politically.[10] Those who came to exert most influence over Wilhelm at this time were also hostile to England, they included the Prince's adjutant Adolf von Bülow and Alfred Count von Walder-see.[11] Under the tutelage of these individuals, by 1883, Wilhelm had become, according to Crown Prince Rudolf of Austria, 'a dyed-in-the wool Junker and reactionary'.[12] This was an outcome which the Crown Princess found almost impossible to accept. She compared herself to 'a hen that has hatched ducklings'[13] and in a letter to her friend Marie Countess Dönhoff, she poured out her hatred of Berlin, its society and its politics and observed despairingly that the 'bitterest and hardest of all is that my son Wilhelm and his wife stand on the other side of this gulf.'[14]

The attitude which Wilhelm had by this point adopted towards his mother and her politics was to remain with him for the rest of his life. Looking back on the role which the Crown Princess had played in Germany, from his exile in Holland, the ex-Kaiser noted that his mother had wished to see a parliamentary régime on the British model established in Germany and to turn the *Reich* into a vassal of Britain which would further British interests in continental Europe.[15] Wilhelm's political activity during the 1880s indicated that he had determined to thwart this aim. The central issue of dispute between Wilhelm and his mother at this time was the Crown Princess's determination, in alliance with her husband and her relatives in London, to arrange a marriage between her daughter, Viktoria, and Prince Alexander of Battenberg. Wilhelm, supported by his grandparents, Kaiser Wilhelm I and Kaiserin Augusta, and by both Fürst Bismarck and his son Herbert, was adamant that he would not tolerate the match.

There were several reasons for his opposition to the marriage. Batten-berg was the product of a morganatic marriage between a Hessian prince and a Polish countess. Wilhelm, along with his grandparents therefore viewed the proposed match as a *mésalliance*. In political terms, he feared that the marriage would create complications between Germany and Russia, as Bulgaria, the country ruled by Prince Alexander, was a Russian satrapy and Battenberg's relations with Tsar Alexander

---

[10] Cecil, *Wilhelm II*, p. 78.   [11] Röhl, *Jugend des Kaisers*, pp. 417–31.   [12] *Ibid.*, p. 421.
[13] The Crown Princess to Queen Victoria, 5 August 1880, *Beloved Mama*, p. 85.
[14] Crown Princess Victoria to Countess Dönhoff, quoted by Cecil, *Wilhelm II*, p. 73; cf. Crown Princess Victoria to Queen Victoria, 7 March 1887, Agatha Ramm (ed.), *Beloved and Darling Child. Last Letters between Queen Victoria and her Eldest Daughter 1886–1901* (Stroud, 1990), pp. 45–6.
[15] Notes by Wilhelm II, Haus Doorn, 28 March 1927, GStA Berlin, BPH 53/165.

III were tense due to the former's wish for greater political independence. In addition, he feared that a marriage alliance between his sister
and Battenberg would increase English influence in the Balkans because
Battenberg's two brothers Louis and Henry had married, respectively,
Queen Victoria's granddaughter, Victoria of Hesse, and daughter,
Princess Beatrice. The Crown Princess was equally determined for the
marriage to take place, seeing it as opening the way to an Anglo-
German dominance in the Balkans once she and the Crown Prince
ascended the throne.[16]

Ultimately, the marriage was frustrated by the deaths, in rapid
succession, in 1888 of Kaiser Wilhelm I and of Kaiser Friedrich III, who
ruled for only ninety-nine days before succumbing to cancer. Wilhelm
wrote to Battenberg on 3 April 1888 to inform him that his first act on
becoming Kaiser would be to banish Battenberg and his sister from
Germany if they were to marry.[17] Forbidding the marriage between
Battenberg and his sister was just one of the indignities which Wilhelm
heaped upon his mother in the immediate aftermath of Kaiser Friedrich's death. He caused the palace in which his father had died to be
surrounded so as to prevent his parents' correspondence from being sent
to England.[18] He also reversed his father's two dying wishes that the
Neues Palais in Potsdam should be renamed Friedrichskron and that the
marriage between Viktoria and Battenberg should be allowed to go
ahead. The impact of these humiliations was too much for Wilhelm's
mother to bear. She accused Wilhelm of exhibiting 'perfectly heartless
disregard' for his sister's feelings by prohibiting the Battenberg marriage. She found this particularly wounding because Wilhelm's father
had given the marriage his blessing. As a consequence of Wilhelm's
behaviour she made clear that she intended 'for the future to hold no
communication' with him 'beyond what is absolutely necessary'.[19]
Thereafter, Victoria retreated from Berlin and lived a reclusive life at
her home, Schloss Friedrichshof, in the Taunus mountains.

---

[16] Röhl, *Jugend des Kaisers*, pp. 517–45; Cecil, *Wilhelm II*, ch. 3; Cecil, 'History as Family Chronicle',
pp. 100–1; Norman Rich, *Friedrich von Holstein: Politics and Diplomacy in the Era of Bismarck and
Wilhelm II*, 2 vols. (Cambridge, 1965), I, pp. 145–242; Kollander, 'Politics for the Defence?',
28–46; the Crown Princess to Queen Victoria, 16 May 1884, *Beloved Mama*, p. 166.

[17] Cecil, *Wilhelm II*, p. 118; Röhl, *Jugend des Kaisers*, pp. 787–821.

[18] He failed in this aim as the letters had already been given to Sir Frederick Ponsonby, Queen
Victoria's assistant private secretary, by the Crown Princess. Some of them were later published.
Sir Frederick Ponsonby (ed.), *The Letters of the Empress Frederick* (London, 1928).

[19] Kaiserin Friedrich to Wilhelm II, 7 November 1888, GStA Merseburg HA Rep. 52 T Nr 13; cf.
Kaiserin Friedrich to Wilhelm II, 29 October 1888, *ibid*; Kaiserin Friedrich to Queen Victoria,
16 August 1888, *Beloved and Darling Child*, pp. 75–6.

It was Wilhelm's conduct towards his parents which first created serious difficulties in his relationship with his English grandmother, Queen Victoria. She first learned of Wilhelm's rudeness towards his mother, through her son Arthur, Duke of Connaught, in November 1881. The Queen echoed the concerns of her son about Wilhelm's behaviour.[20] It was, however, the Battenberg marriage which led to a growth in the hostility between the Queen and her eldest grandson. Queen Victoria favoured the match and was offended by Wilhelm's description of it as a *mésalliance*, particularly as her youngest daughter, Beatrice, had married Heinrich Battenberg in 1884.[21] The Queen declared that Wilhelm deserved 'a good "skelping"'[22] and in 1885 she refused to allow him or his brother Heinrich to visit her in England because of their mutual hostility to Battenberg. Wilhelm responded by referring to his grandmother, in conversation with Herbert Bismarck, as an 'old hag'.[23]

By 1887, Wilhelm's dislike for his grandmother and for England had reached dangerous proportions. On a visit to his friend, Philipp Count zu Eulenburg, in June of that year, Wilhelm spoke in insensitive terms about his grandmother and in a hostile way about England. Eulenburg recorded that his royal guest had said of Queen Victoria, 'It is high time that the old woman dies.' When Eulenburg drew attention to the anti-English views of another of his guests, Wilhelm reportedly remarked 'That pleases me . . . One can never have enough hatred for England.'[24] It is little wonder then that the visit which Wilhelm paid to England for Queen Victoria's Golden Jubilee later that year was a disaster. Wilhelm had only been invited at the last minute because Vicky had persuaded her reluctant mother that his exclusion would cause political complications.[25] During the jubliee celebrations the Queen did not hide her disapproval of Wilhelm's conduct towards his parents and handled him and Dona coldly. Wilhelm's hostility towards England also led Lord Salisbury, the prime minister, to believe that Germany might turn towards Russia when Wilhelm became Kaiser, a prospect which he viewed with apprehension.[26]

[20] Röhl, *Jugend des Kaisers*, pp. 402–3; Queen Victoria to the Crown Princess, 27 December 1884, *Beloved Mama*, p. 175.

[21] Cecil, 'History as Family Chronicle', pp. 100–1; Röhl, *Jugend des Kaisers*, p. 527.

[22] Queen Victoria to the Crown Princess, 13 February 1885, *Beloved Mama*, p. 183.

[23] Holstein, diary entry, 16 October 1885, *HP*, ii, p. 254.

[24] *EK*, i, p. 225.

[25] Queen Victoria to Crown Princess Victoria, 21 and 28 March 1887, and Crown Princess to Queen Victoria, 2 April 1887, *Beloved and Darling Child*, pp. 46–7, 48–50.

[26] Röhl, *Jugend des Kaisers*, pp. 672–8.

Relations between Wilhelm and Queen Victoria remained difficult during his first years as Kaiser.[27] This was due in large measure to the influence which Wilhelm's mother, Vicky, exercised over the Queen. Both women regretted that Fritz had not lived longer, and contrasted Wilhelm's conduct as Kaiser unfavourably with that which they believed his father would have adopted.[28] However, gradually, under the influence of Lord Salisbury, the Queen began to take a more diplomatic line towards her Prussian grandson.[29] Salisbury was himself no admirer of the Kaiser. He described Wilhelm on one occasion as an 'ultra human' who was 'as jealous as a woman because he does not think the Queen pays him enough attention'.[30] But he knew how to handle the Queen and the 'capricious moods' which tended to influence her attitudes towards questions of foreign policy.[31] Thus, under his guidance, she took a moderate line when the Kaiser sent a telegram to Kruger, the president of the Boer republic, in 1896,[32] and she gave Wilhelm the honorary positions in the Royal Navy and the British Army which he craved. Shortly before the Kaiser's arrival in England for a visit in 1889, Queen Victoria awarded him the rank of admiral of the fleet. Wilhelm professed himself to be 'overwhelmed', and remarked in a letter to the British ambassador: 'Fancy wearing the same uniform as St. Vincent and Nelson; it is enough to make one quite giddy.'[33] Similarly, in 1894, Wilhelm said that he was 'deeply moved' when the Queen made him an honorary colonel in the Royals.[34] He attached an importance to these honours which was far out of proportion to their true significance, seeing them as signs of his grandmother's special favour towards him and desire for close co-operation between Britain and Germany.[35] In reality, the colonelcy in the Royals, like the rank of admiral, had been given to the Kaiser by the Queen only with great

[27] Cecil, 'History as Family Chronicle', p.102.
[28] Kaiserin Friedrich to Queen Victoria and Queen Victoria to Kaiserin Friedrich, 3 and 6 October 1896, *Beloved and Darling Child*, pp. 195–6.
[29] Zara Steiner, *The Foreign Office and Foreign Policy* (Cambridge, 1969), pp. 201–2; Paul M. Kennedy, *The Rise of the Anglo-German Antagonism 1860–1914* (London, 1980), pp. 400–1; Cecil, 'History as Family Chronicle', p. 102.
[30] Lord Salisbury to Sir Frank Lascelles, 10 May 1899. Lascelles Papers PRO FO 800/9; quoted, in part, by Cecil, *Wilhelm II*, p. 280.
[31] Lord Esher, journal entry, 14 March 1895, Esher Papers, Churchill College, Cambridge, ESHR 2/10.
[32] Queen Victoria to Kaiser Wilhelm II, 5 January 1896, and Queen Victoria to the Prince of Wales, 11 January 1896, *LQV*, III, pp. 8–9, 18–20.
[33] Wilhelm II to Sir Edward Malet, 14 June 1889, *ibid.*, I, p. 504.
[34] Wilhelm II to Queen Victoria, 24 April 1894, *ibid.*, II, p. 395.
[35] Wilhelm II to Brigadier General W. H.-H. Waters, 24 April 1928, W. H.-H. Waters, *Potsdam and Doorn* (London, 1935), pp. 95–7.

reluctance, after pressure from Berlin, and when Wilhelm visited England in August 1894, and was distressed not to be greeted by representatives of the regiment, nobody had the nerve to tell him that they had forgotten that he was their colonel-in-chief.[36]

Queen Victoria was not unaware of her grandson's faults. She knew of his passion for political intrigue,[37] which took the form, in her case, of Wilhelm writing letters to her warning against the allegedly anti-English actions of the Russians.[38] Eventually, she sought to neutralise the potential damage of her grandson's actions by warning Nicholas II against Wilhelm's 'mischievous and unstraightforward proceedings'.[39] Her personal distaste for the Kaiser was also revealed in her failure to invite Wilhelm to her Diamond Jubilee in 1897 or to her eightieth birthday celebrations in May 1899. Despite the vicious and insensitive terms in which he had spoken of Queen Victoria in the 1880s, Wilhelm seems to have retained a great deal of inherent respect for his grandmother and this persisted until the end of his life. He would declare, not withstanding evidence to the contrary, many years after the Queen's death, that he had been her favourite grandson and spoke of her as his 'unparalleled grandmama'.[40] Towards the end of Queen Victoria's life, Wilhelm wrote his grandmother a letter full of admiration, making clear his view that she respected him not only as a grandson, but also as a monarch.[41] Wilhelm's deferential demeanour at Queen Victoria's death-bed and funeral reflected the extent of his affection for his grandmother, and his conviction, expressed in a comment on a diplomatic despatch from London, that 'Her Majesty always does the right thing at the right moment.'[42]

It would have been inconceivable for Wilhelm to speak of his uncle, Albert Edward, Prince of Wales, in such glowing terms. Queen Victoria had been able to act as a positive influence upon Wilhelm in large

---

[36] Col. Swaine to Sir Henry Ponsonby, 13 January 1894, *LQV*, II, p. 345; Major-General Sir Leopold Swaine, *Camp and Chancery in a Soldier's Life* (London, 1926), pp. 215–16.

[37] Queen Victoria to Grand Duke Ernst Ludwig of Hesse, 15 March 1892, HStA Darmstadt, D 24 33/5.

[38] Wilhelm II to Queen Victoria, 8 December 1891, and Wilhelm II to Queen Victoria, 29 December 1898, *LQV*, II, pp. 82–4 and III, pp. 323–5.

[39] Queen Victoria to Tsar Nicholas II, 1 March 1899, *ibid.*, III, pp. 343–4.

[40] Waters, *Potsdam and Doorn*, p. 7.

[41] Wilhelm II to Queen Victoria, 2 February 1899, *LQV*, III, p. 337; Lascelles to Queen Victoria, 24 December 1898, *ibid.*, p. 322.

[42] Wilhelm II's comment on Metternich to Bülow, 8 March 1900, PA Bonn, England Nr 81 Nr 1 Bd 6.

measure because of the respect and admiration which he possessed for her. In this sense, she had been able to play a mediating role in relations between London and Berlin. No such affection existed between the Kaiser and his Uncle Bertie. Indeed, in the years after Albert Edward's accession to the British throne in 1901, as King Edward VII, Wilhelm's suspicion of his uncle added to his distrust of Britain. Similarly, Edward's distaste for his nephew, which initially was largely a personal matter, came to take on a political importance. Thus, in the first decade of the twentieth century the volatile relationship between the British monarch and the Kaiser became a further factor which accentuated the antagonism between Britain and Germany.

Wilhelm's negative view of his uncle in comparison with Queen Victoria is revealed in comments which he made on a newspaper cutting, regarding Edward VII, following the latter's death. In June 1912, the British paper, *The Nation*, brought a new biography of Edward VII by Sir Sidney Lee to the attention of its readers.[43] The Kaiser made a point of underlining all the references to his uncle's negative character traits which appeared in the newspaper article's summary of Lee's biography, for instance in its reference to the 'bad consequences' of Edward VII's education which, the paper noted, had 'partly spoilt' the King's character.[44] The ill-feeling between Wilhelm and his uncle was essentially a matter of incompatible personalities. Hermann Baron von Eckardstein, who was for many years a diplomat at the German embassy in London, believed that the personal vanity of both Edward and Wilhelm made it difficult for them to get on.[45] Wilhelm himself remarked on one occasion that he and his uncle were so different that 'it was scarcely to be expected that anything like a cordial friendship would exist between us'.[46] Yet the reasons for the ill-feeling between uncle and nephew went much deeper than this. Various personal, dynastic and political factors must also be taken into consideration.

Wilhelm's alienation from his uncle was a by-product of his quarrel with the Crown Princess, who was very close to Albert Edward, her

---

[43] *The Nation*, with marginalia by Wilhelm II, 8 June 1912, PA Bonn England Nr 81 Nr 1 geheim. Bd 1. Sir Sidney Lee's biography was at that time appearing as a supplement in the *Dictionary of National Biography*, it was published in book form in the 1920s; Sir Sidney Lee, *King Edward VII: A Biography*, 2 vols. (London, 1925–7).

[44] Wilhelm II 's marginalia on *The Nation*, 8 June 1912, PA Bonn England Nr 81 Nr 1 geheim. Bd 1.

[45] Hermann Freiherr von Eckardstein, *Persönliche Erinnerungen an König Eduard aus der Einkreisungszeit* (Dresden, 1927), pp. 14–15; cf. Hugo Graf Lerchenfeld-Köfering, *Kaiser Wilhelm II. als Persönlichkeit und Herrscher, eine Rückschau*, ed. Dieter Albrecht (Regensburg, 1985), p. 25; Wilhelm von Stolberg to Metternich, 1 June 1906, PA Bonn England Nr 78 geheim. Bd 8.

[46] Wilhelm II quoted by Cecil, 'History as Family Chronicle', p. 102.

younger brother. There is some evidence that Wilhelm and the Prince of Wales argued during a visit which Wilhelm paid to his uncle at Sandringham in November 1881.[47] However, the role which Albert Edward played in promoting the Battenberg marriage was probably the principal factor in the deterioration in the relationship between the two in the 1880s. The Prince of Wales was a firm advocate of the marriage and even travelled to Berlin with Prince Alexander von Battenberg on one occasion to try to persuade Kaiser Wilhelm I to agree to the match. This was resented by both Kaiserin Augusta and Albert Edward's nephew, Prince Wilhelm.[48] The Prince of Wales's visit occurred in May 1884. Later the same month, Wilhelm paid a visit to Tsar Alexander III in Russia.[49] Wilhelm's first recorded denunciation of his uncle was made in a letter to the Tsar sent from the Kremlin on 25 May 1884. The close proximity between this date and Albert Edward's visit to Berlin as a supporter of the Battenberg marriage would suggest that Wilhelm's determination to prevent the match lay at the roots of his early hostility to the Prince of Wales. The attack on his uncle was also linked to more general warnings against the Crown Prince and Princess, which would also lend weight to this theory.[50] Significantly, the first letter which Wilhelm sent to the Tsar after his return to Germany made a direct reference to the Prince of Wales's mission to Berlin on behalf of Battenberg and his own determination to prevent the marriage.[51]

By March 1885, Wilhelm's denunciations of his uncle had become even more extreme. He warned the Tsar against Albert Edward's 'false and intriguing character'.[52] This view of Albert Edward was to remain a basic conviction of Wilhelm's for the rest of his life and influenced him against England in the first decade of the twentieth century. It seems unlikely that the Prince of Wales learned of his nephew's intrigues against him at the time, for a letter which he addressed to Wilhelm, inviting him to Sandringham, sent in August 1885, was very friendly in tone.[53] However, Albert Edward was Alexander III's brother-in-law, and it is probable that details of Wilhelm's letters were eventually

[47] Sir Sidney Lee, *King Edward VII*, I, p. 475; Cecil, 'History as Family Chronicle', p. 114, note 41.
[48] Röhl, *Jugend des Kaisers*, pp. 527–9.
[49] *Ibid.*, pp. 433–40.
[50] Prince Wilhelm to Tsar Alexander III, 25 May 1884 (copy), GStA Berlin BPH 53/11; cf. Alexander III to Prince Wilhelm, 7/19 May 1885, GStA Merseburg HA Rep. 53 J Lit. R Nr 6.
[51] Prince Wilhelm to Tsar Alexander III, 19 June 1884 (copy), GStA Berlin BPH 53/12.
[52] Prince Wilhelm to Tsar Alexander III, 13 March 1885 (copy), GStA Berlin BPH 53/13.
[53] Albert Edward, Prince of Wales, to Prince Wilhelm, 18 August 1885, GStA Merseburg HA Rep. 53 J Lit. G Nr 11.

communicated to the Princess of Wales by her sister, the Tsarina Marie Feodorovna.[54]

Nonetheless, in October 1885, at a meeting between the Prince of Wales and Wilhelm in Budapest, Albert Edward was obliged to inform his nephew that he would be unable to receive him at Sandringham. This was the result of Queen Victoria's cancellation of a visit by Wilhelm and his brother Heinrich on account of their opposition to the Battenberg marriage.[55] Wilhelm's account of his meeting with his uncle also contained one of his first denunciations of Albert Edward's private life. Wilhelm had been hunting with Crown Prince Rudolf at Mürzsteg and the Prince of Wales had been obliged to wait for him at Pest. Wilhelm told Herbert Bismarck that in the interim, Albert Edward 'led such a fast life . . . that even the Hungarians shook their heads'.[56] This was but the first example of the moralising hypocrisy with regard to his uncle's private life, which was to become an obsession of Wilhelm's during his reign as Kaiser. A Bavarian diplomat reported back to Munich in 1901 that Edward VII's sexually free-wheeling lifestyle 'shocked' Wilhelm,[57] and Bernhard von Bülow told Admiral Tirpitz in early 1905 that the Kaiser had offended the British monarch by interrogating him about his private life.[58] Wilhelm's moralising, having come to the King's attention, thus became a matter of political as well as personal significance.

Wilhelm's disapproving attitude with regard to his uncle's private life may well have been passed down to him by his grandparents, Wilhelm I and Kaiserin Augusta, who both disapproved of the Prince of Wales's adulterous relationships.[59] However, it was the Prince of Wales's political opinions which made him particularly suspect in the eyes of the Prussian royal family. In 1863, Albert Edward had married Princess Alexandra of Schleswig-Holstein-Sonderburg-Glücksburg, the daughter of Prince Christian, the heir to the Danish throne.[60] This created embarrassing political complications, when, in 1864, the Prussian and

---

[54] Giles St Aubyn, *Edward VII: Prince and King* (London, 1979), p. 278.

[55] Holstein, diary entry, 16 October 1885, *HP*, II, pp. 254–5.

[56] *Ibid.*, p.254; cf. Prince Wilhelm to Kaiser Wilhelm I, 30 September 1885. Röhl, *Jugend des Kaisers*, p. 486.

[57] Hugo Graf von Lerchenfeld-Köfering to Kraft Freiherr von Crailsheim, 25 January 1901, Isabel V. Hull, *The Entourage of Kaiser Wilhelm II 1888–1918* (Cambridge, 1982), p. 21; Lerchenfeld, *Kaiser Wilhelm II.*, p. 25; cf. Röhl, *Jugend des Kaisers*, pp. 482–93; Wilhelm II's marginalia on the *Vossische Zeitung*, 26 September 1912. PA Bonn England Nr 81 Nr 1 geheim. Bd 1.

[58] Note by Tirpitz, 4 January 1905. Kohut, *Wilhelm II and the Germans*, p. 13.

[59] Kennedy, *Anglo-German Antagonism*, p. 127.

[60] Sir Philip Magnus, *King Edward the Seventh* (London, 1964), pp. 67–8.

Austrian armies seized Schleswig-Holstein from Alexandra's father, who had ascended the throne as King Christian IX. The war left the Princess of Wales with a bitterness against Prussia which remained with her for the rest of her life.[61] The Prince of Wales also expressed outrage at the annexation[62] and, in 1866, when Prussia went to war against Austria, he made no secret of his support for the Habsburgs.[63] In addition, he supported France in the war of 1870, and was known to be a Francophile – all in all, a politically unreliable customer to German eyes. The Princess of Wales developed a dislike for Wilhelm which, coupled with her known antipathy towards Germany, became a matter of common knowledge in Berlin.[64] She regarded Wilhelm as a 'fool' and said so openly.[65] Although her influence over her husband was limited, she none the less became one voice which warned Albert Edward against his Prussian nephew.[66]

Of perhaps greater importance was the animosity with which Dona, Wilhelm's wife from 1881 onwards, viewed the Prince and Princess of Wales. In 1919, Wilhelm's cousin, Ernst Ludwig, the Grand Duke of Hesse, told a German diplomat that Dona had been responsible for many of the difficulties between Wilhelm and his English relatives.[67] Other sources confirm this. She disapproved of Albert Edward's private life and sought to prevent her husband and her children from coming into contact with his 'immoral' influence.[68] A further complicating factor was that Alexandra and Dona disliked each other, not least because both their families considered themselves to be the legitimate

---

[61] St Aubyn, *Edward VII*, p. 91; Magnus, *Edward the Seventh*, pp. 81–8.

[62] St Aubyn, *Edward VII*, p. 90.   [63] Magnus, *Edward the Seventh*, p. 93–6.

[64] Georgina Battiscombe, *Queen Alexandra* (London, 1969), pp. 174–9, 226, 283; Holstein to Radolin, 15 October 1889, *HP*, III, no. 294, pp. 316–17; Hohenlohe to Wilhelm II, 10 June 1895, Chlodwig Fürst zu Hohenlohe-Schillingsfürst, *Denkwürdigkeiten der Reichskanzlerzeit*, ed. Karl Alexander von Müller (Berlin, 1931), p. 76; Lord Esher, journal entry, 23 November 1899, Esher Papers, ESHR 2/10; Götz Graf von Seckendorff to Wilhelm II, 7 July 1902. GStA Merseburg HA Rep. 53 J Lit. S Nr 19; Eckardstein to Bülow, 17 September 1902, PA Bonn England Nr 78 geheim. Bd 6; Paul Cambon to Delcassé, 29 January 1903, *DDF*, III, no. 49, pp. 65–8; Hardinge to Knollys, 16 March 1908, RA W 53/29; Hardinge to Knollys, 25 January 1909, RA W 54/162; Wangenheim to Kiderlen-Wächter, 4 May 1911, PA Bonn England Nr 81 Nr 1 geheim.; W. H-H Waters, *'Private and Personal': Further Experiences of a Military Attaché* (London, 1928), p. 215.

[65] Holstein to Eulenburg, 30 November 1896, *HP*, III, no. 587, p. 660; Paul Cambon to Delcassé, 29 January 1903, *DDF*, 2nd series, III, no. 49, p. 67.

[66] Bernhard Fürst von Bülow, *Memoirs*, English translation, 4 vols. (London, 1931), I, p. 338; Paul Cambon to Delcassé, 29 January 1903, *DDF*, 2nd series, III, no. 49, p. 67.

[67] Prietz to the Prussian ministry of foreign affairs, 29 May 1919, PA Bonn Hessen Nr 56 Nr 1 geheim. Bd 2.

[68] Bülow, *Memoirs*, I, pp. 301, 339, 498, 501–2, II, pp. 237–8; Eulenburg to Bülow, 26 September 1901, *EK*, III, no. 1454, pp. 2030–4; Metternich to Wilhelm II, 9 September 1901, GStA Merseburg HA Rep. 53 J Lit. M Nr 4.

claimants to the Danish throne.[69] Wilhelm himself, on one occasion told Bernhard von Bülow: 'My wife has a fanatical hate for the British majesties.'[70]

Much of the personal antagonism which developed between Albert Edward and Wilhelm can be attributed to Wilhelm's treatment of his mother in the aftermath of the death of Kaiser Friedrich III.[71] Wilhelm had kept his uncle informed in the closing stages of Fritz's terminal illness,[72] and when the Prince of Wales travelled to Berlin for his brother-in-law's funeral, he formed a favourable impression of Wilhelm's intentions.[73] However, by November of the same year, in view of Wilhelm's scandalous treatment of his mother, Albert Edward had changed his view about the new Kaiser. 'His conduct towards you is simply revolting,' the Prince of Wales informed Kaiserin Friedrich. 'But alas! he lacks the feelings and usages of a gentleman! Qualities which his ever to be regretted father and also his grandfather possessed to a high degree.'[74]

Another event which occurred in 1888 and must be seen as being of key importance in the deterioration of the relationship between uncle and nephew was a misunderstanding which took place involving the Prince of Wales and Wilhelm when they both visited Austria in the autumn of that year. The origins of the dispute related to remarks which the Prince of Wales had made to Herbert Bismarck whilst in Berlin for Kaiser Friedrich's funeral. The Prince asked the latter whether there was any truth in a rumour that Fritz, had he lived, would have returned Alsace-Lorraine to France.[75] He also asked whether the late Kaiser would have considered returning North Schleswig to Denmark and sequestered property to the Princess of Wales's brother-in-law, the Duke of Cumberland.[76] The remarks, while perhaps well intentioned, were politically injudicious in the extreme, and simply confirmed the prevalent impression in Berlin that Albert Edward's French, Danish and Hanoverian sympathies made him an enemy of the *Reich*. Wilhelm said nothing about it at the time, but in a speech at Frankfurt an der Oder on 15 August 1888, he referred to intolerable insults that his father would have considered giving up lands won by the Prussian army.[77]

[69] Bülow, *Memoirs*, I, p. 339.   [70] Cecil, *Wilhelm II*, p. 267.   [71] Bülow, *Memoirs*, I, p. 338.
[72] Prince Wilhelm to Albert Edward, Prince of Wales, 12 June 1888, GStA Berlin BPH 53/349.
[73] The Prince of Wales to Queen Victoria, 18 June 1888, *LQV*, I, pp. 418–9.
[74] The Prince of Wales to Kaiserin Friedrich, November 1888, St Aubyn, *Edward VII*, p. 278.
[75] The Prince of Wales to Prince Christian of Schleswig-Holstein, 3 April 1889, *LQV*, I, p. 489.
[76] Magnus, *Edward the Seventh*, p. 205.   [77] *Ibid.*, p. 205.

At Vienna in October 1888, the Prince of Wales was asked by the British ambassador to leave the city during a visit which Wilhelm was to pay to the Austrian capital. Albert Edward formed the impression that his nephew had refused to see him. Although Wilhelm had warned the Austrians against the Prince by stating that he was unreliable and would leak information to Copenhagen and St Petersburg, the decision to ask Albert Edward to leave may have been taken by the Austrians themselves. However, no one has ever discovered the whole truth about the episode.[78] Nevertheless, Albert Edward went away from Vienna believing that he had been slighted by Wilhelm.

It was in the aftermath of the incident that the Kaiser's resentment of his uncle's remarks at his father's funeral were brought to the attention of the British royal family.[79] Queen Victoria was outraged by Wilhelm's accusations, particularly the latter's complaint that his uncle did not treat him with enough respect. She hoped that the quarrel would not have political repercussions, but as she informed Lord Salisbury: 'the Queen much *fears* that, with such a hot-headed, conceited, and wrong-headed young man, devoid of all feeling, this may at ANY moment become impossible'.[80] A concerted effort was subsequently made to limit the damage caused by the dispute between Albert Edward and Wilhelm. However Wihelm refused to apologise to his uncle, nor to admit that he had been a fault. Therefore it fell to Queen Victoria, acting on Salisbury's advice, to accept her grandson's denial, and to invite Wilhelm to pay a visit to Britain. The British prime minister saw this as the only solution if a lasting breach between Britain and Germany were to be avoided.[81] The honour of the Prince of Wales had thus been sacrificed in the interests of harmonious relations between the British and the new Kaiser.[82] Although relations between uncle and nephew appeared to improve as a result of the Kaiser's visit to

---

[78] Cecil, 'History as Family Chronicle', p. 118, note 96.
[79] Memorandum by the Marquis of Salisbury, 13 October 1888, Queen Victoria to Salisbury, 15 October 1888, *LQV*, I, pp. 438–41; Holstein to Hatzfeldt, 7 October 1888, *HNP*, II, no. 397, pp. 697–9.
[80] Queen Victoria to Salisbury, 15 October 1888, *LQV*, I, p. 441.
[81] Herbert Bismarck to the Earl of Rosebery, 11 December 1888, Rosebery Papers, National Library of Scotland, Edinburgh, MS 10004; Holstein to Hatzfeldt, 26 February 1889, *HNP*, II, no. 421, pp. 727–8; Magnus, *Edward the Seventh*, p. 212; Queen Victoria to the Prince of Wales, 7 February 1889, Prince of Wales to Prince Christian of Schleswig-Holstein, 3 April 1889, Prince Christian to the Prince of Wales, 8 April 1889, *LQV*, I, pp. 467–8, 489, 491–2; Queen Victoria to Wilhelm II, 25 May 1889, GStA Berlin BPH 53/156.
[82] Sir Francis Knollys to Prince Christian, 8 June 1889, *LQV*, I, p. 501; Queen Victoria to Kaiserin Friedrich, 14 August 1889, *Beloved and Darling Child*, p. 92.

England,[83] there is no doubt that the Prince of Wales did not fully accept his nephew's denial of ill-will towards him. It is interesting to note, for example, that in November 1908, when Edward found out about derogatory remarks which Wilhelm had made about him to an American journalist, his thoughts, and those of his son, Prince George, turned towards the incident which had occurred at Vienna twenty years before.[84]

In the years following the Vienna incident, Wilhelm's suspicion of the Prince of Wales seems to have increased. He continued to condemn his uncle's private life and expressed outrage at trivial breaches of etiquette.[85] The annual summer visits which the Kaiser paid to Cowes, for the yachting regatta, in the years down to 1895, also created friction between him and his British relatives. Although Wilhelm's visit to the regatta in 1890 'went off very well',[86] his hosts came to dread his descent on the Isle of Wight in future years. As early as 1892, Queen Victoria's private secretary was suggesting to the British ambassador that he 'could hint' to the Kaiser 'that these regular annual visits are not quite desirable'.[87] Albert Edward resented the arrogant attitude which Wilhelm adopted at the yachting regatta, and dubbed him the 'Boss of Cowes'.[88] Wilhelm responded by referring to Albert Edward as the 'old peacock',[89] while Albert Edward was known among the Kaiser's entourage simply as 'fat Wales'.[90] Matters reached their lowest ebb in 1895 when the Prince of Wales was blamed for encouraging Lord Salisbury to snub the Kaiser during his visit to the regatta and for failing to treat his nephew with sufficient respect.[91]

[83] E. F. Benson, *The Kaiser and his English Relations* (London, 1936), pp. 76–7; Herbert Bismarck to Rosebery, 4 and 15 August 1889, Rosebery Papers, MS 10004.
[84] Esher, journal entry, 22 November 1908, Esher Papers ESHR 2/11; Fritz Fischer, 'Exzesse der Autokratie – das Hale-Interview Wilhelms II. vom 19. Juli 1908', in *Deutschlands Sonderung von Europa 1862–1945*, ed. Wilhelm Alff (Frankfurt am Main, 1984), pp. 53–78; Ralph R. and Carol Bresnahan Menning, '"Baseless Allegations": Wilhelm II and the Hale Interview of 1908', *Central European History* 16, 4 (1983), 368–97.
[85] Cecil, 'History as Family Chronicle', p. 104; Eulenburg to Bülow, 23 September 1905, *EK*, III, no. 1506, p. 2114; Prince of Wales to Wilhelm II, 6 December 1891, PA Bonn England Nr 81 Nr 1a geheim. Bd 3.
[86] Knollys to Rosebery, 12 August 1890, Rosebery Papers, MS 10039.
[87] Sir Henry Ponsonby to Sir Edward Malet, 24 June 1892, *LQV*, II, p. 125.
[88] Hermann Freiherr von Eckardstein, *Ten Years at the Court of St James*, English translation (London, 1921), p. 55; cf. *ibid.*, pp. 119–20; Eckardstein to Hatzfeldt, 31 July 1899, *HP*, IV, no. 702, pp. 146–7.
[89] *Ibid.*, pp. 56–60.
[90] Ernst Jäckh (ed.), *Kiderlen-Wächter der Staatsmann und Mensch. Briefwechsel und Nachlass*, 2 vols. (Stuttgart, Berlin and Leipzig, 1924), I, pp. 125, 130.
[91] Alfred von Kiderlen-Wächter to Holstein, 7 August 1895, *HP*, III, no. 482, p. 538; Hermann Freiherr von Eckardstein, *Lebenserinnerungen und politische Denkwürdigkeiten*, 2 vols. (Leipzig, 1920), I, pp. 209–14;

It was not only personal quarrels, however, which contributed to the deterioration in the relations between Wilhelm and his uncle in the years between 1888 and 1895. Political factors also played a role. German diplomats alleged that the Prince of Wales was aiming to bring about an alliance between Britain and Russia, directed against Berlin.[92] Yet, in reality, the political views of the Prince of Wales were broadly in sympathy with Germany for most of the late 1880s and early 1890s. It is doubtful that he would have disagreed with the desire expressed by his younger brother, Arthur, Duke of Connaught,[93] to Wilhelm at the time of the latter's accession, to 'always see our two *great* countries united for the good of the world'.[94] Although the Duke of Connaught's love of Germany was particularly strong – even in 1939 he remained proud of being a Prussian field marshall – and he was regarded by Wilhelm as his '*favourite* uncle',[95] his views were not unrepresentative of the British royal family at the time, brought up as they had been in a tradition of Anglo-German friendship.

In 1890 and 1891, the Prince of Wales made an attempt to improve his relations with Wilhelm and to make a positive contribution to Anglo-German friendship. In March 1890, he paid a highly successful visit to Berlin in the company of his younger son, Prince George.[96] The favourable outcome of the Prince's visit encouraged the prime minister, Lord Salisbury, to open the negotiations with Berlin which led to the signing of the Heligoland-Zanzibar Treaty.[97] In the following year, Wilhelm paid his first state visit to England as Kaiser and Albert Edward did his best to ensure that this passed off successfully.[98] In the following year, in urging his friend, the Liberal politician, the Earl of Rosebery, to accept the foreign office in Gladstone's government, Albert Edward's main concern was with the machinations of France and Russia rather than Germany.[99] There is also no evidence that the

---

[92] Holstein to Hugo von Radolin, 15 October 1889, *HP*, III, no. 294, pp. 316–17; Röhl, *Jugend des Kaisers*, pp. 739–40; Lee, *Edward VII*, I, pp. 692–3; Holstein to Hatzfeldt, 30 November 1894, *HNP*, II, no. 620, p. 1006; Werder to Hohenlohe, 27 December 1894. PA Bonn England Nr 81 Nr 1a geheim. Bd 3.

[93] Arthur, Duke of Connaught, 1850–1942, married to Princess Luise Margarete of Prussia, 1860–1917.

[94] Arthur, Duke of Connaught, to Wilhelm II, 17 June 1888. GStA Berlin BPH 53/191.

[95] Sir John W. Wheeler-Bennett, *Knaves, Fools and Heroes. In Europe between the Wars* (London, 1974), pp. 181, 186; cf. Wilhelm II, *My Memoirs*, English translation (London, 1922), p. 99.

[96] Prince Albert Victor, Duke of Clarence, to Wilhelm II, 11 April 1890, GStA Berlin BPH 53/250; Lee, *King Edward VII*, I, pp. 659–62.

[97] *Ibid.*, pp. 662–5.

[98] The Prince of Wales to Prince Louis of Battenberg, 13 July 1891, Broadlands Archives, Southampton University, MB1/T75.

[99] The Prince of Wales to the Earl of Rosebery, 14 August 1892, *LQV*, II, p. 144.

Prince of Wales's efforts to improve Britain's relations with Russia had an anti-German motive.[100] The distaste which the Prince of Wales had for Wilhelm personally dated back to the mid 1880s, however by 1895 it had become more pronounced, as manifested in his displeasure at his nephew's appearances at the Cowes regatta, and his frustration at the political stupidity of many of his nephew's public utterances.[101] Nevertheless, up until that point, Albert Edward's antipathy towards the *Reich*'s ruler had not been transformed into political opposition to the German empire. Despite German fears on this point, the evidence does not support a characterisation of Albert Edward as a Germanophobe at this time. Indeed what is striking is the extent to which Albert Edward went out of his way to be accommodating towards his nephew, despite Wilhelm's disrespectful conduct towards him. This was motivated by the Prince's willingness to put personal considerations aside in the interests of cordial relations with Germany.[102] However, in Wilhelm's case, there can be little doubt that he had retained the political suspicions towards his uncle which he had articulated in his letters to Alexander III in the mid 1880s. In a life famous for inconsistency, hatred of Albert Edward was one of the few constant views which the Kaiser held. It can best be summed up in a remark which Wilhelm himself made on a diplomatic despatch in the summer of 1895: 'Wherever H.R.H. has his hand in the game, there is always a new intrigue against us.'[103] However, in January 1896, the Kaiser was to launch a thunderbolt, which altered the attitude of the British royal family and the British people towards him, and gave rise, for the first time, to serious political doubts in the Prince of Wales about the direction in which Wilhelm was taking Germany.

The telegram which the Kaiser sent to President Kruger of the Transvaal republic in January 1896 was a powerful manifestation of Wilhelm's hostility towards England. He had felt slighted by Lord Salisbury over the latter's conduct towards him during his visit to England in the summer of 1895 and wished to gain some revenge on the English. The abortive Jameson Raid by British mine speculators on to the territory of

---

[100] Magnus, *Edward the Seventh*, pp. 246–9; Lee, *King Edward VII*, I, pp. 692–4; W. H-H. Waters, *'Secret and Confidential': The Experiences of a Military Attaché* (London, 1926), p. 135; Hatzfeldt to Hohenlohe, 27 February 1895. PA Bonn England Nr 81 Nr 1a geheim. Bd 3.
[101] Queen Victoria to Kaiserin Friedrich, 22 September 1891, *Beloved and Darling Child*, p. 132.
[102] Queen Victoria to Kaiserin Friedrich, 21 March 1887, *ibid.*, p. 47.
[103] Wilhelm II's comment on Voigts to the German foreign office, 7 June 1895, PA Bonn England Nr 81 Nr 1a geheim. Bd 3.

the Transvaal provided the perfect opportunity. The Kaiser may also have wished to gain revenge over the Prince of Wales, whose friends, the Jewish financiers, Alfred Beit and Sir Ernest Cassel, he believed, incorrectly, were behind the Jameson raid.[104] Initially, the Kaiser had wanted to land German troops on the east African coast and to declare a German protectorate over the Transvaal. He stated that he was prepared for war with England, but only on land. It was only after an intervention from the state secretary of the German foreign office, Freiherr von Marschall, that the Kaiser agreed to send a telegram instead. The telegram was drafted by Marschall, with the help of Paul Kayser, the head of the colonial department, and was signed by Wilhelm only reluctantly.[105]

Even in this modified form, however, the impact of the telegram on Wilhelm's relations with the British royal family and on Germany's relations with Britain was disastrous.[106] The Prince of Wales viewed the Kaiser's action 'as a most gratuitous act of unfriendliness'[107] and urged Queen Victoria to administer 'a good snubbing' to Wilhelm.[108] The Queen, however, decided that it would be wiser to take a more moderate course, and wrote her grandson a rebuke which was comparatively mild in the circumstances.[109] Her reasons for acting in this way were based on an astute judgement of the Kaiser's character. On 11 January, she told the Prince of Wales that reprimands did not work with Wilhelm whose 'faults come from impetuousness (as well as conceit); and calmness and firmness are the most powerful weapons in such cases'.[110]

The letter which the Kaiser sent to the Queen justifying the Kruger telegram was moderate in tone, and denied that his action had been directed against England.[111] However, Wilhelm's draft for the letter was less conciliatory in tone and better reflected his true feelings. It implied that the unfavourable press comment which he had received in the British papers during his visit to England in 1895 had angered him considerably. This would seem to suggest that the telegram was in part

---

[104] Cecil, *Wilhelm II*, p. 288; Lee, *King Edward VII*, I, p. 730.

[105] John C. G. Röhl, *Germany without Bismarck: The Crisis of Government in the Second Reich, 1890–1900* (London, 1967), pp. 165–6; Rudolf Vierhaus (ed.), *Das Tagebuch der Baronin von Spitzemberg* (Göttingen, 1960), diary entry, 5 January 1896, pp. 339–41.

[106] O. J. Hale, *Publicity and Diplomacy – with special reference to England and Germany 1890–1914*, reprint (London, 1964), pp. 105–20; Lee, *King Edward VII*, I, pp. 723–4.

[107] Sir Francis Knollys to Sir Arthur Bigge, 4 January 1896, *LQV*, III, pp. 7–8.

[108] Lee, *King Edward VII*, I, p. 724.

[109] Queen Victoria to Wilhelm II, 5 January 1896, *LQV*, III, pp. 8–9.

[110] Queen Victoria to the Prince of Wales, 11 January 1896, *ibid.*, p. 20.

[111] Wilhelm II to Queen Victoria, 8 January 1896, Lee, *King Edward VII*, I, pp. 726–7.

a response to this. In the draft he referred to the anger of the German people at 'the *Standard* articles which appeared when I was at Cowes & which were very unkind to me personally'.[112] His true attitude towards the English at this time was revealed in the letter which he wrote to Tsar Nicholas II on the day before he sent the telegram to Kruger. That letter had been very anti-English in tone and, in it, he had vowed: 'I never shall allow the British to stamp out the Transvaal.'[113] Lacking a powerful fleet, the Kaiser could only use words against Britain in January 1896. However, afterwards, his determination to create a navy which could challenge Britain increased.[114] Significantly, those who advocated naval expansion had been the ones who had pressed him to send the telegram to President Kruger.[115] It is also interesting to note that less than three weeks after the Kaiser sent his telegram to Kruger, Holstein was already reporting to Hatzfeldt that the Kaiser wished to exploit the tense atmosphere between Germany and England in order to press for naval expansion.[116]

If the Kruger telegram affair marks a watershed in the Kaiser's attitude towards England, it was no less of one in terms of the attitude of the Prince of Wales towards Wilhelm and Germany. The Prince was not convinced by Wilhelm's explanation at the time,[117] and even many years later, after re-reading his nephew's letter to Queen Victoria, he described it as 'a lame defence'.[118] Following the Kruger telegram crisis, the ill-feeling between Wilhelm and his English relatives continued to fester. In April 1896, the Duke of York told the Kaiser that he would not be welcome in Cowes that summer. Wilhelm was reportedly greatly angered by this. He, in turn, believed that English public opinion had been artifically whipped up against him 'by the Prince of Wales and mine speculators'.[119]

Reports of Albert Edward's hostility towards Germany continued to circulate in the years afterwards,[120] and evidence also emerged of a sharp alteration in Wilhelm's feelings towards Britain. The distrust

---

[112] Wilhelm II to Queen Victoria (draft), 8 January 1896, PA Bonn England Nr 81 Nr 1. geheim. Bd 1.
[113] Wilhelm II to Nicholas II, 2 January 1896, *BKW*, pp. 300–1.
[114] Cecil, *Wilhelm II*, p. 290; Röhl, *Germany without Bismarck*, pp. 166–71.
[115] Kennedy, *Anglo-German Antagonism*, p. 221.
[116] Holstein to Hatzfeldt, 22 January 1896, *HNP*, II, no. 668, pp. 1068–70; Spitzemberg, *Tagebuch*, diary entry, 15 January 1896, p. 341.
[117] Lee, *King Edward VII*, I, p. 727; cf. Hohenlohe, note, 9 February 1896, *DdR*, pp. 169–70.
[118] Esher, journal entry, 21 November 1908, Esher Papers, ESHR 2/11.
[119] Holstein to Hatzfeldt, 25 April 1896, *HNP*, II, no. 680, p. 1083.
[120] Münster to Hohenlohe, 23 February 1898, *DdR*, p. 431; Lee, *King Edward VII*, I, pp. 734–5.

which characterised the Kaiser's relations with his English relatives undoubtedly contributed to his suspicion of British overtures for an alliance with Germany in the spring of 1898.[121] The Kaiser's mother, in a rare political appeal to her son, wrote to him, on 29 May of that year, enthusiastically advocating such a project, stressing 'the *immense* importance of an alliance – between the 2 great Germanic & Protestant nations, wh. for 50 years has been the dream, of so *many* true patriots'.[122] Wilhelm's response to his mother's letter leaves no doubt that the accumulated bitterness of his treatment by his English relatives, and the attacks made on him in Britain at the time of the Kruger telegram, had prejudiced him against co-operation with England. He claimed that he had long been a friend of England, but that the British had failed to respond in kind: 'instead of thanks or help in our colonizing enterprises I got nothing whatever, and for the last 3 years I have been abused, ill-treated and a butt to any bad joke any musikhall singer or fishmonger or pressman thought fit to let fly at me'. In any case, he feared that an alliance with England might lead to a situation where Germany alone would face France and Russia in a continental war.[123]

The Kaiser's ill-humour towards Britain persisted after the alliance negotiations ground to a halt. A political disagreement between Britain and Germany over the future of the Samoan Islands played a role in this,[124] but dynastic factors were of not inconsiderable importance. Wilhelm continued to believe that the Prince of Wales was hostile towards him,[125] and a quarrel developed between the Kaiser and his English relatives over the succession in Coburg, where the son of the Duke had recently died.[126] The Kaiser was reportedly irritated that Queen Victoria sought to settle the matter without consulting him and

---

[121] Kennedy, *Anglo-German Antagonism*, pp. 231–5; Peter Winzen, *Bülows Weltmachtkonzept. Untersuchungen zur Frühphase seiner Aussenpolitik, 1897–1901* (Boppard am Rhein, 1977), pp. 163–75; *HP*, IV, nos. 645–71.

[122] Kaiserin Friedrich to Wilhelm II, 29 May 1898, GStA Merseburg HA Rep. 52 T Nr 13; cf. Kaiserin Friedrich to Hatzfeldt, 30 May 1898, *HNP*, II, no. 725, pp. 1162–4; Holstein to Hatzfeldt, 8 June 1898, *ibid.*, no. 727, p. 1166.

[123] Wilhelm II to Kaiserin Friedrich, 1 June 1898, *HP*, IV, no. 657, pp. 83–4; cf. Holstein to Hatzfeldt, 31 May 1898, *ibid.*, no. 655, p. 80 Holstein to Hatzfeldt, 25 May 1898 and 11 June 1898, *HNP*, nos. 723, 728, pp. 1160, 1167–8; Wilhelm II to Nicholas II, 30 May 1898, *BKW*, pp. 309–11; Kaiserin Friedrich to Wilhelm II, 3 June 1898, PA Bonn Preussen Nr 1 Nr 1d geheim. Bd 1; Winzen, *Bülows Weltmachtkonzept*, p. 175.

[124] Paul M. Kennedy, *The Samoan Triangle. A Study in Anglo-German-American Relations, 1878–1900* (Dublin, 1974), pp. 178–239; Kennedy, *Anglo-German Antagonism*, pp. 235–9.

[125] Eulenburg to Bülow, 11 July 1898, *EK*, III, no. 1378, pp. 1904–5; Cecil Rhodes to the Prince of Wales, March 1899, *LQV*, III, pp. 349–51.

[126] The Duke himself was Queen Victoria's son, Alfred, Duke of Edinburgh (from 1893 Duke of Saxe-Coburg and Gotha), 1844–1900.

did not inform him directly of the decision which she had made.[127] Wilhelm insisted that the heir to the Duke of Coburg should serve in the German army, which effectively ruled out the Queen's choice of her son, the Duke of Connaught, who was unwilling to give up his position in the British army.[128] Tension over the Coburg succession and Samoa were not the only factors which caused disagreement between the Kaiser and his British relatives at this time. He greatly resented his exclusion from the celebrations for Queen Victoria's eightieth birthday in May 1899, particularly as one of his German cousins, the Grand Duke of Hesse, was invited and he was not. This seemed, in Wilhelm's view, to contradict the Queen's claim that her birthday was going to be marked only by the close family circle.[129]

Wilhelm blamed Lord Salisbury for preventing him from going to England for the Queen's birthday and told the British military attaché that 'while the latter remained Prime Minister, it would be impossible for him to come to England'.[130] If this was indeed his attitude, the Queen remarked dryly, her grandson would have to 'wait a long time' before returning to Britain.[131] However, eventually, she thought better of this and it was decided that Wilhelm would come to England in November 1899.[132] Despite the Prince of Wales's exasperation at the Kaiser's behaviour since his accession, he was still able to put his personal feelings aside in the interest of improved Anglo-German dynastic and political relations. Albert Edward took an active interest in the arrangements for his nephew's visit to England and was anxious to make it a success. On 27 September, he wrote to Lascelles, expressing his pleasure that the Queen had invited the Kaiserin as well as the Kaiser. He told the ambassador: 'I did my very best to bring it about.' He also asked Lascelles to find out if the Kaiser would like to visit him at Sandringham,[133] a place where Wilhelm had not stayed since 1880. The

---

[127] Fürstin Marie Radziwill, *Briefe vom deutschen Kaiserhof 1889–1915*, German translation (Berlin, 1936), 4/5 April 1899, p. 167.

[128] Colonel Grierson to Lascelles, 3 May 1899, *LQV*, III, p. 358.

[129] Holstein to Hatzfeldt, 13 May 1899, *HNP*, II, no. 757, p. 1226; Wilhelm II's marginalia on Golz to Hohenlohe, 8 May 1899. PA Bonn England Nr 81 Nr 1 Bd 6.

[130] Grierson to Lascelles, 3 May 1899, *LQV*, III, p. 358.

[131] Queen Victoria to Kaiserin Friedrich, 9 May 1899, *Beloved and Darling Child*, pp. 228–9; cf. Queen Victoria to Wilhelm II, 18 May 1899, GStA Merseburg HA Rep. 52 W 3 Nr 11; Wilhelm II to Queen Victoria, 27 May 1899, Queen Victoria to Wilhelm II, 12 June 1899, *LQV*, III, pp. 375–9, 381–2.

[132] Wilhelm II to Queen Victoria, 22 July 1899 and Queen Victoria to Wilhelm II, 23 July 1899, *LQV*, III p. 388.

[133] The Prince of Wales to Lascelles, 27 September 1899, Lascelles Papers, PRO FO 800/9; cf. Holstein to Hatzfeldt, 4 July 1899, *HNP*, II, no. 766, note 2, p. 1239; Lee, *King Edward VII*, I, p. 745.

Kaiser reportedly '*jumped*' at the prospect of the visit, despite the fact that the Prince of Wales's invitation had only been provisional.[134] However, the Kaiser's visit to England in November 1899 was not accompanied by positive political omens. The outbreak of war between the British and the Boers in South Africa shortly before the start of the visit led to a popular outcry in Germany against it.[135] Many of those in official circles at Berlin were against the visit, including the Kaiserin, who put pressure on her husband to abandon his plans to travel to England.[136] The general feeling before the visit took place was that it might improve relations between the two royal families but would be unlikely to dispel the rivalry and hostility which was coming to dominate Anglo-German relations in the wider political context.[137]

This rivalry and hostility had been fuelled to a large extent by economic competition in the first instance. However, in the aftermath of the Kruger telegram affair, Wilhelm's obsession with creating a navy to challenge that of Britain had come to be of considerable importance. Wilhelm's advisers such as Admiral von Müller and Admiral von Tirpitz made no secret that the navy was to be built in order to break Britain's world domination. In 1897 a series of governmental appointments, which saw Tirpitz become state secretary of the imperial navy office and Bernhard von Bülow become state secretary of the German foreign office, and the introduction of a Navy Bill into the Reichstag initiated the policy. The trouble was that although Wilhelm himself was credited by Tirpitz as being the driving force behind the new *Flottenpolitik*,[138] he was prone to sporadic bouts of Anglophilia when he either denied or forgot the fleet was being constructed against the British empire. His attitude towards the British royal family tended to serve as a barometer as to his perceptions of Anglo-German relations as a whole.

Thus the Kaiser's advisers, the majority of whom lacked his ties of kinship to Britain, found it easier to maintain his support for the new anti-British *Weltpolitik* when the dynastic relationship between Potsdam and Windsor was cool, as for example during the abortive Anglo-German alliance negotiations of 1898, than when it was more cordial, such as in the weeks preceding Wilhelm's visit to England in the autumn

[134] Knollys to Rosebery, 7 October 1899, Rosebery Papers, MS 10039.
[135] Holstein to Hatzfeldt, 26 October 1899, *HNP*, II, no. 796, pp. 1280–90.
[136] Bülow, *Memoirs*, I, p. 301; Holstein to Hatzfeldt, 1 November 1899, *HNP*, II, no. 797, pp. 1293–4.
[137] Holstein to Hatzfeldt, 2 August 1899, *HNP*, no. 773, pp. 1247–9.
[138] Grand Admiral von Tirpitz, *My Memoirs*, 2 vols. (London, 1920), I, p. 156.

of 1899. Bülow for instance emphasized the advantage which Germany would gain by pursuing a policy of the 'free hand' while building up her naval forces. In a letter to the Kaiser on 19 August 1898, he wrote: 'The ideal for us remains . . . the solid and independent position between England and Russia set out by Your Majesty, autonomous in relation to both, but with the possibility, as soon as it suits Your Majesty, to align ourselves with one or other of them.' At the time, Wilhelm was in full agreement with this policy.[139]

Yet in a letter to the Kaiser on 6 August 1899, Bülow had to take a different line, in order to counteract the burgeoning enthusiasm which Wilhelm displayed for the British in the months preceding his visit to Windsor, which risked destabilising the policy which Bülow was pursuing. He made clear that he believed that the Kaiser should use his influence with the English to maintain correct relations between the two powers until the German fleet was ready, but should go no further.[140] Shortly, before the Kaiser's visit to England, Bülow informed Wilhelm that the Samoan agreement had been signed. He presented this as a great triumph for German diplomacy. However, Bülow was also keen to emphasize that the agreement implied no alteration to the policy of the 'free hand', and no commitment to England.[141] Bülow sought to stress the private nature of the Kaiser's visit to England. This was done for political reasons, and it was only shortly beforehand that his own presence in the Kaiser's entourage was made public.[142] A considerable degree of cynicism also attached itself to the German attitude towards the visit. A new Navy Bill was to be introduced into the Reichstag in the autumn of 1899, but Wilhelm gave an order that this was not to be done until after his return from England.[143]

The Kaiser's visit to England achieved virtually nothing politically. Bülow was keen to assure British politicians that Germany's intentions were friendly, yet the introduction of the Navy Bill immediately after Wilhelm's return to Berlin exposed the hollowness of this claim.[144] All the visit did was to draw a line under the ill-feeling between the Kaiser and 'the English family', which had been its principal aim.[145] Bülow

[139] Bülow to Wilhelm II, 19 August 1898, GStA Merseburg HA Rep. 53 J Lit. B Nr 16a Bd 1.
[140] Bülow to Wilhelm II, 6 August 1899, GStA Merseburg HA Rep. 53 Lit. B Nr 16a Bd 1.
[141] Bülow to Wilhelm II, 8 November 1899, *ibid.*
[142] Winzen, *Bülows Weltmachtkonzept*, p. 212.
[143] Jagemann to Brauer, 18 November 1899, Walther P. Fuchs (ed.), *Grossherzog Friedrich I. von Baden und die Reichspolitik, 1871–1907*, 4 vols. (Stuttgart, 1968–80), IV, no. 2034, p. 200.
[144] Kennedy, *Anglo-German Antagonism*, p. 239.
[145] Bülow to Hatzfeldt, 15 November 1899, XV, no. 4397, p. 412; Queen Victoria to Kaiserin Friedrich, 25 November 1899, *Beloved and Darling Child*, pp. 240–1.

noted that the Prince of Wales and all Queen Victoria's daughters had expressed their enthusiasm for co-operation between Germany, England and America, believing that this would be the best way to preserve world peace.[146] The visit also saw the re-establishment of outwardly cordial relations between Wilhelm and the Prince of Wales, although Albert Edward's private secretary, Sir Francis Knollys, noted during the course of the visit that it would be 'a great relief' once Wilhelm had gone.[147]

In the year that followed, the British people and royal family came to make a greater distinction between the Kaiser, whom they considered to be friendly towards them, and the German people, who because of their pro-Boer sympathies, they considered to be irremediably hostile. Wilhelm's mother was one of those who held such views. Following her son's visit to England, she wrote: 'I belong to those who *hope* and trust that your visit may be a sign that the Govt*s*. of Germany & England are on good terms, in spite of the ardent wishes of the French to the contrary.' However, in the same letter she made reference to the press attacks being made on the continent, including Germany, against England. She resented these and claimed 'they make one's *blood boil*!',[148] yet they also helped to explain why the hope she expressed for Anglo-German co-operation was so unlikely to be fulfilled.

Wilhelm's own attitude at this time contrasted sharply with those of his subjects. Soon after his return to Germany, he began to bombard the Prince of Wales with letters advising him on the best way to conduct the war in the Transvaal.[149] Albert Edward resented his nephew's intervention and acknowledged Wilhelm's letter curtly.[150] Wilhelm's second intervention irritated his uncle still further, for the 'Weitere Gedankensplitter' which the Kaiser forwarded to him contained what the Prince considered to be a tasteless parallel between British military reverses in South Africa and England's defeat by Australia at cricket.[151] The reception in Berlin of Dr Leyds, the secretary of state to the Transvaal

---

[146] Note by Bülow, 24 November 1899, *GP*, xv no. 4398, p. 418; Eckardstein to Hatzfeldt, 30 November 1899 and Hatzfeldt to Hohenlohe, 2 December 1899, *ibid.*, nos. 4400–1, pp. 420–6.

[147] Knollys to Rosebery, 26 November 1899, Rosebery Papers, MS 10039.

[148] Kaiserin Friedrich to Wilhelm II, 2 December 1899, GStA Merseburg HA Rep. 52 T Nr 13; cf. Kaiserin Friedrich to Wilhelm II, 19 March 1900, *ibid.*; Kaiserin Friedrich to Queen Victoria, 24 October and 2 November 1899, *Beloved and Darling Child*, pp. 238, 238–9.

[149] Wilhelm II to the Prince of Wales, 21 December 1899, RA W 60/26, enclosing 'Notes on the War in the Transvaal', German original RA W 60/28, English translation RA W 60/27.

[150] Lee, *King Edward VII*, I, p. 755.

[151] Wilhelm II to the Prince of Wales, 4 February 1900, RA W 60/66, enclosing 'Weitere Gedankensplitter über den Transvaalkrieg', RA W 60/67; Lee, *King Edward VII*, I, pp. 755–6.

government, on the occasion of the Kaiser's birthday also irritated the Prince and in his reply to Wilhelm's letter he sternly rebuked his nephew.[152] But, in general, the Prince was outwardly grateful for the support which the Kaiser gave to England during the Boer War.[153] This did not mean that the Prince had lost any of the mistrust of Wilhelm and Germany's political leaders which had been awakened in him by the Kruger telegram. The views which he held in private contrasted sharply with those which he expressed to his nephew. The Prince told his friend Lord Rosebery in February 1900, for example, that he was 'inclined to agree' with his private secretary, Sir Francis Knollys, that 'all public men in Germany from the Emperor downwards were liars'.[154]

By the time of Queen Victoria's death in January 1901, the relationship between Wilhelm and the Prince of Wales can best be characterised as one of personal distrust, coupled with growing political suspicion. In the Prince of Wales's case, this did not yet mean that he was determined to oppose Germany politically, though in the years since 1896, his personal dislike of his nephew had come to have political overtones. He realised though, that with Britain isolated due to her war against the Boers, co-operation with Germany appeared to be the only viable option. There is no reason to doubt that the Kaiser's attitude towards his uncle remained one of considerable personal and political suspicion. Wilhelm's role in the initiation of *Weltpolitik* and *Flottenpolitik* also indicated that his outward expressions of Anglophilia hid a desire to challenge the British empire's global supremacy. This was, for a time, masked by the favourable attitude which he adopted towards the new King and Britain in the months after Queen Victoria's funeral. However, the death of the Queen and the accession of his uncle as Edward VII marked the starting point for a deterioration in the relations between the two royal families which was to prove irreversible and politically damaging.

There can be little doubt that the Kaiser's demeanour at Queen Victoria's death-bed and funeral indicated that he had been deeply attached to his grandmother. His English relatives had been irritated when he had intimated his intention of coming to England, but Wilhelm won them over by behaving 'in a most dignified and admirable

---

[152] The Prince of Wales to Wilhelm II, 8 February 1900. Lee, *King Edward VII*, 1, pp. 758–9.
[153] The Prince of Wales to Wilhelm II, 7 March 1900, PA Bonn England Nr 78 geheim. Bd 3.
[154] The Prince of Wales to Rosebery, 19 February 1900, Rosebery Papers, MS 10039. Christopher Hibbert, *Edward VII: A Portrait* (London, 1976), p. 273.

manner.'[155] The *rapprochement* between Wilhelm and Edward VII during the former's stay in England in early 1901 was political as well as personal. Eckardstein, the first secretary of the London embassy, reported that the King and the Kaiser were in full accord in matters of politics. The new King was hostile to France and Russia and favoured co-operation with Germany.[156] This corresponded with Wilhelm's own anti-Russian sentiments at the time.[157] At the same time, Wilhelm tried to convince the British foreign secretary that he formed the 'balance of power' in Europe and that the British should shape their policy accordingly.[158] In addition, he made two gestures of a highly Anglophile nature. At a lunch at Marlborough House, in the presence of Edward VII, he stressed the benefits which would result from an Anglo-German alliance,[159] and he also awarded the Order of the Black Eagle to Lord Roberts, the commander-in-chief of the British army.[160]

The problem was that the Kaiser's Anglophile sentiments were at odds with the views of his subjects and political advisers. Bülow, who succeeded Hohenlohe as chancellor in October 1900, had clearly set out the aims of his foreign policy in a letter to the Kaiser in August 1900. The letter had made clear his obsession with breaking England's world power and his desire to see Germany succeed to that position.[161] Such a policy was incompatible with the utterances which the Kaiser made during his stay in England.[162] Eulenburg, who also had no love of England, watched in horror as the Kaiser prolonged his visit and showed few signs of wishing to return to Germany. Eulenburg observed ironically that the Kaiser was only able to remain in England for so long because Queen Victoria was no longer there to ask him to leave,[163] and lamented the dreadful effect of Wilhelm's pro-English sympathies on German public opinion.[164]

[155] Sir Frederick Ponsonby, *Recollections of Three Reigns* (London, 1951), p. 82; cf. Wilhelm II to Eulenburg, 5 February 1901, *EK*, III, no. 1444, p. 2014; G. K. A. Bell, *Randall Davidson. Archbishop of Canterbury*, 2 vols. (Oxford, 1935), I, pp. 353–7; Michaela Reid, *Ask Sir James: Sir James Reid, Personal Physician to Queen Victoria and Physician-in-Ordinary to Three Monarchs* (London, 1987), pp. 209–12.
[156] Eckardstein to the German foreign office, 29 January 1901, *GP*, XVII, no. 4986, pp. 23–4.
[157] Metternich to Bülow, 22 January 1901, *HP*, IV, no. 765, pp. 217–18.
[158] Wilhelm II to Bülow, 29 January 1901, *GP*, XVII, no. 4987, pp. 28–9.
[159] Arthur Gould Lee, *The Empress Frederick Writes to Sophie, Letters 1889–1901*, 2 vols. (London, 1955), II, p. 11.
[160] Eckardstein, *Ten Years*, pp. 196–7.
[161] Bülow to Wilhelm II, 6 August 1900, GStA Merseburg HA Rep. 53 J Lit. B Nr 16a Bd II.
[162] Metternich to Bülow, 22 January 1901, *HP*, IV, no. 765, pp. 217–18.
[163] Eulenburg to Bülow, 6 February 1901, *EK*, III, no. 1445, pp. 2014–15.
[164] Eulenburg to Bülow, 16 February 1901, *ibid.*, no. 1446, p. 2015; cf. Bülow, *Memoirs*, I, pp. 498, 501–2; Radziwill, *Briefe*, 31 January/1 February 1901, pp. 196–7.

However, relations between Wilhelm and Edward VII were un-doubtedly better in the few months after Queen Victoria's death than they were ever to be afterwards. In a letter to his nephew on 13 February 1901, the King emphasised that Wilhelm's visit had made a profound impression on the royal family and the British people.[165] The King also sought to institute a separate dynastic diplomatic channel between London and Berlin, hoping that this would enable him to 'smooth matters down' if a divergence of opinion arose between the two govern-ments. The Kaiser seemed eager to take up this proposal.[166] The King's relations with his nephew remained excellent until the end of 1901. As late as Christmas Day of that year, he wrote of his desire to see an 'Entente Cordiale' with Wilhelm, while simultaneously expressing re-gret at the 'jealousies & Anglophobism on the part of Germany'.[167] The Kaiser appeared to share his uncle's views on the need for co-operation between Britain and Germany, and stressed the racial similarities of the two peoples:

I gladly reciprocate all you say about the relations of our two Countries and our personal ones; they are of the same blood, and they have the same creed and they belong to the great Tutonic [*sic*] Race, which Heaven has entrusted with the culture of the world; . . . that is I think grounds enough to keep Peace and to foster *mutual* recognition and *reciprocity* in all that draws us together, and to sink everything which could part us-!

The Kaiser dismissed the Anglophobe utterances of the German press, with words which were at once dismissive, boastful and threatening:

The Press is awful on both sides, but here it has nothing to say, for I am the sole arbiter and master of German Foreign Policy and the Government and Country *must* follow me, even if I have to 'face the musik' [sic] – May Your Government never forget this, and never place me in the jeopardy to have to choose a course which could be a misfortune to both them and us.[168]

However, the seeds of renewed ill-feeling between the two monarchs were present in this exchange of letters. Each blamed the other side for the friction between Britain and Germany. A dispute which arose between the two governments in January 1902 indicated that the two royal courts could not insulate themselves from the wider antagonism between Britain and Germany, notably as expressed in the press. It undermined the fragile dynastic reconciliation that had occurred in

[165] Edward VII to Wilhelm II, 13 February 1901, GStA Berlin BPH 53/195.
[166] Lascelles to Edward VII, 13 April 1901, RA X37/40.
[167] Edward VII to Lascelles, 25 December 1901, RA X37/49.
[168] Wilhelm II to Edward VII, 30 December 1901, RA X37/51.

1901. The background to this was an exchange of insults between Joseph Chamberlain, the British colonial secretary, and Bülow. In a speech at Edinburgh in October 1901 Chamberlain had defended the British army's conduct of the South African campaign, and had drawn attention to the fact that the armies of other nations had been abused in the past for 'barbarity' and cruelty', citing, rather injudiciously, the German army during the Franco-Prussian war.[169] This met with an angry response from Bülow, who in his so-called 'Granit-Rede' to the Reichstag on 10 January 1902 stated that the German nation would not tolerate attacks upon the honour of the German army.[170]

The matter might have ended there, but for the fact that Edward VII had intended to send his son to Berlin for the Kaiser's birthday. In view of the tense atmosphere between Britain and Germany, he now thought of cancelling this visit thus provoking a diplomatic crisis.[171] Both the foreign secretary, Lord Lansdowne, and the British ambassador at Berlin, Sir Frank Lascelles, sought to dissuade the King from taking such a step and instead urged that his letter to the Kaiser be framed in such a way as to leave the matter open.[172] The King's letter to the Kaiser was, however, very strongly worded and somewhat offensive in nature, implying that the Prince of Wales might be insulted by the German public. In addition, he rebuked the Kaiser for his attack on Chamberlain and noted his regret that the German government had done so little to counteract anti-English feeling among the German people.[173] Lansdowne seemed to feel that the King should have ignored the remarks made by the Kaiser in his letter of 6 January, and told Lascelles that he still hoped that a conciliatory line from the Kaiser would avoid cancellation of the Prince of Wales's visit.[174] Lascelles, in turn, stated categorically in a letter to Lord Knollys that he was opposed to the postponement of the Prince's visit due to the offence which it would give to the Kaiser, whom he still considered to be pro-English, and because of the damage which it would cause to Anglo-German relations.[175]

---

[169] Lee, *King Edward VII*, II, p. 133.   [170] *Ibid.*, p. 137.
[171] Edward VII to Lascelles, 25 December 1901, RA X37/49; Wilhelm II to Edward VII, 6 January 1902. RA X37/52; Lascelles to Edward VII, 28 December 1901, RA X37/50; Knollys to Lascelles, 7 January 1902. RA X37/53; Lansdowne to Knollys, 10 January 1902, RA W 42/47; Lansdowne to Lascelles, 17 January 1902, Lascelles Papers, PRO FO 800/10; Knollys to Lansdowne, 11 January 1902, RA W 42/49.
[172] Lansdowne to Knollys, 14 January 1902, RA W 42/48.
[173] Edward VII to Wilhelm II, 15 January 1902, RA W 42/58.
[174] Lansdowne to Lascelles, 17 January 1902, Lascelles Papers, PRO FO 800/10.
[175] Lascelles to Knollys, 17 January 1902, RA W 42/61; Lascelles to Lansdowne, 14 January 1902, Lansdowne Papers, PRO FO 800/129.

The situation turned to farce when it was revealed that the King's letter to the Kaiser, informing him of his decision to postpone the Prince of Wales's visit, had been mislaid by a palace servant. Lascelles informed the Kaiser on 22 January of the King's decision. Wilhelm reacted with 'considerable irritation, and talked about another Fashoda and the possibility of having to recall Count Metternich'.[176] Such a calamitous outcome was avoided, however, because the King under pressure from Lansdowne and the prime minister, Lord Salisbury, agreed to back down, provided that the Kaiser sent him a conciliatory telegram intimating his desire to receive the Prince of Wales.[177] This having been achieved, the visit proceeded without incident. Indeed, in a conversation with Bülow during the visit, the Prince of Wales made clear that King Edward wished to see good relations restored between Britain and Germany.[178]

The events of January 1902 had indicated that the dynastic relationship could not be divorced from the wider political context. The Anglo-German antagonism was making itself felt through rivalry between the two powers and through the attitude adopted by the press and public opinion in both countries. This, in turn, had a negative impact on the personal relationship between the Kaiser and King Edward, as each believed that the other was in a position to influence the press in a favourable direction. Their mutual failure to stem the rising tide of press hostility led to recriminations in the years that followed, thus worsening, still further, their attitude towards each other.[179] This was all the more serious because, paradoxically, as Anglo-German relations deteriorated, the relationship between the two courts took on an added significance for it represented one of the few remaining mechanisms for maintaining close links between the two powers. This was recognised by

---

[176] Lascelles to Lansdowne, 24 January 1902, Lascelles Papers, PRO FO 800/10; Sir Frank Lascelles: report on conversation with the German Emperor, 22 January 1902, RA W 42/64.

[177] Lansdowne to Edward VII, 22 January 1902, RA W 42/63; Knollys to Lansdowne, 22 January 1902, RA W 42/65; Lascelles to Lansdowne, 24 January 1902, Lascelles Papers, FO 800/10.

[178] Wilhelm II to Edward VII, 28 January 1902, RA W 42/70; Bülow, *Memoirs*, I, pp. 548–50; Sir Harold Nicolson, *King George the Fifth. His Life and Reign* (London, 1952), pp. 76–8.

[179] Cf. Wilhelm II's comment on Metternich to the German foreign office, 29 January 1903, *GP*, XVII, no. 5140, note 1, p. 282; Lascelles to Lansdowne, 6 February 1903. Lansdowne Papers, PRO FO 800/129; Spitzemberg, diary entry, 12 February 1905, *Tagebuch*, p. 445; minute by Edward VII on Lascelles to Grey, 3 January 1906, *BD*, III, no. 225, pp. 206–7; Bihourd to Rouvier, 1 January 1906, *DDF*, 2nd series, VIII, no. 304, pp. 420–1; Wilhelm II to Bülow, 30 December 1905, Bülow, *Memoirs*, II, pp. 183–7; Alfred Beit to Lascelles, 29 December 1905. Lascelles Papers PRO FO 800/13; Edward VII to Wilhelm II, 23 January 1906 and 5 February 1906, PA Bonn England Nr 78 geheim. Bd 8; Wilhelm II to Edward VII, 1 February 1906, RA X37/62; Paul Cambon to Bourgeois, 11 May 1906, *DDF*, 2nd series, X, no. 51, pp. 71–3; Knollys to Lascelles, 16 May 1906, Lascelles Papers, PRO FO 800/13; Wilhelm II's comment on Bülow to Wilhelm II, 6 March 1908, *GP*, XXIV, no. 8187, p. 40.

the German ambassador to London, Metternich, in a perceptive report in February 1902. He believed that only the Kaiser represented a positive asset to Germany in a context of Anglo-German press hostility and political antagonism:

The only thing which to some extent still preserves the much loosened bond between Germany and England is the person of H.M. the Kaiser. If the force of circumstances should ever make H.M. oppose England publicly on some issue at dispute, I am firmly convinced that the last bond would be broken. We should have to reckon with England's declared enmity for a generation.[180]

Significantly, the Kaiser himself seems to have concurred with this assessment. In conversation with Szögyény-Marich, the Austrian ambassador to Berlin, in August 1902, Wilhelm expressed 'his great regret that the relations between England and Germany were so unsatisfactory'. However he also observed that Edward VII was 'personally very well disposed towards' Germany. The Kaiser had been invited by the King to visit England in November 1902 and hoped that the visit 'might be productive of good'. However Lascelles, who reported Wilhelm's remarks to London, recognised that the relationship of trust between the two monarchs was of only limted value given the deteriorating political relations between Britain and Germany. The ambassador feared that the Kaiser's desire to see the visit succeed would not be shared by his subjects, who were hostile to England 'and strongly dislike the Emperor's English proclivities'. He noted that Wilhelm's own entourage were hostile to the forthcoming royal visit, and that German public opinion would react in a hostile manner to it.[181] Such concerns were amply borne out when, shortly before the visit was due to take place, a major diplomatic incident arose between Berlin and London. A group of Boer generals were touring Europe and, in view of the pro-Boer feeling in Germany, the Kaiser came under pressure to receive them. The fact that he did not was in large measure due to pressure from Edward VII, who gave his nephew to understand that the deplorable effect that this would have in Britain would place Wilhelm's visit to England in jeopardy.[182] The details of what followed need not be rehearsed here, suffice to say that the Kaiser refused to receive the generals and was reportedly extremely annoyed with Bülow for having

---

[180] Metternich to Bülow, 21 February 1902, *HP*, IV, no. 799, pp. 253–4 cf. Rosen to Richthofen, 31 March 1904, PA Bonn England Nr 78 geheim. Bd 7.
[181] Lascelles to Lansdowne, 23 August 1902, Lansdowne Papers, PRO FO 800/129; cf. Lascelles to Lansdowne, 28 February 1902, *ibid.*
[182] Knollys to Lascelles, 2 October 1902, RA W 42/122.

proposed that he do so. Warnings that such an act would have risked the abandonment of his visit to England were undoubtedly a decisive influence on Wilhelm's decision.[183]

The Kaiser's visit to England passed off without serious incident, but it underlined that displays of *bonhomie* between the two royal families could not serve as a vehicle for a political *rapprochement* between Britain and Germany. The British press remained savage in its attacks upon Germany, although Wilhelm personally was largely exempted from criticism.[184] During his visit to Sandringham, Wilhelm had tried to convince the British prime minister, Arthur Balfour, of Germany's need for a large navy. He claimed that it was a 'living example of the unity of the Empire' and that it was not directed against any other power.[185] The Kaiser was, nonetheless, shaken to discover the extent of Germano-phobia in England. He believed that Joseph Chamberlain was the chief orchestrator of this and that the latter had all classes of the population behind him. He noted that his own reception had been 'warm and kind' but appreciated, like other observers, that the English now made a distinction between him personally and the German government generally. Above all, he advised Bülow to institute a less overtly hostile policy towards England, for the all important question of naval armaments dictated this. 'Therefore caution! They have thirty-five armoured ships in service here and we only have eight!!'[186]

Yet even the relationship between the Kaiser and the King, which Metternich had singled out in February 1902 as being the bright spot in an otherwise gloomy picture of bilateral tension, appeared to be again under strain. Before the visit, Edward had been most anxious to ensure that Wilhelm brought only a small retinue with him to England, suggesting that the King regarded receiving his nephew as a wearisome duty rather than a pleasure.[187] Matters of a private nature also showed in

[183] Holstein, diary entry, 7 November 1902, *HP*, IV, no. 811, pp. 268–71; Waters, *'Private and Personal'*, p. 232; Eckardstein to the German foreign office, *GP*, XVII, no. 5096, pp. 229–31; Holstein to Ida von Stülpnagel, November 1902, Helmut Rogge (ed.), *Friedrich von Holstein: Lebensbekenntnis in Briefe an eine Frau* (Berlin, 1932), p. 216; Lascelles to Knollys, 5 October 1902, RA W 42/123; Knollys to Lascelles, 4 October 1902, RA W 42/125; Lascelles to Knollys, 5 October 1902, RA W 42/127; Edward VII to Knollys, 8 October 1902, RA W 42/131; Lansdowne to Balfour, 8 October 1902, Lansdowne Papers, PRO FO 800/129.
[184] The Marquis de Noailles to Delcassé, 9 November 1902, *DDF*, 2nd series, II, no. 475, pp. 588–90; Paul Cambon to Delcassé, 11 November 1902, *ibid.*, no. 480, pp. 600–2.
[185] Metternich to the German foreign office, 9 November 1902, PA Bonn Deutschland Nr 138 geheim. Bd 5.
[186] Wilhelm II to Bülow, 12 November 1902, *GP*, XVII, no. 5031, pp. 115–17.
[187] Edward VII to Lascelles, 28 August 1902, RA W 42/107c; Arthur Davidson to Lascelles, 23 September 1902, Lascelles Papers, PRO FO 800/11.

1902 and early 1903 that the Kaiser continued to view Edward VII with less respect than he had Queen Victoria. In the autumn of 1902, for example, he was outraged to learn that the King had decided to give Osborne House on the Isle of Wight, where Queen Victoria had died, to the Royal Navy. The King had no use for it. Part of it was to be used as a training centre for naval cadets and another part as a convalescent home for servicemen.[188] Wilhelm regarded the decision as an insult to the deceased Queen's memory. He expressed his rage in a comment on a report from the German naval attaché in London in December 1902:

It is as if I wanted to turn Babelsberg into the Potsdam Cadets' House or the Unter den Linden Palace into a casino!! It is downright shameless and outrageous! To destroy the most personal private property and the most holy place in which she lived, where we spent our youth, two years after her death in such a manner!![189]

In February 1903, rumours circulated that during a cruise off the coast of Norway, the previous summer, Wilhelm had denounced King Edward in front of a group of Americans. The Kaiser was reported to have said 'that if he (the Emperor) had done what King Edward has done, he would have been turned out of his country', a comment which reflected Wilhelm's moral condemnation of his uncle's private life. He had also, allegedly, condemned England as 'a rotten country'.[190] Wilhelm's comments had been particularly injudicious as one of those on board the American yacht was an English honorary consul, Humphreys Owen, who had reported full details of the Kaiser's remarks to the British foreign office.[191] It is not known whether details of the Kaiser's remarks were communicated to the King at the time. This is unlikely as in the summer of 1902, Edward VII was recovering from a serious operation on his appendix. However, in February 1903, details of the Kaiser's remarks were made public in the *National Review*.[192] The King may have learned of the Kaiser's attacks upon him then. Wilhelm, of course, denied ever having made the comments attributed to him, and dismissed the allegations as 'an infamous lie'.[193] However, the weight of evidence tends to leave little doubt that Wilhelm did make the

---

[188] Lee, *King Edward VII*, II, pp. 19–21.
[189] Wilhelm II's comment on Coerper to Admiral von Tirpitz, 27 December 1902. PA Bonn England Nr 81 Nr 1 geheim. Bd 1; cf. Wilhelm II's marginalia on Metternich to Bülow, 11 August 1902, *ibid.*
[190] Metternich to Bülow, 4 February 1903, PA Bonn England Nr 81 Nr 1 geheim. Bd 1.
[191] Gordon Brook-Shepherd, *Uncle of Europe: The Social and Diplomatic Life of Edward VII* (London, 1975), pp. 117–18.
[192] Mr. A. Maurice Low to the editor of the *National Review*, 3 February 1903, RA W 43/49.
[193] Bülow to Metternich, 12 February 1903, PA Bonn England Nr 81 Nr 1 geheim. Bd 1.

comments, and they would certainly have been in keeping with the view of Edward which he had held since the 1880s.

Despite the personal hostility with which the Kaiser viewed his uncle, there is little sign, from the evidence available, that Wilhelm considered Edward VII to be hostile to Germany politically in 1902 and the early part of 1903. Indeed, the Kaiser and many German diplomats and courtiers seem to have regarded the King as being politically sympathetic towards Germany at this time, in contrast to the British people as a whole, who were perceived to be increasingly Germanophobe, and even to Queen Alexandra and the Prince of Wales, who were also viewed as hostile to the *Reich*.

Count Seckendorff, who accompanied Prince Heinrich to London in July 1902, sent back a pessimistic report to the Kaiser on British attitudes towards Germany. He pointed to growing Anglo-German rivalry in the commercial sphere as a source of tension. The English were envious of German commercial success and the Germans had an inferiority complex. He also noted the corrosive effect of press hostility on Anglo-German relations, particularly with regard to the influence of the Germanophobe stance of *The Times* on its readers in the British upper classes. He seemed to believe that only the good relations between the Kaiser and the King formed a durable link between the two powers, but feared that this might not last if King Edward were to die prematurely:

It is difficult under these conditions to draw an advantage from the good relations between both the high princely families. Your Majesty knows how well-disposed King Edward has become towards Your Majesty. We must all hope that God still deigns to grant him a long life.

He feared that Prince George would not be so sympathetic towards the *Reich*. 'I am not entitled to maintain that the Heir to the Throne harbours anti-German sentiments – it appears so. That he is under the influence of His Mother cannot be doubted.'[194] Seckendorff's opinions were echoed two months later by the Marquis de Soveral, the Portuguese minister in London, and a close friend of the British royal family. Soveral shared Seckendorff's view that Queen Alexandra and the Prince of Wales were anti-German. However the Portuguese diplomat believed that Edward VII's own sentiments were very different. 'I fear', Soveral stated, 'that King Edward is the only true friend that Germany still has in England. He is a real, loyal friend to your Kaiser

---

[194] Seckendorff to Wilhelm II, 7 July 1902, GStA Merseburg HA Rep. 53 J Lit. S Nr 19.

and besides holds on to the tradition of friendship for Germany dating from his youth.'[195]

Such judgements persisted into 1903, and were shared by Wilhelm himself, which is quite remarkable in the light of the pathological hatred with which he came to view the King towards the end of the latter's life. In March 1903, for example, the Kaiser informed Bülow that Edward VII had become tired of the persistent attacks being made by *The Times* against Wilhelm and Germany. The King had tried, in vain, to put a stop to these. Edward VII was, according to Wilhelm's account, 'very deeply disappointed and grieved'.[196] This was hardly the action of a Germanophobe. Similarly, in August 1903, the Prussian envoy in Karlsruhe, Karl von Eisendecher, who was also well acquainted with English conditions, sent a report to the Kaiser which again depicted Edward VII as sympathetic towards Germany. However, Eisendecher feared, correctly, that the support of the British court would not be of sufficient weight to arrest the general direction of British policy towards *rapprochement* with France and Russia.[197]

The reaction of the Kaiser and German diplomats to Edward VII's spring cruise of 1903, which ended with his historic visit to Paris, provides the best example of their view of the King as Germanophile. The visit was credited by many contemporary observers with creating the atmosphere for the Anglo-French *entente* of 1904[198] but, at the time, the Germans did not see the King's diplomatic activities as a threat to the *Reich*. In April 1903, Edward VII paid a visit to Lisbon, prior to going to Paris and Rome. During a reception for the *corps diplomatique*, Edward VII spent noticeably more time with Tattenbach, the German minister in Lisbon, than with the representatives of the other powers. He stressed his high opinion of Metternich and of the Kaiser. Tattenbach interpreted the King's special favour as being indicative of his desire for good Anglo-German relations. Wilhelm, while accepting this, appreciated the main reason for his uncle's graciousness towards Germany's diplomatic representative. 'The behaviour of H.M. calls our attention to the fact that he fears his journey to Rome and Paris could be misunderstood by us and interpreted badly!'[199] Wilhelm's comments on a second report sent by Tattenbach to Berlin reinforce the impression that he saw

[195] Eckardstein to Bülow, 17 September 1902, PA Bonn England Nr 78 geheim. Bd 6.
[196] Wilhelm II to Bülow, 30 March 1903, *ibid.*
[197] Eisendecher to Wilhelm II, 9 August 1903, *HNP*, II, p. 1378, note 6.
[198] See ch. 3.
[199] Tattenbach to Bülow, with marginalia by Wilhelm II, 7 April 1903. PA Bonn England Nr 81 Nr 1 Bd 11a.

Edward VII as pro-German at this time. Soveral, who was also in Lisbon at the time of the King's visit, repeated the assertion which he had made to Eckardstein the previous year about Edward's Germanophile views. The Kaiser noted his agreement with this. Soveral told Tattenbach that King Edward would never agree to an anti-German coalition. The Kaiser, surprisingly, also agreed with this, although he believed that it would be difficult for the King to resist his people and parliament should such an eventuality arise. Soveral also gave his view that the King's visit to Paris would not lead to a change in relations between Britain and France, and claimed that the King of Portugal had great respect for Wilhelm. The Kaiser was sceptical, but, interestingly, related Soveral's words to the pro-German feelings of the King's recent guest, Edward VII: 'I do not believe it! Only apparent because King Edward is friendly towards Germany.'[200]

The attitude which German diplomats adopted when the King visited Paris at the beginning of May 1903 also lends support to the idea that they still believed him to be friendly towards Germany. Hugo Prince von Radolin, the German ambassador to Paris, reported, before the King's arrival, that Edward VII's visit might bring about a *détente* in Anglo-French relations, but that the cornerstone of French foreign policy would remain the alliance with Russia.[201] It never seems to have occurred to Bülow that the success of the King's visit would have potentially negative consequences for Anglo-German relations. He believed that the British desire for *rapprochement* with France was a policy directed against Russia rather than Germany and, in any case, he felt that it was questionable that the policy would succeed.[202]

The conspicuous failure of King Edward to counter-balance his visits to Paris and Rome with a similar one to Berlin began to raise doubts in the German capital as to the real attitude of the King towards the *Reich* as 1903 progressed. In May 1903, the Kaiser told the British military attaché, Colonel Waters, that he was 'hurt and disappointed' that his uncle had failed to visit Berlin since his accession. He also criticised King Edward's desire to play a role in foreign affairs, which Wilhelm claimed his uncle 'did not understand'.[203] The King had told Lascelles that he did not have time to meet the Kaiser during 1903, but that a visit might

---

[200] Tattenbach to Bülow, with marginalia by Wilhelm II, 17 April 1903, *ibid.*
[201] Radolin to Bülow, 29 April 1903, *GP*, xviii(ii), pp. 842–3.
[202] Winzen, *Bülows Weltmachtkonzept*, pp. 405–6. Kennedy, *Anglo-German Antagonism*, p. 267.
[203] Waters, *Potsdam and Doorn*, pp. 89–90; cf. Prinet to Delcassé, 26 April 1903, *DDF*, 2nd series, iii, no, 201, pp. 277–8; Sir Frederick Ponsonby to Lascelles, 18 August 1903, Lascelles Papers, PRO FO 800/11; Radziwill, *Briefe*, 7/8 September 1903, pp. 237–8.

be arranged for 1904, an excuse which the British ambassador found unconvincing.[204] Wilhelm's bitter reaction to an English newspaper report on the success of a visit by King Victor Emmanuel of Italy to London, in November 1903, also indicated his frustration and depression as to the likelihood of his being received by King Edward in a similar fashion. He ordered that the article be preserved: 'so that once I officially return King Edward VII's visit to me we can compare whether I will be party to the same "splendid sincerity"'.[205]

The gradual deterioration in Germany's diplomatic position was having an influence on the Kaiser's attitudes by the autumn of 1903. This manifested itself in a number of ways, not least of which was Wilhelm's growing disenchantment with Edward VII and Britain. His frustration on the diplomatic front found expression in a strongly worded attack on the calibre of German ambassadors abroad, who he believed lacked influence with the governments of the states to which they were accredited. He believed that if this situation were to endure the consequences for Germany would be disastrous. 'If this continues we will find ourselves surprised one day by a "Global Coalition" against us.' He noted, further, that initial signs of this danger were emerging from London.[206] Yet Wilhelm had only himself to blame for the level of British hostility towards Germany, for his own policies since his accession had been responsible to a large extent for creating alarm in Britain as to the course of German policy, most notably as a result of his *Flottenpolitik*. Wilhelm's 'first and fundamental idea' at this time 'was to destroy England's position in the world to the advantage of Germany'. The naval build-up was an integral part of this strategy.[207] It was these policies, rather than the poor quality of German diplomats or the attitude of Edward VII, which accounted for the deterioration in Anglo-German relations.

The Kaiser's frustration and anger at Germany's emerging diplomatic encirclement, and at his uncle's failure to add Berlin to his itinerary of royal visits, led him to make a public outburst which caused considerable irritation to Edward VII and the British people. In a speech at Hanover on 19 December 1903, Wilhelm referred to the Battle of Waterloo, and claimed that the British would have lost the battle had

[204] Bihourd to Delcassé, 27 September 1903, *DDF*, 2nd series, III, no. 445, p. 590.
[205] Wilhelm II's marginalia on *The Standard*, 18 November 1903, PA Bonn England Nr 81 Nr 1 Bd 12.
[206] Wilhelm II's marginalia on Monts to Bülow, 20 October 1903, PA Bonn Russland Nr 82 Nr 1 Bd 50.
[207] Spitzemberg, diary entry, 14 March 1903, *Tagebuch*, p. 428.

it not been for the intervention of Marshal Blücher and the Prussian and Hanoverian forces. This led to fierce criticism of the Kaiser in the British press.[208] Edward VII reacted angrily to his nephew's statements, which he regarded as 'foolish, injudicious & historically untrue', and wondered what motivated Wilhelm to say 'such unnecessarily foolish things'.[209] The King had to be restrained by his advisers from protesting to his nephew about the speech, and they, in turn, could only hope that a meeting between the two monarchs scheduled to take place in 1904 would remove the ill-feeling which had re-emerged between them.[210]

Before the meeting between the King and the Kaiser, British diplomacy scored a major triumph, with the signing in April 1904 of the Anglo-French agreement.[211] Baroness Spitzemberg was one of those who recognised the damage which the agreement had caused to Germany's international position, describing it as 'one of the most serious defeats for German diplomacy since the Dual Alliance'.[212] The Kaiser and Bülow seem to have reacted more pragmatically, at least at first, to the signing of the agreement. Wilhelm was sceptical as to the likelihood that a comparable agreement could be concocted between Britain and Germany. He wrote on a report, which raised this possibility: 'No! because we are too similar, and are going to be stronger than the French.'[213] Nonetheless, the Kaiser appreciated that the agreement gave both the British and the French more room for manoeuvre. By contrast, Bülow felt that the *entente* might last for the duration of the Russo-Japanese War, but would fall apart during the peace negotiations, because England would support the Japanese, and Russia the French.[214]

The chancellor's view proved to be hopelessly over-optimistic. At the beginning of May, Tattenbach, German minister in Lisbon, reported that Edward VII was now eager to see an understanding between Britain and Russia.[215] A few days later, this was confirmed by the German ambassador at St Petersburg, Count von Alvensleben. He had heard, on good authority, that there had been a noticeable *détente* in Anglo-Russian relations, which was to a great extent attributable to the

[208] Paul Cambon to Delcassé, 22 December 1903, *DDF*, 2nd series, iv, no. 137, pp. 198–9.
[209] Knollys to Lascelles, 23 December 1903, Lascelles Papers, PRO FO 800/12.
[210] Cf. Lascelles to Knollys, 25 December 1903, RA W 44/18; Knollys to Lascelles, 11 January 1904, Lascelles Papers, PRO FO 800/12; Lee, *Edward VII*, ii, p. 292.
[211] See ch. 3.
[212] Spitzemberg, diary entry, 15 April 1904, *Tagebuch*, p. 439.
[213] Wilhelm II's marginal comment on Metternich to Bülow, 9 April 1904, *GP*, xx(i), no. 6375, p. 14.
[214] Wilhelm II to Bülow, 19 April 1904; Bülow to Wilhelm II, 20 April 1904, *ibid.*, nos. 6378–9, pp. 22–4.
[215] Tattenbach to Bülow, 2 May 1904, *ibid.*, no. 6382, pp. 26–7.

personal influence of Edward VII, and reflected the British desire to show solidarity with the European powers against the 'yellow peril'. Wilhelm, by now suspicious of British intentions, noted that the King might be seeking an improvement in relations with Russia, but did not appear to want one with Germany.[216]

Edward VII's state visit to the Kaiser at Kiel in June 1904 was motivated in large measure by a desire to limit the damage caused to Anglo-German relations by the signing of the Anglo-French agreement. It was, however, in no way seen as a prelude to a political agreement between Britain and Germany. Paul Cambon, the French ambassador to London, appreciated this. He noted that the British people remained very suspicious of Germany and viewed the King's visit to the Kaiser with indifference bordering on hostility. The visit was best seen as a damage limitation exercise, motivated by Edward's desire not to give his 'impressionable and impulsive' nephew a feeling of isolation.[217]

Friedrich von Holstein was sceptical as to the likely benefits of the Kiel visit. However, Germany's diplomatic position had become so desperate that he believed that 'right now even a momentary, somehow generally recognizable success, would be very important'.[218] The King's visit appeared at the time to be a success. He and the Kaiser exchanged toasts and made speeches in which they both expressed a desire for Anglo-German friendship.[219] In conversation with Bülow, the King showed himself to be critical and mistrustful of Russian policy in the Far East. The British monarch also tried to convince the chancellor that the Anglo-French agreement was not directed against Germany. He told Bülow that there was no reason for a similar understanding with the *Reich*, but that he wished to see all sources of disagreement removed between Britain and other powers.[220]

Both the Kaiser and Edward VII expressed satisfaction at the outcome of their discussions. Wilhelm telegraphed to his aunt, Grand Duchess Luise of Baden: 'The King's visit passed off very satisfactorily and I hope it will be a further support to peace.'[221] Edward VII told Paul

---

[216] Alvensleben to Bülow, 11 May 1904, with marginalia by Wilhelm II, *GP*, xix(i), no. 6033, pp. 177–80; cf. Wilhelm II's comment on Bernstorff to Bülow, 5 May 1904, PA Bonn England Nr 81 Nr 1 Bd 12.
[217] Paul Cambon to Delcassé, 9 June 1904, *DDF*, 2nd series, v, no. 204, pp. 236–7.
[218] Holstein to Bülow, 25 June 1904, *HP*, iv, no. 828, p. 291.
[219] The German Emperor's speech at Kiel, 25 June 1904, RA W 44/114a; King Edward's answer, 25 June 1904, RA W 44/114b.
[220] Note by Bülow, 26 June 1904, *GP*, xix(i), no. 6038, pp. 186–8; cf. Bülow to Holstein, 29 June 1904, *HP*, iv, no. 829, p. 292.
[221] Wilhelm II to Grand Duchess Luise of Baden, 29 June 1904, GStA Berlin BPH 53/69.

Cambon that he believed he had managed to reassure Bülow and the Kaiser about the Anglo-French *entente*, and conceded that this had been the main purpose of his journey to Kiel. The King admitted that he had been aware of sensitivities in France regarding his visit, and said that it was because of these that he had wanted to give the visit a sporting and family character, and not a political one.[222] Yet, even a few weeks after the visit had taken place, it had become evident that it had not brought about any improvement in Anglo-German relations, and by the autumn, the animosity between Edward and the Kaiser was again coming to the fore. Robert Count von Zedlitz-Trützschler, the comptroller of the Prussian royal household, who had been present at Kiel, noted that the effect of the visit had been minimal:

Everyone is pretending that we are on the best possible terms with England, and that the rulers have, at any rate for the time being, cleared up all difficulties. As a matter of fact, however, all the differences between the English and the German peoples remain as they were, and such talk only serves to stimulate the zeal of all who make it their business to fan the fire of dissension.[223]

Bülow also appreciated that the visit had not brought about any real change in English attitudes towards Germany. Although he felt that an attempt to improve relations with England should be a priority for Germany, as he was convinced that any threat to the *Reich*'s security would come from that power,[224] the chancellor advised the Kaiser that all attempts should be made to cultivate good relations with Russia, the power which the chancellor had long regarded as Germany's natural partner: 'As long as the sentiment in England remains as hostile to us as it apparently unfortunately still is, we must as before carefully cultivate our relations with . . . Russia.'[225]

By the autumn of 1904, the joint efforts of Bülow and the Kaiser to win over the Tsar to co-operation with Germany appeared to bearing fruit,[226] and had become a cause of concern at the British court, not least to Edward VII, for it made his own ambition to secure an Anglo-Russian *entente* more difficult. The King's suspicion of his nephew's

---

[222] Paul Cambon to Delcassé 9 July 1904, *ibid.*, no. 261, p. 304; cf. Maurice Paléologue, *The Turning Point; Three Critical Years 1904–1906*, English translation (London, 1935), diary entry, 11 July 1904, pp. 99–100; Lascelles to Knollys, 27 May 1904, Lascelles Papers, PRO FO 800/12; Wilhelm II to Edward VII and Edward VII to Wilhelm II, 19 June 1904, *ibid.*

[223] Robert Graf von Zedlitz-Trützschler, *Twelve Years at the Imperial German Court*, English translation (London, 1924), diary entry, 21 July 1904, p. 80.

[224] Bülow to Wilhelm II, 15 July 1904, *GP*, XIX(i), no. 6043, pp. 203–4.

[225] Bülow to Wilhelm II, 2 August 1904. GStA Merseburg, HA Rep. 53J Lit. B Nr 16a Bd III.

[226] Cf. McLean, 'Monarchy', chs. 3 and 4.

intrigues against him at St Petersburg was one of the major causes of the quarrel between uncle and nephew, which was to see relations between the two monarchs deteriorate to an unprecedented extent by the spring of 1905. On 7 September 1904, Lord Esher, a close friend of the King's, wrote of his concern that 'a secret and very intimate understanding' already existed between Germany and Russia.[227] Later in the same month, following the publication of a report in *The Times*, Edward VII himself began to fear that this might be the case,[228] and although Lascelles insisted that no understanding existed between Germany and Russia,[229] British suspicions on this matter remained.[230] Confirmation that these concerns were justified was given in a report by Sir Charles Hardinge, the British ambassador to St Petersburg, in a letter to the King on 5 November. The ambassador wrote: 'It is said here that the German Emperor sends a message every day from Berlin with a letter for the Emperor . . . there is no doubt that Germany is making strenuous efforts to establish very close relations here and to eventually oust France.'[231] At the same time, Wilhelm sought to accentuate Nicholas II's mistrust of England by drawing to his attention various ways in which the English were aiding the Japanese in their war against Russia.[232] Less judiciously, Wilhelm denounced Edward VII at the first audience which he gave to the Russian military plenipotentiary, Colonel Schebeko. This move was highly damaging politically, for Schebeko immediately reported the Kaiser's remark to the French military attaché, General Moulin.[233]

On 22 October 1904, the Russian fleet, on its way to the Far East, fired on British fishing boats in the North Sea, off the Dogger Bank. This precipitated a crisis in Anglo-Russian relations which threatened to bring about a war between these two powers.[234] The British press, and senior British naval figures, such as the first sea lord, Admiral Fisher,

---

[227] Lord Esher to Maurice Brett, 7 September 1904, Maurice V. Brett (ed.), *Journals & Letters of Reginald, Viscount Esher*, 4 vols. (London, 1934–8), II, p. 62.
[228] Lansdowne to Edward VII, 19 September 1904, RA W 44/205.
[229] Lascelles to Knollys, 19 September 1904, RA W 45/2.
[230] Sir Cecil Spring-Rice to Lascelles, 27 September 1904, Lascelles Papers, PRO FO 800/12.
[231] Hardinge to Edward VII, 7 November 1904, Hardinge Papers, University Library, Cambridge, vol. 6.
[232] Wilhelm II to Nicholas II, 10 October 1904, *BKW*, pp. 345–6.
[233] Paléologue, *The Turning Point*, diary entry, 29 October 1904; Boutiron to Delcassé, 24 October 1904, *DDF*, 2nd series, v, no. 385, p. 464; Zedlitz, *Twelve Years*, diary entry, 10 December 1904, p. 112.
[234] See ch. 3.

blamed Germany for inciting Russia against Britain, thus precipitating panic in Germany that the British were going to attack.[235] The so-called War Scare of 1904/5 not only led to a deterioration in relations between Britain and Germany, but also to a growth in the ill-feeling between the Kaiser and King Edward. Metternich, in a letter to the King's private secretary, denied that Germany had any responsibility for the action of the Russian fleet at Dogger Bank. He repudiated the rumour as 'a mere fabrication without a shadow of truth', noting further that, 'the inventors have attained their purpose in making the English people once more believe in Germany's dark designs against them'. He feared that a profound change in the British attitude to the *Reich* was occurring: 'with regard to Germany there is a desire to create an atmosphere of dislike and exasperation which might lead to the most serious consequences'.[236]

Such disingenuous protestations of innocence failed to remove the tension between the two powers. On 15 December 1904, Bülow informed Holstein that both the German naval and military attachés in London were convinced that England was contemplating an attack on Germany.[237] The Kaiser shared these fears. Dynastic factors played a role in his attitude at this time. He saw two minor violations of etiquette by the British royal family towards himself and the Kaiserin as evidence that Edward VII favoured war. He was greatly angered by the tardiness with which Queen Alexandra answered a telegram which he and the Kaiserin had sent to congratulate her on her birthday, and he also saw the failure of the British royal family to send a telegram to congratulate the Kaiserin on her birthday as a warning that the English were about to mount an attack.[238]

Both Metternich and Lascelles tried to convince the Kaiser that the British had no intention of attacking Germany, but to no avail.[239] Wilhelm's anxiety persisted. On 26 December a report reached Berlin, which claimed that Edward VII was greatly disturbed by the strong terms in which the Kaiser had recently spoken against England.

[235] Jonathan Steinberg, 'The Copenhagen Complex', *Journal of Contemporary History* 1 (1966), 23–46; Barbara Vogel, *Deutsche Russlandpolitik: Das Scheitern der deutschen Weltpolitik unter Bülow 1900–1906* (Düsseldorf, 1973), p. 203.
[236] Metternich to Knollys, 5 November 1904, RA W 45/72.
[237] Bülow to Holstein, 15 December 1904, *HP*, IV, no. 869, p. 317; Steinberg, 'The Copenhagen Complex', pp. 33–9.
[238] Cf. Wilhelm II's marginalia on Queen Alexandra to Wilhelm II, 5 December 1904, PA Bonn England Nr 81 Nr 1 Bd 13; Zedlitz, *Twelve Years*, diary entry, 10 December 1904, p. 112.
[239] Cf. Lascelles to Lansdowne, 23 December 1904, Lansdowne Papers PRO FO 800/129; Lascelles to Lansdowne, 25 December 1904, Steinberg, 'The Copenhagen Complex', p. 38; Lascelles to Lansdowne, 28 December 1904, *BD*, III, no. 65, pp. 56–8; Bülow to Wilhelm II, 26 December 1904, *GP*, XIX(i), no. 6157, pp. 372–3.

Wilhelm dismissed the allegation as 'Lies out of Petersburg and Paris'. He asserted that he was committed to good relations with England, and noted: 'I must write to H.M. that I unfortunately know how I have been slandered in relation to him.'[240] On 15 January 1905, Bülow informed Holstein that the Kaiser was still concerned about English attitudes and wanted to inform Lascelles that the German fleet had never been mobilized, and to tell him, for the King's information, 'that Russia and France were trying to sow enmity between England and Germany'.[241] Edward VII, by contrast, had been perplexed by the whole episode,[242] and when Metternich visited the King at Windsor, he found the latter to be in conciliatory mood towards Germany. Edward told the German ambassador that the war scare had been 'senseless', and he stressed his desire to live in peace with all powers, including Germany. Metternich, however, believed that the crisis would not be the last.[243] The pessimistic German ambassador proved to be a more perceptive observer than the optimistic British monarch.

In March 1905, Wilhelm II landed at Tangiers in Morocco, against his own initial instincts, and under pressure from Bülow.[244] This action initiated a crisis in Germany's relations with France and Britain, for it was a direct challenge to the *entente* between those two powers, which had involved British recognition of the pre-eminence of France's claim in Morocco in return for a guarantee of French support for British claims in Egypt. On a dynastic level, the Kaiser's landing in Morocco resulted in a breach between Wilhelm and Edward VII which was never healed satisfactorily before the King's death, thus destroying the residual political value of the close family ties between the British and Prussian courts. Edward VII was already 'full of mistrust of the Emperor and his doings' before the Kaiser's visit to Tangiers, in large measure due to Wilhelm's attempt to win over the United States by inciting that power against Britain.[245] Wilhelm's landing at Tangiers, thus, simply confirmed the King's suspicion of his nephew.

[240] Wilhelm II's marginalia on Alvensleben to Bülow, 26 December 1904, *GP*, XIX(i), no. 6158, pp. 374–5.

[241] Bülow to Holstein, 15 January 1905, *HP*, IV, no. 875, p. 323.

[242] Knollys to Lascelles, 27 December 1904 and Lansdowne to Lascelles, 13 January 1905. Lascelles Papers, PRO FO 800/12.

[243] Metternich to the German foreign office, 28 January 1905. PA Bonn England Nr 81 Nr 1 Bd 13.

[244] Wilhelm II to Bülow, 21 March 1905 and Bülow to Wilhelm II, 20 March 1905, *GP*, XX(i), nos. 6564–5, pp. 263–4; Norman Rich, *Friedrich von Holstein; Politics and Diplomacy in the era of Bismarck and Wilhelm II*, 2 vols. (Cambridge, 1965), II, pp. 692–4.

[245] Knollys to Lascelles, 21 March 1905, Lascelles Papers, PRO FO 800/12; cf. Spring-Rice to Knollys, 25 March 1905, RA W 45/122; Bülow, *Memoirs*, I, pp. 564–5; Magnus, *Edward the Seventh*, p. 342.

Lord Lansdowne caught the mood of the British people in describing the Kaiser's 'Tangier escapade as an extraordinarily clumsy bit of diplomacy'. He was convinced that Wilhelm had been greatly angered by the Anglo-French agreement, and by the failure of the British to concoct a similar understanding with Germany about Egypt.[246] The French chargé d'affaires saw the hostile reaction of the British press and people to the Kaiser's action as symptomatic of the almost universal suspicion with which the British now viewed Germany. He noted, significantly, that the British court had also been party to this trend. At the time of Queen Victoria, the court had remained 'very Germanic in habit and sentiment'. This was no longer the case. Edward VII had little sympathy for Wilhelm, whom he found disagreeable on a personal level, and the King's views, in turn, had influenced those of his courtiers and of English high society.[247] Thus, the ill-feeling between the Kaiser and the King had led to the disappearance of the dynastic friendship which had acted as a check to Anglo-German distrust during the Victorian era.

The King's reaction to the Kaiser's landing at Tangiers also confirmed this to be the case. Edward VII was well-informed about Wilhelm's views at this time, because his nephew had expressed himself in frank terms on diplomatic questions in a conversation with Prince Louis of Battenberg on the day after his visit to Tangiers. Battenberg immediately communicated details of the Kaiser's statements to the King. Wilhelm had justified his action as a defence of the principle of the 'open door' in Morocco. He spoke of his belief that the world would eventually be divided between the Teutons and Slavs, and made a thinly-veiled threat against the French. 'As to France,' he informed Battenberg, 'we know the road to Paris, and we will get there again if needs be. They should remember that no fleet can defend Paris.'[248] This statement, like his landing in Morocco, represented a clear challenge to the Anglo-French *entente*. Edward VII's reply to Battenberg's report showed that he had finally lost patience with Wilhelm:

I consider that the Tangiers incident was one of the most mischievous & uncalled for events which H.M. G.E. has ever undertaken. It was a gratuitous insult to 2 Countries – & the clumsy theatrical part of it – would make me laugh were the matter not a serious one. It was a regular *case* of 'Bombastes

[246] Lansdowne to Lascelles, 9 April 1905, Lascelles Papers, PRO FO 800/12.
[247] Geoffray to Delcassé, 9 April 1905, *DDF*, 2nd series, VI, no. 264, pp. 328–31.
[248] Prince Louis of Battenberg, notes of a conversation with HM the German Emperor on board HMS *Drake*, Gibraltar, 1 April 1905, Lansdowne Papers, PRO FO 800/130.

Furioso'! I suppose G.E. will never find out as he will never be told how ridiculous he makes himself – In all he said to you there is throughout a want of sincerity.

The final statements which the King made to Prince Louis indicated that he had lost all faith in the Kaiser. 'I have tried to get on with him & shall nominally do my best till the end – but trust him – *never*. He is *utterly false* & the bitterest foe that E[ngland] possesses!'[249]

The resolute support which King Edward gave to the French foreign minister, Théophile Delcassé, during the period which followed can be attributed in large measure to his belief that Wilhelm II could not be trusted and that Britain and France should act together over Morocco. He also wished to show personal support for Delcassé, particularly after learning that the Kaiser was behind an intrigue to force the latter from office.[250] Edward VII visited Paris twice in the spring of 1905, and on the second occasion he had two meetings with the French foreign minister. Delcassé came away convinced that Britain would support France in a war with Germany.[251] These discussions aroused the Kaiser's suspicion. He was not inclined to take the King's assurance that Britain did not want war with Germany at face value,[252] and continued to declare: 'The English Fleet cannot protect Paris from our conquest!'[253]

Yet disagreements over Morocco were but one of many sources of tension between the King and the Kaiser during 1905. Other, less well-known, factors need to be examined in order to gain a full understanding of the motivations behind the personal and political quarrel between them.[254] Various dynastic issues contributed to the ill-feeling between uncle and nephew at this time. At the beginning of March, King Edward had agreed that the Prince of Wales would attend the wedding of Crown Prince Wilhelm at Berlin on 6 June 1905. However, two weeks later, the King reneged on this pledge, ostensibly because he wished his son to remain in England during a visit by the King of Spain.[255] The real reason may have been the King's anger at what he saw as Wilhelm's intrigues against Britain.[256]

[249] Edward VII to Prince Louis of Battenberg, 15 April 1905, Broadlands Archives, MB1/T75.
[250] Bertie to Edward VII, 22 April 1905, RA W 46/1.
[251] Cf. ch. 3.
[252] Wilhelm II's marginalia on Radolin to Bülow, 1 May 1905, *GP*, xx(ii), no. 6848, pp. 616–17.
[253] Wilhelm II's comment on Bernstorff to Bülow, 22 April 1905, PA Bonn England Nr 78 geheim. Bd 7.
[254] Fritz Fellner, 'Die Verstimmung zwischen Wilhelm II. und Eduard VII. im Sommer 1905', *Mitteilungen des Österreichischen Staatsarchivs* 11 (1958), 501–11.
[255] Lee, *King Edward VII*, II, p. 335.
[256] Knollys to Lascelles, 21 March 1905, Lascelles Papers, PRO FO 800/12.

This decision was met with considerable dismay at Berlin,[257] and Lascelles sought, in vain, to reverse it. He tried to reassure Knollys about the Kaiser's attempts to win over the Americans, which he believed had already failed, and stressed the political damage which would result if the Prince of Wales did not attend the Crown Prince's wedding. Lascelles also drew attention to the Kaiser's complaints that Prince George had not yet visited the German regiment of which he had been created colonel-in-chief in 1902.[258] The Prince of Wales reacted angrily to Lascelles's letter. He described the ambassador's complaints as 'bosh', and commented: 'It is a pity that the Emperor should always go out of his way to find fault & make complaints.' The Prince concluded by criticising the political views of the British ambassador: 'Although I like Lascelles very much, I fear he has become too German in his ideas for my taste.'[259] The ambassador was left with no option but to communicate the King's original excuse to the Kaiser's *Hausminister*, and to announce that Prince Arthur of Connaught, the son of the Duke of Connaught, would attend the Crown Prince's wedding as Edward VII's representative.[260]

The matter did not end there, however. Wilhelm had been greatly angered by his uncle's decision, and when Prince Arthur arrived in Berlin for the Crown Prince's wedding, an incident occurred between the Kaiser and Lascelles at the railway station which led the latter, in despair, to contemplate resigning as British ambassador. Wilhelm avoided political topics with Lascelles. When, towards the end of their conversation the ambassador informed him that he was about to leave for England and asked if he had any message for King Edward, the Kaiser replied negatively in an uncharacteristically brusque and unfriendly tone. Wilhelm then turned his back on Lascelles in order to speak to others.[261] It was immediately after this that the ambassador went to see Bülow and told him of his desire to resign, the chancellor tried to calm Lascelles down and assured him that the Kaiser did not harbour any hostility towards him personally. Wilhelm was, instead, greatly angered by the tone of the British press and government towards Germany and himself. Bülow told Lascelles that he was convinced that England had offered France a treaty of alliance, which he believed the

[257] Fellner, 'Die Verstimmung', 504.
[258] Lascelles to Knollys, 24 March 1905, RA W 45/146.
[259] George, Prince of Wales, to Knollys, 26 March 1905, RA W 45/147.
[260] Knollys to Lascelles, 9 May 1905; Lascelles to Count August zu Eulenburg, 11 May 1905, Lascelles Papers, PRO FO 800/12.
[261] Szögyény-Marich to Vienna, 14 June 1905, Fellner, 'Die Verstimmung', 504.

latter had refused. Lascelles told his Austrian colleague, Szögyény, that after ten years as British ambassador he had failed to maintain, or improve, good relations between England and Germany and wondered if it wouldn't be better if he were to ask to be recalled.[262]

King Edward's snub to the Kaiser over the Crown Prince's wedding, and the latter's subsequent anger was but one instance of a personal dispute which came to have wider political ramifications. Another source of ill-feeling between uncle and nephew in 1905 concerned the status of the King's cousin, Lord Edward Gleichen, as British military attaché at Berlin. Gleichen was closely related to both King Edward and Wilhelm's consort, Kaiserin Augusta Viktoria. He was the grandson of Queen Victoria's half-sister, who had married Prince Ernst of Hohen-lohe-Langenburg, and was therefore the first cousin of the Kaiserin.[263] Although a German by birth, he had been brought up in England and served in the British army. He enjoyed the special favour of Edward VII, who, soon after his succession, persuaded the foreign secretary to add Gleichen's name to the list of potential military attachés,[264] with Gleichen being appointed to Berlin in August 1903. Bülow recalled that both Gleichen and another favourite of King Edward's, Prince Louis of Battenberg, were distrusted in Germany for having betrayed their German origins,[265] and Gleichen himself admitted that he was handled coldly by German officers during his time at Berlin.[266] Gleichen succeeded, unintentionally, in offending the Kaiser in a number of ways, such as by passing German military literature which was offensive to Britain to the war office in London, through minor ceremonial violations, and most seriously by visiting the capitals of the German states which possessed their own armies without prior authorisation from Berlin.[267] Edward VII resented his nephew's discourteous treatment of Gleichen, and initially resisted German attempts to have him removed as British military attaché.[268]

However, Gleichen was eventually transferred from Berlin to Washington in early 1906. Even at the time of Gleichen's recall King

---

[262] *Ibid.*, 505–6; cf. Bülow to Metternich, 11 June 1905, *GP*, xx(ii), no. 6857, pp. 628–30; Bihourd to Rouvier, 11 June 1905, *DDF*, 2nd series, vii, no. 38, pp. 36–9.

[263] Lord Edward Gleichen, *A Guardsman's Memories* (Edinburgh, 1932), pp. 7, 275.

[264] Lansdowne to Knollys, 29 July 1901, RA W 42/23; Wilhelm II to Edward VII, 16 August 1903, RA X37/57.

[265] Bülow, *Memoirs*, ii, p. 24.   [266] Gleichen, *Guardsman's Memories*, p. 262.

[267] *Ibid.*, pp. 262–5, 270–1; Lascelles to Knollys, 2 March 1905, RA W 45/121; Knollys to Lascelles, 7 March 1905. Lascelles Papers, PRO FO 800/12; Bülow to Metternich, 22 July 1905, *GP*, xx(ii), nos. 6866–7, pp. 643–7.

[268] Edward VII quoted in Knollys to Lascelles, 27 July 1904, Lascelles Papers, PRO FO 800/12.

Edward and the Kaiser were unable to agree about his merits as a military attaché. Metternich reported that the King had said: 'Count Gleichen experienced good and bad weather in Berlin. He means well and . . . has left many friends behind among the German officers.' Wilhelm strongly contested this point: 'That is absolutely not the case! on the contrary!'[269] Still, Gleichen's departure for America did remove one source of dispute between the two monarchs.

A further issue, unconnected with the Moroccan crisis, which contributed to the ill-feeling between the King and the Kaiser in 1905, was the contrasting attitude which they took to the separation of Norway and Sweden. King Edward believed that Wilhelm was intriguing against his preferred candidate for the Norwegian throne, his nephew and son-in-law, Prince Charles of Denmark. The King came under pressure from the Norwegian representative in Copenhagen and from British diplomats at the legation there to use his influence in favour of the Prince. The concern that otherwise Germany might seek to interfere played a role in these calculations. As a result Edward VII made strenuous efforts to persuade Prince Charles to take up the throne and to secure British recognition for him.[270] The Kaiser and his entourage viewed the prospect of the King of England's son-in-law on the Norwegian throne with dismay, believing that English influence would then become dominant in Norway.[271] The Kaiser himself had favoured a candidate from the Swedish royal house, and his initial opposition to Prince Charles angered Edward VII considerably.[272] The disagreement between the two monarchs over the Norwegian throne was thus one example of an area where a clash of dynastic interests contributed to the ill-feeling between the Kaiser and the King. The Kaiser's continuing condemnation of Edward VII's private life also played a role in fuelling the King's anger and distrust towards him. During the Kiel Week in 1905, Wilhelm publicly condemned the relationship between his uncle and the latter's mistress, Mrs Alice Keppel. This became known in London and caused considerable irritation to the King.[273]

[269] Metternich to Bülow, 4 February 1906, PA Bonn England Nr 78 geheim. Bd 8.
[270] Cf. Stephen Leech to Knollys, 30 June 1905, RA W 46/54; Knollys to the Hon. Alan Johnstone, 30 July 1905, RA W 46/75; Edward VII to Johnstone, 3 August 1905, RA W 46/145; Knollys to Johnstone, 8 August 1905, RA W 46/194; Ponsonby to Hardinge, 21 August 1905, Hardinge Papers, vol. 7.
[271] Helmuth von Moltke, *Erinnerungen, Briefe, Dokumente, 1877–1916* (Stuttgart, 1922), 18 July 1905, p. 324.
[272] Note by Mühlberg, 1 August 1905, *GP*, xx(ii), no. 6868, pp. 648–9; Lascelles to Lansdowne, 3 August 1905, Lansdowne Papers, PRO FO 800/130.
[273] Metternich to Bülow, 19 October 1905, Bülow, *Memoirs*, II, p. 182.

As a result of the ill-feeling between the two monarchs, Edward VII refused to pay a visit to Wilhelm on his way to Marienbad in August 1905. This brought the dispute between them into the public domain and contributed to a worsening of the atmosphere between Britain and Germany, already strained by the Moroccan crisis. Although the quarrel between Edward and Wilhelm was patched up in early 1906, relations between them never fully recovered from the low-ebb which they reached in the late summer of 1905. It was in the years that followed that the Kaiser became obsessed by the fear that Edward VII wished to encircle the *Reich*, and King Edward's attitude towards Germany also became noticeably less conciliatory in the last years of his life.

The King's political distrust of the Kaiser was absolute in the summer of 1905. On 15 July, in a letter to Prince Louis of Battenberg, he made a thinly veiled reference to Wilhelm, which was also very disparaging. 'As regards the "bull in the china shop" policy of a certain most energetic but tactless not to say dangerous Sovereign! I think it is best to say nothing- though the subject is one which I think the world in general are against.'[274] The Kaiser's sister, Crown Princess Sophie of Greece, was 'deeply alarmed' by the anti-German sentiments which she found at the British court in July 1905. She believed that King Edward's annoyance with Germany was 'momentary' and would pass. Metternich was convinced that the best way to remove tension between the Kaiser and the King would be to arrange a meeting between them.[275] After talking to Seckendorff, who had recently returned from England, Bülow also became aware of the extent of King Edward's suspicion of Germany and of the Kaiser. Seckendorff stated that the King had lost all trust in Wilhelm because of Germany's Morocco policy.[276]

On 8 August, Lord Knollys wrote to Lascelles, informing the ambassador that the King would not meet the Kaiser on his way to Marienbad. The reasons given only corresponded in part to the truth. Knollys stated: 'The King, notwithstanding what the Emperor says about him, would have no personal feeling against a meeting, but it could not take place just now.' The first reason was that a visit to the Kaiser could not be fitted into the King's travel plans. This was a spurious excuse, for in subsequent years Edward VII had no trouble in arranging visits to Wilhelm on his journeys to and from Bohemia. The second reason was more plausible. The King did not wish to upset the French, who had

[274] Edward VII to Prince Louis of Battenberg, 15 July 1905, Broadlands Archives, MB1/T75.
[275] Metternich to Bülow, 25 July 1905, Bülow, *Memoirs*, II, pp. 121–2.
[276] Bülow to Metternich, 22 July 1905, *GP*, xx(ii), no. 6866, pp. 641–6.

recently sent their navy on a visit to the British Channel ports, and he believed that if he were to meet Wilhelm this would have 'a very bad effect' in France.[277] Lascelles, still eager to pursue the increasingly fruitless task of conciliating the two monarchs, told Knollys that he believed a meeting between the King and the Kaiser would be 'productive of much good'.[278] The chances of such a meeting taking place were removed when the King told Metternich that he could not meet the Kaiser until the Moroccan crisis had ended satisfactorily. However, in order to show that he was not a Germanophobe, the King proposed instead to invite the Crown Prince and Princess of Prussia to Windsor in November.[279] Metternich's account of his conversation with Edward VII showed that he was not convinced by the King's claims that he had nothing against his nephew. Instead, the ambassador stated that he was aware from other sources that the King's attitude was characterised by 'a profound ill-feeling . . . against German policy and unfortunately also particularly against the person of His Majesty the Kaiser'.[280]

An attempt was made by Count Seckendorff, acting at the Kaiser's behest, to get the King to change his mind.[281] This, however, ended in recrimination. The King found Seckendorff's intervention 'impertinent' and got Knollys to write a strongly worded reply to the former's letter, refuting the charges made therein. The King maintained, despite overwhelming evidence to the contrary, that he had 'no quarrel . . . of any kind' with the Kaiser, and stated, unconvincingly: 'I am on the same terms that I have always been since my accession.'[282] The King's refusal to contemplate a meeting only seemed to fuel Wilhelm's anger against his uncle. The Kaiser's friend, Prince Max Fürstenberg, told Tschirschky that Wilhelm had spoken about his uncle in terms which could not be repeated.[283] At the same time, British press criticism of Germany and her ruler had contributed to an intensification of Wilhelm's *Englandhass*. He wrote bitterly on a despatch that the British press seemed to view Germany as 'a benighted country ruled by a bloodthirsty tyrant'.[284] Edward VII, by contrast, proceeded to Marienbad, via

[277] Knollys to Lascelles, 8 August 1905, Lascelles Papers, PRO FO 800/12.
[278] Lascelles to Knollys, 11 August 1905, *ibid.*
[279] Knollys to Lascelles, 14 August 1905, Lascelles Papers, PRO FO 800/12.
[280] Metternich to Bülow, 14 August 1905, *GP*, xx(ii), no. 6870, p. 655.
[281] Seckendorff to Edward VII, 15 August 1905, RA W 46/231.
[282] Edward VII to Knollys, 18 August 1905, RA W 46/252; cf. Edward VII to Lascelles, 20 August 1905. RA X37/61; Knollys to Seckendorff, 23 August 1905, RA W 46/285.
[283] Tschirschky to Bülow, 22 August 1905, Bülow, *Memoirs*, II, pp. 146–7.
[284] Wilhelm II's marginal comment on Bernstorff to Bülow, 18 August 1905, PA Bonn England Nr 78 Bd 31; cf. Wilhelm II's marginalia on Radolin to the German foreign office, 9 August 1905, PA Bonn England Nr 81 Nr 1 Bd 14.

the hunting lodge of the Austrian Emperor, Franz Joseph, at Ischl. In a letter to his friend, the financier Sir Ernest Cassel, the King could not help contrasting the congenial Austrian ruler with his troublesome German counterpart. 'I stayed a few hours at Ischl on my way here to pay the E. a visit & found H.M. in excellent health & we had some very interesting conversations – Would to God that other Sovereigns were as sensible as he is.'[285]

Despite the ever worsening quarrel between the King and the Kaiser, there still remained the possibility of reconciliation through a visit by the Crown Prince and Princess of Prussia to England. However, this suggestion was vetoed by Wilhelm in a manner which caused considerable offence to Edward VII. The Kaiser had been irritated by the King's invitation to the Crown Prince. He felt that he should have been consulted about the visit and he also raised moral objections as a reason for forbidding it. He accused the King of inviting his son 'behind his back', and of having a double purpose, namely 'to divide father and son, second, to secure (according to an old English recipe) a member of the family here, who would serve him as spy and observer and whom he could use in his own interests just as he thought fit'.[286] The Kaiserin also resented the King's invitation to the Crown Prince and wondered why Edward VII visited President Loubet of France frequently, but never paid a visit to his nephew, Wilhelm.[287] The Crown Prince was therefore forced to decline the King's invitation, because of his father's objections.[288] Edward VII wrote back expressing his regret and blaming the Kaiser: 'Another year it will probably be the same story as I have reason to believe that your Father does not *like* your coming to England!'[289]

Sir Frederick Ponsonby, the King's assistant private secretary, who was with him in Marienbad when he received the Crown Prince's letter, was left in no doubt as to the extent of the King's displeasure. Ponsonby informed Lascelles that the King was 'very angry' at the Crown Prince's refusal.[290] Wilhelm's mood was no more conciliatory than that of his uncle. He had been angered by the remarks which King Edward had made in his letter to the Crown Prince. He told Lascelles that 'the

---

[285] Edward VII to Cassel, 17 August 1905, Cassel Papers, Broadlands Archives, MB1/X2.
[286] Tschirschky to Bülow, 22 August 1905. Bülow, *Memoirs*, II, p. 146; cf. Lascelles to Edward VII, 13 September 1905, RA W 47/206.
[287] Sir Almeric Fitzroy, *Memoirs*, 2 vols. (London, 1925), I, diary entry, 8 August 1905, p. 263.
[288] Crown Prince Wilhelm of Prussia to Edward VII, copy (undated) in Lascelles Papers, PRO FO 800/12.
[289] Edward VII to Crown Prince Wilhelm of Prussia, 5 September 1905, GStA Berlin BPH 54/132; Lascelles Papers, PRO FO 800/12.
[290] Ponsonby to Lascelles, 27 August 1905, Lascelles Papers, PRO FO 800/12; cf. Ponsonby to Hardinge, 30 August 1905, Hardinge Papers, vol. 7.

remarks about himself amounted almost to a personal insult', and believed that the King was seeking a quarrel with him.[291] Wilhelm manifested his displeasure at his uncle and Britain in another way at this time. He sought to exploit a visit by the Royal Navy to Germany's Baltic ports as a means of increasing support within the *Reich* for naval expansion. At the same time, he duplicitously tried to persuade the King that he saw this naval visit as an opportunity to encourage Anglo-German co-operation.[292] Wilhelm's real attitude towards the Royal Navy and its visit to the Baltic coast was revealed in a letter which he sent to the Tsar and in instructions which he submitted to the German foreign office prior to the visit. He wrote to Nicholas on 22 August, denouncing Edward VII as the 'Arch intriguer – and mischief-maker', and noted: 'His fleet is in the act of visiting our shores and I think this will open the eyes of many Germans who are still loth to vote money for the extension of our Fleet; we shall send many down by rail and steamer to take an object lesson. They will I hope learn to understand the necessity of building a strong fleet.'[293] He had already telegraphed to the German foreign office in order to ensure that cheap rail fares would allow as many Germans as possible to travel to Swinemünde to see the Royal Navy.[294] Yet in his conversation with Lascelles on 8 September 1905, the Kaiser had complained hypocritically that King Edward had failed to acknowledge the warm reception which the Royal Navy had received in German waters.[295]

King Edward was in no mood to accept responsibility for the quarrel with Wilhelm. In a letter to Knollys, he gave his reaction to the remarks which the Kaiser had made about him to Lascelles. He stated that he had had every right to invite the Crown Prince to England and noted: 'The G.E.'s most silly remarks on that point are beside the question. The real truth is that he was jealous at my asking his son at all.' Edward believed that the tone of Wilhelm's remarks was one of 'peevish complaint' against him, and he did not think that there was any prospect of a meeting between them until 1906, and then only if the Kaiser desisted in thinking up imaginary grievances against him and stopped intriguing against England.[296]

---

[291] Lascelles to Knollys, 9 September 1905, Lascelles Papers, PRO FO 800/12; Lascelles to Lansdowne, 12 September 1905, *ibid.*

[292] Wilhelm II to Edward VII, 4 September 1905. PA Bonn England Nr 78 geheim. Bd 8.

[293] Wilhelm II to Nicholas II, 22 August 1905, *BKW*, p. 377.

[294] Wilhelm II to Excellenz von Budde, 15 August 1905, PA Bonn England Nr 78 Bd 31.

[295] Lascelles to Edward VII, 13 September 1905, RA W 47/206.

[296] Edward VII to Knollys, 17 September 1905, RA W 47/253; cf. Knollys to Lascelles, 22 September 1905, RA W 47/315; Metternich to Bülow, 2 October 1905, *GP*, xxii, no. 6871, pp. 659–62.

By September 1905, the quarrel between the King and the Kaiser had become a matter of concern to members of the British cabinet and also to members of the Kaiser's entourage. Lord Lansdowne told Lascelles that he believed that King Edward was partly to blame for the deterioration in his relations with Wilhelm: 'He talks & writes about his Royal Brother in terms which make one's flesh creep, and the official papers which go to him whenever they refer to H.I.M., come back with all sorts of accusations of a most incendiary character.'[297] On the German side, Philipp Eulenburg made clear his anxiety about the possible political damage which could result if the ill-feeling between King Edward and Wilhelm were to persist. He warned Bülow that Edward VII's hostility towards the Kaiser was one of the most serious obstacles facing German diplomacy, and observed 'the *strongest* spring of future action – even political action – is always personal'.[298]

The Kaiser remained distrustful of his uncle politically. He told Eulenburg that he believed that the King was behind France's Morocco policy, and wished to bring about a Franco-German war from which only England would profit.[299] King Edward, by contrast, continued to maintain that no meeting between himself and Wilhelm could take place until Anglo-German relations improved, and allowed Knollys to publish a statement refuting rumours that he intended to visit Wilhelm, to his nephew's evident indignation.[300] However, signs by the autumn of 1905 that the Kaiser's dream of an alliance with Russia had proved a chimera caused Wilhelm to demand measures to improve Germany's relations with Britain. He wrote to Bülow from Glücksburg on 12 October 1905 in pessimistic fashion on this topic. The Kaiser was inclined to place some of the blame for the poor state of Anglo-German relations on Metternich, whom he felt had failed to gain sufficient influence in the diplomatic and court circles of the British capital, and much of the rest on Edward VII's entourage. Prince Arthur of Connaught, who like Wilhelm was in Glücksburg to attend the wedding of the Duke of Coburg, gave the Kaiser a gift from Edward VII and passed on the King's continuing grumbles about his nephew's refusal to allow the Crown Prince to visit England. Wilhelm finally admitted the real reason for his own anger. Prince Arthur told the Kaiser, with regard to Edward VII's attitude: 'he is unhappy that my son was not allowed to

[297] Lansdowne to Lascelles, 25 September 1905, Lascelles Papers, PRO FO 800/12; cf. Lansdowne to Balfour, 23 August 1905, F. R. Bridge, *Great Britain and Austria-Hungary 1906–1914. A Diplomatic History* (London, 1972), p. 12, note 98, p. 237.
[298] Eulenburg to Bülow, 23 September 1905, *EK*, III, no. 1506, p. 2114.
[299] Note by Eulenburg, 25 September 1905, *ibid.*, no. 1509, pp. 2115–16.
[300] Zedlitz, *Twelve Years*, diary entry, 9 October 1905, p. 147.

come as he would have had an excellent "reception"! I replied that I would not have doubted that for a moment, but "first the *father*, then the *son*"! He laughed but he understood me.'[301]

As 1905 drew to a close, there seemed few signs of reconciliation between Edward and Wilhelm. The English-born Princess Daisy of Pless found herself on the receiving end of King Edward's hostility towards Germany when she attended the Newmarket races. She found the King's conduct towards her uncharacteristic, and concluded that 'he must hate the Germans'.[302] Intermediaries were also blamed for the persisting ill-feeling between the two monarchs. The French chargé d'affaires in London, M. Geoffray, believed that the Kaiser's choice of Lord Lonsdale as his closest friend in England did not help matters, for Edward VII viewed the latter with disdain. This point was echoed by the Grand Duke of Baden who felt that unofficial advisers of both monarchs had caused many of the problems in the relationship between them.[303] Bülow tried to reassure the Kaiser that Anglo-German relations were improving by submitting a report to him by Metternich which drew attention to the activities of certain pro-German organisations in London. Wilhelm was, however, unimpressed, and noted that no princes, friends or relatives of Edward VII were involved in these groups. As far as he was concerned only a sign that the King himself had altered his attitude towards Germany would suffice.[304]

A partial reconciliation did occur between the Kaiser and the King at the beginning of 1906,[305] but despite superficial appearances much of the antagonism between uncle and nephew remained. In this sense the events of 1905 marked a watershed in the relations between them. From

---

[301] Wilhelm II to Bülow, 12 October 1905, PA Bonn Deutschland Nr 131 Nr 4 Bd 5.

[302] Diary entry, 1 November 1905, D. Chapman Huston (ed.), *The Private Diaries of Daisy Princess of Pless 1873–1914*, reprint (London, 1950), p. 140.

[303] Geoffray to Rouvier, 9 November 1905, *DDF*, 2nd series, VIII, no. 117, pp. 159–60; Eisendecher to Bülow, 1 November 1905, *Grossherzog Friedrich I.*, IV, no. 2526, pp. 608–9; cf. Wilfrid Scawen Blunt, *My Diaries. Being a Personal Narrative of Events 1888–1914*, 2 vols. (London, 1919–20), II p. 352 (diary entry, 9 February 1911); Bülow to Holstein, 13 May 1903, *HP*, IV, no. 816, p. 275; Bülow to Wilhelm II, 25 May 1903, GStA Merseburg HA Rep. 53 J Lit. B Nr 16a vol. II; Bülow, *Memoirs*, II, p. 29; Lonsdale to Wilhelm II, 4 August 1898, 6 October and 7 November 1901, GStA Merseburg HA Rep. 53 J Lit. L. Nr 9; Memorandum by Hardinge, 19 August 1907, *BD*, VI, no. 25, p. 45; Hardinge to Lascelles, 26 August 1907, Lascelles Papers, PRO FO 800/13; Edward VII to Hardinge, 1 September 1907, Hardinge Papers, vol. 9; Lascelles to Knollys, 2 October 1905, Lascelles Papers PRO FO 800/12; Stolberg to Metternich, 1 June 1906, PA Bonn England Nr 78 geheim. Bd 8.

[304] Wilhelm II's comment on Bülow to Wilhelm II, 3 December 1905, *GP*, xx(ii), no. 6882, p. 681.

[305] Cf. Edward VII to Wilhelm II, 23 January 1906, PA Bonn England Nr. 78 geheim. Bd 8; Wilhelm II to Edward VII, 1 February 1906, RA X37/62.

that time onwards, Wilhelm was not prepared to trust Edward VII and became obsessed with the idea that his uncle wished to destroy the *Reich*. Similarly, although the King made great efforts to get on with his nephew, from 1906 onwards, he never showed the same desire for co-operation with Germany as he had, at various times, in the first years of his reign.

The initial hopes of a political reconciliation between Edward and Wilhelm were focussed on the attempts to resolve the Moroccan crisis at the Algeciras conference. At the beginning of February 1906, Wilhelm was still optimistic that it would result in a favourable outcome for Germany.[306] However, as time progressed, and Germany found herself increasingly isolated at the conference, he became angered by what he saw as the duplicitous conduct of Edward VII and the British. A visit paid by King Edward to Paris and subsequent meeting with King Alphonso of Spain at Biarritz were taken as evidence by Wilhelm that his uncle's political intrigues against him were reviving.[307] Zedlitz noted in his diary on 13 March 1906 that Wilhelm's hostility towards Edward VII had resurfaced, and that this coincided with a deterioration of his confidence over Morocco:

He is furious at the machinations of his uncle, the King of England, against him, and ascribes all rumours which crop up now and again as to meetings between the King and himself to English intrigues. Their object is, he says, to prove unmistakeably to the world that such interviews are impossible.[308]

The Kaiser's growing disenchantment with Edward VII was revealed in his tendency to believe ever wilder rumours about his uncle. For instance, in April 1906, he seemed to accept, in a fatalistic manner, a false report that his uncle was about to visit Italy for the purpose of detaching that country from Germany.[309] Similarly, he accepted another false report that King Edward was going to visit Nicholas II in order to prepare the ground for an Anglo-Russian agreement.[310] Germany's diplomatic humiliation at the Algeciras conference, where all the powers deserted her aside from Austria, was widely seen in Germany

---

[306] Wilhelm II to Grand Duchess Luise of Baden, 1 February 1906, GStA Berlin BPH 53/76.
[307] Wilhelm II's marginal comment on Metternich to the German foreign office, 1 March 1906. PA Bonn England Nr 81 Nr 1 Bd 15; Wilhelm II's comment on Stumm to Bülow, 7 March 1906, *ibid.*; Wilhelm II's comment on Stumm to Bülow, 9 March 1906. *GP*, xxi(i), no. 7082, p. 268;
[308] Zedlitz, *Twelve Years*, diary entry, 13 March 1906, pp. 161–3.
[309] Wilhelm II's marginalia on Monts to the German foreign office, 1 April 1906. PA Bonn England Nr 81 Nr 1 Bd 16.
[310] Wilhelm II's comment on Radolin to Bülow, 14 April 1906, *ibid.*

as being a triumph for Edward VII.[311] In the aftermath of Algeciras, Friedrich von Holstein concluded that the British monarch was the most skillful diplomat in Europe, whereas the Kaiser was the least competent.[312]

The Kaiser also blamed Edward VII for the débâcle of Algeciras. Wilhelm, recalling the events of 1906 more than twenty years later, blamed King Edward and the latter's unofficial ambassador at Algeciras, Mackenzie Wallace, for Germany's defeat at the conference. He also claimed that it was from that moment onwards that the 'encirclement' of the *Reich* had begun.[313] The visit which the King had paid to Paris in early March 1906 was also a fertile breeding ground for German suspicions. Radolin believed that sinister motives had lain behind this: 'Under the cover of making a "private trip", he helped along many a serious treaty, although this is naturally kept secret.'[314]

In order to counteract such suspicions, arrangements were made for a visit by Edward VII to the Kaiser in the summer of 1906, but neither the British nor the German side expected much good to come out of it, and in the end, despite some reduction in the tension between the two powers, these predictions proved to be correct.[315] The troubled dynastic relationship between the two countries was one factor which ensured this. Even members of the British royal family who were, in general, favourably disposed towards Wilhelm had begun to express doubts about his political judgement by 1906. Edward VII's sister, Louise, Duchess of Argyll, was one such individual. She wrote to the Kaiser in April 1906, warning him about the damaging political consequences of his speeches.[316]

The meeting between Edward and Wilhelm at Friedrichshof in August 1906 did nothing to bring about a fundamental political and personal reconciliation between them. By the spring of 1907, the Kaiser's suspicion of his uncle had returned with even greater force than previously, and he seemed to interpret every visit which King Edward

---

[311] Holstein to Maximilian von Brandt, 10 April 1906, *HP*, IV, no. 959, p. 410; memorandum by Holstein, 17 May 1906, *ibid.*, no. 983, p. 427.

[312] Holstein to Ida von Stülpnagel, 12 June 1906, Rogge (ed.), *Holstein: Lebensbekenntnis*, p. 258.

[313] Note by Wilhelm II, 28 March 1927, GStA Berlin BPH 53/165.

[314] Radolin to Holstein, 8 May 1906, *HP*, IV, no. 976, p. 421. The British account of the King's visit to Paris lends no support to this claim. Bertie to Grey, 5 March 1906, *BD*, III, no. 327, p. 284.

[315] Lascelles to Grey, 18 May 1906, Grey Papers, PRO FO 800/61; Knollys to Louis Mallet, 18 June 1906, Grey Papers, PRO FO 800/103; Metternich to Bülow, 4 May 1906, *GP*, XXI(ii), no. 7180, pp. 424–7; Bülow to the German foreign office, 13 August 1906, *ibid.*, no. 7193; Hardinge to Grey, 16 August 1906, *BD*, III, no. 425, p. 370; Ponsonby, *Recollections*, p. 182.

[316] Louise, Duchess of Argyll, to Wilhelm II, 7 April 1906. GStA Merseburg HA Rep. 53J Lit. A Nr 8.

paid to foreign countries as being motivated by his desire to establish a coalition of powers against Germany.[317] Edward VII, being a more discreet individual, displayed fewer outward signs of hostility towards his nephew. However, by late 1906, he had become convinced that the Kaiser's reckless personality and his tendency to surround himself with sycophantic advisers represented a potential threat to world peace.[318]

The keen interest which King Edward took in Russian affairs in 1906–7 reflected his disillusion with Germany, and contributed to the Kaiser's suspicion of him.[319] Edward VII's attitude towards Germany at this time, however, fell well short of the fanatical opponent presented in German propaganda. The Italian foreign minister, Tittoni, gave a realistic assessment of the British monarch's view of Germany and the Kaiser in 1907. He had held discussions with the King during his visit to Italy in the spring of 1907, and gave the French ambassador a reassuring assessment of the British monarch's opinions: 'King Edward is . . . not in the least bellicose. His nephew irritates him greatly; . . . but he would willingly live on good terms with the Germans.' Edward would, Tittoni asserted, use his considerable influence in Europe to maintain peace.[320]

Wilhelm's own attitude towards his uncle and England was more complex than one might initially think from a cursory examination of the sources. Raymond Lecomte, the chargé d'affaires at the French embassy in Berlin, who was party to a particularly violent outburst by the Kaiser against Edward VII and the British in March 1907, made some observant remarks about Wilhelm's attitude. The Kaiser's suspicions had been awakened by the Anglo-Japanese alliance, the Anglo-French *entente* and by the negotiations between Britain and Russia, then in progress, which resulted in the signing of an agreement between those two powers in August 1907. Lecomte believed that Wilhelm's hostile comments about Edward VII should not be taken too seriously as in reality, the Kaiser loved England, regretted the poor state of Anglo-German relations, and was offended by what he saw as his uncle's tendency to ignore him.[321] King Edward's failure to visit Berlin remained a source of considerable resentment to the Kaiser, as he saw this as a snub and a glaring omission in view of the large number of

---

[317] Wilhelm II's comment on Monts to Bülow, 18 April 1907, *GP*, xxi(ii), no. 7215, p. 497; Wilhelm II's comment on Stumm to Bülow, 27 April 1907, *ibid.*, no. 7217, p. 501; Grand Duchess Luise of Baden to Wilhelm II, 13 May 1907, GStA Merseburg HA Rep. 53 J Lit. B Nr 83.

[318] Paléologue, *The Turning Point*, diary entry, 29 November 1906, p. 327.

[319] Wilhelm II's comments on Stumm to Bülow, 17 April 1907, PA Bonn Russland Nr 82 Nr 1 Bd 55.

[320] Barrère to Pichon, 19 May 1907, *DDF*, 2nd series, xi, no. 3, p. 7.

[321] Lecomte to Pichon, 21 March 1907, *DDF*, 2nd series, x, no. 440, pp. 703–4.

European capitals which the King had visited since 1903. Edward VII's willingness, or otherwise, to visit the German capital became the criterion by which Wilhelm judged his uncle's desire to improve Anglo-German relations. Wilhelm remarked when the issue of such a visit was raised in the *Westminster Gazette* in August 1907: 'that is absolutely essential!'[322]

The fact that King Edward found his nephew so disagreeable on a personal level was one of the major factors in his reluctance to meet Wilhelm on anything other than an infrequent basis. The King's reluctance to discuss politics when he met Wilhelm also reflected the fact that he did not feel that he could talk openly when in the latter's company.[323] Although Wilhelm did finally visit England on a state visit in 1907, this resulted in an improvement in relations between the two monarchs and countries which was more apparent than real. No political agreement could be found between the two governments, and on the increasingly sensitive question of naval armaments, the rivalry between the two countries was actually growing in intensity.[324] Various events during the course of 1908 were to indicate that on a political level, too, the animosity between the Kaiser and the King was intensifying rather than diminishing.

The first such incident was the Kaiser's decision in February 1908 to send a letter to the first lord of the British admiralty, Lord Tweedmouth, about the level of German naval estimates. He did so without consulting Bülow,[325] and partly in response to an imprudent letter sent by Edward VII's friend, Lord Esher, to the Imperial Navy League, and subsequently printed in *The Times*, in which the latter had claimed that every German, from the Emperor downwards, wished to see the dismissal of Admiral Fisher.[326] The Kaiser had written to his uncle to inform him that he had communicated with Tweedmouth.[327] This, however, did not prevent the King from replying in indignant terms. He told Wilhelm: 'Your writing to my First Lord of the Admiralty is a "new

[322] Wilhelm II's marginal comments on Metternich to Bülow, 6 August 1907, PA Bonn Russland Nr 82 Nr 1 Bd 55.
[323] Hardinge to Grey, 21 August 1907, *BD*, VI, no. 26, pp. 46–7; Hardinge to Knollys, 22 August 1907, RA W 52/11.
[324] Jonathan Steinberg, 'The Kaiser and the British: The State Visit to Windsor, November 1907', in *Kaiser Wilhelm II: New Interpretations*, ed. Röhl and Sombart, pp. 136–9; cf. ch. 4.
[325] Lascelles to Grey, 27 February 1908, *BD*, VI, no. 88, p. 138; Esher, journal entry, 14 March 1908, Esher Papers, ESHR 2/11.
[326] Wilhelm II to Tweedmouth, 16 February 1908, *GP*, XXIV, no. 8181, pp. 32–5; Tweedmouth to Wilhelm II, 20 February 1908, *ibid.*, no. 8182, p. 35.
[327] Wilhelm II to Edward VII, 14 February 1908, Esher Papers, ESHR 10/53.

departure", and I do not see how he can prevent our press from calling attention to the great increase in the building of German ships of war, which necessitates our increasing our navy also.'[328] Edward VII's anger was also directed against Esher, whom he blamed for having precipitated the crisis, and this resulted in a temporary removal of royal favour from Esher.[329]

The matter might have ended there, if the military correspondent of *The Times*, Colonel à Court Repington, had not revealed the existence of the Kaiser's letter in that newspaper on 6 March 1908. This was a move which he had co-ordinated with Lord Esher in order to force the Liberal government to take a stronger line on the naval question.[330] There is no evidence that Edward VII had anything to do with this revelation. Indeed, he was not even in England, having left for Paris and Biarritz. This did not stop the Kaiser from blaming his uncle for *The Times* article. He declared that his uncle was 'concerned that the letter' was making 'a calming impression'.[331] Others in Germany were less charitable towards the Kaiser's action. Princess Radziwill speculated that Wilhelm might be mentally ill, and felt that King Edward would be wringing his hands with pleasure at his nephew's folly.[332]

In reality, the episode had caused Edward VII considerable exasperation. The King's irritation was directed against Wilhelm, Tweedmouth and Esher in equal measure[333] and, contrary to the Kaiser's suspicions, he greatly regretted what had occurred, as did Lord Knollys, his private secretary.[334] One of the King's friends, the financier Ernest Cassel, told Metternich that the British monarch regretted Esher's original remarks and Repington's revelations in *The Times*, particularly as he had felt that Anglo-German relations were improving. The Kaiser was unimpressed. He criticised his uncle for not rebuking Esher five weeks previously when the letter in which the King's friend had made his original remarks had been published. Wilhelm also refused to take responsibility

---

[328] Edward VII to Wilhelm II, 22 February 1908, *GP*, XXIV, no. 8183, p. 36.
[329] Edward VII to Esher, 19 February 1908, Esher Papers, ESHR 6/2; Esher, journal entries, 19 and 20 February 1908, ESHR 2/11.
[330] Repington to Esher, 5 March 1908, Esher Papers, ESHR 10/53; Bülow to Wilhelm II, 6 March 1908, *GP*, XXIV, no. 8186, p. 39; Metternich to Bülow, 7 March 1908, *ibid.*, no. 8190, p. 42.
[331] Wilhelm II's comment on Bülow to Wilhelm II, 6 March 1908, *GP*, XXIV, no. 8187, p. 40.
[332] Princess Radziwill to General di Robilant, 10 March 1908, *This Was Germany. An Observer at the Court of Berlin. Letters of Princess Radziwill to General di Robilant, 1908–1915*, English translation, ed. Cyril Spencer Fox (London, 1937), p. 22.
[333] Geoffray to Pichon, 12 March 1908, *DDF*, 2nd series, XI, no. 310, pp. 521–3.
[334] Edward VII to Hardinge, 10 March 1908, Hardinge Papers, vol. 14; Knollys to Esher, 8 March 1908, Esher Papers, ESHR 10/50.

for the naval race between England and Germany, and instead blamed 'the insane "Dreadnought" Policy of Sir J. Fisher and His Majesty' for bringing this about.[335] Although disagreeing with the tactics employed by Esher and Repington, the King did support their general aim of ensuring that Britain's naval and military forces would be prepared for any eventuality including conflict with Germany. Esher noted in his journal on 14 March 1908 that, as a consequence of the Tweedmouth letter controversy, Balfour had succeeded in drawing a declaration from Asquith that Britain would lay down enough ships in the following three years to maintain naval superiority over Germany.[336] Edward VII also approved of this result.[337]

The King's support for such measures did nothing to dispel the conviction of the Kaiser and a large section of the German people that he was working towards the *Reich*'s encirclement. Wilhelm himself reacted to the visit which Edward VII paid to Nicholas II at Reval in 1908 by interpreting it as a sign that his uncle wanted to provoke a war.[338] The Kaiser's friend, the shipping magnate Albert Ballin, visited London in early July 1908. Wilhelm was comforted by the impressions which Ballin had gained, and reported them to Bülow in terms which revealed his own paranoia in relation to King Edward: 'Impressions from London favourable. City and commercial circles as before totally against any war. Anger and dissatisfaction about the travel and *entente* enterprise of the King growing strongly. The ministry's relations with the King strained for the same reason.'[339] Yet Bülow formed a somewhat different picture of Edward VII's attitudes when he spoke to Ballin personally. Ballin was of the view that the King took every opportunity to make snide remarks about Wilhelm, but he also felt that with time Edward VII was likely to favour more peaceable policies towards Germany. Ballin's preferred solution to the broader crisis in Anglo-German relations was, however, one which Wilhelm would not contemplate, namely, a naval agreement with England.[340]

Edward VII's visit to Reval and seeming lack of willingness to visit Berlin were not the only sources of grievance which the Kaiser held

---

[335] Wilhelm II's comment on Metternich to Bülow, 8 March 1908, *GP*, XXIV, no. 8193, p. 46.
[336] Esher, Journal Entry, 14 March 1908, Esher Papers, ESHR 2/11.
[337] Edward VII to Hardinge, 17 March 1908, Hardinge Papers, vol. 14; Edward VII to Fisher, 17 March 1908, Arthur J. Marder (ed.), *Fear God and Dread Nought. The Correspondence of Admiral of the Fleet Lord Fisher of Kilverstone*, vol. II *Years of Power, 1904–1914* (London, 1956), p. 170.
[338] Wilhelm II's comment on Metternich to Bülow, 25 June 1908, *GP*, XXV(ii), no. 8821, note 3, p. 481.
[339] Wilhelm II to Bülow, 6 July 1908, *GP*, XXIV, no. 8214, p. 91.
[340] Bülow to Wilhelm II, 15 July 1908, *ibid.*, no. 8216, pp. 96–9.

against his uncle in the summer of 1908. He had also been outraged by the King's nomination of Sir Fairfax Cartwright, the British minister in Munich, as British ambassador to Berlin. The main reason for the Kaiser's objections were not known to the King when he decided on the appointment and he could therefore in no way be held responsible for the dispute. Cartwright had allegedly written a book many years previously which the Germans considered a 'libel on Berlin society', and this made him an unsuitable candidate in German eyes.[341] The King accepted this, albeit with some reluctance,[342] and played a key role in finding a candidate acceptable to the Kaiser by putting pressure on a reluctant Sir Edward Goschen to exchange the congenial surroundings of the Vienna embassy for Berlin.[343]

The resolution of the ambassador question was the only positive aspect to an otherwise profoundly gloomy picture of deteriorating relations between the Kaiser and the King, as between Britain and Germany. A meeting between the two monarchs at Friedrichshof in August 1908 was little short of disastrous, as the Kaiser, during a heated conversation on the naval question with Hardinge, refused to contemplate any alteration to the German naval construction programme and threatened war should the English try to interfere. This brought the magnitude of the German threat into sharp focus for the King, who believed that Britain had no alternative but to keep on building ships at twice the rate of the *Reich*.[344] His own doubts about Wilhelm personally remained as strong as ever. After reading a report of a lecture which the Kaiser had given the British military attaché on the merits of Germany's economy and military organisation, the King gave expression to his irritation with his nephew: 'The Emperor evidently wished to impress on the "gallant Colonel" that there was only one country wh[ich] excelled in civilization and practical benefits for mankind! and that was Germany.'[345]

The extent of Edward VII's suspicion of the Kaiser and Germany was revealed in remarks which he made in conversation with Clemenceau during a meeting between the two men at Marienbad in late August 1908. The King told Clemenceau that in the light of the Kaiser's intransigence there was 'no hope' of a naval agreement between Britain

---

[341] Grey to Edward VII, 27 June 1908, RA W 53/112.
[342] Edward VII to Wilhelm II, 13 July 1908, GStA Merseburg HA Rep. 53 J Lit. G Nr. 11.
[343] Christopher Howard (ed.), *The Diary of Sir Edward Goschen 1900–1914* (London, 1980), diary entry, 12 August 1908, p. 31, pp. 175–6.
[344] Cf. ch. 4.
[345] Edward VII's minute on Colonel Trench to Lascelles, 12 August 1908, *BD*, VI, p. 178.

and Germany. Edward VII declared further that he thought that peace in Europe could be maintained for a further five or six years and echoed Clemenceau's fear that a certain impulsive sovereign – Wilhelm – might launch an escapade some day which would inevitably lead to conflict. By this time, the King's commitment to the *entente* with France was absolute. He spoke of the need for Britain to construct a strong army which could aid France against Germany.[346] Later in the same year, when Lord Esher held discussions about the aid which Britain might extend to France in the event of war, he assured the French military attaché that the King would use his influence in favour of British intervention.[347] The King's attitude remained not that of a warmonger but that of a monarch keen to assure that Britain would be prepared for all eventualities.[348]

The King's response to the intransigence of his nephew on the naval question was thus a measured and pragmatic one. The Kaiser's behaviour at this time does not fit this description. He was prepared to believe preposterous rumours that Edward VII had tried to persuade Franz Joseph, the Austrian Emperor, to abandon the alliance with Germany in favour of co-operation with England. In fact all that had occurred was that the King and Hardinge had sought to persuade Franz Joseph and Aehrenthal to put pressure on Germany over the naval armaments issue. This request had been declined.[349] Wilhelm now saw his principal task as being to prevent his uncle from bringing about Germany's encirclement: 'Stop the King! That is now what is most essential,'[350] was his assessment of the required objective. Every set-back for the *Reich* in the diplomatic arena was now ascribed by him to the Machiavellian machinations which he attributed to his Uncle Bertie. When Prince Ferdinand of Bulgaria unexpectedly declared himself Tsar in September 1908, Wilhelm automatically assumed that Edward VII was responsible. 'The Prince is wholly in his hands and is working with him', he wrote, and further declared: 'That is an Anglo-Russian coup from Marienbad directed against the consolidation of Turkey and our capital.'[351]

---

[346] Clemenceau to Pichon, 29 August 1908, *DDF*, 2nd series, XI, no. 434, pp. 749–52; Edward VII to Hardinge, 25 and 29 August 1908, Hardinge Papers, vol. 14; Edward VII's minute on Goschen to Grey, 29 August 1908, *BD*, VI, no. 100, p. 158.

[347] Lt. Colonel Huguet to General Picquart, 9 November 1908, *DDF*, 2nd series, XI, p. 933.

[348] Holstein to Bülow, 3 September 1908, *HP*, IV, no. 1125, pp. 560–1.

[349] Bridge, *Great Britain and Austria-Hungary*, pp. 102–5, 269–71.

[350] Wilhelm II's comment on Stumm to Bülow, 8 September 1908, PA Bonn England Nr 78 Bd 66.

[351] Wilhelm II's comments on Jenisch to the German foreign office, 26 September 1908. PA Bonn England Nr 81 Nr 1 Bd 19.

The publication of remarks made by the Kaiser about Britain in the *Daily Telegraph* 'interview' of 28 October 1908 served to damage still further Edward VII's view of his nephew.[352] In the 'interview', the Kaiser was quoted as describing the English as 'mad as March Hares' for refusing to accept his protestations of friendship for Britain. He also made claims to have aided the British cause in the South African War by sending battle plans to the British royal family and by refusing to take part in a continental league against England. He also contrasted his own Anglophilia with that of the majority of his subjects. The domestic implications of the *Daily Telegraph* affair are not relevant here, other than to state that they led to a political crisis which almost brought about Wilhelm's abdication as Kaiser.[353] King Edward reacted to Wilhelm's remarks with irritation rather than anger. He described the Kaiser's revelations about Franco-Russian overtures to Germany against England during the Boer War as 'malicious' but he did not think that these would 'in any way alter our (present) good relations with France & Russia.'[354]

The *Daily Telegraph* interview had simply exposed publicly what the King had long known, that Wilhelm's judgement was less than astute in the political sphere. The contents of an interview which the Kaiser had given to an American journalist, Dr Hale, while in Norway on 19 July 1908, which became known in November 1908, provided confirmation to the King that his nephew hated him.[355] Rumours about the contents of the Kaiser's conversation with Hale reached British diplomatic sources soon after it had taken place. Sir Arthur Herbert, the British envoy extraordinary at Christiania, reported to Hardinge that in conversation with an American journalist, the Kaiser had been 'very bitter in his denunciation of Great Britain'.[356] By mid October, when Valentine Chirol, the foreign editor of *The Times*, met Holstein, the former was able to inform the latter that Wilhelm had allegedly declared that

---

[352] *HP*, I, pp. 203–7.
[353] Terence F. Cole, 'The *Daily Telegraph* Affair and its Aftermath: the Kaiser, Bülow and the Reichstag, 1908–1909', in *Kaiser Wilhelm II: New Interpretations*, ed. John C.G. Röhl and Nicolaus Sombart (Cambridge, 1982), pp. 249–68; Katharine A. Lerman, *The Chancellor as Courtier. Bernhard von Bülow and the Governance of Germany 1900–1909* (Cambridge, 1990), pp. 210–47; Lamar J. R. Cecil, *Wilhelm II: Emperor and Exile 1900–1941* (Chapel Hill, NC, and London, 1996), pp. 123–45.
[354] Edward VII to Hardinge, 30 October 1908. Hardinge Papers, vol. 14; cf. Knollys to Esher, 29 October 1908, Esher Papers, ESHR 10/50; Esher journal entries, 28, 29 October 1908, 2, 5, 12 November 1908, Esher Papers, ESHR 2/11.
[355] Fischer, 'Exzesse der Autokratie', pp. 53–78; Menning and Menning, '"Baseless Allegations"', pp. 368–97.
[356] Sir Arthur Herbert to Hardinge, 31 July 1908. Hardinge Papers, vol. 11; Herbert to Hardinge, 7 August 1908, *ibid.*

'Germany and America had the same task of working together against England'.[357]

The Hale interview was due to appear in *Century Magazine* in the United States on 1 November 1908, but as a consequence of the outcry in Germany over the Kaiser's *Daily Telegraph* interview, whose contents it contradicted because of its Anglophobic tone,[358] it was suppressed prior to publication. This did not prevent some of the Kaiser's remarks about King Edward from becoming known. The British ambassador to Paris, Sir Francis Bertie, gave Hardinge an account of Wilhelm's comments to Hale:

> To him the Emperor is represented to have expressed the greatest contempt for the King of England and his entourage; to have stated that England was rotten and marching to her ruin and ought to be wiped out, and that he considered war between Germany and England as inevitable and to have said 'let it come'.

Edward VII described this information as 'curious'.[359]

Unfortunately, as Lord Esher noted,[360] the Kaiser's remarks were bound to come to public knowledge in the end and this occurred when *The Observer* published a résumé of the Hale interview on 22 November 1908. When King Edward learned the gist of Wilhelm's remarks about him, he was understandably offended and considered cancelling his state visit to Berlin, scheduled for February 1909.[361] Metternich issued a denial, stating that the interview 'was an invention from beginning to end, & that the words which H.M. is alleged to have said, have never been spoken'.[362] Edward VII accepted this assurance, without believing a word of it. 'I am however convinced in my mind', he wrote to Knollys, 'that the words attributed to the G.E. by Dr. Hale are perfectly correct. I know the E. *hates me* & never loses an opportunity of saying so (behind my back).'[363] The matter was thus at an end, but it had provided King Edward with renewed confirmation of Wilhelm's duplicity.

The King's state visit to Berlin in February 1909 went some way towards healing the rift between uncle and nephew, and the King told Cassel shortly afterwards that it had been 'in every respect a success'.[364]

---

[357] Memorandum by Holstein, 18 October 1908, *HP*, IV, no. 1143, p. 584.
[358] Fischer, 'Exzesse der Autokratie', pp. 59–70.
[359] Bertie to Hardinge, with minute by Edward VII, 11 November 1908, Hardinge Papers, vol. 11.
[360] Esher, journal entry, 21 November 1908, Esher Papers, ESHR 2/11.
[361] Esher, journal entry, 22 November 1908, *ibid.*; Hardinge to Knollys, 20 November 1908, RA W 54/132; Hardinge to Goschen, 25 November 1908, Hardinge Papers, vol. 13.
[362] Metternich to Knollys, 24 November 1908, Hardinge Papers, vol. 14.
[363] Edward VII to Knollys, 25 November 1908, RA W 53/37.
[364] Edward VII to Cassel, 19 March 1909, Cassel Papers, MB1/XI.

However, this was true only on a superficial level, for the naval arms race between Britain and Germany was intensifying, and despite a tentative intervention by the King on this issue, in conversation with Wilhelm during the visit, the Kaiser showed no desire to compromise in the months which followed.[365] The British minister in Dresden had expressed the hope that the King's visit to Berlin would put an end to German attempts to depict him as the mastermind behind the *Reich*'s 'encirclement'.[366] However, the hostile reaction in Germany in May 1909, when Edward VII visited the King of Italy, suggested that the King remained the *bête noire* for a large section of German public opinion.[367]

Edward VII's political suspicion of Germany, during the winter of 1908–9, was strengthened by the role which he came to believe that the German government had played in encouraging the Austrian annexation of Bosnia–Herzegovina. As early as 23 October 1908, he had stated his conviction that Germany had 'aided & abetted Austria' with a view towards isolating Britain, France and Russia and excluding them from influence in the Balkans.[368] Following the resolution of the Bosnian Crisis in March 1909, in circumstances of humiliation for Russia, the King was incandescent with fury against the Germans, remarking that Germany was now Britain's 'bitterest foe'.[369]

There were other instances where Edward VII adopted an attitude of scepticism and hostility towards Germany during the last year of his life. The King dismissed the acting state secretary of the German foreign office, Kiderlen-Wächter, as a 'humbug' when he told Goschen that he was not averse to an understanding with England.[370] When Daisy Princess of Pless passed on a message from the Kaiser, stating the latter's desire to see a treaty between England and Germany, the King expressed opposition on the grounds that the French and Russians would object.[371] Edward VII's hostile view of Germany was shared by the most influential members of his entourage in the latter years of his life. Those such as Fisher, Esher, Hardinge and Soveral who had ready access to the King were all convinced Germanophobes, and those friends of the

---

[365] Memorandum by Hardinge, *BD*, VI, pp. 230–2; Bülow to Tschirschky, 13 February 1909, *GP*, XXVIII, no. 10262, p. 889; Metternich to Bülow, 3 March 1909, *ibid.*, no. 10266, pp. 93–9.
[366] Findlay to Hardinge, 18 February 1909, Hardinge Papers, vol. 15.
[367] Goschen to Hardinge, 1 May 1909, Hardinge Papers, vol. 15.
[368] Edward VII to Hardinge, 23 October 1908, Hardinge Papers, vol. 14.
[369] Edward VII to Hardinge, 28 March 1909, Hardinge Papers, vol. 18.
[370] Edward VII's minute on Goschen to Hardinge, 26 March 1909, Hardinge Papers, vol. 15.
[371] Pless, *Diaries*, 14 December 1909, p. 233.

King who were more sympathetic towards Germany tended to be ones valued for social and not political reasons. Soveral, for example, was described by the Princess of Pless as 'a firebrand against Germany'.[372] By contrast, the Austrian ambassador to London, Count Mensdorff, was valued by the King as a congenial acquaintance rather than as a political like-mind. As Edward VII told Hardinge on one occasion: 'Our good friend Mensdorff is a great success socially but as regards politics he is not strong enough or up to the mark.'[373]

While there were signs in the last few months of his life that Edward VII was prepared to take a more conciliatory attitude towards the Kaiser personally,[374] there is little evidence that this had any influence on his attitude towards Germany politically. The King was, as in 1905, irritated in the autumn of 1909 by Wilhelm's refusal to let the Crown Prince visit England, and again took the view 'that it was of no use to ask him, as his father obviously never would spare him'.[375] Despite this grievance, Edward VII did make some attempt to improve his personal relations with Wilhelm. The King sent the Kaiser a friendly letter on the occasion of the latter's birthday in January 1910. This had pleased Wilhelm, who was particularly gratified that the King had raised political matters 'for the first time in 21 years'.[376]

When Metternich visited the King at Windsor he also found him to be a supporter of peaceful co-existence with Germany. The ambassador believed that the King was favourably disposed towards the Kaiser and the imperial government.[377] Wilhelm's reply to his uncle's letter sought to exploit this personal *rapprochement* for political ends. When one contrasts the Kaiser's words with the reality of Anglo-German political estrangement, they seem completely hollow. He wrote:

Your remark 'that it is essential for the Peace of the world that we should walk shoulder to shoulder for the good of civilization & the prosperity of the world' strikes a familiar note in my heart. This wish has always been the leading maxim of my policy & the goal which I have ardently striven to reach.[378]

It did not take long for this reconciliation to end in recrimination, like all those which had preceded it. On 17 February 1910, the German ambassador to Vienna reported, falsely, that the aim of British and French

---

[372] *Ibid.*   [373] Edward VII to Hardinge, 24 March 1908. Hardinge Papers, vol. 14.
[374] Mensdorff to Aehrenthal, 27 July 1909 *ÖUA*, II, no. 1694, pp. 419–20.
[375] Esher, journal entry, 8 October 1909, Esher Papers, ESHR 2/12.
[376] Goschen to Grey, 3 February 1910, *BD*, VI, no. 329, p. 438. The Kaiser's statement was an exaggeration, as the King's letters often alluded to politics, albeit usually only in passing.
[377] Metternich to Bethmann Hollweg, 30 January 1910, PA Bonn England Nr 78 geheim. Bd 25.
[378] Wilhelm II to Edward VII, 31 January 1910, RA X37/65.

policy was to detach Austria from Germany. Wilhelm accepted this renewed depiction of his uncle as 'Der Einkreiser' and remarked that this exposed the duplicity of the King's claim to want good relations with the *Reich*.[379]

Wilhelm was wrong on this occasion, but he was correct in suspecting that his uncle remained hostile to Germany. A few weeks before his death, King Edward sent a letter to Hardinge in which he made severe criticisms of German foreign policy: 'The way Germany is intriguing ags*t*. us & Russia is really too bad. They must have "a finger in every pie" & interfering with us everywhere at the same time being surprised that we do not like them! It is the old Bismarckian policy wh. is not yet dead.'[380] Several months after Edward VII's death, Lord Esher wrote an article for the *Deutsche Revue* about the late monarch in which he sought to present the King in a favourable light to the hostile German people.[381] Knollys, while approving of the purpose of the article, believed that it misrepresented Edward VII's true feelings about Germany. 'From numerous conversations with him, I should have said he felt towards Germany as 999 Englishmen out of 1000 do; very considerable mistrust.'[382]

Wilhelm II had appreciated this.[383] In a curious remark to Goschen in January 1910, he had referred to his uncle as 'the strong man',[384] reflecting the inferiority complex which lay at the root of his hostility towards Edward VII. The King's death thus came as a relief to him, although he managed to cover this up when he went to the British embassy to pay his condolences.[385] In a telegram to the chancellor, Bethmann Hollweg, Wilhelm made his true feelings clear. He believed that with the King's death, they could expect a quieter period in Europe. His uncle, he claimed, would be mourned principally by the French and the Jews.[386] Admiral von Tirpitz took an even more blunt attitude towards the King's death. It represented, he reputedly declared,

[379] Wilhelm II's marginalia on Tschirschky to Bethmann Hollweg, 17 February 1910, *GP*, XXVII(ii), no. 9910, p. 464; Note by Aehrenthal on his conversations with Wilhelm II and Bethmann Hollweg at Berlin on 22–5 February 1910, *ÖUA*, II, no. 2024, pp. 724–7.
[380] Edward VII to Hardinge, 5 April 1910, Hardinge Papers, vol. 20.
[381] The article, entitled 'King Edward VII and Foreign Affairs', is printed in Viscount Esher, *The Influence of King Edward and Essays on Other Subjects* (London, 1915), pp. 49–60.
[382] Knollys to Esher, 17 September 1910, Esher Papers, ESHR 4/3.
[383] Wilhelm II to Nicholas II, 21 April 1911, *BKW*, p. 408.
[384] Goschen to Hardinge, 28 January 1910, Hardinge Papers, vol. 20; *BD*, VI, no. 328, p. 437.
[385] Goschen to Hardinge, 13 May 1910, Hardinge Papers, vol. 20.
[386] Wilhelm II to Bethmann Hollweg, 7 May 1910, PA Bonn England Nr 78 geheim. Bd 25; *GP*, XXVIII, pp. 321–2; Crozier to Pichon, 6 June 1910, *DDF*, 2nd series, XII, no. 508, p. 791.

'the removal of a great obstacle in the way of Germany's aims'.[387] Wilhelm considered the new King, his cousin George V, to be much less of a threat. He was a country gentleman, without political knowledge, whose lack of foreign languages would direct him towards remaining at home. This would make his known suspicion of Germany less problematic than that of Edward VII.[388] For these reasons, the Kaiser was hopeful that dynastic relations between Berlin and London would now improve, and in the initial years of the new King's reign this was indeed the case.[389]

Towards Edward VII, however, the Kaiser's hatred remained undimmed and persistent. In May 1913, he made clear, in conversation with the British naval attaché, that he held the late King responsible for the creation of the *entente*,[390] and in July 1914, he made the extraordinary claim that his uncle, by that time dead for more than four years, had been instrumental in bringing about the crisis which was about to spark off the First World War. 'Edward VII is stronger after his death than am I who am still alive!' he declared.[391] Germany's defeat and his own abdication and flight into exile only intensified Wilhelm's need to find scapegoats for the catastrophe, and again his uncle's name was to the fore. After the failure of Operation *Michael* in 1918, Germany's last great offensive on the Western Front, Wilhelm had visions of all his English and Russian relatives 'marching past and mocking him.'[392] We can assume that King Edward was prominent among them. He attacked Edward VII in his own ghost-written memoirs,[393] and in the last year of his life, he declared, in a letter to a friend, that Edward VII had been the

---

[387] Sir Cecil Spring-Rice, memorandum on the political situation at Berlin: Admiral v. Tirpitz etc., August 1910. Hardinge Papers, vol. 20.

[388] Görlitz (ed.), *Müller: Aufzeichnungen*, p. 78; Paul Cambon to his son Henri, 7 May 1910, Cambon, *Correspondance*, II, pp. 298–9; Metternich to Bülow, 24 May 1910, *GP*, XXVIII, no. 10391, p. 331; Vierhaus (ed.), *Spitzemberg: Tagebuch*, diary entry, 7 May 1910, p. 521; Mensdorff to Aehrenthal, 13 May 1910, *ÖUA*, II, no. 2169, pp. 867–8. Esher, journal entry, 23 April 1908, Esher Papers, ESHR 2/11; Prince of Wales to Hardinge, 24 August 1908, Hardinge Papers, vol. 14; Prince of Wales to Esher, 4 January 1909 and 31 March 1909, Esher Papers, ESHR 6/5.

[389] Cf.ch. 4; Goschen to Hardinge, 10 May 1910, Hardinge Papers, vol. 20; Knollys to Esher, 27 September 1912, Esher Papers, ESHR 10/52; Kenneth Rose, *King George V* (London, 1983), pp. 163–5; Nicolson, *King George the Fifth*, pp. 180–2.

[390] Captain Watson to Goschen, 12 May 1913, *BD*, X(ii), no. 475, p. 701.

[391] Wilhelm II's comment on Pourtalès to Bethmann Hollweg, 29 July 1914. Imanuel Geiss (ed.), *July 1914. The Outbreak of the First World War. Selected Documents*, English translation (London, 1967), no. 135, p. 295.

[392] Admiral von Müller, diary entry, 23 July 1918. Walther Görlitz (ed.), *The Kaiser and His Court. The Diaries, Note Books and Letters of Admiral Georg Alexander von Müller Chief of the Naval Cabinet, 1914–1918*, English translation (New York, 1964), p. 374.

[393] Wilhelm II, *Memoirs*, pp. 112–13, 122–5.

servant of Satan and had engineered not just the First, but also the Second World War with the help of Jewish freemasonry and high finance. The victory of the Nazis, which he saw as inevitable and welcome,[394] would provide him with ultimate revenge over his long-deceased Uncle Bertie.

The ill-feeling between Edward VII and the Kaiser was of considerable political significance. During the reign of Queen Victoria, the dynastic relationship between London and Berlin had remained, in the main, good. Wilhelm's respect for his grandmother meant that she was one of the few people whose opinions he would listen to. By contrast, between the Kaiser and Edward VII there existed considerable mutual suspicion dating back to the Battenberg marriage controversy of the mid 1880s, and the events of 1888–9. In the early years of his reign, King Edward made considerable efforts to remain on satisfactory terms with Wilhelm. However, as time moved on a succession of quarrels and misunderstandings of both a political and personal nature alienated the King, firstly from his nephew, and secondly, from Germany. The growing bilateral tension between Britain and Germany, notably as manifested in the press and public opinion, played a role in this. However, Wilhelm's own behaviour was the decisive factor in the process. His constant intrigues against his uncle and Britain were clumsy and indiscreet in their execution and his intransigence on the question of naval armaments led the King to conclude that the Kaiser was Britain's enemy, for all the hollow protestations of friendship with which he might pepper his letters to Windsor. Edward VII was for Wilhelm a ready-made scapegoat when Germany's diplomatic position began to disintegrate, from 1905 onwards. Blaming King Edward for this and depicting him as 'Der Einkreiser' provided an easy way of avoiding any analysis of his own responsibility.

Edward VII was never the decisive figure in Britain's foreign policy establishment. However, he did possess considerable personal prestige both at home and on the continent. In addition, through his role in senior diplomatic appointments, he was able to influence the make-up of the British foreign service. It is striking that those who enjoyed the royal favour, in the last years of the King's life, such as Hardinge, Bertie

394 Wilhelm II to Alwina Gräfin von der Goltz, 28 July 1940, Willibald Gutsche, 'Illusionen des Exkaisers: Dokumente aus dem letzten Lebensjahr Kaiser Wilhelms II. 1940/41', *Zeitschrift für Geschichtswissenschaft* 10 (1991), 1028–9.

and Spring-Rice among the diplomats, and Fisher, Esher and Soveral, among the King's entourage, were without exception suspicious, if not hostile, towards Germany. By alienating his uncle, the Kaiser had helped to push the British monarch into the camp of Germany's enemies, thus destroying the possibility that the King would act as a Germanophile influence in London. In addition, Edward VII's poor relations with the Kaiser made him reluctant to seek to influence the latter's policies at a time when this would have been to Britain's advantage, most notably on the issue of naval armaments.

Similarly, Wilhelm's pathological hatred of Edward VII influenced him against Britain. This was something of considerable importance in view of the Kaiser's role as the ultimate arbiter of decision-making in Germany. Until 1903, Wilhelm had concurred with the views of his diplomats that Edward VII was friendly towards Germany. He saw the King's subsequent hostility as a personal betrayal, and this helps to explain the vehemence with which he denounced his uncle from 1905 onwards. The breakdown in relations between the British and Prussian courts removed one of the few mechanisms which bound Britain and Germany together. For much of the nineteenth century, dynastic ties had been an asset to Anglo-German relations. Sadly, in the first decade of the twentieth century, as relations between the two monarchs deteriorated, they lost this function and became a political liability. For this reason alone the often petty disputes between the Kaiser and King Edward cannot be dismissed as trivial or irrelevant. They contributed to an atmosphere of ill-feeling, which encouraged the two monarchs to support policies which fuelled the Anglo-German antagonism and ultimately led to war.

Figure 1 Victoria, Kaiserin Friedrich, March 1891.

Figure 2 Queen Victoria, 1893.

Figure 3 A group photograph taken at Coburg, April 1894, at the time of the wedding of Princess Victoria Melita of Saxe-Coburg-Gotha and Ernest Louis, Grand Duke of Hesse. Seated at the front are Kaiser Wilhelm II, Queen Victoria, and the Tsarevich Nicholas of Russia stands behind the Kaiser in a bowler hat.

Figure 4 Queen Victoria's funeral procession, Windsor, February 1901. Walking behind the coffin are King Edward VII, Kaiser Wilhelm II and Arthur, Duke of Connaught.

Figure 5 Kaiser Wilhelm II, 1901.

Figure 6 King Edward VII, *c.* 1902.

Figure 7 Queen Alexandra, *c.* 1903.

Figure 8 King Edward VII and Tsar Nicholas II on board the imperial yacht
Standart, Reval, June 1908.

Figure 9　Royal party at Windsor, during the Kaiser's visit, November 1907. In the foreground are King Edward VII, Arthur, Duke of Connaught, and Kaiser Wilhelm II.

Figure 10 Tsar Nicholas II, signed and dated 'Cowes, Aug. 1909'.

Figure 11 Group photograph of the British and Russian royal families, taken at Barton Manor, 4 August 1909.

Figure 12 Nine sovereigns at Windsor for the funeral of King Edward VII, 20 May 1910. Standing (left to right): Haakon VII of Norway, Ferdinand of Bulgaria, Manuel II of Portugal, Wilhelm II of Germany, George I of Hellenes, Albert I of Belgium. Seated (left to right): Alfonso XIII of Spain, George V, Frederick VIII of Denmark.

Figure 13 King George V, 1912.

Figure 14 Kaiserin Augusta Victoria, 1913.

Figure 15 King George V (right) with Tsar Nicholas II in Berlin, May 1913, for the wedding of Princess Victoria Louise of Prussia and Ernest Augustus, Duke of Brunswick.

CHAPTER 3

King Edward VII and British diplomacy, 1901–1910

As we have seen, the death of King Edward VII in May 1910 was regarded at the time as an important political event. Many of the King's contemporaries saw it as marking the end of an era during which the British monarch had taken a leading role in the creation and implementation of his country's foreign policy. For some observers, notably in Germany, the King's death came as a relief, for he was perceived to have been the architect of *Einkreisung*, the process which had led to the *Reich*'s diplomatic isolation.[1] Others, such as Paul Cambon, the French ambassador to London, took a different view. Cambon described the King's death as 'un grand malheur pour l'Angleterre'. Edward VII had been, in the ambassador's view, England's pre-eminent statesman, and had possessed a special competence in matters of foreign policy.[2] Lord Esher, a close friend and adviser to Edward VII, echoed Cambon's assessment of the King's significance: 'He had an instinct for statecraft which carried him straight to the core of a great problem, without deep thought or profound knowledge of the subject. He had one supreme gift, and this was his unerring judgement of men and women.'[3]

The statesmen who served in governments during Edward VII's reign were some of the first to question the idea that he had played a significant part in the formation and implementation of British foreign policy. In 1915, Arthur Balfour, who had been the Conservative prime minister from 1902 to 1905, wrote to Lord Lansdowne, who had served in the same government as foreign secretary, that he had been puzzled to read a history of pre-war diplomacy which attributed the policy of *entente* to Edward VII. Balfour recalled the King's role as having been a much less significant one: 'during the years which you and I were his

[1] See ch. 2.
[2] Paul Cambon to his son, 7 May 1910, Henri Cambon (ed.), *Paul Cambon: Correspondance, 1870–1924*, 3 vols. (Paris, 1940), II, p. 299.
[3] Esher, journal entry, 7 May 1910, Esher Papers, Churchill College, Cambridge, ESHR 2/12.

141

Ministers, he never made an important suggestion of any sort on the larger questions of policy.'[4] Similarly, in his memoirs, Sir Edward Grey, the foreign secretary in the Liberal government of 1905 to 1914, dismissed as a 'legend' the idea that British foreign policy had been due to Edward VII's 'initiative, instigation and control.' According to Grey, the King, 'not only accepted that policy must be that of his Ministers, but he preferred that it should be so'.[5]

Professional historians have tended to accept the judgements of Balfour and Grey. The author of one influential work on British foreign policy in the early years of the twentieth century has written with regard to the role of Edward VII: 'The great diplomatic developments of his reign . . . were negotiated by his Ministers and their diplomacy owed nothing to him.'[6] This interpretation has become the orthodox view of the King's role in British diplomacy and has contributed to Edward VII's virtual absence in modern analyses of British foreign policy during his reign.[7] In contrast, Edward VII's life has proved a fruitful subject for royal biographers, most of whom have been balanced in their judgements,[8] though one biography in particular undermined its case by giving the impression that Edward VII had masterminded the policy of *entente* and by misinterpreting the workings of the British constitution, to the extent of implying that the King acted, on occasion, like an absolute monarch.[9]

Diplomatic historians have applied false terms of reference when examining Edward VII's role in international relations. If diplomacy is understood solely by the narrow, and old-fashioned, definition of negotiations between the ministers and bureaucrats of the Great Powers, then the role of the monarch is bound to be marginalised. For even in a state where the monarch possessed considerable authority over the executive, such as Wilhelmine Germany, the sovereign took only a peripheral part in day-to-day decision making, and instead intervened

---

[4] Quoted in Lord Newton, *Lord Lansdowne* (London, 1929), p. 293.
[5] Viscount Grey of Fallodon, *Twenty-five Years, 1892–1916*, 2 vols. (London, 1925), I, p. 205.
[6] G. W. Monger, *The End of Isolation: British Foreign Policy, 1900–1907* (London, 1963), p. 263.
[7] Paul M. Kennedy, *The Rise of the Anglo-German Antagonism, 1860–1914* (London, 1980), pp. 400–3; Zara S. Steiner, *The Foreign Office and Foreign Policy, 1898–1914* (Cambridge, 1969), pp. 202–7; Zara S. Steiner, *Britain and the Origins of the First World War* (London, 1977); M. L. Dockrill and C. J Lowe, *The Mirage of Power. British Foreign Policy, 1902–1914* (London, 1972).
[8] Sir Sidney Lee, *King Edward VII*, 2 vols. (London, 1925–27); Sir Philip Magnus, *King Edward the Seventh* (London, 1964); Giles St Aubyn, *Edward VII. Prince and King* (London, 1979).
[9] Gordon Brook-Shepherd, *Uncle of Europe. The Social and Diplomatic Life of King Edward VII* (London, 1975), pp. 182, 247.

at specific times when he wished to see the course of policy changed, or the office-bearers replaced.[10] Such a definition is even more inappropriate when applied to the British monarchy during the reign of Edward VII because political power had long passed to the executive and the monarch's role was restricted to an advisory capacity. When a wider definition of diplomacy is applied, Edward VII appears as a more important figure. He retained powers in several areas which allowed him to influence the course of British foreign policy and to play a positive role in the cultivation of Britain's relations with the other European powers. The King retained a large measure of influence over diplomatic appointments. He possessed a considerable degree of freedom with regard to his dealings with the diplomats and ministers of foreign countries. Most importantly, by virtue of his position, Edward VII played a crucial role in his country's dealings with the sovereigns of the other Great Powers, many of whom were his close relatives. It is through an examination of these areas that a true picture of Edward VII's role in British diplomacy emerges.

Edward VII's influence was brought to bear most prominently in political terms in the sphere of Anglo-French relations. He had been an enthusiastic supporter of Anglo-French co-operation since his youth, a fact which had caused disquiet in some foreign capitals, notably Berlin.[11] Within a year of coming to the throne, and frustrated by the difficulty of reaching an understanding with Germany, he had come to the conclusion that it would be in Britain's interests to seek an agreement with France, which would involve a recognition by France of Britain's pre-eminent place in Egypt, in return for British acceptance of Morocco as a French sphere of influence.[12] However, in the spring of 1902, the mood in France towards England remained hostile, due to French sympathy for the Boers, with whom the British were still at war in South Africa. As a consequence, the French press made clear that a visit from Edward VII to Paris would not be welcome.[13] By the end of 1902, Joseph Chamberlain, the colonial secretary, had come to the conclusion that Britain's international position had been so weakened by the South

[10] John C. G. Röhl, *Kaiser, Hof und Staat: Wilhelm II. und die deutsche Politik* (Munich, 1987), pp. 116–40; English translation: *The Kaiser and his Court. Wilhelm II and the Government of Germany* (Cambridge, 1994), pp.107–30.
[11] See ch. 2.
[12] Hermann Freiherr von Eckardstein, *Ten Years at the Court of St James*, English translation (London, 1921), pp. 228–30.
[13] Radolin to Bülow, 21 March 1902, PA Bonn England Nr 81 Nr 1 Bd 9.

African war, that it would be desirable to seek agreements with France and Russia. However, Balfour and Lansdowne were much more sceptical.[14]

The intelligence which Edward VII was receiving in the autumn of 1902 indicated that there was burgeoning enthusiasm in France for an understanding with England. On 2 November 1902, the King's brother-in-law, King George of the Hellenes, wrote to him following a visit to Paris, informing him that President Loubet[15] had spoken of his wish that the French people 'might understand clearly that it only could be in the interest of France to be on the most intimate footing with England'.[16] Edward VII's own desire for an agreement with France came across in discussions which he held with Paul Cambon, the French ambassador to London, at Windsor in January 1903. The King emphasized that he believed that the affairs of Morocco should be settled exclusively by England, France and Spain, and that Germany, whose interests in Morocco were minor, should be left out of the discussions. The Austrian ambassador, Count Deym, who was also at Windsor, told Cambon that King Edward was favourably disposed towards France and using his influence with the British government in favour of an *entente cordiale* with her. At the same time, the King had spoken in flattering terms of Théophile Delcassé, the French foreign minister, to whom he attributed much of the improvement in Anglo-French relations.[17]

Behind the scenes, the King was making plans for a state visit to the French capital. The arrangements for Edward VII's visit to Paris were made in the greatest possible secrecy. Initially, not even Queen Alexandra and Lord Knollys, the King's private secretary, were aware of his plan. Unusually, the King did not inform the British ambassador to Paris, Sir Edward Monson, nor his ministers, of his intentions. Instead, the preliminary negotiations were carried on between Colonel Stuart-Wortley, the British military attaché in the French capital, and President Loubet.[18] The first individual, other than Stuart-Wortley and Loubet, to be informed of the King's intentions was Luis de Soveral, the Portuguese minister in London, and a close friend of the British royal family. On 1 March 1903, he was summoned to Buckingham Palace by the King. The latter informed him of his plan to pay visits to the King of

[14] Monger, *The End of Isolation*, pp. 107–14.
[15] Emile Loubet, 1838–1929. French President, 1899–1906.
[16] King George of the Hellenes to Edward VII, 2 November 1902, RA W 43/3a.
[17] Paul Cambon to Delcassé, 29 January 1903, *DDF*, 2nd series, III, no. 49, pp. 65–8.
[18] St Aubyn, *Edward VII: Prince and King*, pp. 320–1.

Portugal at Lisbon, the King of Italy at Rome, and the President of the French republic at Paris. In a telegram to the King of Portugal, Soveral noted that Edward VII had told him that 'political considerations of the highest order' lay behind his decision. The King had told him that the secrecy surrounding his trip was necessary because of the suspicion which the visits could produce in 'the powers of the North', Germany and Russia.[19]

By early March, Sir Edward Monson had begun to suspect that Edward VII was using a private channel in order to communicate with the French President. On 11 March 1903, he wrote to Lord Lansdowne, in some confusion after receiving a curious communication from Stuart Wortley, enquiring after the dates of a visit which President Loubet was to pay to Algiers and its likely duration. 'His message implied that he had been charged to procure this information for the King.' Monson speculated that if the enquiry had originated from the King it would have been communicated to him and not to the military attaché, but he made clear that, in his view, a visit by the King to France would be 'most welcome.'[20] The extent of the foreign secretary's ignorance about the King's plans was revealed in a letter which he wrote to Monson on the same day. Lansdowne stated that he felt sure that the King would prefer to meet Loubet at Cannes, rather than at Paris.[21] This impression was corrected by the King himself in a note which he penned in his own hand, indicating that he wished to meet the French President at Paris on 2 and 3 May.[22] President Loubet exhibited 'unmistakeable delight' at the prospect of the King's visit and 'said that a visit from the King would in the present temper of France do an amount of good which is probably not realised in England', drawing attention to the immense popularity which Edward VII had enjoyed in Paris as Prince of Wales.[23]

In his memoirs, Sir Frederick Ponsonby, Edward VII's equerry and assistant private secretary, recalled that Lord Lansdowne and the British foreign office had opposed the King's decision to visit Paris in 1903 for fear that he would meet with a hostile reaction from the French crowds.[24] However, political considerations as well as security fears

---

[19] Soveral to King Dom Carlos of Portugal, 1 March 1903, Brook Shepherd, *Uncle of Europe*, pp. 153–5.

[20] Sir Edward Monson to Lord Lansdowne, 11 March 1903. Lansdowne Papers, FO 800/125.

[21] Lansdowne to Monson, 11 March 1903, *ibid.*

[22] Note by Edward VII, 13 March 1903, *ibid.*

[23] Monson to Lansdowne, 13 March 1903, *ibid.*; Knollys to Monson, 17 March 1903, *ibid.*

[24] Sir Frederick Ponsonby, *Recollections of Three Reigns* (London, 1951), p. 169; Lord Hardinge of Penshurst, *Old Diplomacy* (London, 1947), p. 87.

motivated Lansdowne's attitude. The impetus for closer Anglo-French relations had come disproportionately from the French side, and in particular from Delcassé. Since the Fashoda crisis of 1898, when Britain and France had been on the verge of war over a dispute relating to their mutual territorial claims in the Nile valley, the French foreign minister had gradually become convinced of the advantages of a colonial agreement between the two powers.[25] By contrast, in March 1903, Lord Lansdowne sent two letters to Edward VII emphasizing that the British government had no intention of reaching an understanding with France over the partition of Morocco, suggesting a more lukewarm attitude on the British side.[26] The King's visit to Paris was to transform the atmosphere between the two powers and allow this impasse to be broken.

At the time of Edward VII's arrival in Lisbon, in the first week of April, Soveral and the members of the King's entourage revealed to the French minister in the Portuguese capital, M. Rouvier, that the King saw his visit to Paris as being of immense political importance, and aimed at contributing towards an Anglo-French *rapprochement*.[27] During his visit to Lisbon, the King stressed to Rouvier how much he was looking forward to meeting President Loubet and visiting Paris.[28] After Edward VII's departure from Portugal, King Dom Carlos confirmed to the French minister that the British monarch's decision to visit Paris was his alone. Furthermore, in conversation with Rouvier, Soveral had stressed the strong anti-German sentiment existing in England and the popularity with which a *rapprochement* with France would be welcomed there. Rouvier believed that Soveral's views echoed those of King Edward.[29]

Nevertheless, it is doubtful that Edward VII himself saw his visit to Paris as being in any way directed against Germany. At Lisbon, the King went out of his way to be courteous to the German minister, Tattenbach, stressing his desire to see friendly relations between Britain and Germany. Wilhelm II, who read Tattenbach's report, accepted the King's assurances, though he doubted that Edward's sentiments were shared by the British government, people and press.[30] In a conversation

[25] Christopher Andrew, *Théophile Delcassé and the Making of the Entente Cordiale. A Reappraisal of French Foreign Policy, 1898–1905* (London, 1968); Gordon A. Craig and Alexander L. George, *Force & Statecraft: Diplomatic Problems of our Time*, 2nd edition (Oxford, 1990), pp. 251–4.

[26] Lansdowne to Edward VII, 7 March 1903, RA W 43/60; Lansdowne to Knollys, 9 March 1903, RA W 43/61.

[27] Rouvier to Delcassé, 5 April 1903, *DDF*, 2nd series, III, no. 161, p. 219.

[28] Rouvier to Delcassé, 12 April 1903, *ibid.*, no. 177, p. 243.

[29] Rouvier to Delcassé, 12 April 1903, *ibid.*, no. 178, pp. 244–6.

[30] Wilhelm II's comment on Tattenbach to Bülow, 7 April 1903, PA Bonn England Nr 81 Nr 1 Bd 11a.

with Tattenbach, following Edward VII's departure from Lisbon, Soveral emphasised that the British monarch was favourably disposed towards Germany and that the King's trip to Paris would not lead to a fundamental improvement in Anglo-French relations. This statement was in direct contradiction to the comments made by Soveral to Rouvier, and was no doubt made in order to allay German suspicions.[31]

Edward VII was in no way assured of a unanimously warm reception in Paris. Monson reported to Lansdowne that the Anglophobe press was active in opposing the King's journey to the French capital.[32] Nevertheless, the King's visit to Paris was a resounding success, surpassing all expectations. The Hon. Charles Hardinge, who accompanied the King as minister-in-attendance, and whose rise within the foreign office had been assisted by royal patronage,[33] described the visit as the 'turning point' in Anglo-French relations.[34] Edward VII's speeches during the visit, which had been written by Hardinge, but echoed the King's own views, made clear his desire to see greater co-operation between Britain and France, and made an excellent impression on his hosts.[35] During discussions with Loubet and Delcassé during the visit, the King appears to have overstepped his constitutional role by emphasising his desire to see an Anglo-French agreement, and, if possible, also a colonial agreement between England and Russia. It was Edward VII's attitude, more than anything else, which convinced Delcassé that an agreement with Britain was possible.[36]

Thus, the King's visit to Paris acted as a catalyst, which persuaded Delcassé to open negotiations with London, and it also created the atmosphere of good-will, which was necessary before such an understanding could be arrived at.[37] The positive effect of the King's visit to the French capital was reinforced by a return visit paid by President Loubet to London in July 1903. On 6 July 1903, Delcassé wrote to Lansdowne stressing his eagerness for an agreement with England based on their respective rights in Egypt and Morocco. Balfour told the King

[31] Tattenbach to Bülow, 17 April 1903, *ibid.*
[32] Monson to Lansdowne, 24 April 1903. Lansdowne Papers, PRO FO 800/125.
[33] Hardinge, *Old Diplomacy*, p. 84; Dockrill and Lowe, *The Mirage of Power*, p. 19; Monger, *The End of Isolation*, p. 101; Steiner, *The Foreign Office*, pp. 91–2, 102, 203–4.
[34] Hardinge, *Old Diplomacy*, pp. 95–6.
[35] Lee, *King Edward VII*, II, pp. 236–43; Magnus, *Edward the Seventh*, pp. 308–12; St Aubyn, *Edward VII: Prince and King*, p. 325; P. J. V. Rolo, *Entente Cordiale. The Origins and Negotiation of the Anglo-French Agreements of 8 August 1904* (London, 1969), pp. 164–6.
[36] Andrew, *Théophile Delcassé*, pp. 208–9; St Aubyn, *Edward VII*, II, pp. 326–7; Rolo, *Entente Cordiale*, pp. 166–7.
[37] Monson to Lansdowne, 15 May 1903, Lansdowne Papers, PRO FO 800/125.

that the British cabinet were 'unanimous in their wish to proceed with the negotiations'.[38] During the course of Loubet's visit, Edward VII appears to have spoken with the same candour as during his own visit to Paris. Delcassé recalled that they had agreed that it was 'necessary to organize a vast coalition which could stand up to Germany if the necessity arose'. The discussions also dealt with Anglo-Russian relations. The King had stated: 'Russia is indispensible if Germany is to be kept in awe of us', and had asked Delcassé to use his influence at St Petersburg in favour of Anglo-Russian friendship.[39]

At the time of the signing of the Anglo-French agreement in April 1904, there was a general feeling in both countries that King Edward VII's visit to Paris had played a major part in smoothing the way towards a *rapprochement*. Lansdowne made this clear in a letter to Monson, on the day after the agreement had been concluded,[40] and his views were echoed by others.[41] However, the significance of the King's intervention was best put by Paul Cambon, the French ambassador in London. He remarked that, 'any clerk at the Foreign Office could draw up a treaty', but that it was only Edward VII, 'who could have succeeded in producing the right atmosphere for a rapprochement'.[42] The King appreciated that the success of the detailed negotiations was due to the efforts of Lansdowne and Delcassé, and he congratulated both of them on their work.[43] However, he was also realistic enough to appreciate that his visit to Paris had helped to prepare the ground for the Anglo-French agreement.[44]

In the years following the signing of the *entente*, Edward VII's commitment to it remained absolute. During the first Moroccan crisis in 1905/6, when the German government tried to undermine Anglo-French relations by challenging France's claims in Morocco, the King gave strong support to the French foreign minister, Delcassé, and the French position. He was outraged by Wilhelm II's landing at Tangiers,

---

[38] Andrew, *Théophile Delcassé*, pp. 210–1.
[39] Maurice Paléologue, *The Turning Point. Three Critical Years, 1904–1906*, English translation (London, 1935); diary entry, 26 May 1904, pp. 83–4.
[40] Lansdowne to Monson, 8 April 1904, RA W 44/61.
[41] Vicomte d'Harcourt to Sir E. C. Phipps, 2 April 1904, RA W 44/49; Crozier to Goschen, 11 April 1904, RA W 44/65; Hardinge, *Old Diplomacy*, p. 96; Ponsonby, *Recollections*, p. 173.
[42] Quoted in St Aubyn, *Edward VII: Prince and King*, p. 329.
[43] Edward VII to Lansdowne, 7 April 1904, RA W 44/54; Lansdowne to Edward VII, 13 April 1904, RA W 44 /85; Paul Cambon to Delcassé, 21 April 1904, DDF, 2nd series, v, no. 47, pp. 55–6.
[44] Cambon to Delcassé, 21 April 1904, *ibid*.

which precipitated the crisis,[45] and by German attempts to force Delcassé from office, which he learned of from the British ambassador to Paris, Sir Francis Bertie.[46] The King showed his support for the French position by meeting President Loubet on his way to join the royal yacht for the start of his Mediterranean cruise, an encounter to which *The Times* ascribed 'special and unmistakeable significance'.[47] During his cruise, the King sent a telegram to Delcassé, encouraging him not to give in to German threats and resist the temptation to resign.[48]

While passing through Paris, on his way back to England, Edward VII had two long and well-publicised meetings with Delcassé. The King made clear that he believed that the Franco-German dispute over Morocco should be settled by negotiation,[49] a view which he repeated to the German ambassador in the French capital, Hugo Prince von Radolin.[50] However, one of the King's closest French friends, the Marquis de Breteuil, confirmed to Maurice Paléologue, a secretary in the French foreign ministry, that Edward VII had stated that France's Moroccan policy was 'beyond reproach from the point of view of international law'. Breteuil was also 'morally certain' that the King would support British intervention, on the French side, in the event of war between France and Germany, though the ultimate decision would be made by the British government.[51]

Throughout the Moroccan crisis, Edward VII gave his whole-hearted backing to the French and was mindful of French sensitvities, not least over his relationship with his nephew, the Kaiser. The King still adhered to the view which he had expressed to Paul Cambon in January 1903, namely that the affairs of Morocco should be settled between England, France and Spain. He made this evident in a conversation with Paul Cambon in June 1905. The King urged Cambon to oppose German demands for a conference to settle the Moroccan crisis. He believed that if France were to accept this, it would constitute an unacceptable humiliation. Wilhelm II was, in the King's view, only interested in his *amour propre*, and a firm stance would force him to back down.[52]

In August 1905, the King gave his support to a visit by the French fleet

---

[45] See ch. 2. [46] Sir Francis Bertie to Edward VII, 22 April 1905, RA W 46/1.
[47] Andrew, *Théophile Delcassé*, p. 280.
[48] Delcassé to Bompard, 25 April 1905, *DDF*, 2nd series, VI, no. 353, pp. 418–19.
[49] Paléologue, *The Turning Point*, diary entries, 2 and 7 May 1905, pp. 239, 242.
[50] Radolin to Bülow, 1 May 1905, *GP*, xx(ii), no. 6848, pp. 616–17.
[51] Paléologue, *The Turning Point*, diary entry, 20 May 1905, p. 250.
[52] Paul Cambon to Rouvier, 14 June 1905, *DDF*, 2nd series, VII, no. 58, pp. 65–6.

to the ports of the English Channel coast, which reinforced the friendly feeling between Britain and France, as well as sending a powerful message of Anglo-French solidarity to Berlin.[53] One of the many reasons for Edward VII's refusal to meet the Kaiser on his way to the Bohemian spa of Marienbad in the late summer of 1905 was his desire not to upset the French.[54] The King, in turn, was rewarded for his support for France with the confidence of the French government. This was most clearly illustrated by the events of December 1905. The coming to power of a Liberal government in Britain during that month gave rise to fears in Paris about the stability of the Anglo-French *entente*. The French were particularly concerned that if the Earl of Rosebery were to be appointed foreign secretary instead of the pro-French Sir Edward Grey, 'he would try to come to some arrangement with Germany.'[55] Although Grey was chosen, the King represented a reassuring figure for the French during the period of transition. On 18 December 1905, M. Rouvier, the French foreign minister, wrote to Paul Cambon informing him that King Alphonso of Spain had become convinced following a visit to Berlin that Wilhelm II was planning an imminent act of aggression against France. The Kaiser had tried to persuade the Spanish monarch to station troops on France's southern frontier in order to tie down some of the French army. Rouvier believed that the alarming nature of this information necessitated that Edward VII be informed, drawing attention to the strength of the King's commitment to Anglo-French co-operation. Significantly, he did not believe that the new Liberal government should be told, seeing this as premature.[56]

Cambon was received by Edward VII on 20 December 1905. The King was alarmed by the information which the ambassador gave him and authorised Cambon to inform Grey and the prime minister, Sir Henry Campbell-Bannermann. However, Edward told the ambassador not to divulge that King Alphonso was the source of the information. The King, who had an acute appreciation of the Kaiser's character, continued to believe that Wilhelm would not risk a war over Morocco. The first sea lord, Admiral Sir John Fisher, was convinced, the King informed Cambon, that the German fleet was not capable of taking on the Royal Navy. The French ambassador was not fully reassured and

[53] Edward VII to Sir Ernest Cassel, 17 August 1905, Cassel Papers, Broadlands Archives, Southampton University Library, MB1/X2; Rouvier to Lansdowne, 14 August 1905, RA W 46/228; Lansdowne to Rouvier, 14 August 1905, RA W 46/229.

[54] Knollys to Lascelles, 8 August 1905; Knollys to Lascelles, 14 August 1905; Knollys to Lascelles, 23 September 1905, Lascelles Papers PRO FO 800/12.

[55] Bertie to Knollys, 5 December 1905, RA W 47/353.

[56] Rouvier to Paul Cambon, 18 December 1905, *DDF*, 2nd series, VIII, no. 246, pp. 335–6.

pressed the King as to the military assistance which Britain would extend to France in the event of a German attack. Edward VII, who as a constitutional sovereign was not in a position to offer military guarantees, answered evasively, but gave the impression that the new Liberal government was unlikely to provide ground troops to assist the French, but might provide naval support.[57]

Edward VII continued to give his full backing to France during the early months of 1906, when the Algeciras conference, convened to settle the Moroccan crisis, was in session. Sir Donald Mackenzie Wallace, the former foreign editor of *The Times*, passed through Paris in January 1906 on his way to Algeciras. While in the French capital, Wallace was able to give President Loubet an assurance that the King shared his belief in the need to maintain the *entente*.[58] In late January, Edward VII received Cambon at Windsor, along with three individuals whose commitment to Anglo-French co-operation was absolute, Grey, Sir Charles Hardinge, the recently appointed permanent undersecretary at the foreign office, and Sir Francis Bertie, the British ambassador to Paris.[59] In addition, when the King passed through Paris, on his way to Biarritz, in March 1906, he assured M. Fallières, Loubet's successor as French President, and the foreign minister, Rouvier, that Britain could be relied upon, and that there was no substance to reports emanating from Germany that Britain wished to provoke a Franco-German war.[60]

One historian has suggested that Edward VII's attitude was far from consistent in the first months of 1906. He has drawn attention to an improvement in relations between the King and his nephew the Kaiser at the beginning of that year, and attempts by courtiers and the foreign office to dissuade Edward from meeting Wilhelm during his Mediterranean cruise in the spring of 1906, to imply that the King's attitude towards Germany became more conciliatory at this time.[61] Such a view is not supported by the sources. While it is true that an exchange of letters between the King and the Kaiser, at the beginning of 1906, did lead to a temporary improvement in their personal relationship,[62] there

---

[57] Paul Cambon to Rouvier, 21 December 1905, *ibid.*, no. 262, pp. 359–66.
[58] Sir Donald Mackenzie Wallace to Lord Knollys, 14 January 1906, RA W 48/9.
[59] Paul Cambon to his son, 27 January 1906. Cambon, *Correspondance*, ii, p. 207; Paul Cambon to Rouvier, 25 January 1906, *DDF*, 2nd series, ix(i), no. 55, pp. 88–91.
[60] Bertie to Grey, 5 March 1906, *BD*, iii, no. 327, p. 284.
[61] Monger, *The End of Isolation*, p. 262.
[62] Edward VII to Wilhelm II, 23 January 1906, PA Bonn England Nr 78 geheim. Bd 8; Wilhelm II to Edward VII, 1 February 1906, RA X37/62.

is no evidence that it resulted in a political *rapprochement* between them. Edward VII received the German ambassador to London, Count Wolff-Metternich, at Buckingham Palace, on 4 February 1906. Metternich's report, on his conversation with the King, was annotated several times by Wilhelm II. Thus the views of the two monarchs on the subject of the Moroccan crisis can be contrasted directly. Their opinions were at odds with one another on every important issue, with the King defending the actions of the French at Algeciras and elsewhere. From the German viewpoint, the only positive aspect of Edward VII's stance was his desire to see the Moroccan crisis solved through concessions from both Paris and Berlin.[63]

The King's willingness to meet the Kaiser during his Mediterranean cruise was an error of judgement, but not a sign that he had become pro-German politically. It reflected the fact that his family obligations and political interests were not always in harmony, and also a lack of appreciation on Edward VII's part that every act of his was seen as being of political significance. He gave way once Hardinge and Knollys brought the certainty of French objections to such a meeting to his attention.[64] The King had in no way wished to betray the French, and, at worst, had been guilty of naivity. Edward VII's support for the French position on Morocco had remained steadfast throughout.[65] It should also be noted in this context that, by the middle of March 1906, the Kaiser had again become hostile to Edward VII, believing that the King wished to thwart German ambitions in Morocco at all costs, and was trying to enlist the support of the Spanish, as well as the French, for this purpose.[66] Germany's eventual humiliation at the Algeciras conference, when she was left completely isolated, aside from the support of Austria, was seen by Friedrich von Holstein as confirmation of Edward VII's political sagacity. The King had predicted all along that the Kaiser would give in, and he had proved to be correct.[67]

In the years that followed, down to his death in 1910, King Edward continued to do all that he could, in a supportive capacity, to strengthen

---

[63] Metternich to Bülow, 4 February 1906, PA Bonn England Nr 78 geheim. Bd 8.

[64] Hardinge to Knollys, 22 February and 5 March 1906, RA W 48/65 and RA W 48/79; Knollys to Hardinge, 4 March 1906, Hardinge Papers, University Library, Cambridge, vol. 9.

[65] Hardinge to Lascelles, 26 February 1906, Lascelles Papers, PRO FO 800/13.

[66] Robert Graf von Zedlitz-Trützschler, *Twelve Years at the Imperial German Court*, English translation (London, 1924), diary entry, 13 March 1906, p. 160; Wilhelm II's comments on Stumm to Bülow, 9 March 1906, *GP*, xxi(i), no. 7082, p. 268; Wilhelm II to Bülow, 11 February 1906, *HP*, iv, no. 933, p. 395.

[67] Holstein to Maximilian von Brandt, 10 April 1906, memorandum by Holstein, 17 May 1906, *HP*, iv, nos. 959, 983, pp. 410–1, 427.

the links between Britain and France. Thus, when the King eventually did meet Wilhelm II, at Friedrichshof, in the summer of 1906, both he and his entourage went out of their way to play down the visit's significance, and to emphasize its private character; stressing that the Anglo-French *entente* remained secure.[68] When the King and the Kaiser again met in Germany, at Wilhelmshöhe in August 1907, Hardinge assured Paul Cambon beforehand that Edward had only agreed to the visit because Wilhelm had insisted upon it and that the King would avoid politics in his discussions with his nephew.[69] After his visit to Wilhelm II at Wilhelmshöhe and to Franz Joseph, the Emperor of Austria, at Bad Ischl, ever mindful of French sensitivities, the King received the French premier, Georges Clemenceau at Marienbad. The prospect of the interview caused concern to German diplomats,[70] but Wilhelm von Stumm, the *Geschäftsträger* at the German embassy in London, appreciated correctly that the purpose of the King's invitation to Clemenceau was to show that his meetings with the German and Austrian emperors had in no way undermined Anglo-French relations.[71] Both Hardinge and Grey were delighted by the King's decision to meet the French premier, an invitation made on his own initiative.[72]

Edward VII established a relationship of trust with Clemenceau, similar to that which he had previously enjoyed with Théophile Delcassé. When passing through Paris on his way to Biarritz, in March 1908, he met Clemenceau and the French Foreign Minister, Pichon. The King told Hardinge that his meeting with the two French statesmen had been a success, and that Pichon had agreed to accompany President Fallières on an official visit to England the following May.[73] The principal topic of political conversation between the King and his two guests was Morocco and Edward VII 'expressed to them the pleasure he felt at the co-operation of France with Spain'.[74] Hardinge complimented the King on his decision to meet Clemenceau and Pichon, seeing it as politically beneficial.[75]

[68] Paul Cambon to M. Bourgeois, 26 June 1906, *DDF*, 2nd. series, x, no. 120, pp. 186–9; Geoffray to Bourgeois, 22 August 1906, *ibid.*, no. 187, p. 287; Paul Cambon to Bourgeois, 29 August 1906, *ibid.*, no. 192, p. 287.

[69] Paul Cambon to M. Pichon, 8 August 1907, *DDF*, 2nd series, xi, no. 123, p. 209.

[70] Graf Brockdorff-Rantzau to Bülow, 20 August 1907, *GP*, xxiv, no. 8163, p. 9.

[71] Wilhelm von Stumm to Bülow, 22 August 1907, *ibid.*, no. 8164, pp. 9–10.

[72] Hardinge to Edward VII, 26 August 1907. RA W 52/15; Edward VII to Hardinge, 30 August 1907, Hardinge Papers, vol. 9.

[73] Edward VII to Hardinge, 10 March 1907, Hardinge Papers, vol. 14.

[74] Sir Arthur Davidson to Hardinge, 6 March 1908, *ibid.*

[75] Hardinge to Edward VII, 7 March 1908, RA W 53/21.

Although the evidence is sketchy, it seems that Edward VII and Clemenceau also discussed the contentious question of the military assistance which Britain would offer to France in the event of war between the latter country and Germany, during their meeting in Paris. In a letter to Hardinge in April 1907, Edward VII had drawn attention to Clemenceau's concerns about a rumour that the British prime minister, Campbell Bannerman, had stated, 'that England would refuse sending Forces to the assistance of France when in need of it.' The prime minister had denied making such an announcement, but the King remained sceptical, believing that Clemenceau would not have 'invented such a statement'.[76] In April 1908, following Edward VII's meeting with Clemenceau, Sir Frederick Ponsonby wrote to Lord Esher, the King's close friend, and a member of the Committee of Imperial Defence, on the contentious issue of army reform. The King believed, Ponsonby reported, that Britain had become 'the laughing stock of Europe', because of the lack of preparedness of her armed forces.[77]

King Edward's enthusiasm for greater Anglo-French military cooperation increased during 1908, particularly as a consequence of his disastrous meeting with the Kaiser at Friedrichshof in August of that year, when Wilhelm II made clear, in conversation with Hardinge, that under no circumstances would he give in to British pressure for an agreement limiting the pace of German naval construction. This, more than anything else, convinced Edward VII that no political accommodation was possible with Germany.[78] During his subsequent stay at Marienbad, the King held discussions with Clemenceau, and, on this occasion, spoke with great frankness on matters of foreign and military policy. Clemenceau had stated, in an interview with the journalist H. Wickham Steed, shortly before his meeting with Edward VII, that he was greatly concerned by the limited nature of the support which the British would be able to give France on land in the event of a German attack.[79] The King sent a transcript of Steed's interview to Hardinge, and emphasised his sympathy with Clemenceau's fears.[80]

Edward VII spoke candidly to Clemenceau when they met on 26 August 1908. He asserted that Britain would continue to build battle-

[76] Edward VII to Hardinge, 27 April 1907, Hardinge Papers, vol. 9.
[77] Ponsonby to Esher, 11 April 1908, Esher Papers, ESHR 6/2.
[78] Edward VII to Cassel, 15 August 1908, Cassel Papers, MB1/xi; Edward VII's minute on Cartwright to Grey, 14 August 1908, *BD*, vi, no. 114, p. 180.
[79] H. Wickham Steed, *Through Thirty Years*, 2 vols. (London, 1924–5), i, pp. 284–8.
[80] Edward VII to Hardinge, 25 August 1908, Hardinge Papers, vol. 14.

ships, at a faster rate than Germany, until the latter power agreed to a compromise solution to the naval race. The King also stressed that he supported Clemenceau's view on the need for Britain to have a strong army, as well as a large fleet, but he was sceptical as to the British government agreeing to such a policy.[81] The steadfast nature of the King's commitment to the *entente* and desire to see it strengthened militarily, was underlined in a conversation between Lord Esher and the French military attaché, Lieutenant Colonel Huguet, in November 1908. Esher told Huguet that he was convinced that the King would favour British intervention on the side of France in the event of a Franco-German war, and that Edward VII's attitude would be shared by Sir Edward Grey.[82] The King's views did not change in the final eighteen months of his life, and he opposed German offers for a naval agreement linked to a British promise of neutrality in the event of a continental war.[83]

Edward VII's role in Anglo-French relations can thus be seen to have been broadly positive. He was not solely responsible for the creation of the *entente cordiale*, nor should he be given the credit for the negotiation of the Anglo-French agreement, nor for British policy towards France during his reign. These accolades must be accorded to his ministers. Nevertheless, it was the King's visit to Paris in May 1903 which helped to remove the atmosphere of suspicion between the two powers and create the good-will which was a pre-condition of agreement between them. In the years following the signing of the *entente*, in April 1904, he remained a consistent supporter of France, notably during the Moroccan crisis, and established relationships of trust with Loubet, Delcassé and Clemenceau, to the benefit of Anglo-French relations.

Edward VII's attitude towards Russia was characterised by an ambivalence which was absent from his view of France. He expressed doubts, in a letter to Lord Lansdowne in December 1902, about the wisdom of reaching a colonial agreement with Russia,[84] but his active support remained crucial if such an accord were to be arrived at, for only through the King could the Tsar be reached, and no understanding

---

[81] Clemenceau to Pichon, 29 August 1908, *DDF*, 2nd series, XI, no. 434, pp. 749–52; Edward VII to Hardinge, 29 August 1908, Hardinge Papers, vol. 14; Edward VII to Sir Ernest Cassel, 3 September 1908, Cassel Papers, MB1/X1; Edward VII's minute on Goschen to Grey, 29 August 1908, *BD*, VI, no. 100, p. 158.
[82] Lt. Colonel Huguet to General Picquart, 9 November 1908, *DDF*, 2nd series, XI, p. 933.
[83] Knollys to Hardinge, 13 November 1909, Hardinge Papers, Vol. 18.
[84] Monger, *The End of Isolation*, p. 109.

would be possible without Nicholas II's approval. By the autumn of 1903, the King had overcome his initial doubts as to the desirability of an Anglo-Russian *rapprochement*,[85] and was willing to give it his encouragement.

Nicholas II was Edward VII's nephew by marriage, being the son of Queen Alexandra's sister, Dagmar, the consort of Tsar Alexander III, known in Russia as Tsarina Marie Feodorovna. These family ties had been reinforced in 1894 through Nicholas's marriage to Princess Alix of Hesse, who was Edward's niece, being the daughter of his sister Princess Alice. Edward visited Russia in November 1894, as Prince of Wales, for the funeral of his brother-in-law, Alexander III. In the years that followed, the Prince of Wales did succeed in winning the young Tsar's trust and subsequently they began to correspond on a regular basis.[86] Nevertheless, despite the warmth of their friendship, the Prince of Wales and the Tsar had reservations about each other. The Prince habitually described his nephew as being 'weak as water'.[87] Nicholas's doubts about his uncle related more to the raffish company which the latter kept.[88]

After the Prince of Wales came to the throne in 1901, he and Nicholas exchanged letters about the South African War. The Tsar believed that British policy was unjust and he appealed to his uncle to stop the bloodshed.[89] In his reply, Edward VII vigorously defended the conduct of the British forces.[90] Despite this disagreement, Nicholas was generally favourably disposed towards Edward VII, a statement which could not be made about his attitude to Britain and its political system. When the Kaiser's brother, Prince Heinrich of Prussia, visited the Tsar at his hunting lodge at Spala, in Poland, in the autumn of 1901, he found that Nicholas's warm feelings for Edward VII were not matched by a respect for Britain's constitution and the British monarch's political role. Nicholas was distrustful of England politically, contemptuous of the British parliamentary system, and regarded Edward VII as 'having no right to say anything in his own country'.[91] Nevertheless, between 1903

---

[85] This may have been due, in part, to the influence of his friend, Charles Hardinge, at that time under secretary of state at the foreign office. The latter had become convinced of the desirability of a colonial agreement with Russia by 1903. Hardinge, *Old Diplomacy*, p. 84.

[86] Magnus, *Edward the Seventh*, pp. 246–9.

[87] *Ibid.*, p. 249.

[88] Nicholas II to Marie Feodorovna, 27 June/9 July 1894, Edward J. Bing (ed.), *The Letters of Tsar Nicholas and Empress Marie*, English translation (London, 1937), p. 84.

[89] Nicholas II to Edward VII, 22 May/ 4 June 1901, RA W 42/11.

[90] Edward VII to Nicholas II, 19 June 1901, RA W 42/16.

[91] Note by Bülow, 4 November 1901, *GP*, xviii(i), no. 5399, pp. 34–5.

and the conclusion of the Anglo-Russian convention in 1907, Edward VII played an important part in convincing the Tsar of the benefits of an understanding between their two countries.

Exploratory talks took place between Sir Charles Hardinge and Count Alexander Benckendorff, the Russian ambassador to London, at Windsor Castle in November 1903, concerning the possibility of an Anglo-Russian understanding. Hardinge made clear, in a letter to Lord Knollys, that the support given by Edward VII, during the latter's conversation with the Russian ambassador, was likely to be of greater benefit, particularly in influencing the attitude of Nicholas II.[92] The outbreak of the Russo-Japanese War in February 1904 temporarily put an end to the possibility of an agreement between Britain and Russia, for Britain had made an alliance with Japan in 1902, and the war caused an upsurge in anti-English hostility in Russia. Nevertheless, shortly after the outbreak of the war, Lansdowne asked the King to speak to Benckendorff, before the ambassador's departure for St Petersburg, in order to give him an assurance that Britain had remained neutral during the early stages of conflict.[93] In his conversation with the Russian ambassador, the King told Benckendorff to inform Nicholas II that Britain would not intervene in the war.[94]

The King took other measures, on his own initiative, to ensure that the diplomatic lines of communication between London and St Petersburg would not be broken as a consequence of the war in the Far East. Principal among these was his strong support for the candidacy of his friend, the Hon. Charles Hardinge, as the new British ambassador to Russia. The sphere of senior diplomatic appointments was one of those in which the sovereign retained considerable power. Edward VII used that power in order to force Hardinge's candidacy on a reluctant foreign office.[95] Hardinge's appointment was announced on 15 February 1904, and the King wrote to congratulate him, emphasizing the role which he had played in securing his friend's nomination.[96]

Soon after the signing of the Anglo-French agreement, in April 1904, Edward VII discussed the possibility of a similar agreement with Russia in talks with Alexander Isvolsky, the Russian minister in Copenhagen, while on a visit to the Danish capital. Isvolsky was the rising man in the

[92] Hardinge to Knollys, 29 November 1903, RA W 44/10.
[93] Lansdowne to Edward VII, 18 February 1904, RA W 44/34.
[94] Paul Cambon to Delcassé, 20 February 1904, *DDF*, 2nd series, IV, no. 297, pp. 389–90.
[95] Hardinge, *Old Diplomacy*, p. 97.
[96] Edward VII to Hardinge, 15 February 1904, Hardinge Papers, vol. 7; Lansdowne to Scott (copy), February 1904, *ibid.*

Russian diplomatic service, having the Tsar's mother, the Dowager Empress Marie as his patron,[97] and the King may have sought out Isvolsky in the expectation that he would eventually become Russian foreign minister.[98] The King and Isvolsky met at the British legation in Copenhagen on 12 April 1904. Two days later, Isvolsky sent a report of the conversation to the Russian foreign minister, Count Lamsdorf. Edward VII stressed his desire to see the Anglo-French *entente*, which had been concluded during his stay in the Danish capital, complemented by a similar agreement with Russia. He made clear that Hardinge's mission as British ambassador to Russia would be to establish cordial relations between the two countries and then to reach an understanding on all the questions dividing Britain and Russia around the globe. The King appreciated that such an understanding could not be reached until after the conclusion of the Russo-Japanese War and he emphasised that he and the British government would do all that they could to ensure that the conflict did not escalate.[99]

Lord Lansdowne gave his full support to the King's initiative, which conformed with the government's policy.[100] Following his return to London, the King received the Russian ambassador, Count Benckendorff, and informed him of what had taken place at Copenhagen.[101] The King sought to reinforce the improvement in Anglo-Russian relations by entrusting Hardinge with a personal letter for Nicholas II, when the former left for St Petersburg to take up his duties as ambassador.[102] In his letter to the Tsar, the King stressed that Britain would not intervene as mediator in the Russo-Japanese War unless both powers desired it. He also recommended Isvolsky to Nicholas as, 'a man of remarkable intelligence & who is I am sure one of your ablest & most devoted servants'. In doing so, Edward reiterated his hope that at the end of the conflict between Russia and Japan, Britain and Russia would be able to come to 'a lasting agreement . . . similar to the one which we have lately concluded with France'.[103] In a letter to Lord Knollys, following his arrival in the Russian capital, Hardinge noted that his own close links to the British court, and the role which the King had played in his

[97] Charles Louis Seeger (ed.), *The Memoirs of Alexander Iswolsky. Formerly Russian Minister of Foreign Affairs and Ambassador to France*, English translation (London, 1920), p. 22.
[98] M. Bompard to Delcassé, 4 May 1904, *DDF*, 2nd series, v, no. 89, pp. 106–7.
[99] Isvolsky to Count Lamsdorf, 14 April 1904, Lee, *King Edward VII*, ii, pp. 284–6; Crozier to Delcassé, 12 April 1904, *DDF*, 2nd series, v, no. 15, pp. 17–19.
[100] Lord Lansdowne to Edward VII, 13 April 1904, RA W 44/85.
[101] Lansdowne to Sir Cecil Spring-Rice, 22 April 1904, *BD*, iv, no. 183, pp. 188–9.
[102] Edward VII to Hardinge, 12 May 1904, Hardinge Papers, vol. 7.
[103] Edward VII to Nicholas II, 12 May 1904, RA W 44/95.

appointment, had contributed to the warmth of his reception in official circles at St Petersburg.[104] At his audience with the Tsar, with the aid of the King's letter, Hardinge managed to gain Nicholas's support for the policy of an Anglo-Russian *entente*.[105] The ambassador found a useful ally at the Russian court in the Tsar's mother, the Dowager Empress Marie Feodorovna, who assured Hardinge that she would use her influence in favour of Anglo-Russian friendship.[106]

The King's decision to send Prince Louis of Battenberg to Russia in August 1904, as his representative at the christening of the Tsarevitch Alexei, was another move designed to improve Anglo-Russian relations through dynastic channels. Battenberg was the director of British naval intelligence. He was also married to the Tsarina's sister, Princess Victoria of Hesse, who was the niece of Edward VII. Thus, he was able to speak to the Tsar with greater candour and on a more equal basis than could any diplomat. He was not only Nicholas II's relative, but also his personal friend.[107] The King stressed to Lansdowne that Prince Louis's visit was 'quite a private mission'. However, it is clear that he saw it as having political overtones. 'You know how able & discreet he is', Edward wrote in relation to Battenberg, 'so I am in hopes that his visit may be productive of good – if he is able to have some private conversation with the Emperor and Lamsdorff [sic]'.[108] Edward's offer to be one of the Tsarevitch's godfathers also had a political dimension. Knollys believed that the suggestion 'would at this particular moment be appreciated & would create a better feeling in Russia towards us'.[109]

Sir Charles Hardinge appreciated the potential benefit of Prince Louis's visit for Anglo-Russian relations. He was convinced that the Prince would gain ready access to the Tsar, and that as a consequence he would be able to articulate British views accurately, something which Hardinge believed did not always occur 'when they have to pass thro' the intermediary of Ct. Lamsdorff'. Hardinge had also tried to persuade Lansdowne, who was sceptical about the value of Prince Louis's visit,[110] that it would 'have a beneficial effect'.[111] This seemed to be confirmed

104 Hardinge to Knollys, 25 May 1904, RA W 44/103.
105 Hardinge to Edward VII, 27 May 1904, Hardinge Papers, vol. 6; Ponsonby to Hardinge, 2 June 1904, Hardinge Papers, vol. 7.
106 Hardinge to Queen Alexandra, 4 June 1904, Hardinge Papers, vol. 6.
107 Richard Hough, *Louis and Victoria: The First Mountbattens* (London, 1974), pp. 184–6; Hardinge to Knollys, 10 August 1904, RA W 44/194.
108 Edward VII to Lansdowne, 21 August 1904, RA W 44/195a.
109 Knollys to Hardinge, 24 August 1904, Hardinge Papers, vol. 7.
110 Monger, *The End of Isolation*, p. 171.
111 Hardinge to Edward VII, 18 August 1904, Hardinge Papers, vol. 6.

soon after Prince Louis's arrival in St Petersburg, when Hardinge informed the King that his decision to send a representative to the Tsarevitch's christening had been warmly welcomed by the Russians.[112]

At the King's behest, Prince Louis wrote a detailed report on his discussions with Nicholas II and Lamsdorf, following his return from Russia. Prince Louis had been given a letter by the King for Nicholas II, requesting that the Tsar discuss Anglo-Russian relations with him, and he had also been charged with a friendly personal message from Edward VII to Lamsdorf. In general, Prince Louis found the Tsar 'very calm, moderate, conciliatory & fully appreciating the position in which our Government found themselves'. Lamsdorf was, Battenberg reported, 'very optimistic as to the ultimate establishment on a lasting basis of a good understanding between the two countries'.[113] Edward VII regarded Prince Louis's visit as a resounding success, as did Hardinge.[114] The friendly assurance given by Battenberg to the Tsar on Edward VII's behalf also appear to have had a beneficial effect on the attitude of Nicholas II towards Britain. On 16 October 1904, Hardinge informed Lord Knollys that he had learned from a Russian acquaintance 'that the Emperor had spoken enthusiastically of the King and in a generally friendly way of England'.[115]

The attack made by the Russian Baltic fleet on British fishing vessels on the Dogger Bank on the night of 21 October 1904 caused a crisis in Anglo-Russian relations, which nearly led to war between the two countries, and undermined the efforts made by the King and Hardinge to maintain cordial relations with St Petersburg. The Russians had, unbelievably, mistaken the trawlers for Japanese torpedo boats, and particular outrage was caused by their failure to lend assistance to the crews of the damaged vessels.[116] The majority of the British cabinet were prepared to go to war with Russia, but some diplomats, notably Hardinge, who believed that such a conflict would be warmly welcomed by Berlin, did their utmost to ensure that the dispute was settled peacefully.[117]

Towards the end of the crisis, when it appeared likely that the dispute

---

[112] Hardinge to Edward VII, 25 August 1904, RA W 44/196.
[113] Prince Louis of Battenberg, memorandum on his visit to Russia, 28 August 1904. RA W 44/198.
[114] Ponsonby to Hardinge, 30 August 1904, Hardinge Papers, vol. 7; Hardinge to Lansdowne, 1 September 1904, Hardinge Papers, vol. 6.
[115] Hardinge to Knollys, 16 October 1904. RA W 45/30.
[116] Lee, *King Edward VII*, II, p. 301
[117] Monger, *The End of Isolation*, pp. 172–3.

would be settled by international arbitration, Knollys wrote to Hardinge, implying that throughout Edward VII had been determined to see peace maintained.[118] In making this claim, the King's private secretary was being somewhat economical with the truth. In reality, Edward VII, outraged by the behaviour of the Russians, initially supported the cabinet 'hawks', and went along with Lord Lansdowne's demand for full reparations and an apology from the Russian government and an enquiry into the incident. His attitude underwent a change when he learned that the behaviour of the Russians had been the result of a tragic case of mistaken identity, and when he appreciated that if a compromise solution were not reached, then the alternative might be war.[119] Thereafter, the King's behaviour did correspond to that depicted by Knollys, and he opposed what he saw as the needlessly provocative policy of 'shadowing' the Russian Baltic fleet, and gave his full support to Hardinge's efforts to find a peaceful solution.[120]

The King's caution, he told Paul Cambon, had been motivated to a large extent by the fear that Nicholas II would give in to the war party at St Petersburg. He also seemed concerned about the possibility of a Russian attack on India in the event of a conflict. Cambon, in turn, drew attention to fears that Germany wished to incite an Anglo-Russian war, and warned the King about Wilhelm II's attempts to turn the Tsar against France and Britain. Edward VII responded by stating that he was aware of his nephew's intrigues at St Petersburg, and was considering writing to the Tsar, in order to counteract Wilhelm's letters.[121] Hardinge believed strongly that such a gesture would be beneficial and although it is not known whether a letter was sent, his reasons for advocating the course provide an excellent illustration of the key role which Hardinge believed Edward VII played in Anglo-Russian relations. He asserted that only the King could convince the Tsar and Lamsdorf of the merits of co-operation with Britain, something which was more necessary than ever in view of the Kaiser's assiduous wooing of Nicholas II.[122]

Edward VII continued to support the objective of an understanding between Britain and Russia,[123] but the circumstances did not again

[118] Knollys to Hardinge, 15 November 1904, Hardinge Papers, vol. 7.
[119] Lee, *King Edward VII*, II, pp. 301–4.
[120] Knollys to Hardinge, 15 November 1904, Hardinge Papers, vol. 7; Hardinge to Knollys, 24 November 1904, RA W 45/76.
[121] Paul Cambon to Delcassé, 17 November 1904, *DDF*, 2nd series, V, pp. 535–40.
[122] Hardinge to Knollys, 24 November 1904, Hardinge Papers, vol. 6.
[123] Hardinge to Lansdowne, 30 May 1905, *BD*, IV, no. 189, pp. 195–6.

become favourable until the conclusion of peace between Russia and Japan in August 1905. Two months later, on 21 October 1905, the King sent a telegram to Hardinge, asking the ambassador to communicate his desire for an Anglo-Russian *rapprochement* to Nicholas II.[124] At his audience with the Tsar, Hardinge passed on this message, which Nicholas received warmly. In addition, Hardinge stressed the British government's desire to maintain friendly relations with Russia. Both the British and the French were concerned at this time by signs of the predominance of German influence at the Russian court, and, in order to counteract this, Hardinge drew the Tsar's attention to the possibility of British participation in a much needed loan for Russia. It was these financial pressures, above all else, that forced Nicholas II to agree to the policy, warmly advocated by Lamsdorf and Benckendorff, of *rapprochement* with England.[125]

In the first months of 1906, Edward VII came under pressure from the Tsar and the Russian premier, Sergei Witte, to visit Russia, in order to negotiate an understanding between the two countries. This idea, as well as exhibiting a misunderstanding of the powers of a constitutional sovereign, also represented a security risk, for revolutionary upheavals continued unabated in Russia. Both Hardinge and Lord Knollys advised against such a visit in the circumstances and, in a note on 22 March 1906, Edward VII confirmed that he would not travel to Russia at that time.[126] Nevertheless, both Hardinge, who in January 1906, thanks partly to the King's influence, had taken up the post of permanent under-secretary at the foreign office, and the new Liberal foreign secretary, Sir Edward Grey, were convinced that Edward VII's intervention with the Tsar would be crucial, if the Anglo-Russian negotiations were to succeed.[127] After the King vetoed the idea of a visit to Russia in 1906, Grey wrote to Knollys, stating that a meeting between King Edward and the Tsar remained necessary if an Anglo-Russian *entente* were to become a reality, for only through the King could Nicholas II be reached.[128]

[124] Edward VII to Hardinge, 21 October 1905, RA W 47/325.
[125] Hardinge to Lansdowne, 24 October 1905. *BD*, IV, no. 202, pp. 215–16.
[126] Spring-Rice to Knollys, 16 January 1906, RA W 48/10; Boutiron to Delcassé, 10 January 1906, *DDF*, 2nd series, VIII, no. 378, p. 499; Spring-Rice to Grey, 26 January 1906, Grey Papers, PRO FO 800/72; Spring-Rice to Grey, 15 March 1906. *BD*, IV, no. 208, pp. 222–4; memorandum by Edward VII, 22 March 1906, RA W 48/97.
[127] Hardinge to Edward VII, 13 March 1906, RA W 48/84a.
[128] Sir Edward Grey to Lord Knollys, 28 March 1906, Grey Papers, PRO FO 800/103.

Although Edward VII played no real part in the detailed negotiations of the Anglo-Russian agreement, he did do his best to smooth matters by cultivating his personal relationships with the key figures in the political world at St Petersburg, Isvolsky, who replaced Lamsdorf as Russian foreign minister in the spring of 1906, and Nicholas II. In October 1906, when Isvolsky was on a visit to Paris, the King wrote to Hardinge suggesting that the Russian foreign minister be invited over to London to hold discussions on outstanding questions between the two countries.[129] Hardinge and Grey both expressed doubts about the wisdom of the King's suggestion, believing that such an invitation would be premature, given the on-going negotiations between London and St Petersburg.[130] However, the King eventually got his way, and although Isvolsky was unable to accept the invitation to London,[131] he was greatly flattered by the courtesy which the King had shown towards him. Hardinge later recalled that the invitation had been most beneficial politically.[132] The move had been particularly astute as it followed closely on a minor crisis in Anglo-Russian relations. There had been a danger that a delegation of Labour and radical Liberal MPs would go on a visit to Russia to lend their support to the members of the Duma, the Russian parliament, then in conflict with the Tsarist authorities. Grey, firmly backed by Hardinge, Lord Knollys and the King, had managed to prevent this, knowing that it would have caused great harm, notably by alienating Nicholas II from Britain.[133]

Edward VII also promoted an atmosphere of good-will between the British and Russian royal families, which served to counteract Nicholas II's distaste for Britain politically. Two individuals acted as intermediaries in this regard. They were Sir Arthur Nicolson, the British ambassador at St Petersburg, who had succeeded Hardinge in that post, with the approval of the King,[134] in January 1906, and Sir Donald Mackenzie Wallace, who spoke Russian fluently and had better contacts in St. Petersburg than did Nicolson,[135] including ready access to the Tsar

[129] Edward VII to Hardinge, 19 October 1906, Hardinge Papers, vol. 9.
[130] Hardinge to Edward VII, 20 October 1906, RA W 50/24.
[131] Paul Cambon to Bourgeois, 24 October 1906, *DDF*, 2nd series, x, no. 242, pp. 362–3.
[132] Hardinge, *Old Diplomacy*, p. 133.
[133] Grey to Knollys, 4 October 1906, RA W 50/16; Hardinge to Edward VII, 9 October 1906, RA W 50/18; Hardinge to Edward VII, 10 October 1906, RA W 50/19; Sir Donald Mackenzie Wallace to Knollys, 10 October 1906, RA W 50/20; Hardinge to Knollys, 13 October 1906, RA W 50/21.
[134] Sir Arthur Nicolson to Knollys, 25 November 1905, RA W 47/340.
[135] Steiner, *Foreign Office*, p. 188.

himself. The Dowager Empress Marie Feodorovna continued to act as a pro-English influence over her son, the Tsar, and in March 1907, she paid her first visit to England for more than thirty years, as the guest of her sister Queen Alexandra. Her visit was exploited for political purposes by the foreign office, with royal approval, in order to increase popular support in Britain for the policy of *entente* with Russia.[136] Sir Donald Mackenzie Wallace visited St Petersburg twice during 1907. The fact that he enjoyed Edward VII's friendship allowed him to gain audiences with members of the imperial family. On both occasions, he was able to ascertain that the Tsar and his mother were committed to the policy of *rapprochement* with Britain, and favourably disposed towards the British royal family.[137]

The conclusion of the Anglo-Russian convention on 31 August 1907 was warmly welcomed by Edward VII. He was the first to acknowledge that the credit for this agreement went in the first instance to Grey, Hardinge and Nicolson.[138] Nevertheless, the King made his own contribution to cordial Anglo-Russian relations by inviting Isvolsky to visit him during his stay at Marienbad, shortly after the conclusion of the agreement.[139] Hardinge expressed pleasure at the prospect of the interview, particularly as it followed so closely after a meeting between the King and Clemenceau, thus drawing attention to the solidarity between England, Russia and France. He suggested that the King use his considerable charm to flatter the Russian foreign minister: 'As M. Isvolsky is essentially a vain man, it could do no harm to emphasise the role which he personally has played in bringing the negotiations to a satisfactory conclusion.'[140] The King's discussions with Isvolsky were wide-ranging in nature, concerning many of the subjects dealt with in the Anglo-Russian agreement, such as India and Central Asia. The Russian foreign minister was of the view that remaining issues could be settled 'with a loyal disposition on both sides', a sentiment which was readily reciprocated by the King.[141]

Although due allowance must be made for sycophancy, Edward VII's

[136] Hardinge to Knollys, 4 March 1907, RA W 51/40; Hardinge to Knollys, 9 March 1907, RA W 51/41.
[137] Sir Donald Mackenzie Wallace, Memorandum on Audience with the Czar. 29 March 1907, RA W 51/59; Sir Donald Mackenzie Wallace to Knollys, 6 June 1907, RA W 51/110.
[138] Edward VII to Hardinge, 1 September 1907. Hardinge Papers, vol. 9; Hardinge to Nicolson, 4 September 1907, *BD*, IV, no. 520, p. 580.
[139] Hardinge to Edward VII, 26 August 1907, RA W 52/15.
[140] Hardinge to Edward VII, 1 September 1907, RA W 52/18.
[141] Note dictated by the King upon His Majesty's interview at Marienbad with M. Isvolsky, 8 September 1907, Hardinge Papers, vol. 9.

role in the Anglo-Russian *rapprochement* did not go unacknowledged. Both Hardinge and Sir Edward Goschen, the British ambassador in Vienna, who had been British minister in Copenhagen at the time of Edward VII's initial interview with Isvolsky in the Danish capital in April 1904, praised the contribution made by the King. In a letter to Edward VII on 4 September 1907, Hardinge noted, with regard to the transformation in Britain's international position, which had occurred since the King's succession:

I venture to express the opinion that no Sovereign has ever, by peaceful methods, contributed more than Your Majesty to the pursuit of a successful foreign policy and to the predominance of his country in the Councils of Europe. When a comparison is made of the position of England abroad in 1900 and what this country now occupies Your Majesty has every reason for a feeling of profound satisfaction.[142]

Goschen was more realistic in his assessment of the King's contribution. In his own conversation with Isvolsky at Marienbad, the ambassador had drawn attention to the fact that the agreement had been 'foreshadowed' in a conversation between Edward VII and Isvolsky at Copenhagen in April 1904,[143] by implication suggesting that the King had shown foresight in cultivating his friendship and trust.

The ties between Russia and Britain were further reinforced by Edward VII's visit to Nicholas II at Reval in June 1908. By meeting the Tsar, the King left himself open to attack from Labour and radical Liberal MPs, who continued to oppose the Anglo-Russian *rapprochement*.[144] His visit to Reval also caused considerable alarm in Berlin, where it was seen as completing Germany's encirclement.[145] Before going to Reval, King Edward came under pressure from the leading members of the Rothschild banking family to raise the issue of the maltreatment of the Russian Jews with the Tsar. Lord Knollys gave Lord Rothschild an evasive answer, noting that the King would have to consult with Hardinge, who again served as minister-in-attendance, and Nicolson, before making a decision.[146] The Rothschilds were not the only ones to try to

[142] Hardinge to Edward VII, 4 September 1907, RA W 52/20.
[143] Sir Edward Goschen to Grey, 6 September 1907, RA W 52/21.
[144] Hardinge to Knollys, 2 June 1908, RA W 53/96; Grey to Knollys, 4 June 1908, RA W 53/100; Knollys to the Master of Elibank, 18 June 1908, Elibank Papers, National Library of Scotland, Edinburgh, MS 8801.
[145] Metternich to Bülow, 27 May 1908, PA Bonn England Nr. 81 Nr. 1 Bd. 18; Wilhelm II's comment on Pourtalès to Bülow, 9 June 1908, *GP*, xxv(ii), no. 8803, pp. 448–50.
[146] Lord Rothschild, Alfred and Leopold Rothschild to Edward VII, 3 June 1908, RA W 53/98; Knollys to Lord Rothschild, 3 June 1903, RA W 53/99.

influence the agenda of the King's meeting with the Tsar. In addition, King Edward's friend, the financier, Sir Ernest Cassel, tried to persuade the King to ask the Tsar to allow him to participate in a new loan for Russia. Cassel pressed his concerns at a dinner with the King on the eve of the latter's departure for Reval.[147] Hardinge wrote to Knollys on 4 June 1908, advising strongly that the King should not raise either the Rothschilds' or Cassel's request during the Reval visit, pointing to the potential political damage which this would cause.[148]

Edward VII's visit to Reval achieved its political objectives. Hardinge recorded that the King's visit had caused great satisfaction to the Tsar, and had been of great benefit to Anglo-Russian relations. This sentiment was echoed by members of Nicholas II's suite, who contrasted the relaxed atmosphere between Edward VII and the Tsar with the tension which tended to dominate encounters between Nicholas and the Kaiser.[149] However, three actions of the King's during the visit left him open to criticism subsequently. First, he raised the concerns of the Rothschilds, in a general way, during a conversation with the Russian Premier, P. A. Stolypin. Secondly, against Hardinge's advice, the King mentioned Cassel's request to the Tsar, who agreed to receive the financier if he should visit Russia.[150] Although, the King exercised great tact in raising these matters, it was inappropriate of him to bring up these private concerns during a state visit. The third action taken by the King was most serious of all. He bestowed the rank of honorary admiral of the fleet on Nicholas II, without first consulting the British government.[151] The move was astute politically, as it caused considerable satisfaction to the Tsar,[152] but it was unconstitutional. The King's friend Lord Esher, who had echoed the concerns of the leader of the opposition, Arthur Balfour, about the constitutional impropriety of the King making the politically controversial visit to the Tsar, unaccompanied by Sir Edward Grey,[153] saw the three instances outlined above as evidence

[147] Anthony Allfrey, *Edward VII and his Jewish Court* (London, 1991), pp. 216–17.
[148] Hardinge to Knollys, 4 June 1908, RA W 53/101.
[149] Hardinge, visit to the Emperor of Russia at Reval in June, 1908, *BD*, v, no. 195, p. 243; A. A. Mossolov, *At the Court of the Last Tsar* (London, 1935), pp. 210–2; George, Prince of Wales, to Hardinge, 18 June 1908, Hardinge Papers, vol. 14; Ponsonby, *Recollections*, pp. 194–6.
[150] Hardinge to Knollys, 13 June 1908, RA W 53/104.
[151] Hardinge to Asquith, 10 June 1908, Hardinge Papers, vol. 14.
[152] Admiral Sir John Fisher to Reginald Mackenna, 12 June 1908, A. J. Marder (ed.), *Fear God and Dread Nought. The Correspondence of Admiral of the Fleet Lord Fisher of Kilverstone*, 3 vols. (London, 1952–7), II, no. 130, p. 181; Sir Donald Mackenzie Wallace, memorandum on conversation with the Emperor, 10 December 1908, RA W 54/138.
[153] Esher, journal entry, 30 May 1908, Esher Papers, ESHR 2/11.

of the dangers involved when the sovereign travelled abroad without the foreign secretary. Esher accepted Knollys's assurance that the King had not intended to act unconstitutionally on the admiral of the fleet question, but he was scornful of Cassel's attempts to influence the King in favour of his own financial interests.[154]

However, such controversy seems minor when set against the visit's success. It fulfilled Grey's objective, outlined in March 1906, of reinforcing the Anglo-Russian *rapprochement* through direct contact between the King and Nicholas II. The solidity of the Anglo-Russian *entente* was put to the test a few months after the Reval visit when Austria-Hungary annexed Bosnia-Herzegovina. This act was particularly humiliating for Russia, as the Russians saw themselves as the protectors of the south Slavs, and also due to the fact that Isvolsky had been double-crossed by the Austrian foreign minister, Count Aehrenthal. Aehrenthal had obtained Isvolsky's tacit support for the annexation by promising to support Russian demands for the opening of the Dardanelles. By going ahead with the annexation of Bosnia, before Isvolsky had been given a chance to obtain the support of the other powers for Russia's own ambitions in the Straits, Aehrenthal had destroyed the Russian foreign minister's credibility, and also weakened the prestige of Nicholas II, who had backed Isvolsky's deal with his Austrian counterpart, without informing the other Russian ministers.[155]

Edward VII had again shown his favour for Isvolsky by meeting the Russian foreign minister at Marienbad in August 1908. During this visit, the King arranged for Isvolsky to come to London in October 1908.[156] While in London, the circumstances of his visit having been altered by the Austrian annexation of Bosnia, Isvolsky begged Edward VII and the British government to make concessions over the Dardanelles, and to take measures to reinforce his position with the Tsar. The King was unable to persuade the cabinet to agree to the immediate opening of the Straits to Russian ships,[157] but, acting on a suggestion by Hardinge,[158] he did write to the Tsar, stressing his commitment to Anglo-Russian co-operation, and urging Nicholas not to sack Isvolsky.[159] The letter helped to strengthen Isvolsky's position and the Tsar retained him as foreign minister. Nicholas subsequently wrote an effusive reply to

---

[154] Esher, journal entry, 13 June 1908, *ibid.*   [155] See ch. 1.
[156] Edward VII to Hardinge, 25 August and 29 August 1908, Hardinge Papers, vol. 14; Hardinge to Edward VII, 31 August 1908, RA W 54/15.
[157] Magnus, *Edward the Seventh*, p. 416.
[158] Hardinge to Nicolson, 28 October 1908. Hardinge Papers, vol. 13.
[159] Magnus, *Edward the Seventh*, p. 417.

Edward VII's letter, expressing his pleasure at the political co-operation between Russia and England, and his determination to prevent the Bosnian crisis developing into a general war.[160] Edward VII's decision to write to the Tsar had thus been of considerable benefit, both in helping to save Isvolsky from dismissal, and in reinforcing the relationship of trust between the two monarchs.

Edward VII intervened for a second time on Isvolsky's behalf at the end of the Bosnian crisis in March 1909. He was angered by the Russian foreign minister's decision to give in to pressure from Berlin and accept the Austrian annexation of Bosnia-Herzegovina. Nevertheless, the crisis had convinced the King of the need for unity between the *entente* powers.[161] Edward VII believed that Russia's humiliation over Bosnia would end Isvolsky career as a 'public man'.[162] However, the King's belief that the alternatives to Isvolsky were singularly unappealing led him to support the successful efforts of his sister-in-law, the Dowager Empress Marie, to persuade her son to retain Isvolsky as foreign minister.[163] His desire to receive a visit from the Tsar at Cowes in the summer of 1909 was also motivated by his belief that everything should be done to preserve the Anglo-Russian *entente*. The King viewed the visit as being 'politically of the highest importance'.[164] The subsequent meeting between the two monarchs was the last significant event in Anglo-Russian relations in which Edward VII was a participant.[165]

Edward VII's contribution to the Anglo-Russian *rapprochement* was less significant than that which he made to the Anglo-French *entente*. He possessed a suspicion of the tsarist empire, typical of Englishmen who had grown up in the nineteenth century, and he opposed the policy of *rapprochement*, when it was first suggested by Lansdowne in 1902. Nevertheless, he overcame these initial doubts, and came to appreciate the advantages of co-operation with St Petersburg. As in the case of his actions towards France, the King's greatest attribute was his ability to win and retain the trust of the key political figures. In Russia, this meant Nicholas II and Isvolsky. His decision to seek out Isvolsky while in Copenhagen in April 1904 was inspired and the enthusiasm which he

[160] Nicholas II to Edward VII, 5/18 November 1908, Hardinge Papers, vol. 14.
[161] Edward VII to Hardinge, 28 March 1909, Hardinge Papers, vol. 18.
[162] Edward VII to Hardinge, 2 April 1909, *ibid.*
[163] Marie Feodorovna to Nicholas II, 25 March/7 April 1909 and 30 March/12 April 1909, Bing (ed.), *The Letters of Tsar Nicholas*, pp. 241–4.
[164] Edward VII to Hardinge, 1 May 1909, Hardinge Papers, vol. 18.
[165] Metternich to Bülow, 14 July 1909, PA Bonn Russland Nr. 82 Nr. 1 Bd. 57; Grey to Knollys, 25 July 1909, RA W 55/50; Sir Donald Mackenzie Wallace to Knollys, 7 August 1909, RA W 55/53.

expressed for a political understanding on that occasion helped to convince the then Russian foreign minister, Count Lamsdorf, that the British were seriously interested in an agreement with Russia.

His actions during the Russo-Japanese War, with the notable exception of his initial belligerent attitude after the incident on the Dogger Bank in October 1904, were of some significance in keeping the diplomatic lines of communication open at a time when there was much distrust of England in Russia and when the Germans, and notably Wilhelm II, were making assiduous efforts to convince the Tsar to agree to an alliance with Berlin. It was largely due to Edward VII's influence that Hardinge, one of Britain's most able diplomats, was chosen as ambassador to St Petersburg in February 1904. The latter's commitment to improved Anglo-Russian relations and his close connections to the British court allowed him to play a positive role, most notably by working actively for a compromise solution over the Dogger Bank dispute. The King's assurance to Count Benckendorff that he would not undertake anything against Nicholas II was also of considerable political value, because, as a fellow monarch, the King's words carried greater force with the Tsar than would those of a diplomat or politician. Similarly, Edward's decision to send Prince Louis of Battenberg to St. Petersburg in August 1904, although initially opposed by Lansdowne, was an inspired one. Prince Louis, as the Tsar's relative, and a fellow member of Europe's supra-national royal family, was able to talk more openly to Nicholas than any diplomat, and was therefore in a better position to convince the latter of Britain's desire for closer relations.

The King's actions were of less significance in the years after 1906. But even then, his role in furthering Anglo-Russian co-operation was a largely positive one. He continued to cultivate Isvolsky and his meetings with the Russian foreign minister were acknowledged as beneficial by Hardinge and Grey. Both Isvolsky and the Tsar's chief minister, Peter Stolypin, came to admire Edward VII and to acknowledge the importance of the role which the King had played in fostering good relations between Britain and Russia.[166] In addition, Nicholas II's personal sympathy for Edward VII and his belief in his uncle's good faith helped to counteract the distaste which the Tsar undoubtedly felt for the British Liberal government and parliamentary system. This, in turn, had a beneficial impact on Anglo-Russian relations, as did the interviews between the two monarchs at Reval in 1908 and Cowes in 1909.

[166] Memoranda by the Master of Elibank on conversations with Stolypin and Isvolsky, 19 and 23 January 1909, Elibank Papers, MS 8801.

A perception built up in continental Europe before Edward VII's death that he had been responsible for the course taken by British foreign policy during his reign, and particularly for the encirclement of Germany. Historical research has since proved that this was a complete myth. It arose, principally, as a consequence of three factors – a misunderstanding of the British constitution, a misinterpretation of Edward VII's numerous visits abroad, and a tendency to equate the predominantly anti-German views of the King's advisers with those of Edward VII himself, which were more ambiguous, in the early years of his reign at least.

Of those who misunderstood Edward VII's political role, few were more distinguished than the political theorist Max Weber. At the time of the *Daily Telegraph* affair, in November 1908, he wrote to a friend contrasting the role of the British monarch and the German Kaiser, in their two countries: 'The King of England has a sense of dignity and *power*,' Weber asserted, 'the German Emperor has vanity and satisfies himself with the *appearance* of power.'[167] The comptroller of the Prussian royal household, Robert Count von Zedlitz-Trützschler, also believed that Edward VII was responsible for British policy.[168] However, Weber and Zedlitz were not the only individuals to overestimate Edward VII's importance. Others who did so included Théophile Delcasse, Tittoni, the Italian foreign minister, King Alphonso XIII of Spain and, not least, Kaiser Wilhelm II.

The numerous visits paid by Edward VII to continental Europe during his short reign had the greatest impact in creating the myth that the King controlled British foreign policy. These visits were only rarely of considerable political significance, an obvious case being Edward VII's visit to Paris in May 1903, and in general, as Grey observed in his memoirs, they were not made the occasion for significant changes in policy.[169] Although Edward VII discussed political questions with foreign sovereigns and statesmen with a candour that would be unheard of in a constitutional sovereign today, controversial matters were normally left to his minister-in-attendance who was, on numerous occasions, his friend Sir Charles Hardinge. The fact that the King rarely travelled abroad accompanied by a cabinet minister, and never with his foreign secretary, was largely responsible for giving the false impression

[167] Max Weber to Friedrich Naumann, 12 November 1908, M. Rainer Lepsius and Wolfgang J. Mommsen (eds.), *Max Weber: Briefe, 1906–1908* (Tübingen, 1990), p. 695.
[168] Zedlitz, *Twelve Years*, diary entry, 21 July 1904, pp. 80–1.
[169] Grey, *Twenty-five Years*, I, pp. 149–51.

that he was conducting Britain's foreign relations. The practice of the King going abroad without the foreign secretary was the subject of much controversy even at the time.[170] However, Sir Edward Grey's reluctance to accompany the King on his visits to foreign sovereigns did not, as one historian has suggested, result from a belief, on the part of the foreign secretary, that such meetings were politically irrelevant.[171] The chief reason which explained Hardinge's frequent presence in the royal entourage was the fact that Hardinge and Edward VII were personal friends, and the King found the latter's company congenial. Grey accepted this, and did not desire to go against Edward VII's wishes.[172]

However, there were a number of occasions when the King's practice of travelling abroad without Grey caused disagreements between the foreign office and the palace, and contributed to suspicions in Europe as to the true character of Edward VII's political role. In February 1907, Grey and the King clashed over the latter's desire that Hardinge accompany him on a visit to the King of Spain at Cartagena, scheduled for April 1907.[173] Grey eventually yielded in the face of pressure from the King and Hardinge.[174] Nevertheless, the absence of a cabinet minister in the King's entourage during his Mediterranean cruise in 1907 was made the subject of a question in the House of Commons,[175] and the hysterical reaction of the German press, in particular, to Edward VII's meetings with the Kings of Spain and Italy was probably greater than it would otherwise have been because the absence of a foreign minister allowed German newspaper editors to present the visits as part of the King's personal scheme of encirclement.[176]

Despite the political controversy which surrounded the King's visits to Spain and Italy in the spring of 1907, Grey appears to have moderated his attitude to the practice of Hardinge's presence as the foreign office representative in Edward VII's entourage during the latter's visits abroad. Before Edward VII's visits to the Kaiser and the Emperor of Austria in the summer of 1907, the foreign secretary made clear to Hardinge that he was content to accept the latter as the King's minister-in-attendance.[177] As has been noted, Grey's failure to accompany

[170] Lord Fitzmaurice to Lascelles, 21 September 1906, Lascelles Papers, PRO FO 800/13.
[171] Monger, *The End of Isolation*, pp. 261–4.
[172] Hardinge, *Old Diplomacy*, p. 192.   [173] Hardinge to Knollys, 17 February 1907, RA W 51/22.
[174] Hardinge to Knollys, 18 February 1907, RA W 51/23.
[175] Hardinge to Edward VII, 2 May 1907, RA W 51/75; Hardinge, *Old Diplomacy*, p. 137.
[176] Lascelles to Grey, 19 April 1907, *BD*, VI, no. 15, p. 28; Wilhelm II's comments on Monts to Bülow, 18 April 1907, *GP*, XXI(ii), no. 7215, pp. 496–7; Edward VII to Hardinge, 27 April 1907, Hardinge Papers, vol. 9.
[177] Hardinge to Knollys, 19 July 1907, RA W 52/9.

Edward VII on his visit to the Tsar at Reval in June 1908, a meeting
which was widely seen both in Britain and Germany as being of
considerable symbolic significance, both in terms of Anglo-Russian
relations and the balance of power in Europe, led to renewed criticism
of the arrangement whereby Hardinge, and not the foreign secretary
accompanied the King.[178]

By the summer of 1908, every action of Edward VII was scrutinised
by the German press for evidence that he was pursuing the *Reich*'s
encirclement. This necessitated precautions on the part of the King.
Thus, when the former French foreign minister, Théophile Delcassé,
paid a visit to London in June 1908, Hardinge stressed to Lord Knollys
that the King's audience with him should be kept private due to the
possibility of a hostile reaction from Berlin.[179] Sadly, these precautions
proved to be futile. The German press condemned Edward VII's
decision to receive Delcassé as a provocative act, and one French
diplomat reported that the Germans believed that the King was determined to destroy the *Reich*'s battlefleet with the help of France and
Russia.[180] Such fanciful notions were not adhered to in Britain. However, following the failure of Edward VII and Hardinge to extract
concessions from the Kaiser over the issue of naval armaments at
Friedrichshof in August 1908, some elements in the London press began
to criticise the King's visits abroad from a different perspective. Wilhelm
von Stumm of the German embassy in London reported to Berlin on 10
September 1908 that the Liberal paper *The Nation* had asserted that
Edward VII's visits abroad, notably that to Reval, had damaged Britain's relations with Germany and Austria, and had not contributed to
tranquility in Europe, nor to the reputation of the Liberal government.
Hardinge's status as minister-in-attendance was also, as Stumm noted,
the object of particular criticism, as the former was not responsible to
parliament.[181]

As a consequence of these criticisms, the practice was altered when
Edward VII went to Berlin in February 1909. In addition to Hardinge,
he was accompanied by the colonial secretary, Lord Crewe. By 1909,
Grey was more alive than at the start of his tenure as foreign secretary to
the potential dangers, not least for the reputation of the monarchy, in

---

[178]   On Reval, see above.
[179]   Hardinge to Knollys, 22 June 1908, RA W 53/110.
[180]   M. Ferrand, French consul at Stuttgart, to M. Pichon, 3 July 1908, *DDF*, 2nd Series, XI, no. 397,
        pp. 685–7.
[181]   Stumm to Bülow, 10 September 1908, PA Bonn England Nr 81 Nr 1 Bd 19.

allowing the King too great a level of freedom in his dealings with foreign statesmen. Thus, when the German chancellor, Theobald von Bethmann Hollweg, requested a meeting with Edward VII during the latter's stay at Marienbad in the summer of 1909, the foreign secretary advised that the suggestion be refused, on the grounds that such an audience would be too sensitive politically.[182]

The King's tendency to travel abroad without a cabinet minister was not the only factor which contributed to a misunderstanding of his constitutional role and political opinions by foreigners. In addition, Edward VII's views were often confused with those of his entourage, thus contributing to the perception, which was false, during the early years of his reign at least, that he was hostile to Germany. Edward VII relied for advice on a group of unofficial advisers. The most important of these were Lord Knollys, the King's private secretary, Viscount Esher, the lieutenant governor of Windsor Castle and member of the committee of imperial defence, Sir Charles Hardinge, and Admiral Sir John Fisher, the first sea lord from 1904 onwards. Others who advised the King included Sir Donald Mackenzie Wallace and the Marquis de Soveral, the Portuguese minister in London. The characteristic which all these individuals shared was a scepticism about the objectives of German foreign and military policy. All of them had become resolutely anti-German by the time of the King's death. It is true that Edward VII also had friends who were pro-German, notably Alfred de Rothschild, Sir Ernest Cassel and the Austrian ambassador to London, Count Mensdorff. It has been suggested, by one historian, that their influence largely offset that of the anti-Germans in the King's entourage.[183] As will be seen, this is a view which finds minimal support in the sources. The extent to which these individuals were pro-German, and the level of their influence over Edward VII, has been grossly exaggerated.

Of the King's friends, Lord Esher was among the most anti-German. His influence over Edward VII is hard to quantify as he refused high office on a number of occasions, preferring to bring his views to bear behind-the-scenes. Nevertheless, his journals and letters bristle with condemnation of the German empire and of Kaiser Wilhelm II, whom he loathed. In September 1906, he wrote to his son: '*L'Allemagne c'est l'Enemi* – and there is no doubt on the subject. They mean to have a powerful fleet, and commercially to beat us out of the field, before ten

[182] Grey to Goschen, 31 July 1909, Grey Papers, PRO FO 800/61.
[183] Kennedy, *The Rise of the Anglo-German Antagonism*, p. 402.

years are over our heads.'[184] By December 1907, his views on the threat posed by Germany had, if anything, become more firmly held.[185] Esher was no less critical in his assessment of the character of the Kaiser, concluding at the time of the *Daily Telegraph* affair that Wilhelm II was mentally unstable. 'I am sure that the taint of George III is in his blood', Esher declared.[186] Esher's influence over Edward VII was particularly strong in the sphere of military policy. It was due in part to Esher's influence that the King had become a strong supporter of British intervention on the side of France, in the event of a continental war, by the time of his death. The need to ensure that the British army was prepared for such an eventuality was an issue raised in the correspondence between them, and was discussed by the two men at Balmoral in September 1909.[187]

Esher's suspicion of Germany was manifested most prominently and publicly in the winter of 1908, when he wrote to the Imperial Navy League, defending the policies of Admiral Fisher, and asserting that everyone in Germany, from the Emperor downwards, wished to see Fisher's dismissal as first sea lord. This intervention in the politically sensitive sphere of naval policy was followed by the Kaiser's letter to the first lord of the admiralty, Lord Tweedmouth, in which Wilhelm rebuked Esher and asserted that the German navy did not represent a threat to Britain. The Tweedmouth letter affair caused lasting damage to Anglo-German relations. Edward VII was angered by the actions of both his nephew, the Kaiser, and of Lord Esher. Wilhelm II was convinced that Esher's views represented those of Edward VII himself, whereas the King, although sympathising with Esher's objective, namely to persuade the Liberal government to maintain the strength of the Royal Navy, had been furious at the method which his friend had employed.[188]

The King's rebuke to Esher did not prevent the Kaiser from assuming on a later occasion that Esher spoke for Edward VII. In January 1909, Gerald du Maurier's play *An Englishman's Home* opened in London. It told the story of a foreign invasion of England. The 'foreigners' depicted in the play were unnamed, but they were clearly supposed to be German. Esher, and the proprietor of the *Daily Mail*, Lord North-

---

[184] Viscount Esher to Maurice Brett, 6 September 1906, Maurice V. Brett (ed.), *The Journals and Letters of Reginald, Viscount Esher*, 4 vols. (London, 1934–8), II, p. 183.
[185] Esher, journal entry, 3 December 1907, *ibid.*, p. 267.
[186] Esher, journal entry, 21 November 1908, Esher Papers, ESHR 2/11.
[187] Esher, journal entry, 8 September 1909, Esher Papers, ESHR 2/12.   [188] See ch. 2.

cliffe, hoped to use the play's popularity to boost recruitment to the Territorial Army, of which Esher was chairman in London.[189] Esher gave his enthusiastic views on the play to a correspondent of the *Daily Mail*, and they were published in that paper on 29 January 1909. Wilhelm II read the article, and automatically assumed that Esher's views echoed those of the King. 'That is all systematic!', the Kaiser wrote, 'and comes from near the King to whom Lord Esher is an intimate friend.'[190] On this occasion, Wilhelm's suspicion was justified, for Edward VII undoubtedly sympathised with Esher's concern that Britain prepare militarily for all eventualities, including the possibility of war with Germany.[191]

Lord Knollys was another of the King's advisers who was seen by the Kaiser to exercise a malevolent influence over Edward VII.[192] However, Edward VII's private secretary had opinions on international relations which were much more complex than the Kaiser appreciated. Like Esher, he realised that Germany posed a threat to Britain's security and prosperity. However, he believed that a show-down between the two countries lay far in the future.[193] In addition, although broadly in favour of the policy of *entente*, he favoured the maintenance of good relations with Berlin, and became increasingly irritated by what he saw as the excessive sensitivity of the foreign office towards the French.[194] Like Edward VII himself, Knollys came to the conclusion that Germany was Britain's implacable enemy only in the few years preceding 1910. However, after the King's death, Knollys's growing resentment of France and Russia, and a perception that they were able to dictate British policy, led him to become an advocate of improved Anglo-German relations.[195] Thus, it is difficult to see him as a true anti-German by conviction.

Admiral Sir John Fisher was a prominent figure in Edward VII's entourage who was seen in Berlin as an anti-German influence on the King. In March 1907, the Kaiser declared to a French diplomat that

---

[189] Peter Fraser, *Lord Esher. A Political Biography* (London, 1973), pp. 203–6.
[190] Wilhelm II's comment on the *Daily Mail*, 29 January 1909, PA Bonn England Nr 78 geheim. Bd 17.
[191] Fraser, *Esher*, pp. 205–6.
[192] Wilhelm II's comment on Metternich to Bülow, 7 November 1905, PA Bonn England Nr 81 Nr 1 Bd 15; Wilhelm II to Bülow, 10 October 1905, PA Bonn Deutschland Nr 131 Nr 4 Bd 5; Wilhelm II's comments on Metternich to Bülow, 1 November 1907, PA Bonn Preussen Nr 1 Nr 40 Bd 15.
[193] Knollys to Esher, 8 September 1906, Esher Papers, ESHR 10/49.   [194] *Ibid.*
[195] Letters of Knollys to Esher, 27 September 1912, 26 October 1912 and 10 November 1912, Esher Papers, ESHR 10/52.

Fisher was Edward VII's 'mauvais génie', and along with the King was seeking to provoke a continental war.[196] The Kaiser was correct to be suspicious of Fisher, who realised the threat posed by the German navy to British security earlier than did many observers. On several occasions, Fisher tried to persuade Edward VII of the merits of a pre-emptive strike, to destroy the nascent German fleet in its ports. Despite their personal friendship, the King was not prepared to give his support to such an initiative, rebuking the first sea lord on one occasion by declaring: 'My God, Fisher, you must be mad!'[197] However, although Edward VII acted as a restraining influence on Fisher, Wilhelm had every right to characterise the first sea lord as an individual who sought to counsel the King against Germany.[198]

Esher and Fisher were not the only members of the King's circle whose influence upon him can be broadly characterised as anti-German. Sir Donald Mackenzie Wallace, who advised Edward VII on Russian affairs, also occasionally submitted his views on Germany to the palace. In October 1907, Wallace sent a letter to Lord Knollys, at the King's request, detailing his views of the aims of German foreign policy, specifically in the relation to a book by Emil Reich entitled *Germany's Swelled Head*, which Edward VII had given to him at Balmoral. Wallace's own opinions showed that he too had become a Germanophobe influence in royal circles: 'What we have, as a nation, to fear is, I submit, not megalomania of the vulgar type called *Swelled Head*, but the quiet persistent carrying out of a well-considered policy which aims at destroying our naval supremacy, with a view to appropriating a large portion of our colonial Empire.'[199]

In the field of foreign policy and diplomacy, the individual who worked most closely with Edward VII, particularly in the years after 1906, was Sir Charles Hardinge. As mentioned previously, Hardinge's career had benefited from the King's friendship and his ties to the court. He and Edward VII corresponded regularly on matters of foreign policy, and, although in basic agreement, Hardinge was often able to persuade the King to take the course of action thought most appropriate by the foreign office. As permanent under secretary of the foreign office between 1906 and 1910, Hardinge had an influence second only to Sir Edward Grey over the shaping of British policy, and

---

[196] Note by M. Lecomte, March 1907, *DDF*, 2nd series, x, p. 704.
[197] Marder (ed.), *Fear God and Dread Nought*, II, p. 20.
[198] *Ibid.*, pp. 103, 107, 169, 191–2.   [199] Wallace to Knollys, 1 October 1907, RA W 52/32.

his closeness to Edward VII served to strengthen his position.[200] Like the majority of Edward VII's friends, he came to be a strong believer in the reality of the 'German threat', and the need for Britain to take preventive measures to counteract it. He explained the logic of his position in a letter to Sir Frank Lascelles, the British ambassador to Berlin, whose Germanophile sympathies diverged from Hardinge's own views. Hardinge noted that the Germans freely admitted that their navy was being built 'in order to impose their will' on other powers, and that if the German navy were to reach a greater size than the Royal Navy, Britain's survival as an independent country would be threatened:

Nevertheless, they wish to contest that supremacy, and it is evident that they are extremely anxious that the contest should not take place for some years to come – that is to say until they are ready. The only means by which that day can be indefinitely deferred is by the construction of a very large number of battleships in this country by which the supremacy will still be maintained.[201]

Hardinge's friendship with the King did not just benefit his own career, but also the prospects of those who shared his views. The royal prerogative was still exercised in the sphere of senior diplomatic appointments, and Edward VII showed an almost obsessive interest in them.[202] It is striking that during Edward VII's reign, many of those who benefited from advancement were suspicious of Germany, and eager to see Berlin's aggressive ambitions checked. Two prominent diplomats who were appointed to senior positions, with royal backing, were Sir Francis Bertie and Cecil Spring-Rice. Bertie, as assistant under secretary of the foreign office at the turn of the century, had drawn up a sceptical memorandum, opposing an alliance with Germany. The logic which justified his stance indicated that he was already thinking in terms of a triple *entente*, with the purpose of thwarting German expansionism.[203] Such views proved no impediment to his advancement. In December 1902, Bertie was appointed British ambassador to Rome, an honour for which he thanked the King,[204] and in August 1904, he wrote to thank Edward VII for the key role which the latter had played in securing his appointment to the politically influential position of British ambassador

[200] Steiner, *The Foreign Office*, pp. 91–2, 203–4.
[201] Hardinge to Lascelles, 19 May 1908. Hardinge Papers, vol. 13.
[202] Wilfrid Scawen Blunt, *My Diaries. Being a Personal Narrative of Events 1888–1914*, 2 vols. (London, 1919–20), II, diary entries, 28 July and 31 July 1907, pp. 182, 183.
[203] Sir Francis Bertie, memorandum on alliance with Germany, 27 October 1901, RA W 42/42; Keith Hamilton, *Bertie of Thame: Edwardian Ambassador* (London, 1990), pp. 16–37.
[204] Bertie to Knollys, 27 December 1902, RA W 43/26.

in Paris.[205] Cecil Spring-Rice was another diplomat, belonging to the anti-German tendency, whose career moved forward due to royal favour. At the time of his appointment as British minister in Persia, he wrote to the King acknowledging the latter's role in securing his promotion.[206] Other anti-Germans who secured promotion due to interventions by Edward VII included Sir Arthur Nicolson, who replaced Hardinge as British ambassador in St Petersburg in 1906, and Sir Edward Goschen, who disliked the Kaiser, or 'German Bill' as he disparagingly called him, and was appointed as British ambassador to Vienna in 1905, and to Berlin in 1908.[207] While there is undoubtedly some truth in the assertion that the personal qualities of these individuals influenced the King in their favour to a greater extent than their political opinions,[208] it remains the case that Edward VII used his influence to promote diplomats who were predominantly anti-German, and in this way influenced the character of the British foreign service during his reign.

Edward VII also bestowed special favour on certain members of the diplomatic corps in London. His main friends among them were the Marquis de Soveral, the Portuguese minister in London, Count Benckendorff, the Russian ambassador, and Count Mensdorff, the Austrian ambassador.[209] These friendships did not go unnoticed by the Germans, who sought to find political implications in them.[210] The Kaiser's view of the three diplomats was far from charitable. Wilhelm had offended Soveral by calling him by his nickname, 'the blue monkey', to his face,[211] and he was never prepared to believe the assertions of his diplomats that Soveral was sympathetic towards Germany.[212] Benckendorff was also regarded by the Kaiser as an enemy of Germany and a malevolent influence on Edward VII, and at the time of the Anglo-German war scare in December 1904, he accused Soveral, Benckendorff, and even Mensdorff, of trying to turn Edward VII against him.[213] Wilhelm was partially justified in his suspicions of Benckendorff

---

[205] Bertie to Edward VII, 11 August 1904, RA W 44/190.
[206] St Aubyn, *Edward VII*, p. 289.
[207] Christopher Howard (ed.), *The Diary of Sir Edward Goschen, 1900–1914* (London, 1980), pp. 11, 31.
[208] Edward VII to Hardinge, 13 and 16 September 1906, Hardinge Papers, vol. 9.
[209] Mensdorff, in addition to being Austrian ambassador, was also Edward VII's second cousin. Their common great-grandfather was Prince Francis Frederick of Saxe-Saalfeld-Coburg.
[210] Metternich to Bülow, 9 July 1904, *GP*, XIX(i), no. 6041, pp. 190–2.
[211] Bülow, *Memoirs*, II, p. 37.
[212] Wilhelm II's comments on Tattenbach to Bülow, 17 April 1903, PA Bonn England Nr 81 Nr 1 Bd 11a.
[213] Wilhelm II's comments on Alvensleben to Bülow, 26 December 1904, *GP*, XIX(i), no. 6158.

and Soveral. As has been seen, Benckendorff played a leading role in the diplomatic manoeuverings which led to the signing of the Anglo-Russian Convention in 1907, and acted as an intermediary between King Edward and Tsar Nicholas. Soveral's role was a more ambiguous one. He was closely associated with the plans for Edward VII's visit to Paris in 1903, and had been an enthusiastic supporter of moves towards an Anglo-French understanding, yet at the same time he had sought to assure German diplomats that he wished to see close relations between England and Germany.[214] However, what is not in doubt is that by the end of Edward VII's reign, Soveral had become vehemently hostile to Germany. He, along with Esher, Knollys and Admiral Fisher, belonged to a group who met regularly to discuss the political situation. Following one such dinner, in June 1909, Esher recorded in his journal: 'It was *very* pleasant. No reticences of any sort. Soveral violently hostile to Germany, as usual.'[215] The Kaiser's suspicions of Mensdorff were wide of the mark, but, in any case, the Austrian ambassador was valued by Edward VII primarily as a congenial companion, and the King had a less than flattering view of his political abilities.[216] King Edward's friendship with continental statesmen who were known to be hostile to Germany also caused unease in Berlin. They believed that he had a particular liking for foreign politicians who were hostile to Germany.[217] This assertion had some basis in truth, and it is interesting that the two French and Russia statesmen, with whom the King was on most cordial terms in the second half of his reign, Clemenceau and Isvolsky, were seen by the Germans as enemies.

In contrast, the pro-German friends of Edward VII's were few and far between. Aside from Mensdorff, the most prominent among them were the King's two closest acquaintances in the financial world, Alfred de Rothschild and Sir Ernest Cassel. However, there is no evidence that either of these individuals influenced the King politically. In any case, the extent of their sympathy for Germany has been exaggerated by historians. The Kaiser snubbed Rothschild during a visit to England in 1902, causing the financier lasting offense.[218] Similarly, although Cassel, who had been born in Cologne, was broadly in favour of Anglo-German co-operation, and discussed measures to improve relations between the two countries with the German shipping magnate Albert Ballin, in the

---

[214] See ch. 2. [215] Esher, journal entry, 3 June 1909, Esher Papers, ESHR 2/12.
[216] Edward VII to Hardinge, 24 March 1908, Hardinge Papers, vol. 14.
[217] Metternich to Bülow, 14 August 1905, *GP*, xx(ii), no. 6870, p. 654.
[218] Bülow to Holstein, 16 May 1903, *HP*, iv, no. 816, p. 275.

summer of 1908,[219] he was often at the receiving end of some of King Edward's most severe criticisms of Germany and her ruler,[220] suggesting that Cassel's own pro-German sentiments were somewhat muted.

Observers in Germany were wrong to assume that the opinions of Edward VII's friends and advisers represented those of the King himself. Individuals such as Esher, Fisher and Hardinge were undoubtedly more hostile to Germany than the King, and the latter sometimes acted as a restraining influence upon them. However, it is striking that in the last years of his life, Edward VII surrounded himself with individuals who were predominantly anti-German and supporters of the policy of *entente*. There can be little doubt that by 1908, at the latest, the views of his entourage corresponded closely to those of the King himself. For example, during his discussions with Clemenceau at Marienbad in August of that year, the King told the French premier that he had disowned a friend who had spoken out against the *entente*.[221] Thus, in the last years of Edward VII's life, those pro-Germans among his circle were best to keep their opinions to themselves if they wished to retain his friendship.

A misunderstanding of the workings of the British constitution, a misrepresentation of the purpose and significance of Edward VII's visits abroad, and a tendency to attribute the pronouncements of his advisers to the King himself, thus made up the elements of the myth that the King had been primarily responsible for Germany's encirclement. Edward VII's true political role was considerably more modest. Edward VII's reign saw a decline in the political importance of the British monarchy, notably with the recognition of the office of prime minister in 1905 and the concession of parliament's right to cede British territory, without the prior consent of the sovereign, which occurred at the time of the signing of the Anglo-French agreement in 1904.[222] Lord Knollys and Viscount Esher saw themselves as the guardians of the royal prerogative, and the former, in particular, regarded it as his duty to ensure that the King was consulted by the government. Knollys claimed, in a letter to Esher, in 1905, that Queen Victoria's declining health in her latter years had led to a strengthening of the power of the executive at the

[219] Anthony Allfrey, *Edward VII and his Jewish Court*, p. 254
[220] Edward VII to Cassel, 17 August 1905, Cassel Papers, MB1/X2; Edward VII to Cassel, 15 August 1908, Cassel Papers, MB1/X1.
[221] Clemenceau to Pichon, 29 August 1908, *DDF*, 2nd series, XI, no. 434, p. 752.
[222] Frank Hardie, *The Political Influence of the British Monarchy, 1868–1952* (London, 1970), pp. 78–116.

expense of the crown, a situation which he was confident that Edward VII could correct.[223] However, in April 1906, in a letter to Esher, the King presented a rather different view of his relationship with the Liberal government of Sir Henry Campbell-Bannerman: 'I look with considerable alarm to the way the "P.M." is going on – & needless to say he never brings anything before me – excepting very trifling matters – nor consults me in any *way*'.[224]

There were several reasons as to why the attempts of Knollys and Esher to give the King a greater role in decision-making failed. First, Edward VII lacked the experience of ruling which had been a major asset to Queen Victoria in her later years. This had led her ministers, and Lord Salisbury, in particular, to consult her on questions of foreign policy on a regular basis.[225] In contrast, as Prince of Wales, Edward had developed a reputation of being indiscreet, which resulted in the Queen refusing him access to foreign office despatches until 1892.[226] Knollys's claim that, due to ill-health, Queen Victoria had not been consulted by the government in the last years of her life lacked substance. It was only in the final months of her life that the Queen became physically unable to read despatches, and when the German diplomat, Count Metternich, visited her at Windsor in March 1900, only ten months before her death, he was impressed by her continuing interest in, and knowledge of, all aspects of public life.[227] Nor was there any substance in the charge, made by Knollys, that the Queen's private office had been badly run by her private secretary in later years, Sir Arthur Bigge. Indeed, Sir Frederick Ponsonby believed that it had functioned at least as efficiently, if not more so, than did Edward VII's private office under Knollys.[228]

Thus the factors that militated against Edward VII's prominent involvement in the political process were different from those implied by Knollys. The King lacked an application for desk work, and found reading reports of parliamentary proceedings a chore.[229] He also spent long periods of the year outside London, either visiting friends on their country estates or on the continent.[230] In addition, he failed to establish a strong and trusting relationship with any of his ministers, along the lines of that between Queen Victoria and Lord Salisbury. There was no real

[223] Knollys to Esher, 31 August 1905, Esher Papers, ESHR 10/48.
[224] Edward VII to Esher, 14 April 1906, Esher Papers, ESHR 6/2.
[225] Steiner, *The Foreign Office*, pp. 200–2.   [226] Magnus, *Edward the Seventh*, p. 237.
[227] Metternich to Bülow, 8 March 1900, PA Bonn England Nr 81 Nr 1 Bd 6.
[228] Ponsonby, *Recollections*, p. 102.
[229] Arthur Davidson to Elibank, 2 March 1907, Elibank Papers, MS. 8801.
[230] Magnus, *Edward the Seventh*, pp. 274–5.

warmth between the King and Lord Lansdowne, the foreign secretary in the first years of his reign.[231] Although Edward VII did establish a more satisfactory working relationship with Sir Edward Grey, Grey tended to delegate responsibility for the foreign office's dealings with the court to Hardinge. Despite the convictions of many observers on the continent, the King was, by and large, content to play a supporting role, rather than to involve himself in the formation of policy. However, this was primarily attributable to the fact that he was in fundamental agreement with the foreign policy pursued by his ministers, and thus major disputes did not arise.[232]

Two events, which occurred during 1908, served to illustrate the extent to which Edward VII's practical authority had been exaggerated by many of his contemporaries, notably on the continent. In April 1908, Sir Henry Campbell-Bannermann resigned as prime minister and was succeeded by Herbert Asquith. Edward VII was holidaying in Biarritz at the time and failed to return to London to swear Asquith in as prime minister. Instead, Asquith travelled out to the south of France to see the King. As a consequence of this, King Edward was severely criticised in the British press for a breach of constitutional duty.[233] Even Lord Esher, normally one of the King's most loyal supporters, criticised him for not coming back to London.[234] The newspaper *The Nation* believed that in failing to return from Biarritz, the King had shown that he was nothing more than a 'quantité négligeable' in political terms. However, Wilhelm von Stumm felt that the incident would have beneficial consequences, in convincing people in Germany that Edward VII had neither the power nor the temperament of a Richelieu, and that it was solely the King's ability with people which allowed him, at times, to do service to his country.[235] Stumm's hope turned out to be misplaced, but he did have the distinction of being one of the few Germans to recognise the limited nature of Edward VII's political role.

The second incident in 1908, which indicated that the King's political power was more restricted than many observers believed, was the controversy caused by his decision to bestow an admiralcy on Nicholas

---

[231] Ponsonby, *Recollections*, p. 128; Newton, *Lord Lansdowne*, pp. 233–6, 308–9; Rolo, *Entente Cordiale*, pp. 159–60.
[232] Grey of Fallodon, *Twenty-five Years*, I, p. 205.
[233] *Ibid.*, pp. 252–3. Edward VII to Hardinge, 7 April 1908, Hardinge Papers, vol. 14; Roy Jenkins, *Asquith* (London, 1964), pp. 178–80.
[234] Esher, journal entry, 5 April 1908, Esher Papers, ESHR 2/11.
[235] Wilhelm von Stumm to Bülow, 18 April 1908, PA Bonn England Nr 81 Nr 1 Bd 18.

II at Reval, without first securing the approval of the cabinet. Instead, Asquith was informed of the King's decision after it had been taken, in a letter written by Hardinge, who accompanied Edward VII to Reval as minister in attendance.[236] The King's action caused considerable dismay in London, because it was considered unconstitutional. Edward VII's own reaction to the outcry indicated that he had not appreciated the impropriety of his action.[237] Nevertheless, the fact that the King did not have the right to take such a seemingly trivial action without the prior approval of the cabinet was indicative of the limited nature of his constitutional role.

Although these two incidents revealed that Edward VII's authority was more restricted than many contemporaries believed, this does not imply that he was an insignificant political figure. One observer, Robert Count von Zedlitz-Trützschler, who had previously considered that the King was responsible for British foreign policy, reached a more realistic and balanced conclusion after observing Edward VII during the latter's state visit to Berlin in 1909. Zedlitz noted in his diary:

He allows a great deal of independence to the persons who have been carefully chosen for their duties, and only takes a hand when there is something of special importance to call for his intervention, and then with his age and experience and thorough knowledge of the world he acts very adroitly.[238]

Lord Esher was correct in his assessment that it was Edward VII's knowledge of human nature and ability with people which allowed him to play a role in international relations.[239] This view of Edward VII was echoed by Sir Edward Grey.[240] Edward VII's greatest skill lay in the cultivation of personal relationships, and this proved, on balance, to be an asset to British diplomacy during his reign. The close relationships, based on mutual trust, which the King established with Delcassé, Clemenceau, Isvolsky and Nicholas II helped to create the atmosphere in which political understandings between Britain and France, and Britain and Russia, could be reached, and to strengthen ties between Britain and these two powers once the agreements between them were in existence. Similarly, Edward VII's visits abroad created good-will

---

[236] Hardinge to Asquith, 10 June 1908. Hardinge Papers, vol. 14.
[237] Esher, journal entry, 13 June 1908, Esher Papers, ESHR 2/12.
[238] Zedlitz, *Twelve Years*, diary entry, 12 February 1909, p. 258.
[239] Esher, journal entry, 7 May 1910, Esher Papers, ESHR 2/12.
[240] Grey of Fallodon, *Twenty-five Years*, I, pp. 206–7.

towards Britain on the continent. His state visit to Paris in 1903, in particular, helped to facilitate a political *rapprochement* between Britain and France by removing an atmosphere of mutual suspicion.

Although the King played no direct part in the formation of foreign policy, he did have a key role in the sphere of diplomatic appointments. Edward VII's support worked to the advantage of career diplomats such as Sir Charles Hardinge, Sir Francis Bertie and Sir Arthur Nicolson. Edward VII's backing for this group of diplomats, known collectively as the 'Hardinge Gang', had an important indirect impact on British foreign policy, for the majority of this group were strongly anti-German, and the years of Hardinge's tenure as permanent under-secretary of the foreign office, 1906 to 1910, saw a hardening in London's stance towards Berlin. The King's forceful personality, and prestige as monarch and head of state, enabled him to smooth over difficulties in the sphere of diplomatic appointments. In August 1908, for example, he persuaded Sir Edward Goschen to relinquish his post as British ambassador in Vienna, for the more arduous position of British ambassador to Berlin. Goschen's diary makes clear that he only agreed to the change, with great reluctance, out of loyalty to the King, and a desire to serve his country.[241] It is unlikely that the foreign secretary would have been able to bring pressure to bear on Goschen so effectively as did Edward VII. The King's influence over diplomatic appointments also extended to the area of the representation of foreign powers in London. In August 1909, for example, he intervened with the Austrian government to prevent the recall of his friend Count Mensdorff as Austrian ambassador to London.[242]

Wilhelm II saw Edward VII as the architect of German 'encirclement'. Three years after the King's death, he made this clear in a conversation with the British military attaché.[243] A similar view of Edward VII was presented in German propaganda during the First World War.[244] This image of Edward VII was the product of paranoia. The King had no grand political scheme, at the outset of his reign, beyond a vague desire to see peace maintained in Europe. He was not by nature anti-German, and only became so in the last years of his life as a consequence of German intransigence on the issue of naval arma-

---

[241] Goschen, diary entry, 12 August 1908, Howard (ed.), *The Diary of Sir Edward Goschen*, pp. 175–6.

[242] Bridge, *Great Britain and Austria-Hungary*, p. 22.

[243] Captain Watson to Sir E. Goschen, remarks of His Majesty the Emperor to naval attaché, 12 May 1913, *BD*, XII, no. 475, p. 701.

[244] Oberstleutnant Reinhold Wagner, *Der grösste Verbrecher an der Menschheit im zwanzigsten Jahrhundert; König Eduard VII. von England* (Berlin, 1914).

ments, the *Reichsleitung*'s chosen weapon to achieve the political goal of *Weltmacht*; a policy which the King appreciated represented a threat not just to Britain's security, but also to that of Europe and the wider world. Edward VII, like most Britons, was unconvinced by German assurances that their navy was being constructed to defend Germany's coastline and trade. He reputedly told an acquaintance shortly before his death: 'I know, that is what they say, but it is difficult to believe, considering the size of the fleet they are building.'[245] The King's strong support for measures to ensure that the Royal Navy retained maritime superiority owed much to his scepticism about German intentions.

Edward VII was not responsible for the formation of British foreign policy, and played a largely supportive role. However, there was no real difference between the views of the King and those of his ministers, so disagreements never arose over major issues. They both realised that the policy of *entente* was the most appropriate mechanism for thwarting Germany's expansionist ambitions. The King made a unique, and important, contribution to the creation and maintenance of both the Anglo-French and Anglo-Russian *ententes* by using his charm, his authority and his unrivalled network of contacts to help government policy. He was supported in his efforts by a group of friends, whose careers he in turn promoted, who were, in the main, and with much justification, suspicious of German intentions. Edward VII had appreciated by 1908, at the latest, that no political accommodation was possible between London and Berlin. However, by the time of the King's death, in May 1910, thanks in part to his own efforts, Britain was in a much stronger position, diplomatically and militarily, to resist German aggression than it had been in at the start of his reign. While the Kaiser was wrong to believe that his uncle had been responsible for the policy of *entente*, he was correct in his conviction that the British monarch had played a notable part in preparing the ground for the Anglo-French agreement and the Anglo-Russian understanding, most notably through his cultivation of the key political figures in Paris and St Petersburg, a fact which few modern historians have been prepared to acknowledge.

[245] Edward VII quoted in Metternich to Bülow, 30 January 1910, PA Bonn England Nr 78 geheim. Bd 25.

CHAPTER 4

The limits of dynastic diplomacy: royal visits and Anglo-German relations, 1906–1914

Royal visits in the era before the First World War are rarely examined for their own sake. In general, they are treated only incidentally in most books on international relations before 1914, if indeed they are mentioned at all. This is a pity, because such visits were the public face of royal diplomacy before the First World War, in an age when monarchs remained the divinely ordained centrepieces of the political systems in three of Europe's major states, Austria–Hungary, Germany and Russia, and retained a surprisingly large degree of influence over appointments and the conduct of diplomacy even in Britain. The visits exchanged between Europe's monarchs were regarded at the time as important diplomatic occasions, which were of more than passing interest to the public. They were habitually made the subject of rumour and conjecture, a trend accentuated by the emergence of a mass circulation press during the period. The outcomes of such visits were scrutinised, much in the way that summit meetings between world leaders are today, for evidence of improving or deteriorating personal relationships and political relations. The evidence suggests that royal visits could, in certain contexts, help to clear up misunderstandings between states, and generate the atmosphere of good-will required for political *rapprochement*. King Edward VII's highly successful journeys to Paris in the spring of 1903 and to the Tsar of Russia at Reval in 1908 provide obvious examples of this. The visits, while not being able to effect diplomatic transformations in Britain's relations with France and Russia of their own accord, did play a role in bringing about such changes by creating the atmosphere for improved relations between Britain and these two states, and by complementing British government's policy of *entente*.

However, when one casts an eye over Anglo-German relations between the end of the first Moroccan crisis and the outbreak of the First World War the scene is almost unremittingly bleak. The First Moroccan

Crisis itself accelerated the trend towards confrontation between Britain and Germany, while reinforcing the ties between Britain and France. The years following Germany's diplomatic humiliation at the Algeciras conference saw simply a further growth in the antagonism between London and Berlin. In the sphere of armaments, naval competition between the Royal Navy and the German high seas fleet intensified, with the introduction of the *Dreadnought* and a series of tit-for-tat naval increases. Similarly, in the diplomatic field, with rare exceptions such as the co-operation between the two powers in the Balkans in 1912/13, the trend was towards confrontation rather than compromise. The British government's wooing of Tsarist Russia gave rises to fears of 'encircle-ment' in Germany, which were greeted with *Schadenfreude*, rather than concern, in Britain. The Bosnian crisis of 1908/9 and the second Moroccan crisis of 1911 saw Germany and Britain on opposite sides, and in the latter case close to war. All the attempts which were made to settle the central issue at dispute between the two countries – their confronta-tion over naval armaments – ended in failure, because the Kaiser and Admiral Tirpitz would only accept such an agreement in return for a guarantee of British neutrality in a future continental war. It was, ultimately, unsurprising that Britain sided with France and Russia against Germany when the July crisis of 1914 erupted into a European war.

Yet throughout this period of sharply deteriorating Anglo-German relations, the two closely related royal families continued to exchange visits. King Edward VII met his nephew, Kaiser Wilhelm II, on five occasions between the summer of 1906 and his death in 1910. Three of these meetings were private in character, in so far as that adjective can ever be applied to individuals whose lives were lived out according to royal protocol. However, two took the form of state visits. George V also met the Kaiser on three occasions after his accession – twice in London and once in Berlin. As we have seen, the British government was not averse to exploiting royal visits for political purposes, when the circum-stances suggested that this could bring benefits. This begs the question as to why, despite the almost annual frequency of meetings between the Kaiser and his British relatives, such visits did little to reverse the trend towards confrontation between London and Berlin. Why indeed did Sir Edward Grey come to regard such visits as an irritant, to be kept as 'apolitical' as possible? Why too, despite an apparent willingness to do so, did the Kaiser and the German government fail to make effective use of the dynastic channel to improve relations with Britain? These are two of the main questions which must be answered through an examination of the role of royal visits in Anglo-German relations between the first Moroccan crisis and the Great War.

When Theobald von Bethmann Hollweg succeeded Bernhard Prince von Bülow as German chancellor in the summer of 1909, he entered his new office with a healthy scepticism as to the potential political value of royal visits. Bethmann told the Austrian ambassador to Berlin that although the Kaiser remained convinced that he could bring about an improvement in Anglo-German relations through face-to-face meetings with his British relatives, the reality contradicted this confident assertion.[1] Indeed we must look to the personal dimension of the visits exchanged between Edward VII and the Kaiser when seeking an initial explanation for their failure to improve Anglo-German relations. The two men detested one another. Yet the problem went deeper than a personality clash.

Politics also caused complications in the relationship between the Kaiser and the King. Wilhelm II was convinced from the 1880s onwards that his uncle was hostile to Germany politically, despite the fact that few of his uncle's actions gave credence to this view. The Kaiser developed a paranoia about Edward VII's conduct which made him believe every rumour which was brought to his attention suggesting that his uncle aimed to isolate and humiliate Germany. This sentiment hardened over time, and Wilhelm eventually came to regard Edward VII as the architect of Germany's diplomatic encirclement. It coloured his entire attitude towards British policy. From the time of the first Moroccan crisis onwards, Edward VII similarly viewed Wilhelm as an individual never to be trusted. The hardening in the King's attitude towards Germany which occurred in the last years before his death undoubtedly owed a great deal to his suspicion of his nephew's intentions. The King and the Kaiser's mutual loathing meant that the visits which they exchanged proved to be a poor forum for improving their mutual relations, never mind the relations between Britain and Germany. This is illustrated by the outcome of the meeting between the two monarchs in Germany in the summer of 1906. Although it appeared to have passed off to the satisfaction of both sides,[2] within a few months the

---

[1] Szögyény to Aehrenthal, 3 August 1909, *ÖUA*, II, no. 1701, p. 426.
[2] Memorandum by Tschrischky, 15 August 1906, *GP*, XXI(ii), no. 7196, pp. 453–5; Hardinge to Grey, 16 August 1906, *BD*, III, no. 425, p. 370; Hardinge to Edward VII, 19 August 1906, RA W 49/94.

old animosity between uncle and nephew had reasserted itself. In December 1906 when the Conservative politician Arthur Lee brought disparaging remarks about Wilhelm to Edward VII's attention, the King 'did not pretend to conceal his dislike of his prancing nephew.'[3] Nor had the visit removed the Kaiser's deep-rooted hostility towards his uncle. In March 1907, Wilhelm condemned British foreign policy in a conversation with the French chargé d'affaires at Berlin, Raymond Lecomte, and accused Edward VII and the first sea lord, Admiral Fisher, of seeking to provoke a war among the continental powers.[4] Predictably, if unfortunately, details of the Kaiser's remarks were leaked by the French to their British allies.[5] The King's assistant private secretary, Sir Frederick Ponsonby, noted that there was always an electrical charge in the air when Edward and Wilhelm were together. Ponsonby observed that the encounters passed off best when the two monarchs avoided politics.[6] Sir Charles Hardinge, who invariably accompanied Edward VII on his visits to the Kaiser, as minister-in-attendance, noted the lack of real affection between the King and his Prussian nephew. Hardinge saw this as in marked contrast to the warm rapport between Edward VII and the Austrian Emperor Franz Joseph I.[7] The King seemed to find it difficult to discuss political questions with his nephew. He only broached the question of the naval race directly with Wilhelm on one occasion – during his state visit to Berlin in February 1909. The reports on those discussions, which mainly come from German sources, indicate that the King was insufficiently forthright,[8] to such an extent that Wilhelm was able to write to Archduke Franz Ferdinand that the King seemed unconcerned by the growth of the German navy,[9] a sentiment which conflicted with the reality. The

[3] Alan Clark (ed.), *'A Good Innings'. The Private Papers of Viscount Lee of Fareham* (London, 1974), p. 95.
[4] Note by M. Lecomte, March 1907, enclosure from Lecomte to Pichon, 21 March 1907, *DDF*, 2nd series, x, no. 440, p. 704.
[5] Bertie to Grey, 31 March 1907, *BD*, VII, no. 22, pp. 19–20.
[6] Sir Frederick Ponsonby, *Recollections of Two Reigns* (London, 1951), pp. 182, 258.
[7] Hardinge to Knollys, 22 August 1907, RA W 52/12; Hardinge to Grey, 21 August 1907, *BD*, VI, no. 26, pp. 46–7.
[8] Note by the Kaiser on a conversation with the King of England on navy-building, 12 February 1909, Alfred von Tirpitz, *Der Aufbau der deutschen Weltmacht* (Berlin and Stuttgart, 1924), pp. 122–3; Bülow to Wilhelm II, 12 February 1909, GStA Merseburg HA Rep. 53 J Lit B Nr 16a, vol. IV; Bülow to Tschirschky, 13 February 1909, *GP*, XXVIII, no. 10262, p. 889; W. Görlitz (ed.), *Der Kaiser . . . Aufzeichnungen des Chefs des Marinekabinetts Admiral Georg Alexander von Müller über die Ära Wilhelms II.* (Göttingen, 1965), p. 74; memorandum by Sir Charles Hardinge, 11 February 1909, *BD*, VI, pp. 230–2.
[9] Wilhelm II to Archduke Franz Ferdinand, 12 February 1909, Robert A. Kann, 'Emperor William II and Archduke Francis Ferdinand in their Correspondence', *American Historical Review* 57, 2 (1952), 332.

element of personal loathing and political mistrust which characterised the relationship between Edward VII and the Kaiser was thus one factor, of more than negligible significance, behind the failure of the visits which they exchanged to improve Anglo-German relations. They were able to act civilly in each other's company, but once apart the hatred between them reasserted itself. The King's reluctance to talk frankly on political subjects with his nephew also meant that a diplomatic channel which Edward VII utilised to some effect in his dealings with the Tsar and French and Russian statesmen, such as Clemenceau, Isvolsky and Stolypin, was never exploited effectively during the King's meetings with the Kaiser.

However, contemporary observers were somewhat prone to exaggerate the political significance of the mistrust between Edward VII and Wilhelm. It certainly acted as a further complicating factor in Anglo-German relations, influencing both men against the other's country. However, it cannot provide the central explanation for the failure of royal visits to promote co-operation between London and Berlin. If proof of this is needed, we need look no further than the reign of King George V. George, Wilhelm's cousin, succeeded his father in May 1910. The history of mutual loathing which poisoned the Kaiser's relationship with Edward VII was absent with the new King. Prior to his accession, the Germans had seen George as a Germanophobe, who was under the influence of his fervently anti-Prussian mother Queen Alexandra. They expected him to pursue a more vigorously anti-German policy than his father.[10] However, this misrepresented George V's views. The Germanophobe influence of Queen Alexandra was more than compensated for by the Germanophilia of Queen Mary, who was a regular visitor to Germany and an admirer of Wilhelm II.[11] Additionally, the new King was on excellent terms with the Kaiser's brother, Prince Heinrich,[12] and although Heinrich was not highly regarded in Britain,[13] being seen as primarily an apologist for German naval expansion,[14] this friendship

---

[10] Seckendorff to Wilhelm II, 7 July 1902, GStA Merseburg HA Rep. 53 Lit. S Nr 19.
[11] The Princess of Wales to Wilhelm II, 17 November 1908, GStA Berlin BPH 53/190; Queen Victoria to Kaiserin Friedrich, 6 December 1891, Agatha Ramm (ed.), *Beloved and Darling Child. Last Letters between Queen Victoria and her Eldest Daughter 1886–1901* (Stroud, 1990), p. 136; James Pope-Hennessy, *Queen Mary 1867–1953* (London, 1959), pp. 286, 287–9, 475–9.
[12] John Gore, *King George V. A Personal Memoir*, pp. 286–9; Sir Harold Nicolson, *King George the Fifth: His Life and Reign* (London, 1952), pp. 206–8, 245–7; Grey to Bertie, 10 April 1913, *BD*, x(ii), no. 470, p. 694.
[13] Mensdorff to Berchtold, 11 April 1913, *ÖUA*, VI, no. 6568, p. 108.
[14] Eyre Crowe's minute on Captain Henderson, British naval attaché at Berlin, to Sir Edward Goschen, 27 January 1914, *BD*, x(i), p. 734; cf. Prince Henry of Prussia to Admiral Fisher, 24 March 1908, A. J. Marder (ed.), *Fear God and Dread Nought. The Correspondence of Admiral of the Fleet Lord Fisher of Kilverstone*, vol. II *Years of Power, 1904–1914* (London, 1956), pp. 170–1.

provided a useful diplomatic channel between the British and Prussian courts. George's own attitude towards Germany was ambivalent. He acknowledged the strength of her monarchy and the power of her army,[15] together with the efficiency of her navy, yet simultaneously regarded her as a threat to Britain's security.[16]

His own views on international relations were, however, anachronistic. He favoured a return to isolation, and distrusted the Liberal government's policy of *entente*; telling the German ambassador in the autumn of 1911 that the grouping of powers was not pleasing to him personally. However, as the same ambassador observed, the King had neither the inclination nor the authority to bring about an alteration in British policy.[17] In any case, George V refused to entertain the possibility of a general political agreement with Germany. The King told the Russian foreign minister Sergei Sazonov in October 1912 that the consequences for Germany would be disastrous in any future war at sea with Britain, vowing: 'We shall sink every single German merchant ship we shall get hold of.'[18] During the Balkan crisis in December 1912, when conflict between Austria and Serbia nearly escalated into a European war, George V proved to be a steadfast supporter of France and Russia. He warned the Kaiser's brother, Prince Heinrich, on his own initiative, that Germany could not rely on British neutrality in such a conflict.[19] In so doing, he earned praise from Edward Grey[20] and provoked Wilhelm II's fury.[21] George V told the French ambassador, Paul Cambon, that he had acted in this manner because he

[15] Metternich to Bülow, 23 February 1900, PA Bonn Russland Nr 82 Nr 1 Bd 42.
[16] Esher, journal entry, 23 April 1908, Esher Papers, Churchill College, Cambridge, ESHR 2/11; the Prince of Wales to Esher, 4 January 1909 and 31 January 1909, Esher Papers, EHSR 6/5; the Prince of Wales to Sir Charles Hardinge, 24 August 1908, Hardinge Papers, University Library, Cambridge, vol. 14.
[17] Metternich to Bethmann Hollweg, 25 September 1911, *GP*, XXIX, no. 10650, pp. 244–6.
[18] Report by Sazonov, the Russian foreign minister, to the Tsar on his journey to England, France and Russia, October, 1912. Friedrich Stieve (ed.), *Der diplomatische Schriftwechsel Iswolskis 1911–1910*, 4 vols. (Berlin, 1924), II, p. 291; cf. René Marchand (ed.), *Un livre noir. Diplomatie d'avant-guerre d'après les documents des archives russes: novembre 1910–juillet 1914*, 2 vols. (Paris, 1922–3), II, pp. 347–8.
[19] George V to Grey, 8 December 1912, Grey Papers, PRO FO 800/103; *BD*, X(ii), no. 452, p. 658; cf. Mensdorff to Berchtold, 22 December 1912, *ÖUA*, IV, no. 5028, pp. 213–14; Paul Cambon to Jules Cambon, 21 January 1913, Henri Cambon (ed.), *Paul Cambon: Correspondance 1870–1924*, 3 vols. (Paris, 1940), III, pp. 35–7.
[20] Grey to George V, 9 December 1912, *BD*, X(ii), no. 453, pp. 658–9.
[21] Prince Heinrich to Wilhelm II (annotated by Wilhelm), 11 December 1912, Tirpitz, *Der Aufbau der deutschen Weltmacht*, pp. 363–4; Lerchenfeld to Hertling, 14 December 1912, Ernst Deuerlein (ed.), *Briefwechsel Hertling–Lerchenfeld 1912–1917. Dienstliche Privatkorrespondenz zwischen dem bayerischen Ministerpräsidenten Georg Graf von Hertling und dem bayerischen Gesandten in Berlin Hugo Graf von und zu Lerchenfeld*, 2 vols. (Boppard am Rhein, 1973), I, no. 42, pp. 189–92; Nicolson to Grey, 18 February 1913, *BD*, X(ii), no. 460, pp. 673–4.

wished to remain true to the foreign policy which had been pursued by his father Edward VII.[22]

The King's desire to maintain continuity in foreign policy was not the only factor which limited the chances that the new reign would result in *rapprochement* between London and Berlin. The accession of George V was accompanied by a waning of royal influence in foreign policy and diplomacy. This was partly because the new King, unlike Edward VII, was more interested in the empire than in European affairs,[23] and it can also be attributed to George's failure to construct a court party of the same calibre as that which attached itself to his father.[24] However, the King's Toryism and view that Grey was a 'convinced radical'[25] also contributed to a decline in royal influence as it led to a certain frostiness in his dealings with the foreign office, and the government more generally. Lloyd George, the chancellor of the exchequer, professed to 'detest' court life,[26] and Asquith, the prime minister, did not take the King particularly seriously. The cerebral prime minister referred to George V as a 'nice little man' but lamented his lack of education.[27] On one occasion, he commented disparagingly to his mistress with regard the the King's opinions: 'I don't know a better reflection than his talk of what one imagines to be for the moment the average opinion of the man in the tube'.[28] It appeared at times as if the policy of the government and the policy of the court were pulling in different directions. Disillusionment with the *entente* became apparent among the King's entourage after the second Moroccan crisis of 1911, when a war between Britain and Germany was narrowly avoided. George V's two private secretaries, Lord Knollys and Lord Stamfordham, both believed that Britain's link with France and Russia was leading her inexorably and needlessly towards conflict with Germany.[29] The king himself fretted endlessly about the possibility of war between Britain and Germany,[30] and as a

---

[22] Paul Cambon to M. Jonnart, minister of foreign affairs, 23 January 1913, *DDF*, no. 248, pp. 317–18.

[23] Esher, Journal Entry, 25 August 1910, Maurice V. Brett (ed.), *Journals and Letters of Reginald, Viscount Esher*, 4 vols. (London, 1934–8), III, p. 17.

[24] Admiral Fisher to Arnold White, 22 October 1910, and Admiral Fisher to Edward A. Goulding, 28 January 1911, Marder (ed.), *Fear God and Dread Nought*, II, pp. 342, 354.

[25] Mensdorff to Aehrenthal, 13 May 1910, *ÖUA*, II, no. 2169, pp. 867–8.

[26] Kenneth Rose, *King George V* (London, 1983), p. 92.

[27] H. H. Asquith to Margot Asquith, September 1912, H. H. Asquith, *Letters to Venetia Stanley*, ed. Michael and Eleanor Brock, (Oxford, 1982), p. 43.

[28] Asquith to Venetia Stanley, 18 March 1915, *ibid.*, no. 355, p. 487.

[29] Mensdorff to Berchtold, 29 March 1912, *ÖUA*, IV, no. 3401, pp. 66–7; Knollys to Esher, 26 October and 10 November 1912, Esher Papers, ESHR 10/52.

[30] Mensdorff to Aehrenthal, 27 September 1911 and Mensdorff to Berchtold, 11 October 1912, *ÖUA*, III, no. 2660, pp. 358–9, IV, no. 4043, p. 611; Lord Stamfordham to Winston Churchill, 25 October 1911, *BD*, VII, no. 649, p. 642.

consequence showed markedly greater enthusiasm for meetings with the Prussian royal family than did his ministers, greeting the prospect of a visit to Berlin in 1913 for the wedding of the Kaiser's daughter with genuine pleasure,[31] in contrast to his ministers who regarded it with ill-concealed dread. The King, however, seemed most comfortable in the role of constitutional figurehead, and suppressed his private doubts by supporting the *entente* in public and in conversations with foreign statesmen. His attitude towards Wilhelm was polite, rather than cordial, and the visits which they exchanged were successful on a personal level,[32] but they were essentially apolitical occasions which had no lasting impact on Anglo-German relations.

George V's visit to Berlin in May 1913 for the wedding of Wilhelm's daughter, Viktoria Luise, provides a good illustration of this. Beforehand, the German naval attaché in London had speculated that the King would use the occasion to suggest the basis of a compromise on the naval question to the Kaiser.[33] Instead, aside from limited discussions on Anglo-German relations and the need for stability in the Balkans, George V refrained from politics.[34] The majority of foreign diplomats found him unimpressive,[35] and the King himself seemed most at ease talking to his cousin, Tsar Nicholas II,[36] and discussing the quality of the Prussian royal stables with the Kaiser's Master of the Horse, Baron von Reischach.[37]

If Edward VII and the Kaiser's mutual loathing, and George V's reluctance to involve himself in political controversy provide two

---

[31] Prince Heinrich of Prussia to Wilhelm II, 15 April 1913, PA Bonn England Nr 81 Nr 1 Bd 25.

[32] Goschen to Hardinge, 10 May 1910, Hardinge Papers, vol. 20; Goschen, diary entry, 24 May 1910, C. H. D. Howard (ed.), *The Diary of Edward Goschen 1900–1914* (London, 1980), pp. 205–6; note by Bethmann Hollweg, 23 May 1911, *GP*, XXIX, no. 10562, pp. 120–1; John Gore, *King George V. A Personal Memoir* (London, 1941), pp. 122, 257–8, 278; Wilhelm Widenmann, *Marine-Attaché an der kaiserlich-deutschen Botschaft in London 1907–1912* (Göttingen, 1952), pp. 112–16.

[33] Captain Erich von Müller, naval attaché in London, to the imperial navy office, 28 March 1913. Tirpitz, *Der Aufbau der deutschen Weltmacht*, pp. 385–6.

[34] Goschen to Grey, 28 May 1913, *BD*, x(ii), no. 476, p. 703; Jagow to Tschirschky, 26 and 28 May 1913, *GP*, XXXIV(ii), nos. 13331 and 13340, pp. 864–5, 871–2; Szögyény to Berchtold, 26 May and 3 June 1913, *ÖUA*, VI, nos. 7161 and 7257, pp. 526–7, 583–4; Wilhelm II to Archduke Franz Ferdinand, 27 May 1913, Kann, 'William II and Francis Ferdinand', pp. 348–9; Ponsonby, *Recollections*, pp. 292–9; Goschen, diary entries, 21 and 23 May 1913, Howard (ed.), *Goschen: Diary*, pp. 275–6.

[35] Baron Beyens to Davignon, minister of foreign affairs, 26 May 1913. Jean Stengers, 'Guillaume II et le Roi Albert à Potsdam en novembre 1913', *Bulletin de la Classe des Lettres et des Sciences Morales et Politiques*, 6th series, IV, 7, 12 (1993), 238, note 54; Jules Cambon to Pichon, 26 May 1913, *DDF*, 3rd series, VI, no. 622, p. 725.

[36] Rose, *George V*, p. 166; Nicolson, *King George the Fifth*, p. 216; Jules Cambon to Pichon, 28 May 1913, *DDF*, 3rd series, VI, no. 635, p. 741.

[37] Hugo Baron von Reischach, *Under Three Emperors*, English translation (London, 1927), p. 243.

explanations for the failure of royal visits to improve Anglo-German relations, then the attitude adopted by the press and public opinion towards the visits provides another. An element of chauvinism crept into the attitude adopted by the press in both countries towards questions of international politics. The posturing of newspapers in Britain and Germany soured the atmosphere in which royal visits took place and even on occasion threatened to prevent them from going ahead. After the meeting between Edward VII and the Kaiser in Germany in the summer of 1907, elements of the German press implied that the King had come to Germany as a supplicant, respecting Germany's reluctance 'to beg for the friendship of any Power'.[38] Newspapers on the political right in Britain such as *The Times* and *The Morning Post* gave the visit only limited coverage, and failed to echo the hope of the liberal press that Anglo-German relations would be improved by it.[39] The influence of the press was most apparent in the weeks before Edward VII travelled to Berlin on a state visit in February 1909. The *Daily Mail* printed a fabricated report that the visit had been cancelled, much to the consternation of the British court,[40] and antagonised the Kaiser by printing information about plans for the expansion of the Royal Navy on his birthday, something which he described as 'a gross impertinence'.[41] The Germanophobia and Anglophobia exhibited by the British and German press when incidents flared up between the two countries in the period between royal visits also undermined the benefits of these exchanges. Thus, for example, when the German press attacked Edward VII in the spring of 1907 for visiting Spain and Italy, implying that he had gone to these countries with the aim of recruiting them to an anti-German coalition,[42] the King himself was moved to urge the postponement of a visit to Britain by the Kaiser.[43] Similarly, in the

---

[38] Sir Fairfax Cartwright, British minister in Munich, to Grey, 17 August 1907, *BD*, VI, no. 24, pp. 42–3.

[39] Wilhelm von Stumm to Bülow, 22 August 1907, *GP*, XXV(i), no. 8533, pp. 37–40.

[40] Knollys to Esher, 1 January 1909, Esher Papers, ESHR 10/51.

[41] Wilhelm II's comment on the *Hannoverscher Courier*, 29 January 1909, PA Bonn England Nr 78 geheim. Bd 17.

[42] Lascelles to Grey, 19 April 1907, *BD*, VI, no. 15, p. 28; Barrère to Pichon, 18 April 1907, *DDF*, 2nd series, x, no. 464, pp. 757–9; Monts to Bülow, 18 and 20 April 1907, *GP*, XXI(ii), nos. 7215–6, pp. 497–8; Stumm to Bülow, *ibid.*, no. 7217, pp. 499–501; Stumm to Bülow, 6 May 1907, PA Bonn England Nr 81 Nr 1 Bd 17; Grand Duchess Luise of Baden to Wilhelm II, 13 May 1907, GStA Merseburg HA Rep. 53 J Lit. B Nr 83.

[43] Edward VII to Hardinge, 27 April 1907, Hardinge Papers, vol. 9; Hardinge to Edward VII, 24 April 1907, RA W 51/73; Hardinge to Edward VII, 30 April 1907. RA W51/74; Hardinge to Edward VII, 2 May 1907, RA W51/75; Hardinge to Lascelles, 2 May 1907, Lascelles Papers, PRO FO 800/13.

autumn of 1908, the publication of injudicious remarks by the Kaiser on Anglo-German relations in the *Daily Telegraph*[44] and evidence that an interview which Wilhelm had given to a journalist in which he attacked Edward VII personally was about to appear in an American magazine[45] led British and German courtiers to contemplate the cancellation of Edward VII's visit to Berlin in February 1909.[46] The fleeting conviviality generated by royal visits could not alter the underlying pattern of popular hostility, on the political right in both countries, towards the idea of better Anglo-German relations. The attitude of the press and public opinion must thus be seen as an additional factor behind the failure of the visits to do anything other than generate transient good-will.

Conversely, the reluctance of the British government, in particular, to build upon the success of royal visits with further initiatives to improve relations with Germany also contributed to the failure of the visits to improve the political atmosphere. The journey of the British war minister, R. B. Haldane, to Berlin in September 1906 was a rare example of such a step. It had the blessing of the King, who took a keen interest in Haldane's progress. It also pleased the Kaiser and his entourage.[47] Unfortunately, Haldane made the mistake of being in the German capital on the anniversary of Prussia's victory over France at Sedan, in the Franco-Prussian war. Grey, ever sensitive to French reactions, reprimanded Haldane; implying that the episode had endangered the *entente*.[48] Thereafter Grey's policy of assiduously cultivating the support of the French was pursued, rather than Haldane's desire, as expressed in a letter to Wilhelm II, to see the establishment of 'yet closer relations between Germany and England'.[49] The foreign secretary's terror of

[44] Katharine A. Lerman, *The Chancellor as Courtier. Bernhard von Bülow and the Governance of Germany 1900–1909* (Cambridge, 1990), pp. 210–47; Terence F. Cole, 'The *Daily Telegraph* Affair and its Aftermath: The Kaiser, Bülow and the Reichstag, 1908–1909', in *Kaiser Wilhelm II: New Interpretations*, ed. John C. G. Röhl and Nicolaus Sombart (Cambridge, 1982), pp. 249–68.

[45] The so-called 'Hale Interview' was suppressed prior to publication, cf. Fritz Fischer, 'Exzesse der Autokratie – das Hale-Interview Wilhelms II. vom 19. Juli 1908', in *Deutschlands Sonderung von Europa, 1862–1945*, ed. Wilhelm Alff (Frankfurt am Main, 1984), pp. 53–78; Ralph R. Menning and Carol Bresnahan Menning, '"Baseless Allegations": Wilhelm II and the Hale Interview of 1908', *Central European History* 16, 4 (1983), 368–97.

[46] Hardinge to Goschen, 25 November 1908, Hardinge Papers, vol. 13; Goschen, diary entry, 30 November 1908, Howard (ed.), *Goschen: Diary*, p. 185.

[47] Diary of Mr Haldane's visit to Germany, September 1906, *BD*, III, no. 435, pp. 376–81; Lascelles to Grey, 14 September 1906, *ibid.*, no. 438, p. 389; Arthur Davidson, equerry to King Edward VII, to Haldane, 9 September 1906, Tschirschky to Haldane, 9 December 1906. Haldane Papers, National Library of Scotland, MS 5907.

[48] Grey to Haldane, 3 September 1906, Haldane Papers, MS 5907.

[49] Haldane to Wilhelm II, 26 December 1906, *ibid.*

provoking the French through manifestations of friendliness towards Germany reached new heights of preposterousness in the autumn of 1907 when he vetoed a visit by the band of the Coldstream Guards to the Rhineland on the basis that the visit would be impossible 'without a disturbing effect upon foreign relations'.[50] Neither the King nor Haldane could understand what vital interest was involved in the visit of a military band to Germany,[51] but they had to give way in the face of pressure from Grey, who brought the strenous objections of the French foreign minister, M. Pichon, to their attention.[52] A similar reluctance to follow up royal visits with further political initiatives was discernible after 1910. After the Kaiser's visit to London in May 1911, Sir Edward Goschen noted that King George himself wished to place strict limits on any *rapprochement* with Germany. The ambassador recorded in his diary that the King was 'dead against any binding naval and political arrangement – and told me to try and stop it! . . .'[53] During the course of the same visit Sir Arthur Nicolson reassured the French ambassador that it would alter nothing politically. Nicolson accepted that the Kaiser's visit to London had created a certain *détente* in Anglo-German relations, but noted that such impressions passed whereas political realities remained unchanged.[54]

Perception, misperception and differing expectations all played an important role in influencing the outcome of Anglo-German royal visits. In particular, there was a discrepancy between the manner in which the visits were regarded by the British and Germans. The Kaiser and his courtiers, along with German public opinion and the press, tended to exaggerate the importance of royal visits and their ability to effect a transformation in Anglo-German relations. Thus Edward VII's visit to the Kaiser in the summer of 1906 was described melodramatically in the German press as a last chance to improve relations with Britain.[55] The chief of the Prussian general staff, Helmuth von Moltke, noted in his diary in the summer of 1907 that Edward VII's decision to invite Wilhelm II to Britain in the following autumn represented a 'turning point' in British policy towards Germany.[56] At the time, the Kaiser

---

[50] Grey to Knollys, 6 October 1907, Haldane Papers, MS 5907; cf. Grey to Haldane, 4 October 1907, *ibid.*

[51] Knollys to Grey, 8 October 1907, Grey Papers, FO 800/103.

[52] Grey to Haldane, 6 October 1907, Knollys to Haldane, 8 October 1907, Knollys to Haldane, 9 October 1907, Haldane Papers MS 5907.

[53] Goschen, diary entry, 22 May 1911, Howard (ed.) *Goschen: Diary*, p. 235.

[54] Paul Cambon to Jules Cambon, 23 May 1911, H. Cambon (ed.), *Paul Cambon: Correspondance*, p. 323.

[55] Cartwright to Grey, 20 August 1906, *BD*, III, no. 426, pp. 370–2; Geoffray to Bourgeois, 22 August 1906, *DDF*, 2nd series, x, no. 187, pp. 286–8.

[56] Helmuth von Moltke, *Erinnerungen, Briefe, Dokumente 1877–1916* (Stuttgart, 1922), 7 July 1907, p. 364.

shared Moltke's rose-tinted view. The same pattern of inflated expectation was observable in the enthusiasm with which Wilhelm and his chancellor, Bülow, greeted the prospect of Edward VII's state visit to Berlin in 1909. The Kaiser told his aunt, the Grand Duchess of Baden, that it would have a calming effect on the situation in Europe,[57] and Bülow declared optimistically that 'politically the visit of the King . . . means that the horizon is clearing in the west'.[58]

As late as May 1913, when George V went to Berlin for the wedding of the Kaiser's daughter, Wilhelm himself drew exaggerated conclusions from the cordial discussions which he held with his British cousin and the Tsar. He informed Archduke Franz Ferdinand of Austria–Hungary that: 'Viewed from the political standpoint it went off extremely pleasantly and favourably. King George V, the emperor and I were agreed on an absolutely complete comformity regarding the affairs of the Balkan states.'[59] Yet the discussions between the three monarchs had been non-commital in character. Their joint condemnation of Bulgaria and support for Greece did not contradict the official policy of their governments, and even the Austro-Hungarians seemed unperturbed. Vienna's ambassador in Berlin did not believe that there would be any *rapprochement* between Germany, on the one hand, and Britain and Russia, on the other, as a consequence.[60] However Wilhelm himself took a different view. Princess Marie Radziwill, an astute observer of court life in Berlin before the First World War, wrote to a friend, following the royal wedding:

The Emperor is already thinking of returning the King of England's visit, imagining that the meeting in Berlin has weakened the Triple Entente. It is far too soon. Even if there were any vestige of truth in this hope, the Emperor would only ruin the effect of it by a hasty and perhaps inopportune visit.[61]

Two points can be made with regard to such views. Firstly they exhibited a tendency to exaggerate the importance of royalty politically. Secondly they indicated that the Germans in general, and the Kaiser in particular, misunderstood the character of the British political system, and failed to appreciate that the British monarch possessed only limited

[57] Wilhelm II to Grand Duchess Luise of Baden, 5 February 1909, GStA Berlin BPH 53/81.
[58] Bülow to Wilhelm II, 9 February 1909, GStA Merseburg HA Rep. 53 J Lit. B Nr 16a vol. IV.
[59] Wilhelm II to Franz Ferdinand, 27 May 1913, Kann, 'William II and Franz Ferdinand', p. 348; cf. Goschen to Grey, 28 May 1913, *BD*, X(ii), no. 476, p. 703.
[60] Szögyény to Berchtold, 3 June 1913, *ÖUA*, VI, no. 7259, p. 585.
[61] Princess Marie von Radziwill to General di Robilant, 30 May 1913, Cyril Spencer Fox (ed.), *This Was Germany. An Observer at the Court of Berlin. Letters of Princess Marie Radziwill to General di Robilant, 1908–1915*, English translation (London, 1937), p. 261.

power, even in foreign and military affairs. Thus, in October 1910, Wilhelm informed the British ambassador that he had remained silent on the naval question for several months because he had wished to give George V sufficient time to formulate his policy, little realising that such matters were not in the hands of the court.[62] Similarly in February 1912, the Kaiser's friend, the industrialist Walther Rathenau, recorded a baffling comment by Wilhelm on the question of Anglo-German relations, which throws his misunderstanding of the political role of the British monarchy into sharp relief. 'The Kaiser only wanted to go to Cowes again', Rathenau observed, 'then he would settle everything. The King trusted him. His plan was: the United States of Europe against America. The English are not unsympathetic to this.'[63]

Policy miscalculations were made as a result of such misperceptions. The Kaiser agreed to give the final authorisation for his foreign minister Kiderlen-Wächter's plan to send the gunboat *Panther* to Agadir in the summer of 1911 – the move which sparked off the second Moroccan crisis – because he concluded on the basis of the enthusiastic reception which he received in London in May 1911 from the royal family and the public that the British would not intervene in support of the French in Morocco.[64] Wilhelm's irritation with the British when they gave strong backing to the French in the subsequent crisis stemmed from his belief that he had forewarned George V of the coming action.[65] This was something which the King denied.[66] Similarly the Kaiser's willingness to support the policy of brinkmanship in July 1914 was also influenced by a false assessment of the likely British reaction based on an overestimation of the political authority of the British monarchy. Wilhelm remained reluctant to accept that Britain would intervene, until almost the final moment, because George V gave Wilhelm's brother, Prince Heinrich, an assurance that Britain would do its best to stay out of a European

---

[62] Goschen to Grey, 16 October 1910, *BD*, VI, no. 403, pp. 530–3.

[63] Rathenau, diary entry, 13 February 1912, H. Pogge von Strandmann (ed.), *Walther Rathenau. Notes and Diaries 1907–1922*, English translation (Oxford, 1985), p. 147.

[64] Note by Bethmann Hollweg, 23 May 1911, *GP*, XXIX, no. 10562, p. 120; Lamar J. R. Cecil, *Wilhelm II. Emperor and Exile, 1900–1941* (Chapel Hill, NC, 1996), p. 163; Radziwill to di Robilant, 12 July 1911, Fox (ed.), *This Was Germany*, p. 167; Nicolson to Hardinge, 5 July 1911, *BD*, VII, no. 359, p. 338; Nicolson to Cartwright, 24 July 1911, *ibid.*, no. 418, p. 397.

[65] Jenisch to Bethmann Hollweg, 13 August 1911, *GP*, XXIX, no. 10639, p. 230; Goschen to Grey, 18 August 1911, *BD*, VII, no. 483, p. 457; note by Sir John French, 1911, ibid., no. 490, p. 462; Winston Churchill's note of conversations between the German Emperor and Sir John French, 10 August 1911. Randolph Churchill, *Winston S. Churchill, vol. II Companion, 1907–1911* (London, 1969), Part II, pp. 1107–8.

[66] Mensdorff to Aehrenthal, 29 September 1911, *ÖUA*, III, no. 2669, pp. 366–9.

war.[67] When Sir Edward Grey repudiated the King's statement,[68] Wilhelm remained convinced that it represented the true British policy, telling Admiral Tirpitz: 'I have the word of a king and that is sufficient for me.'[69]

If an overestimation of the political importance of royal visits and their ability to influence bilateral relations was the primary characteristic of the attitude of the Germans, the British side had a more realistic idea of their worth. Edward VII's private secretary Lord Knollys summed up their value succinctly when he wrote in 1906: 'Personally I am not much of a believer in meetings between Sovereigns . . . being of permanent benefit though they may be of *temporary* use in rounding the corners.'[70] The King's meetings with the German Kaiser were regarded as a necessary obligation which could have the consequence of moderating German policy towards Britain but nothing more. This was the rationale behind Sir Charles Hardinge's support for a visit by the Kaiser to Britain in 1907. However, wider considerations, notably the naval competition between Britain and Germany made Hardinge doubt the value of such exchanges: 'I am sceptical that the visit of the German Emperor will do any good, or in fact any other visits, so long as the Navy League maintains its propaganda and holds up England as the bogey whose power at sea has one day to be broken.'[71] Hardinge's increasing pessimism as to the prospects of a naval agreement with Germany led him to take an even bleaker attitude as to the political benefits of royal visits later in the decade. In the autumn of 1908 he wondered whether it would be worthwhile for Edward VII to travel to Berlin on a state visit at all in February of the following year,[72] and at the end of the visit Hardinge informed the Prussian courtier Count Seckendorff that there could be no real trust between Britain and Germany until the naval question was resolved.[73]

[67] Captain von Müller to the imperial navy office, 26 July 1914; Prince Heinrich of Prussia to Kaiser Wilhelm II, 28 July 1914, Max Montgelas and Walther Schücking (eds.), *Outbreak of the World War. German Documents Collected by Karl Kautsky*, English translation (New York, 1924), nos. 207 and 374, pp. 215, 328–9; Lerchenfeld to Hertling, 31 July 1914, Deuerlein (ed.), *Briefwechsel Hertling–Lerchenfeld 1912–1917*, I, no. 113, pp. 321–2.

[68] Lichowsky to the German foreign office, 29 July 1914, *Outbreak of the World War*, no. 368, pp. 321–2.

[69] Alfred von Tirpitz, *My Memoirs*, English translation, 2 vols. (London, 1920), I, p. 275.

[70] Knollys to Mallet, 18 June 1906, Grey Papers, PRO FO 800/103.

[71] Hardinge to Lascelles, 4 June 1907, Lascelles Papers, PRO FO 800/13.

[72] Hardinge to Knollys, 4 October 1908, RA W 54/93a; in taking this line Hardinge was echoing the views of the British court, cf. George, Prince of Wales, to Hardinge, 24 August 1908 and Knollys to Hardinge, 29 August 1908, Hardinge Papers, vol. 14.

[73] Vierhaus (ed.), *Spitzemberg: Tagebuch*, diary entry, 15 February 1909, p. 499.

The official British attitude towards meetings between the Kaiser and the British royal family was almost unremittingly negative. Throughout his tenure as foreign secretary, Sir Edward Grey adopted an attiude towards these exchanges which precluded serious discussion and compromise from the outset. Before Edward VII's meeting with Wilhelm in 1906, Grey stated in a letter to Sir Francis Bertie, the British ambassador to Paris, that no basis existed for an *entente* between London and Berlin,[74] and he instructed Hardinge, who accompanied the King, to stress this in his discussions with the Kaiser and Heinrich von Tschirschky, the state secretary of the German foreign office, who accompanied Wilhelm during the visit.[75] Grey had essentially made his mind up about Germany before coming into office. He believed that she was determined to dominate Europe and hence that there was no room for compromise with her.[76] His sentiments were shared by the most prominent of his officials, such as Hardinge, Bertie and Eyre Crowe, as well as by many of the members of Edward VII's inner circle, such as Viscount Esher and Admiral Fisher. Those in the cabinet who were more willing to accept German assurances of friendship at face value, such as Haldane and John Morley, lacked the influence to impose their views on the foreign office. The British agenda when meetings between King Edward and King George and the Kaiser occurred was thus severely restricted in scope. During the Kaiser's state visit to England in 1907, for example, Grey wrote a memorandum on possible subjects which might arise which was negative in every detail. The foreign secretary indicated that Britain would continue to support France in Morocco, and would not agree to participate in the Kaiser's cherished project of the Berlin–Baghdad railway without first consulting the French and Russians. Even on more personal aspects, he showed a lack of willingness to compromise, indicating his marked reluctance for the King to travel to Berlin on a state visit, and refusing to contemplate the prolongation of Lascelles's term as ambassador to Berlin after 1908, despite the fact that Sir Frank was on excellent terms with the Kaiser.[77] Before this and other royal visits took place, Grey and the foreign office habitually engaged in a damage limitation exercise,

---

[74] Grey to Bertie, 9 July 1906, *BD*, III, no. 420, pp. 361–2.
[75] Cambon to Bourgeois, 26 June 1906, *DDF*, 2nd series, x, no. 120, pp. 186–9.
[76] Zara S. Steiner, *Britain and the Origins of the First World War* (London, 1977); Keith M. Wilson, *The Policy of the Entente. Essays on the Determinants of British Foreign Policy 1904–1914* (Cambridge, 1985).
[77] Memorandum by Grey, November 1907, *BD*, VI, no. 59, pp. 91–2; on the British attitude to the Baghdad railway, see Maybelle Kennedy Chapman, *Great Britain and the Baghdad Railway 1880–1914* (Northampton, MA, 1948).

telling the French and Russian governments that the exchanges of visits between the British and Prussian courts had no wider relevance. The instructions given by Sir Arthur Nicolson to Sir George Buchanan, the British ambassador in St Petersburg, prior to the Kaiser's visit to London in 1911, are typical of the tone which was adopted:

> If you get an opportunity you might inform Sazonow, quite informally, and privately, that the visit of the German Emperor to London . . . has no political significance whatsoever, and is merely a private and family affair . . .. There is no desire or intention on our part to talk politics during his sojourn here, and so I hope there will be no misgivings in Petersburg on the subject. We have also privately told the French what I have mentioned above, and they perfectly understand the reasons and the object of the visit.[78]

The British court was encouraged to follow the government line of downplaying the political significance of Anglo-German royal visits. In the summer of 1906, after meeting the Kaiser at Friedrichshof, King Edward VII assured the French ambassador that his visit to Wilhelm had been a family obligation, devoid of political implications. In order to emphasize this, the King had abstained from wearing a military uniform: behaviour which was most unorthodox for a monarch paying a visit to another sovereign at the time.[79] Similarly, when King George V invited Wilhelm to London in 1911 for the unveiling of the Queen Victoria memorial outside Buckingham Palace, he stressed the apolitical nature of the visit. This was made explicit in the following passage of the letter which he addressed to his Prussian cousin:

> The fact of your presence as dear Grandmama's eldest Grandson would be very much appreciated by us & the family. It will be a purely family gathering. I am not asking any representatives, otherwise the ceremony would assume proportions greater than those within which I wish to keep it . . . I propose that your visit should be quite a private one.[80]

How then can this systematic tendency to play down the political significance of the visits be accounted for? A number of explanations can be advanced. The most obvious one is that Grey and the foreign office could see no advantage in exploiting the visits for political purposes. They had to accept that such visits would take place from time to time because of the close family connections between the Hohenzollerns

---

[78] Nicolson to Buchanan, 28 February 1911, *BD*, x(i), no. 702, pp. 680–1; cf. Goschen to Nicolson, 28 May 1913, *BD*, x(ii), no. 477, pp. 703; Cambon to Bourgeois, 26 June 1906, *DDF*, 2nd series, x, no. 120, pp. 186–9.

[79] Geoffray to Bourgeois, 22 August 1906, *DDF*, 2nd series, x, p. 287.

[80] George V to Wilhelm II, 9 February 1911, GStA Berlin BPH Rep. 53/258.

and the British monarchy, but not that these would give rise to initiatives designed to improve Anglo-German relations.[81] Grey steadfastly pursued the policy of *entente* with France and Russia as a means of containing German power within Europe, and of appeasing Russia in Asia. The policy was predicated upon the belief that the French would abandon Britain if she drew too close to Germany. This helps us account for the repeated and persistent attempts by Grey and his officials to assure the French government that the visits were apolitical occasions. Grey tended to give the French ambassador, Paul Cambon, the impression that the British royal family's meetings with the Kaiser were of no significance,[82] and sometimes his tone verged on the apologetic when he announced that such visits would be taking place. In August 1908, for example, when informing a French diplomat of Edward VII's forthcoming visit to Berlin, Grey was eager to emphasize that he had agreed to it only reluctantly and that it would be abandoned if a major dispute arose between Britain and Germany in the interim.[83] In his memoirs, written after the war, Grey recalled that the British royal family's meetings with the Kaiser had caused him 'a great deal of trouble' because he always had to be mindful of the sensitivities of the French.[84]

The foreign secretary's fear of upsetting the French also explains why, on occasion, he was insistent that visits exchanged between the British royal family and the Kaiser should be followed by summits involving the British monarch and whoever happened to be French President at the time. Thus, President Fallières of France came to London in 1908, shortly after Wilhelm II's state visit to Windsor of November 1907, and in March 1913 Grey invited President Poincaré to visit London the following June,[85] one month after George V and Queen Mary were scheduled to travel to Berlin for the wedding of the Kaiser's daughter, Viktoria Luise. When informing Sir Francis Bertie of the reasons for issuing the invitation to Fallières, Grey emphasised the centrality of political considerations. It would 'show that there was no change in our foreign policy'.[86]

---

[81] Cf. Grey to Bertie, 19 June 1907, *BD*, VI, no. 45, pp. 79–80; Hardinge to Grey, 7 April 1907, *ibid.*, no. 44, pp. 78–9.

[82] Paul Cambon to Pichon, 14 and 16 November 1907, *DDF*, 2nd series, XI, nos. 199–200, pp. 329, 331–4.

[83] de Manneville to Pichon, 22 August 1908, *DDF*, 2nd series, XI, no. 426, p. 738.

[84] Grey of Fallodon, *Twenty-five Years 1892–1916*, 2 vols. (London, 1925), I, pp. 149–50.

[85] Paul Cambon to Pichon, 27 March 1913, *DDF*, 3rd series, VI, no. 79, p. 103; Pichon to Paul Cambon, 29 March 1913, *ibid.*, no. 107, p. 132.

[86] Grey to Bertie, 19 June 1907, *BD*, VI, no. 45, pp. 79–80.

The emphasis which the British government consistently placed on the 'private' and 'family' character of the visits exchanged between the two courts was also motivated by political considerations. Grey had shown through his own utterances and actions, notably with regard to the Anglo-Russian negotiations, that he saw royal visits as a useful complement to government policy when circumstances allowed.[87] Grey did so again in 1914 when he pressurised George V and Queen Mary, who were both reluctant to go, into paying a state visit to Paris, by emphasising that this would serve as a manifestation of the political solidity of the Anglo-French *entente*.[88] Occasionally, he and his officials were forced to concede that Anglo-German royal visits also had a political dimension.

This was revealed most obviously in the autumn of 1907, when Wilhelm II sought to cancel his state visit to England on the grounds that he had 'bronchitis'.[89] King Edward VII urged his nephew to reconsider,[90] and instructed his own private secretary, Lord Knollys, to consult with the prime minister, Sir Henry Campbell-Bannermann, Grey, Hardinge and the German ambassador, Count Metternich. The King felt that the Kaiser's alternative suggestion – that the Crown Prince could visit Windsor in his place accompanied by the Kaiserin – would not be acceptable. 'It would be too evident that he is afraid of coming over just now', Edward wrote, intimating that in his view the 'lawsuit at Berlin', rather than poor health, was the real reason for Wilhelm's reluctance to come to England himself.[91] The King was probably correct, for one of the Kaiser's closest friends, Kuno von Moltke had just lost a libel action against a journalist who had accused him of being homosexual. The scandal tainted Wilhelm's court by association.[92]

Grey agreed with the King's view that the 'painful revelations' about Moltke were behind the Kaiser's wish to abandon his state visit to

[87] See above and ch. 3.
[88] Rose, *George V*, pp. 163–4; Pope-Hennessy, *Queen Mary*, pp. 483–5; Keith A. Hamilton, *Bertie of Thame. Edwardian Ambassador* (London, 1990), pp. 309–10; Ponsonby, *Recollections*, pp. 299–305; Trautmannsdorff to Berchtold, 24 April 1914, *ÖUA*, VII, no. 9608, p. 1085.
[89] Wilhelm II to Edward VII, 31 October 1907, RA W 52/47.
[90] Edward VII to Wilhelm II, 31 October 1907, RA W 52/48.
[91] Edward VII to Knollys, 31 October 1907, RA W 52/46.
[92] On the Eulenburg–Moltke scandals, cf. Isabel V. Hull, *The Entourage of Kaiser Wilhelm II, 1888–1918* (Cambridge, 1982), pp. 109–45; John C. G. Röhl, *Kaiser, Hof und Staat: Wilhelm II. und die deutsche Politik* (Munich, 1987), pp. 35–77; Thomas A. Kohut, *Wilhelm II and the Germans. A Study in Leadership* (Oxford, 1991), p. 108.

England,[93] as did his friend the war Minister, R. B. Haldane.[94] However, the foreign secretary was more concerned with the political implications if the visit were to be abandoned. He urged Sir Frank Lascelles, the British ambassador at Berlin, to 'see Bülow at once and strongly urge upon him the unfortunate result upon public opinion in this country which a postponement of the visit would entail'. Grey believed that such an eventuality would have disastrous consequences and 'might check the improvement in Anglo-German relations which had hitherto been evident'.[95] Jonathan Steinberg has argued convincingly that Grey used the Moltke scandal in Germany to 'exert pressure on the Kaiser.'[96] The Anglo-Russian *entente* had been concluded in August 1907, and Grey needed Wilhelm II's state visit to go ahead in order to avoid accusations from the radical wing of the Liberal Party and the from the pro-German press that the Kaiser had refused to come to Britain in protest at the agreement. The tactic certainly worked. Wilhelm vehemently denied Grey's insinuations about the court scandals, and telegraphed plaintively to Metternich on 1 November: 'That had nothing directly to do with it! . . . Kings are still mere humans and can sometimes be ill!'[97] By the following day, having made a miraculous recovery, Wilhelm had changed his mind and resolved to go to England after all,[98] thus salvaging not only the state visit, but also Grey's standing with the radical wing of his own party.

Similarly, shortly before Edward VII's state visit to Berlin in February 1909, when the King's consort, Queen Alexandra, fell ill, the fear was expressed that it would prove politically damaging if she did not accompany the King to the German capital. The Queen's hostility towards the Prussians was well known and as one observer commented at the time, if she proved unable to travel: 'nobody will give her the credit of the failure being due to her health'.[99] Fortuitously, from a political point of view, the Queen recovered in time to accompany her husband to Berlin. In general, however, the British government persistently sought to play down the value of such visits, encouraging foreign diplomats and statesmen, together with domestic public opinion, to view them as family get-

[93] Grey to Knollys, 1 November 1907, RA W 52/53.
[94] Haldane to his mother, 6 November 1907, Haldane Papers, MS 5978.
[95] Grey to Lascelles, 1 November 1907, *BD*, VI, no. 58, p. 88.
[96] Jonathan Steinberg, 'The Kaiser and the British: the State Visit to Windsor, November 1907', in *Kaiser Wilhelm II: New Interpretations* (Cambridge, 1982), p. 136.
[97] Wilhelm II's marginalia on report of Metternich to Bülow, 1 November 1907, PA Bonn Preussen Nr 1 Nr 40 Bd 15.   [98] Metternich to Bülow, 2 November 1907, *ibid.*
[99] Hardinge to Knollys, 25 January 1909, RA W 54/162.

togethers rather than as political occasions. Paradoxically it was the very political sensitivity of the visits which made the government depict them in this manner.

The arrangements for the visits were the subject of controversy between the foreign office and the court on numerous occasions. This also reflected their political sensitivity. In 1907, for example, Sir Edward Grey urged the King and his private secretary to dissuade the Kaiser from bringing his chancellor, Bülow, and his war minister, General von Einem, to England, fearing that this would turn the visit into a 'regular demonstration' which could subsequently be exploited by the Germans for propaganda purposes against the French. Good relations with Germany, Grey vowed, would only be possible 'on the distinct understanding' that this would not be 'at the expense of our friendship with France'.[100] Even the normally Germanophile Lascelles echoed the foreign secretary, asserting that Bülow's absence from the Kaiser's entourage would serve 'as proof of the slight political importance which the Emperor attached to' the visit.[101] When the controversy first arose, Edward VII had minuted angrily on a document that he was not in a position to dictate who his nephew brought with him to England.[102] A mixture of official and unofficial pressure eventually removed the possibility of Bülow travelling to England as part of the Kaiser's entourage.[103]

However it was not considerations of the international reaction alone which influenced the government's attitude towards the arrangements for royal visits, but also perceptions of the impact which such visits were likely to have on domestic politics. This was revealed most obviously in 1912 during a dispute which arose between the palace and the government over the arrangements and timing of George V's visits to European capitals. Sir Edward Grey was most insistent that the King should go on a state visit to Paris before undertaking a journey to Berlin. This irritated the King, the Queen and the court because they believed that Berlin, as the capital of a monarchy should take precedence over Paris, the capital of a mere republic. Grey argued that if the King went to Berlin first then 'the *entente* would be destroyed' an argument which Lord Knollys found preposterous, and most revealing of the relative state of Anglo-French relations.[104] However, domestic considerations

---

[100] Grey to Lascelles, 18 September 1907, *BD*, VI, no. 48, pp. 81–2; cf. Grey to Haldane, 4 September 1907, Haldane Papers MS 5907; Steinberg, 'The Kaiser and the British', p. 135.
[101] Lascelles to Grey, 20 September 1907, *BD*, VI, no. 49, pp. 82–3.
[102] Grey to Knollys (with a note by Edward VII), 25 August 1907, RA W 52/14.
[103] Hardinge, minute on interview with Count Metternich, 7 October 1907, RA W 52/38; Grey to Lascelles, 4 October 1907, *BD*, VI, p. 84.
[104] Knollys to Esher, 27 September 1912, Esher Papers, ESHR 10/52.

had been just as important as considerations of foreign policy in influencing Grey's attitude; for following the war scare which had accompanied the second Moroccan crisis, many of his own backbenchers were beginning to question the value of tying British policy to that of France and to plead for an accommodation with Germany.[105] The Master of Elibank, the Liberal chief whip, had pointed out that 'a great deal of parliamentary trouble' would be avoided if the King committed himself to going to Paris first.[106] The palace eventually gave way on the matter, and although, as a result of the wedding of the Kaiser's daughter, George V did in fact visit Berlin before Paris, this was a private not a state visit. Grey, for political reasons, was most insistent on this.[107]

However the British government's negative perception of the value of exchanges of royal visits with the Kaiser should not detract from the central problem, namely, that Britain and Germany were pursuing mutually antagonistic policies during the period under discussion, notably in the sphere of naval armaments. This meant that the prerequisite for political *rapprochement* between the two countries – the compatibility of vital interests – was absent. Royal visits were only able to mask this fleetingly, and sometimes not at all. The question of naval armaments was not mentioned at all by either side during the Kaiser's visit to Britain in November 1907. Baron von Schoen, who served as the foreign office representative in Wilhelm II's entourage, admitted that it was too sensitive to be raised.[108] It was mentioned only in passing during Edward VII's visit to Berlin in 1909,[109] yet both sides were aware that the naval arms race was the major subject at dispute between them.

One gains the impression that both powers used royal visits as smokescreens for the pursuit of mutually antagonistic policies. Wilhelm II commented cynically in September 1907, on learning of a visit to Russia by the the British General Sir John French, that the British government was continuing to pursue the 'encirclement' of Germany despite his invitation to Windsor, which he concluded was only a trick designed to deceive those who hoped for an improvement in Anglo-

[105] C. P. Scott, diary entry, 1 December 1911, Trevor Wilson (ed.), *The Political Diaries of C. P. Scott 1911–1928* (London, 1970), p. 56.

[106] The Master of Elibank to Asquith, 25 February 1912, Elibank Papers, National Library of Scotland, Edinburgh, MS 8802.

[107] Nicolson, *King George the Fifth*, p. 216.

[108] Freiherr von Schoen, *The Memoirs of an Ambassador. A Contribution to the Political History of Modern Times*, English translation (London, 1922), pp. 61–2.

[109] Bülow to Tschirschky, 13 February 1909, *GP*, XXVIII, no. 10262, p. 889; memorandum by Hardinge, 11 February 1909, *BD*, VI, pp. 230–2.

German relations.[110] Yet his own policies compounded the problem. Two days after he learnt of French's visit to Russia, he agreed to Admiral von Tirpitz's request for a new Navy Bill, to be introduced into the Reichstag shortly after his return from his visit to England.[111] When the Bill was announced in December 1907, it destroyed the good-will generated by Wilhelm's visit to England, and moved Friedrich von Holstein to write that the Navy Bill had made all the Kaiser's efforts to improve relations with Britain: 'useless and meaningless, and even given them an air of fraud'.[112] The British government also used a royal visit as a smokescreen for the ratcheting up of the naval race. At the time of Edward VII's visit to Berlin in 1909, the cabinet was debating plans to increase the pace of naval construction. These were announced shortly after the visit, leading to a further intensification in the naval rivalry between the two countries.[113]

When controversial matters were raised during the course of meetings between the Kaiser and the British monarch, the effect was inevitably counter-productive. This was illustrated by the outcome of Edward VII's visit to the Kaiser in Germany in the summer of 1908. This was the one occasion when the naval arms race did form the main subject of political discussions during an Anglo-German royal visit. Grey, alarmed at the increase in tension between Britain and Germany, decided to invest the King's visit with a political mission, hoping that the naval agreement with Germany, which had so far eluded the British government, could be achieved through dynastic diplomacy.[114] His actions represent a clear recognition of the potential political value of royal contacts. However, he recognised that the Kaiser might react in a hostile manner when the issue was raised.[115]

Edward VII, showing his usual inclination to avoid a direct confrontation with his nephew, left it to Sir Charles Hardinge to raise the issue of a naval agreement with Wilhelm.[116] Both Hardinge's and the Kaiser's account of the subsequent conversation make depressing reading.

[110] Wilhelm II's comment on Miquel to Bülow, 27 September 1907, *GP*, xxv(i), no. 8537, p. 46.
[111] Volker Berghahn, *Der Tirpitz-Plan. Genesis und Verfall einer innenpolitischen Krisenstrategie unter Wilhelm II.* (Düsseldorf, 1971), pp. 588–9.
[112] Holstein, diary entry, 14 December 1907, *HP*, iv, no. 1067, p. 509.
[113] Zedlitz, *Twelve Years*, diary entry, 10 February 1909, p. 257; Robert K. Massie, *Dreadnought. Britain, Germany and the Coming of the Great War* (London, 1992), pp. 609–25.
[114] Hardinge of Penshurst, *Old Diplomacy* (London, 1947), p. 158; Zara S. Steiner, *The Foreign Office and Foreign Policy, 1898–1914* (London, 1969), p. 89; memoranda by Grey, 28 July 1908, RA W 53/127; 31 July 1908, Hardinge Papers, vol.14; 6 August 1908, RA W 54/4.
[115] Grey to Knollys, 8 August 1908, RA W 54/5.
[116] Knollys to Grey, 9 August 1908, Grey Papers, PRO FO 800/103.

Wilhelm refuted Hardinge's claim that the German high seas fleet would eventually reach parity with the Royal Navy if the *Reich*'s battleship construction programme was not altered, and threatened war if the British tried to force Germany to slow the pace of her naval construction.[117] The stand-off between Hardinge and the Kaiser exposed the fact that when issues of real political substance were raised during Anglo-German royal visits no progress was possible. The Kaiser was not prepared to give up his naval ambitions, and the British could not have security without maritime supremacy. The frank exchange simply resulted in a further widening of the gulf between the two powers. It reinforced the conviction of Hardinge and Grey that no naval agreement was possible, and convinced Edward VII, previously by no means rabidly hostile to Germany, that a war between Britain and Germany would occur within five or six years. In a letter to his friend Sir Ernest Cassel, and in conversation with the French premier, Georges Clemenceau, the King indicated that naval and military preparations would have to be made to meet this eventuality.[118] The hardening in Edward VII's attitude towards Germany in the last two years of his life can in large measure be attributed to the conclusions which he drew from his nephew's remarks to Hardinge. He no longer had any faith in German assurances of friendship and opposed the idea of a political agreement between the two powers when it was raised by the Germans in 1909 because he appreciated that in the event of war on the continent: 'Germany would have the power of demolishing her enemies, one by one, with us sitting by with folded arms, & she would then probably proceed to attack us.'[119]

What conclusions then can be drawn about the role of royal visits in Anglo-German relations before 1914? First, it seems obvious that the visits themselves were unable to bridge the gulf between the powers, despite their frequency and the brief flowering of good-will which they generated in most cases. Between 1906 and 1910 this was due in part to the poor character of the personal relationship between Edward VII

[117] Hardinge to Grey, 15 August 1908, *BD*, VI, no. 116, p. 183; memorandum by Hardinge, 16 August 1908, *ibid.*, no. 117, pp. 184–90; Wilhelm II to Bülow, 13 August 1908, *GP*, XXIV, no. 8226, pp. 126–7.

[118] Edward VII to Sir Ernest Cassel, 15 August 1908, Cassel Papers, Broadlands Archives, Southampton University, MB1/X11; Clemenceau to Pichon, 29 August 1908, *DDF*, 2nd series, XI, no. 434, pp. 749–52; cf. Edward VII's minute on Cartwright to Grey, 14 August 1908, *BD*, VI, no. 114, p. 180; Edward VII to Hardinge, 25 and 29 August 1908, Hardinge Papers, vol. 14; Steed to Bell, 29 August 1908, Anon. *The History of the Times*, 5 vols. (London, 1935–52), III, p. 614.

[119] Knollys to Hardinge, 13 November 1909, Hardinge Papers, vol. 15.

and his nephew the Kaiser, who found it difficult to tolerate each other's company and to discuss controversial political issues. However, under George V no such personal hostility prevailed and yet the visits were of no greater value than in the reign of his father. The attitude adopted by elements of the press and public opinion towards the exchanges of visits provides a further explanation for the failure of the visits to generate an atmosphere of *rapprochement*. Yet this answer also has its limits, for the British government concluded a colonial agreement with Russia in the face of widespread popular hostility, suggesting that the attitude of public opinion was an excuse, not a reason, for the lack of an improvement in Anglo-German relations.[120]

The differing expectations of the two governments with regard to the value of exchanges of royal visits undoubtedly affected their relative value. The Kaiser and the Germans overestimated their significance and vested exaggerated hopes in the ability of royal visits to improve relations with Britain, whereas the British government regarded them as an irritating and embarrassing political complication which could not be avoided because of the close dynastic ties between the British and Prussian courts. However, although it is tempting to argue that the visits failed to have a beneficial impact on Anglo-German relations because of the unremittingly negative attitude adopted towards them by the British government, this would be to miss the key point. Grey was essentially correct. There was no room for an understanding with Berlin, as the Kaiser and Tirpitz were not prepared to offer an acceptable compromise on the naval question. Edward VII's visit to Germany in 1908 simply underlined that this was the case, and even some of Wilhelm II's own advisers eventually became exasperated at his intransigence in naval affairs. Alfred von Kiderlen-Wächter, for example, commented with irritation in January 1911: 'His Majesty is sincere: he wants to have ships, ships, ships and then not to use them, but rather to keep them all in Kiel like a plaything.'[121] When the vital interests of states were in harmony, or could be reconciled, royal visits could assist in the process of *rapprochement*, as indicated by the success of Edward VII's visits to France in 1903 and Russia in 1908. However, in the sphere of Anglo-German relations, such visits could do nothing to dispel the deeply

---

[120] Keith M. Wilson, 'The Foreign Office and the "Education" of Public Opinion before the First World War', *Historical Journal* 26, 2 (1983), 403–11.

[121] Alfred von Kiderlen-Wächter to Hedwig Kypke, 31 January 1911, Ernst Jäckh (ed.), *Kiderlen-Wächter der Staatsmann und Mensch. Briefwechsel und Nachlass*, 2 vols. (Stuttgart, Berlin and Leipzig, 1924), I, p. 79.

rooted antagonism between the two powers. Wilhelm II's determination to construct a navy to rival that of Britain, which was astutely described by President Taft of the USA as 'a piece of vanity, half natural, half personal',[122] and Britain's need for security could not be reconciled. As Helmuth von Moltke stated on one occasion, the relations between states were ultimately determined by vital interests, not dynastic summits.[123] Regrettably, in the case of Britain and Germany, the trend was towards confrontation rather than co-operation. Royal visits could do nothing to reverse this.

[122] President Taft quoted in James Bryce to Hardinge, 10 July 1909, Hardinge Papers, vol. 15.
[123] Moltke, *Erinnerungen*, 4 August 1907, p. 348.

Conclusion

This study has examined the political significance of monarchs in diplomacy on two levels. First, it has concentrated on the importance of the relationships between the monarchs and dynasties, and shown that these had repercussions for the broader political relationships between individual states. Secondly, the book has isolated examples where interventions by monarchs in the spheres of foreign policy and diplomacy were most conspicuous, most notably in the case of the contribution made by Edward VII to the creation and maintenance of the Anglo-French *entente* and the Anglo-Russian agreement, and in Wilhelm II's, ultimately, unsuccessful attempts to reach a political understanding with Nicholas II and Russia.

Certain conclusions can be drawn. The first chapter indicated that Wilhelm II and Nicholas II were the key political figures in German–Russian relations in the years before the First World War. The Kaiser was responsible for the conduct of German *Russlandpolitik*, and his diplomatic incompetence contributed to Berlin's failure to resurrect an alliance with St Petersburg. Similarly, it is impossible to understand Russian policy towards Germany during the period without reference to Nicholas II. He was responsible, as was the Kaiser in Germany, for all government appointments. As a result, all Russia's foreign ministers and diplomats could only retain their posts if they preserved the Tsar's favour. The dynastic ties between the Hohenzollerns and Romanovs, and the residual trust between Wilhelm and Nicholas, prevented an irremediable breakdown in German–Russian relations until the Bosnian crisis of 1908–9. Although Nicholas II's own scepticism as to the advantages of an understanding with Germany ensured that Russia remained committed to her alliance with France, there were other factors that prevented the resurrection of the traditional alliance. The mutual hostility that developed between German and Russian public opinion reduced the possibility of an understanding between the two empires. Such an understanding would have been politically dangerous for the Russian régime, in particular, to contemplate, notably after it had been weakened by the revolutionary disturbances of 1905–6. Clashes of vital interests between the two powers in the Balkans in the last years of peace also reduced the efficacy of royal diplomacy. Therefore, although the Kaiser and the Tsar remained the decisive political actors in the bilateral relationship between their two empires throughout the period before 1914, it is also evident that their freedom of action became more limited as a result of these wider pressures. Ultimately, the German government failed to win over Russia because its diplomatic strategy concentrated too much on the wooing of Nicholas II by the Kaiser and paid too little attention to the sensibilities of Russian public opinion and to Russia's interests in the future of the Balkans and Near East.

Chapter 2 indicated that the personal antagonism which developed between Edward VII and Wilhelm II was of considerable political significance. Edward became alienated from his nephew personally, and this, over time, contributed to his political hostility towards Germany, particularly in the last years of his life. As a result, Edward used his influence over diplomatic appointments to forward the careers of those who were suspicious of German foreign policy. However, Wilhelm's hostility towards his uncle was probably of greater political importance. The Kaiser's firmly held belief that Edward was hostile to him, and constantly intriguing against him, was a major contributory factor in his opposition to any political compromise with Britain, most notably over the issue of the naval armaments. Due to the fact that Wilhelm II was the most important political figure in imperial Germany, the political attitudes which derived from his personal prejudices were obviously of immense significance.

The third chapter sought to probe the extent of Edward VII's involvement in British diplomacy, and to isolate the reasons why many of his contemporaries regarded him as a significant political figure. The analysis indicated that while the King was never able to dictate the course of British foreign policy, he was, by and large, prepared to co-operate with the policy of the government, with which he was in fundamental agreement. In addition, by exploiting his unrivalled connections, his royalty, and his network of influential friends, he was able to help government policy, and thus deserves some of the credit for the success of the policy of *entente*.

Finally the examination of the impact of royal visits on Anglo-German relations in the last years of peace before 1914 indicated that there were limits to the potential efficacy of dynastic diplomacy. While the visits generated good-will between the two peoples and the two royal families, they had only a minimal impact on political relations between Britain and Germany. This resulted in the first instance from the fact that the relationship between the two monarchies was lopsided in terms of their relative power. The Kaiser directed German foreign policy, whereas Edward VII and George V were only able to exert discreet influence on the British government. Wilhelm II and his advisers had a tendency to overestimate the power of the British monarchy and were therefore disappointed and angered when royal summits failed to result in lasting improvements in Anglo-German relations. However, the key factor behind the failure of the visits to bring about good relations between the two powers was that British and German vital interests were in disharmony. Wilhelm II's dream of a German-dominated Europe, backed up by the second largest navy in the world, was simply not compatible, as far as most Britons were concerned, with the survival of the British empire and of Britain itself as an independent nation.

Royal influence in diplomacy remained a political reality in Europe in the last decade of the nineteenth century and the first years of the twentieth. Monarchs did not make decisions divorced from the wider social and political context. Indeed, public opinion, the predilections of advisers, and perceptions of national interest all constrained the ability of monarchs to do exactly as they wished and to achieve the political objectives that they sought. However, this does not detract from the fact that in Germany and Russia, governmental and diplomatic appointments were controlled by the monarch, and thus foreign policy reflected the personal prejudices of the sovereign to a considerable extent. Even in Britain, although the government controlled foreign policy, Edward VII must still be regarded as an important political figure. His visit to Paris in 1903 acted as a catalyst to the Anglo-French *entente*. Similarly, his ability to win the trust of Russian statesmen, and of Nicholas II, assisted the British government's attempt to come to an understanding with Russia. In addition, his involvement in ambassadorial appointments served, indirectly, to strengthen the weight of the anti-Germans in the British foreign policy establishment. The relationships between the monarchs were also of political as well as personal significance. Nicholas II's distaste for the Kaiser ensured the failure of Wilhelm's attempts to win the Tsar's trust. Conversely, Nicholas II's personal affection for his uncle, Edward VII, served to counteract the contempt which he undoubtedly had for the British political system, and played a role in reducing his previous hostility towards Britain. Monarchs were, thus, not decorative non-entities in Europe prior to the First World War, but individuals who retained a prominent role in diplomacy, which has, in the past, been greatly undervalued by historians.

Bibliography

I. UNPUBLISHED SOURCES

1 Geheimes Staatsarchiv Preussischer Kulturbesitz (GStA), Berlin

Brandenburg-Preussisches Hausarchiv:
Rep. 53   Kaiser Wilhelm II
Rep. 54   Crown Prince Wilhelm of Prussia

2 Politisches Archiv des Auswärtigen Amtes (PA), Bonn

Dänemark 32 Nr. 1   Documents concerning the Danish court and Germany
    in the 1880s and 1890s
Deutschland 131   Germany's relations with Russia
Deutschland 131 Nr 4 geheim.   German–Russian negotiations concerning an
    agreement regarding the Russo-Japanese War
England 78   England's relations with Germany
England 78 geheim.   England's relations with Germany
England 81 Nr 1   The British royal family
England 81 Nr 1 secr.   The British royal family
England 81 Nr 1a secr.   The Prince of Wales, 1888–1901
Hessen 56 Nr 1   The Hessian grand-ducal family
Hessen 56 Nr 1 geheim.   The Hessian grand-ducal family
Preussen 1 Nr 1d   Kaiser Wilhelm II
Preussen 1 Nr 1d geheim.   Kaiser Wilhelm II
Preussen 1 Nr 3c   Wilhelm II's correspondence with the Tsar of Russia
Preussen 1 Nr 3s   Wilhelm II's correspondence with the Kings of England
Preussen 1 Nr 40   Wilhelm II's meetings with the Kings of England
Russland 61 geheim.   Russia's relations with Germany
Russland 82 Nr 1   The Russian imperial family
Russland 82 Nr 1 geheim.   The Russian imperial family

3 Hessisches Staatsarchiv (HStA), Darmstadt

Papers of Grand Duke Ernst Ludwig von Hessen und bei Rhein

215

4 Geheimes Staatsarchiv Preussischer Kulturbesitz (GStA), Merseburg

Brandenburg Preussisches-Hausarchiv:
Rep. 52 T   Letters of Kaiserin Friedrich to Kaiser Wilhelm II
Rep. 52 V   Letters of Prince and Princess Heinrich of Prussia to Kaiser Wilhelm II
Rep. 52 W   Letters of Queen Victoria to Kaiser Wilhelm II
Rep. 53 J   Correspondence of Kaiser Wilhelm II

Rep. 89   Files of the *Geheimes Zivilkabinett*

5 Churchill College, Cambridge

Esher Papers

6 University Library, Cambridge

Hardinge Papers

7 Public Records Office (PRO), London

Grey Papers
Lansdowne Papers
Lascelles Papers

8 Broadlands Archives, Southampton University

Prince Louis of Battenberg Papers
Sir Ernest Cassel Papers

9 Royal Archives (RA), Windsor Castle

Papers of King Edward VII

10 National Library of Scotland, Edinburgh

Elibank Papers
Haldane Papers
Rosebery Papers

II. PUBLISHED SOURCES

(a) Government publications

Bittner, Ludwig and Uebersberger, Hans (eds.), *Österreich-Ungarns Aussenpolitik von der Bosnischen Krise 1908 bis zum Kriegsausbruch 1914*, 8 vols. (Vienna, 1930)

Gooch, G. P. and Temperley, Harold (eds.), *British Documents on the Origins of the War, 1898–1914*, 11 vols. (London, 1926–38)

Lepsius, Johannes et al. (eds.), *Die grosse Politik der europäischen Kabinette, 1871–1914. Sammlung der diplomatischen Akten des auswärtigen Amtes*, 40 vols. (Berlin, 1922–7)

Ministère des Affaires Etrangères (ed.), *Documents diplomatiques français, 1871–1914*, 32 vols. (Paris, 1929–62)

(b) Books, Articles and Dissertations

Afflerbach, Holger, 'Wilhelm II as Supreme Warlord in the First World War', *War in History* 5 (1998), 427–49

Anon., *The History of The Times*, vol. III *The Twentieth Century Test, 1884–1912* (London, 1947)

Asquith, H. H., *The Genesis of War* (London, 1923)
Letters to Venetia Stanley, ed. Michael and Eleanor Brock (Oxford, 1982)

Alff, Wilhelm (ed.), *Deutschlands Sonderung von Europa 1862–1945* (Frankfurt am Main, 1984)

Alexander, Grand Duke of Russia, *Once a Grand Duke* (New York, 1932)

Allfrey, Anthony, *Edward VII and his Jewish Court* (London, 1991)

Andrew, Christopher, *Théophile Delcassé and the Making of the Entente Cordiale. A Reappraisal of French Foreign Policy 1898–1905* (London, 1968)

Aronson, Theo, *A Family of Kings: The Descendants of Christian IX of Denmark* (London, 1976)

Balfour, Michael, *The Kaiser and His Times* (London, 1964)

Battiscombe, Georgina, *Queen Alexandra* (London, 1969)

Bell, G. K. A., *Randall Davidson. Archbishop of Canterbury*, 2 vols. (Oxford, 1935)

Benson, E. F., *The Kaiser and his English Relations* (London, 1936)

Berghahn, Volker R., *Germany and the Approach of War in 1914*, 2nd edition (London, 1993)
Imperial Germany, 1871–1914. Economy, Society, Culture and Politics (Oxford, 1994)
Modern Germany. Society, Economy and Politics in the Twentieth Century, 2nd edition (Cambridge, 1987)
Der Tirpitz-Plan. Genesis und Verfall einer innenpolitischen Krisenstrategie unter Wilhelm II. (Düsseldorf, 1971)

Bernstein, H. (ed.), *The Willy–Nicky Correspondence: Being the Secret and Intimate Telegrams Exchanged Between the Kaiser and the Tsar* (New York, 1918)

Bestuzhev, I. V., 'Russian Foreign Policy February–June 1914', *Journal of Contemporary History* 1, 3 (1966), 93–112

Bing, Edward J. (ed.), *The Letters of Tsar Nicholas and the Empress Marie*, English translation (London, 1937)

Blackbourn, David, *Populists and Patricians: Essays in Modern German History* (London, 1987)

Blunt, Wilfrid Scawen, *My Diaries. Being a Personal Narrative of Events, 1888–1914*, 2 vols. (London, 1919–20)

Bogdanor, Vernon, *The Monarchy and the Constitution* (Oxford, 1995)
Brett, Maurice V. (ed.), *The Journals and Letters of Reginald, Viscount Esher*, 4 vols. (London, 1934–8)
Bridge, F. R., *Great Britain and Austria-Hungary 1906–1914: A Diplomatic History* (London, 1972)
'Izvolsky, Aehrenthal, and the End of the Austro-Russian Entente, 1906–8', *Mitteilungen des Österreichischen Staatsarchivs* 29 (1976), 315–62
Brook-Shepherd, Gordon, *Royal Sunset. The Dynasties of Europe and the Great War* (London, 1987)
Uncle of Europe. The Social and Diplomatic Life of Edward VII (London, 1975)
Buckle, George E. (ed.), *The Letters of Queen Victoria*, 3rd series, 3 vols. (London, 1930–2)
Bülow, Bernhard Fürst von, *Memoirs*, 4 vols., English translation (London, 1931)
Buxhoeveden, Baroness Sophie, *Life and Tragedy of Alexandra Feodorovna* (London, 1928)
Cambon, H. (ed.), *Paul Cambon: Correspondance 1870–1924*, 3 vols. (Paris, 1940)
Cannadine, David, 'The Context, Performance and Meaning of Ritual: The British Monarchy and the "Invention of Tradition"', c. 1820–1977', in *The Invention of Tradition*, ed. E. Hobsbawm and T. Ranger (Cambridge, 1983), pp. 101–62
'The Last Hanoverian Sovereign?: The Victorian Monarchy in Historical Perspective, 1688–1988', in *The First Modern Society. Essays in English History in Honour of Lawrence Stone*, ed. A. L. Beier, David Cannadine and James M. Rosenheim (Cambridge, 1989), pp. 127–66
'Kaiser Wilhelm II and the British Monarchy', in *History and Biography. Essays in Honour of Derek Beales*, ed. T. C. W. Blanning and David Cannadine (Cambridge, 1996), pp. 188–202
The Pleasures of the Past (London, 1989)
Cecil, Lamar J. R., 'Coal for the Fleet that Had to Die', *American Historical Review* 69, 4 (1964), 990–1005
The German Diplomatic Service, 1871–1914 (Princeton, 1976)
'History as Family Chronicle: Kaiser Wilhelm II and the Dynastic Roots of the Anglo-German Antagonism', in *Kaiser Wilhelm II: New Interpretations*, ed. John C. G. Röhl and Nicolaus Sombart, (Cambridge, 1982), pp. 91–119
'William II and his Russian "Colleagues"', in *German Nationalism and the European Response 1890–1945*, ed. Carol Fink et al. (Norman, OK, and London, 1985), pp. 95–134
Wilhelm II: Emperor and Exile, 1900–1941 (Chapel Hill, NC, and London, 1996)
Wilhelm II: Prince and Emperor, 1859–1900 (Chapel Hill, NC, and London, 1989)
Chapman, Mabel K., *Great Britain and the Bagdad Railway 1888–1914* (Northampton, MA, 1948)
Chapman Huston, D. (ed.), *The Private Diaries of Daisy Princess of Pless 1873–1914*, reprint (London, 1950)

Churchill, Randolph S., *Winston S. Churchill*, vol. 1 *Young Statesman 1901–1914* (London, 1967)

Winston S. Churchill, vol. 11 *Companion 1907–1914* (London, 1969)

Clark, Alan (ed.), *'A Good Innings'. The Private Papers of Viscount Lee of Fareham* (London, 1974)

Cole, Terence F., 'The *Daily Telegraph* Affair and its Aftermath: The Kaiser, Bülow and the Reichstag, 1908–1909', in *Kaiser Wilhelm II: New Interpretations*, ed. John C. G. Röhl and Nicolaus Sombart (Cambridge, 1982), pp. 249–68

'German Decision-Making on the Eve of the First World War: The Records of the Swiss Embassy in Berlin', in *Der Ort Kaiser Wilhelms II. in der deutschen Geschichte*, ed. John C. G. Röhl, (Munich, 1991), pp. 53–70

'Kaiser versus Chancellor: The Crisis of Bülow's Chancellorship 1905–6', in *Society and Politics in Wilhelmine Germany*, ed. Richard J. Evans, (London, 1978), pp. 40–70

Craig, Gordon A., *Germany, 1866–1945* (Oxford, 1981)

Craig, Gordon A. and George, Alexander L., *Force & Statecraft: Diplomatic Problems of our Time*, 2nd edition (Oxford, 1990)

Dawson, Lionel, *Lonsdale. The Authorised Life of Hugh Lowther Fifth Earl of Lonsdale* (London, 1946)

Deuerlein, Ernst (ed.), *Briefwechsel Hertling–Lerchenfeld 1912–1917. Dienstliche Privat-korrespondenz zwischen dem bayerischen Ministerpräsidenten Georg Graf von Hertling und dem bayerischen Gesandten in Berlin Hugo Graf von und zu Lerchenfeld*, 2 vols. (Boppard am Rhein, 1973)

Dugdale, E. T. S. (ed.), *German Diplomatic Documents, 1871–1914*, English translation, 4 vols. (London, 1928–31)

Dockrill, M. L. and Lowe, C. J., *The Mirage of Power. British Foreign Policy, 1902–1914* (London, 1972)

Duff, David, *Hessian Tapestry* (London, 1967)

Ebel, Gerhard (ed.), *Botschafter Paul Graf von Hatzfeldt: Nachgelassene Papiere 1838–1901*, 2 vols. (Boppard am Rhein, 1976–77)

Eckardstein, Hermann Freiherr von, *Die Isolierung Deutschlands* (Leipzig, 1921)

Lebenserinnerungen und politische Denkwürdigkeiten, 2 vols. (Leipzig, 1920)

Persönliche Erinnerungen an König Eduard aus der Einkreisungszeit (Dresden, 1927)

Ten Years at the Court of St James, English translation (London, 1921)

Edwards, E. W., 'The Franco-German Agreement on Morocco, 1909', *English Historical Review* 78 (1963), 483–513

Eley, Geoff, 'The View from the Throne: The Personal Rule of Kaiser Wilhelm II', *Historical Journal* 28, 2 (1985), 469–85

'Recent Works in Modern German History', *Historical Journal* 23, 2 (1980), 463–81

Reshaping the German Right. Radical Nationalism and Political Change after Bismarck (New Haven and London, 1980)

'Reshaping the Right: Radical Nationalism and the German Navy League, 1898–1908', *Historical Journal* 21, 2 (1978), 327–54

Erdmann, Karl Dietrich (ed.), *Kurt Riezler. Tagebücher-Aufsätze-Dokumente* (Göttingen, 1972)

Esher, Reginald, Viscount, *The Influence of King Edward and Essays on Other Subjects* (London, 1915)

Eubank, Keith, *Paul Cambon. Master Diplomatist* (Norman, OK, 1960)

Evans, Richard (ed.), *Society and Politics in Wilhelmine Germany* (London, 1978)

Evans, R. J. W. and Pogge von Strandmann, H. (eds.), *The Coming of the First World War* (Oxford, 1988)

Fellner, Fritz, 'Die Verstimmung zwischen Wilhelm II. und Eduard VII. im Sommer 1905', *Mitteilungen des Österreichischen Staatsarchivs* 11 (1958), 501–11

Ferguson, Niall, 'Germany and the Origins of the First World War: New Perspectives', *Historical Journal* 35, 3 (1992), 725–52

'Public Finance and National Security: The Domestic Origins of the First World War Revisited', *Past and Present* 142 (1994), 141–68

Ferro, Marc, *Nicholas II: The Last of the Tsars*, English translation (London, 1991)

Fesser, Gerd, *Reichskanzler Bernhard von Bülow* (Berlin, 1991)

Fink, C. et al. (eds.), *German Nationalism and the European Response 1890–1945* (London and Oklahoma City, 1985)

Fischer, Fritz, 'Exzesse der Autokratie – das Hale-Interview Wilhelms II. vom 19. Juli 1908', in *Deutschlands Sonderung von Europa 1862–1945*, ed. Wilhelm Alff (Frankfurt am Main, 1984), pp. 53–78

Germany's Aims in the First World War, English translation (London, 1967)

War of Illusions: German Policies from 1911 to 1914, English translation (London, 1975)

Fisher, H. H. (ed.), *Out of My Past: The Memoirs of Count Kokovtsov*, English translation (Oxford and Stanford, 1935)

Fitzroy, Sir Almeric, *Memoirs*, 2 vols. (London, 1925)

Fox, Cyril Spencer (ed.), *That Was Germany. An Observer at the Court of Berlin. Letters of Princess Marie Radziwill to General di Robilant, 1908–1915*, English translation (London, 1937)

Fraser, Peter, *Lord Esher. A Political Biography* (London, 1973)

Franz, Eckhart G. (ed.), *Ernst Ludwig, Grossherzog von Hessen und bei Rhein, Erinnertes* (Darmstadt, 1983)

French, David, 'The Edwardian Crisis and the Origins of the First World War', *International History Review* 4, 2 (1982), 207–21

'Spy Fever in Britain, 1900–1915', *Historical Journal* 21, 2 (1978), 355–70

Friedberg, Aaron L., *The Weary Titan. Britain and the Experience of Relative Decline 1895–1905* (Princeton, 1988)

Fuchs, Walther P. (ed.), *Grossherzog Friedrich I. von Baden und die Reichspolitik 1871–1907*, 4 vols. (Stuttgart, 1968–80)

Fulford, Roger (ed.), *Beloved Mama. Private Correspondence of Queen Victoria and the German Crown Princess 1878–1885* (London, 1981)

Gall, Lothar, 'Deutsche Gesellschaftsgeschichte', *Historische Zeitschrift* 248 (1989), 365–74

Geiss, Imanuel, *German Foreign Policy, 1871–1914* (London, 1976) (ed.), *July 1914: The Outbreak of the First World War. Selected Documents*, English translation (London, 1967)

Geyer, Dietrich, *Russian Imperialism. The Interaction of Domestic and Foreign Policy 1860–1914*, English translation (Leamington Spa, 1987)

Gilbert, Felix and Large, David C., *The End of the European Era, 1890 to the Present* (London and New York, 1991)

Gilliard, Pierre, *Thirteen Years at the Russian Court*, English translation (London, 1921)

Gleichen, Lord Edward, *A Guardsman's Memories* (Edinburgh, 1932)

Goetz, W. (ed.), *Briefe Kaiser Wilhelms II. an den Zaren 1894–1914* (Berlin, 1920)

Gordon, Michael R., 'Domestic Conflict and the Origins of the First World War: The British and German Cases', *Journal of Modern History* 46 (1974), 191–226

Gore, John, *King George V. A Personal Memoir* (London, 1941)

Görlitz, Walter (ed.), *Der Kaiser ... Aufzeichnungen des Chefs des Marinekabinetts Admiral Georg Alexander von Müller über die Ära Wilhelms II.* (Göttingen, 1965)

(ed.), *The Kaiser and his Court. The Diaries, Note Books and Letters of Admiral Georg Alexander von Müller Chief of the Naval Cabinet, 1914–1918*, English translation (New York, 1964)

Grant, N. F. (ed.), *The Kaiser's Letters to the Tsar* (London, 1920)

Grey, Viscount of Fallodon, *Twenty-five Years, 1892–1916*, 2 vols. (London, 1925)

Gutsche, Willibald, *Ein Kaiser im Exil: Der letzte deutsche Kaiser Wilhelm II. in Holland; Eine kritische Biographie* (Marburg, 1991)

'Illusionen des Exkaisers: Dokumente aus dem letzten Lebensjahr Kaiser Wilhelms II. 1940/41', *Zeitschrift für Geschichtswissenschaft* 10 (1991)

Wilhelm II.: Der letzte Kaiser des deutschen Reiches (Berlin, 1991)

Gwynn, S. (ed.), *The Letters and Friendships of Sir Cecil Spring Rice*, 2 vols. (London, 1929)

Haldane, Richard Burdon, *An Autobiography* (London, 1929)

Before the War (London, 1920)

Hale, O. J., *Publicity and Diplomacy – with special reference to England and Germany 1890–1914*, reprint (London, 1964)

Hamilton, Keith A., *Bertie of Thame: Edwardian Ambassador* (London, 1990)

Harcave, Sidney (ed.), *The Memoirs of Count Witte*, English translation (London and New York, 1990)

Hardie, Frank, *The Political Influence of the British Monarchy, 1868–1952* (London, 1970)

Hardinge, Lord of Penshurst, *Old Diplomacy* (London, 1947)

Herwig, Holger H., 'Clio Deceived. Patriotic Self-Censorship in Germany after the Great War', *International Security* 12, 2 (1987), 5–44

Germany's Vision of Empire in Venezuela 1871–1914 (Princeton, 1986)

'Industry, Empire and the First World War', in *Modern Germany Reconsidered, 1890–1945*, ed. Gordon Martel (London, 1992), pp. 54–73

Hettling, Manfred (ed.), *Was ist Gesellschaftsgeschichte?* (Munich, 1991)

Hibbert, Christopher, *Edward VII: A Portrait* (London, 1976)

Hildebrand, Klaus, *Deutsche Aussenpolitik, 1871–1918* (Munich, 1990)
'Geschichte oder "Gesellschaftsgeschichte"? Die Notwendigkeit einer politischen Geschichtsschreibung von den internationalen Beziehungen', *Historische Zeitschrift* 223 (1976), 328–57
Hinsley, F. H. (ed.), *British Foreign Policy under Sir Edward Grey* (Cambridge, 1977)
Hobsbawn, E. and Ranger, T. (eds.), *The Invention of Tradition* (Cambridge, 1983)
Hohenlohe-Schillingsfürst, Chlodwig Fürst zu, *Denkwürdigkeiten der Reichskanzlerzeit*, ed. Karl Alexander von Müller (Berlin, 1931)
Hosking, Geoffrey, *The Russian Constitutional Experiment* (Cambridge, 1973)
Hough, Richard, *Louis and Victoria. The First Mountbattens* (London, 1974)
Howard, Christopher (ed.), *The Diary of Sir Edward Goschen, 1900–1914* (London, 1980)
Hughes, Judith M., *Emotion and High Politics; Personal Relations at the Summit in Late Nineteenth-Century Britain and Germany* (Berkeley, CA 1983)
Hull, Isabel V., 'Dynastic Ritual and the End of the Monarchy', in *German Nationalism and the European Response, 1890–1945*, ed. Carol Fink et al. (Norman, OK, and London, 1985), pp. 13–43
The Entourage of Kaiser Wilhelm II, 1888–1918 (Cambridge, 1982)
'Kaiser Wilhelm II and the Liebenberg Circle', in *Kaiser Wilhelm II: New Interpretations*, ed. John C. G. Röhl and Nicolaus Sombart (Cambridge, 1982), pp. 193–220
'Persönliches Regiment', in *Der Ort Kaiser Wilhelms II. in der deutschen Geschichte*, ed. John C. G. Röhl (Munich, 1991), pp. 3–23
Ilsemann, Sigurd von, *Der Kaiser in Holland. Aufzeichnungen des letzten Flügeladjutanten Kaiser Wilhelms II.*, 2 vols. (Munich, 1967–8)
Jäckh, Ernst (ed.), *Kiderlen-Wächter der Staatsmann und Mensch. Briefwechsel und Nachlass*, 2 vols. (Stuttgart, Leipzig and Berlin, 1924)
Jakobs, Peter, *Das Werden des Französisch-Russischen Zweibundes, 1890–1914* (Wiesbaden, 1968)
Jarausch, Konrad, *The Enigmatic Chancellor: Bethmann Hollweg and the Hubris of Imperial Germany* (New Haven, 1973)
Jefferson, Margaret M., 'Lord Salisbury's Conversations with the Tsar at Balmoral, 27 and 29 September 1896', *Slavonic and East European Review* 39, 22 (1960)
Jenkins, Roy H., *Asquith* (London, 1964)
Joll, James, *The Origins of the First World War*, 2nd edition (London, 1992)
'Politicians and the Freedom to Choose: The Case of July 1914', in *The Idea of Freedom: Essays in Honour of Isaiah Berlin*, ed. Alan Ryan (Oxford, 1979), pp. 99–115
Kaiser, David E., 'Germany and the Origins of the First World War', *Journal of Modern History* 55 (1983), 442–74
Kann, Robert A., 'Emperor William II and Archduke Francis Ferdinand in Their Correspondence', *American Historical Review* 57, 2 (January 1952), 323–51
Keiger, John, 'Jules Cambon and the Franco-German Détente, 1907–1914',

Historical Journal 26, 3 (1983), 641–59

Keller, Mathilde Gräfin von, *Vierzig Jahre im Dienst der Kaiserin. Ein Kulturbild aus den Jahren 1881–1921* (Leipzig, 1935)

Kennan, George F., *The Decline of Bismarck's European Order: Franco-Russian Relations, 1875–1890* (Princeton, 1979)

    The Fateful Alliance. France, Russia, and the Coming of the First World War (Princeton, 1984)

Kennedy, Paul M., 'The Kaiser and German Weltpolitik: Reflexions on Wilhelm II's Place in the Making of German Foreign Policy', in *Kaiser Wilhelm II: New Interpretations*, ed. John C. G. Röhl and Nicolaus Sombart, (Cambridge, 1982), pp. 143–69

    The Rise of the Anglo-German Antagonism, 1860–1914 (London, 1980)

    The Rise and Fall of British Naval Mastery (London, 1976)

    The Samoan Triangle. A Study in Anglo-German-American Relations, 1878–1900 (Dublin, 1974)

    Strategy and Diplomacy, 1890–1945 (London, 1983)

Knodt, Manfred, *Ernst Ludwig: Grossherzog von Hessen und bei Rhein* (Darmstadt, 1978)

Kocka, Jürgen, 'Überraschung und Erklärung. Was die Umbrüche von 1989/90 für die Gesellschaftsgeschichte bedeuten könnten', in *Was ist Gesellschaftsgeschichte?*, ed. Manfred Hettling (Munich, 1991), pp. 11–21

Kohut, Thomas A., 'Kaiser Wilhelm II and his Parents: An Inquiry into the Psychological Roots of German Policy Towards England before the First World War', in *Kaiser Wilhelm II: New Interpretations*, ed. John C. G. Röhl and Nicolaus Sombart (Cambridge, 1982), pp. 63–89

    Wilhelm II and the Germans. A Study in Leadership (New York and Oxford, 1991)

Kollander, Patricia A., 'Politics for the Defence? Bismarck, Battenberg and the Origins of the *Cartel* of 1887', *German History* 13, 1 (1995), 28–46.

    'The Liberalism of Frederick III', PhD dissertation, Brown University (1992)

Kürenburg, Joachim von, *War Alles Falsch? Das Leben Kaiser Wilhelms II.* (Bonn, 1951)

Lambsdorff, Gustav Graf von, *Die Militärbevollmächtigten Kaiser Wilhelms II. am Zarenhofe 1904–1914* (Berlin, 1937)

Langer, William L., *The Diplomacy of Imperialism, 1890–1902*, 2nd edition (New York, 1965)

Laue, Theodor von, *Sergei Witte and the Industrialization of Russia* (New York, 1969)

Lee, Arthur Gould, *The Empress Frederick Writes to Sophie, Letters 1889–1901*, 2 vols. (London, 1955)

Lee, Sir Sidney, *King Edward VII: A Biography*, 2 vols. (London, 1925–7)

Lees-Milne, James, *The Enigmatic Edwardian. The Life of Reginald, 2nd Viscount Esher* (London, 1986)

Lepsius, M. Rainer and Mommsen, Wolfgang J. (eds.), *Max Weber: Briefe, 1906–1908* (Tübingen, 1990)

Lerchenfeld-Köfering, Hugo Graf von, *Kaiser Wilhelm II. als Persönlichkeit und Herrscher, eine Rückschau*, ed. Dieter Albrecht (Regensburg, 1985)

Lerman, Katherine A., *The Chancellor as Courtier. Bernhard von Bülow and the Governance of Germany, 1900–1909* (Cambridge, 1990)

Lieven, Dominic C. B., *The Aristocracy in Europe, 1815–1914* (London, 1992)

Nicholas II: Emperor of all the Russias (London, 1993)

'Pro-Germans and Russian Foreign Policy, 1890–1914', *International History Review* 2, 1 (1980)

Russia and the Origins of the First World War (London, 1983)

Russia's Rulers under the Old Régime (London and New Haven, 1989)

Loewenberg, Peter, 'Arno Mayer's "Internal Causes and Purposes of War in Europe, 1870–1956" – an Inadequate Model of Human Behavior, National Conflict and Historical Change', *Journal of Modern History* 42 (1970), 628–36

Long, James, 'Franco-Russian Relations during the Russo-Japanese War', *Slavonic and East European Review* 52 (1974), 213–33

McDonald, David M., 'The Durnovo Memorandum in Context: Official Conservatism and the Crisis of Autocracy', *Jahrbücher für Geschichte Osteuropas* 44 (1996), 481–502

United Government and Foreign Policy in Russia 1900–1914 (Cambridge, MA, 1992)

McLean, Roderick R., 'The Kaiser's Diplomacy and the Reconquest of the Sudan', in *Sudan: The Reconquest Reappraised*, ed. E. M. Spiers (London, 1998), pp. 146–62

'Kaiser Wilhelm II and his Hessian Cousins: Intra-state Relations in the German Empire and International Dynastic Politics, 1890–1918', *German History* 19 (forthcoming)

'Monarchy and Diplomacy in Europe, 1900–1910', DPhil thesis, University of Sussex (1996)

McLean, Roderick R. and Seligmann, Matthew S., *Germany from Reich to Republic, 1871–1918* (London, 2000)

Magnus, Sir Philip, *King Edward the Seventh* (London, 1964)

Marchand, René (ed.), *Un livre noir. Diplomatie d'avant-guerre d'après les documents des archives russes, novembre 1910–juillet 1914*, French translation, 2 vols. (Paris 1922–3)

Marder, Arthur (ed.), *Fear God and Dread Nought. The Correspondence of Admiral of the Fleet Lord Fisher of Kilverstone*, 3 vols. (London, 1952–7)

Marks, Sally, '"My Name is Ozymandias": The Kaiser in Exile', *Central European History* 16, 2 (1983), 122–70

Martel, Gordon (ed.), *Modern Germany Reconsidered, 1870–1945* (London, 1992)

Massie, Robert K., *Dreadnought. Britain, Germany and the Coming of the Great War* (London, 1992)

Nicholas and Alexandra (London, 1968)

Mayer, Arno J., 'Internal Causes and Purposes of War in Europe, 1870–1956: A Research Assignment', *Journal of Modern History* 41 (1969), 291–303

The Persistence of the Old Régime: Europe to the Great War (London, 1981)

Mayer, S. J., 'Anglo-German Rivalry at the Algeciras Conference', in *Britain and Germany in Africa. Imperial Rivalry and Colonial Rule*, ed. Prosser Gifford and W. M. Roger Louis (London and New Haven, 1967), pp. 215–44

Mehlinger, Howard D. and Thompson, John M., *Count Witte and the Tsarist Government in the 1905 Revolution* (Bloomington, Indiana, and London, 1971)

Menning, Ralph R. and Menning, Carol Bresnahan, '"Baseless Allegations": Wilhelm II and the Hale Interview of 1908', *Central European History* 16, 4 (1983), 368–97

Middlemas, Keith, *The Life and Times of Edward VII* (London, 1972)

Moltke, Helmuth von, *Erinnerungen Briefe Dokumente 1877–1916: Ein Bild vom Kriegsführung und Persönlichkeit des ersten militärischen Führers des Krieges* (Stuttgart, 1922)

Mommsen, Wolfgang J., 'Domestic Factors in German Foreign Policy before 1914', in *Imperial Germany*, ed. James J. Sheehan (New York, 1976)

Imperial Germany 1867–1918. Politics, Culture, and Society in an Authoritarian State, English translation (London, 1995)

'Kaiser Wilhelm II and German Politics', *Journal of Contemporary History* 25 (1990), 289–316

Monger, G. W., *The End of Isolation. British Foreign Policy, 1900–1907* (London, 1963)

Montgelas, Max and Schücking, Walther (eds.), *Outbreak of the World War. German Documents Collected by Karl Kautsky*, English translation (New York, 1924)

Morley, John Viscount, *Recollections*, 2 vols. (London, 1917)

Morril, Dan L., 'Nicholas II and the Call for the First Hague Conference', *Journal of Modern History* 46, 2 (1974), 296–313

Mossolov, A. A., *At the Court of the Last Tsar*, English translation (London, 1935)

Munz, Sigmund, *King Edward VII at Marienbad: Political and Social Life at the Bohemian Spas*, English translation (London, 1934)

Neilson, Keith, 'Russia', in *Decisions for War, 1914*, ed. Keith M. Wilson (London, 1995), pp. 97–120

Newton, Lord, *Lord Lansdowne: A Biography* (London, 1929)

Nicolson, Harold, *Sir Arthur Nicolson, Bart., First Lord Carnock: A Study in the Old Diplomacy* (London, 1930)

King George the Fifth: His Life and Reign (London, 1952)

Nipperdey, T., 'Wehlers Kaiserreich. Eine kritische Auseinandersetzung', *Geschichte und Gesellschaft* 1 (1975)

Nish, Ian, *The Origins of the Russo-Japanese War* (London, 1985)

Oldenbourg, S. S., *The Last Tsar: Nicholas II, His Reign and His Russia*, 4 vols., English translation (Gulf Breeze, FL, 1975–7)

Oppel, Bernard F., 'The Waning of a Traditional Alliance: Russia and Germany after the Portsmouth Peace Conference', *Central European History* 5 (1972), 318–29

Pakula, Hannah, *Queen of Roumania: The Life of Princess Marie, Grand-Daughter of Queen Victoria* (London, 1984)

Paléologue, Maurice, *Guillaume II et Nicolas II* (Paris, 1935)

The Turning Point. Three Critical Years 1904–1906, English translation (London, 1935)

Pares, Bernard (ed.), *Letters of the Tsaritsa to the Tsar 1914–1916* (London, 1923)

Pflanze, Otto, 'Bismarcks Herrschaftstechnik als Problem der gegenwärtigen Historiographie', *Historische Zeitschrift* 234 (1982), 561–99

Pipes, Richard, *The Russian Revolution, 1899–1919* (London, 1990)

Pogge von Strandmann, H. (ed.), *Walther Rathenau. Notes and Diaries, 1907–1922*, English translation (Oxford, 1985)

Ponsonby, Sir Frederick (ed.), *The Letters of the Empress Frederick* (London, 1928) *Recollections of Three Reigns* (London, 1951)

Radzinsky, Edvard, *The Last Tsar. The Life and Death of Nicholas II*, English translation (London, 1992)

Radziwill, Princess Marie, *Briefe vom deutschen Kaiserhof 1889–1915*, German translation (Berlin, 1936)

Ramm, Agatha (ed.), *Beloved and Darling Child. Last Letters between Queen Victoria and her Eldest Daughter 1886–1901* (Stroud, 1990)

Ransel, David L. (ed.), *The Family in Imperial Russia* (Urbana, Chicago and London, 1978)

Raschdau, Ludwig, *In Weimar als Preussischer Gesandter. Ein Buch der Erinnerungen an Deutsche Fürstenhöfe 1894–1897* (Berlin, 1939)

Rathenau, Walther, *Der Kaiser. Eine Betrachtung* (Berlin, 1923)

Rauchensteiner, Manfred, *Der Tod des Doppeladlers. Österreich-Ungarn und der erste Weltkrieg* (Graz, Vienna and Cologne, 1993)

Reid, Michaela, *Ask Sir James. Sir James Reid, Personal Physician to Queen Victoria and Physician-in-Ordinary to Three Monarchs* (London, 1987)

Reischach, Hugo Baron von, *Under Three Emperors*, English translation (London, 1927)

Retallack, James, 'Wilhelmine Germany', in *Modern Germany Reconsidered, 1870–1945*, ed. Gordon Martel (London, 1992)

Rich, Norman, *Friedrich von Holstein: Politics and Diplomacy in the Era of Bismarck and Wilhelm II*, 2 vols. (Cambridge, 1965)

Rich, Norman and Fisher, M. H. (eds.), *The Holstein Papers*, 4 vols. (Cambridge, 1955–63)

Robbins, Keith, *Sir Edward Grey: A Biography of Lord Grey of Fallodon* (London, 1971)

Rogge, Helmuth (ed.), *Friedrich von Holstein: Lebensbekenntnis in Briefe an eine Frau* (Berlin, 1932)

Röhl, John C. G., 'Admiral von Müller and the Approach of War 1912–1914', *Historical Journal* 12, 4 (1969), 651–89

  'A Document of 1892 on Germany, Prussia and Poland', *Historical Journal* 7 (1964), 143–9

  'An der Schwelle zum Weltkrieg: Eine Dokumentation über den "Kriegsrat" vom 8. Dezember 1912', *Militärgeschichtliche Mitteilungen* 21 (1977), 77–134

  Germany without Bismarck. The Crisis of Government in the Second Reich, 1890–1900 (London, 1967)

  'Germany', in *Decisions for War, 1914*, ed. Keith M. Wilson (London, 1995), pp. 27–54

'Der Kaiser und England', in *Victoria & Albert. Vicky & the Kaiser. Ein Kapitel deutsch-englischer Familiengeschichte*, ed. Wilfried Rogasch (Berlin, 1997), pp. 165–84

Kaiser Wilhelm II. 'Eine Studie über Cäsarenwahnsinn' (Munich 1989)

Kaiser, Hof und Staat: Wilhelm II. und die deutsche Politik (Munich, 1987)

The Kaiser and his Court. Wilhelm II and the Government of Germany (Cambridge, 1994)

(ed.), *Der Ort Kaiser Wilhelms II. in der deutschen Geschichte* (Munich, 1991)

(ed.), *Philipp Eulenburgs politische Korrespondenz*, 3 vols. (Boppard am Rhein, 1976–83)

Wilhelm II.: Die Jugend des Kaisers, 1859–1888 (Munich, 1993); English translation *Young Wilhelm. The Kaiser's Early Life, 1859–1888* (Cambridge, 1998)

Röhl, John C. G. and Sombart, Nicolaus (eds.), *Kaiser Wilhelm II. New Interpretations* (Cambridge, 1982)

Rolo, P. J. V., *Entente Cordiale. The Origins and Negotiation of the Anglo-French Agreements of 8 April 1904* (London, 1969)

Rose, Kenneth, *King George V* (London, 1983)

Ryan, Alan (ed.), *The Idea of Freedom: Essays in Honour of Isaiah Berlin* (Oxford, 1979)

St Aubyn, Giles, *Edward VII: Prince and King* (London, 1979)

Savinskii, A., 'Guillaume II et la Russie, ses dépêches à Nicolas II, 1903–1905', *Revue des deux Mondes* 92, 12 (December 1922), 765–802

Sazonov, Sergei, *Fateful Years, 1909–1916*, English translation (London, 1928)

Schelking, Eugene de, *Recollections of a Russian Diplomat. The Suicide of Monarchies (William II and Nicholas II)* (New York, 1918)

Schoen, Wilhelm Freiherr von, *The Memoirs of an Ambassador. A Contribution to the Political History of Modern Times*, English translation (London, 1922)

Schöllgen, Gregor, *Escape into War? The Foreign Policy of Imperial Germany*, English translation (Oxford, 1990)

Die Macht in der Mitte Europas. Stationen deutscher Aussenpolitik von Friedrich der Grosse bis zur Gegenwart (Munich, 1992)

Schulte, Bernd F., *Vor dem Kriegsausbruch 1914. Deutschland, die Türkei und der Balkan* (Düsseldorf, 1980)

'Zu der Krisenkonferenz von 8. Dezember 1912 in Berlin', *Historisches Jahrbuch* 102 (1982), 183–97

Schüssler, Wilhelm, *Die Daily-Telegraph-Affaire: Fürst Bülow, Kaiser Wilhelm und die Krise des zweiten Reiches 1908* (Göttingen, 1952)

Seeger, Charles L. (ed.), *The Memoirs of Alexander Iswolsky. Formerly Russian Minister of Foreign Affairs and Ambassador to France*, English translation (London, 1920)

Seligmann, Matthew S., 'The Development and Objectives of German Southern African Policy 1893–1899', DPhil. dissertation, University of Sussex (1995)

Sinclair, Andrew, *The Other Victoria. The Princess Royal and the Great Game of Europe* (London, 1981)

Sommer, Dudley, *Haldane of Cloan. His Life and Times, 1856–1928* (London, 1960)

Sösemann, Berndt (ed.), *Theodor L. Wolff. Tagebücher 1914–1919*, 2 vols. (Boppard am Rhein, 1984)

Spiridovitch, General Alexandre, *Les dernières années de la cour de Tsarskoie-Selo*, 2 vols. (Paris, 1928)

Spring, D. W., 'Russia and the Franco-Russian Alliance, 1905–14: Dependence or Interdependence', *Slavonic and East European Review* 66 (1988), 564–92

Stafford, David, 'A Moral Tale: Anglo-German Relations, 1860–1914', *International History Review* 4, 2 (1982), 249–63

Steinberg, Jonathan, 'Diplomatie als Wille und Vorstellung: Die Berliner Mission Lord Haldanes im Februar 1912', in *Marine und Marinepolitik im kaiserlichen Deutschland 1871–1914*, ed. Wilhelm Deist and Herbert Schottelius (Düsseldorf, 1972), pp. 263–82

'The Copenhagen Complex', *Journal of Contemporary History* 1 (1966), 23–46.

'Germany and the Russo-Japanese War', *American Historical Review* 75, 7 (1970), 1965–86

'The Kaiser and the British: The State Visit to Windsor, November 1907', in *Kaiser Wilhelm II: New Interpretations*, ed. John C. G. Röhl and Nicolaus Sombart (Cambridge, 1982), pp. 121–41

'The Kaiser's Navy and German Society', *Past and Present* 28 (1964), 102–10

Yesterday's Deterrent: Tirpitz and the Birth of the German Battlefleet (London, 1965)

Steiner, Zara S., *Britain and the Origins of the First World War* (London, 1977)

The Foreign Office and Foreign Policy, 1898–1914 (Cambridge, 1969)

Stengers, Jean, 'Guillaume II et le Roi Albert à Potsdam en novembre 1913', *Bulletin de la classe des lettres et des sciences morales et politiques de l'Academie Royale de Belgique*, 6th series, VI 7, 12 (1993), 227–53

L'action du roi en Belgique depuis 1830. Pouvoir et influence (Brussels, 1992)

Stieve, Friedrich (ed.), *Der diplomatische Schriftwechsel Iswolskis 1911–1914*, 4 vols. (Berlin, 1924)

Stone, Norman, *Europe Transformed, 1878–1919* (London, 1983)

'Moltke–Conrad: Relations between the Austro-Hungarian and German General Staffs, 1909–14', *Historical Journal* 9, 2 (1966), 201–28

Swaine, Sir Leopold, *Camp and Chancery in a Soldier's Life* (London, 1926)

Taylor, A. J. P., *The Struggle for Mastery in Europe, 1848–1918* (London, 1954)

Tirpitz, Alfred von, *Der Aufbau der deutschen Weltmacht* (Berlin and Stuttgart, 1924)

My Memoirs, English translation, 2 vols. (London, 1920)

Topham, Anne, *Chronicles of the Prussian Court* (London, 1926)

Verner, Andrew M., *The Crisis of the Russian Autocracy. Nicholas II and the 1905 Revolution* (Princeton, 1990)

Vierhaus, Rudolph (ed.), *Das Tagebuch der Baronin von Spitzemberg* (Göttingen, 1960)

Vacha, Robert (ed.), *The Kaiser's Daughter: Memoirs of H.R.H. Viktoria Luise, Duchess of Brunswick and Lüneburg, Princess of Prussia*, English translation (London, 1977)

Vogel, Barbara, *Deutsche Russlandpolitik: Das Scheitern der deutschen Weltpolitik unter Bülow 1900–1906* (Düsseldorf, 1973)

Vorres, Ian, *The Last Grand-Duchess: Her Imperial Highness Grand Duchess Olga Alexandrovna, 1882–1960* (London, 1964)
Wagner, Reinhold, *Der grösste Verbrecher an der Menschheit im zwanzigsten Jahrhundert; König Eduard VII. von England* (Berlin, 1914)
Waters, W. H-H., *Potsdam and Doorn* (London, 1935)
  'Private and Personal': Further Experiences of a Military Attaché (London, 1928)
  'Secret and Confidential': The Experiences of a Military Attaché (London, 1926)
Wehler, Hans-Ulrich, *The German Empire 1871–1918*, English translation (Leamington Spa, 1985)
  'Psychoanalysis and History', *Social Research* 47 (1980)
Wheeler-Bennett, Sir John W., *Knaves, Fools and Heroes. In Europe between the Wars* (London, 1974)
  Three Episodes in the Life of Kaiser Wilhelm II (Cambridge, 1956)
Wickham Steed, H., *Through Thirty Years, 1892–1922*, 2 vols. (London, 1924–5)
Widenmann, Wilhelm, *Marine-Attaché an der kaiserlich-deutschen Botschaft in London 1907–1912* (Göttingen, 1952)
Wilhelm II, *My Memoirs: 1878–1918*, English translation (London, 1922)
Williams, Beryl, 'The Strategic Background to the Anglo-Russian Entente of August 1907', *Historical Journal* 12, 3 (1966), 360–73
Williamson, Samuel R., *Austria-Hungary and the Origins of the First World War* (London, 1991)
  'Influence, Power and the Policy Process: The Case of Franz Ferdinand', *Historical Journal* 17, 2 (1974), 417–34
  'The Origins of World War I', *Journal of Interdisciplinary History* 28, 4 (1988), 795–818
Wilson, Keith M. (ed.), *Decisions for War, 1914* (London, 1995)
  Empire and Continent: Studies in British Foreign Policy from the 1880s to the First World War (London, 1987)
  'The Foreign Office and the "Education" of Public Opinion before the First World War', *Historical Journal* 26, 2 (1983), 403–11
  The Policy of Entente. Essays on the Determinants of British Foreign Policy, 1904–1914 (Cambridge, 1985)
  'Sir Eyre Crowe on the Origin of the Crowe Memorandum of 1 January 1907', *Bulletin of the Institute of Historical Research* 56, 134 (1983), 238–41
Wilson, Trevor (ed.), *The Political Diaries of C. P. Scott 1911–1928* (London, 1970)
Winzen, Peter, *Bülows Weltmachtkonzept. Untersuchungen zur Frühphase seiner Aussenpolitik, 1897–1901* (Boppard am Rhein, 1977)
  'Prince Bülow's *Weltmachtpolitik*', *Australian Journal of Politics and History* 22, 2 (1976), 227–42
  'Zur Genesis von Weltmachtkonzept und Weltpolitik', in *Der Ort Kaiser Wilhelms II. in der deutschen Geschichte*, ed. John C. G. Röhl (Munich, 1991)
Wortman, Richard, 'The Russian Empress as Mother', in *The Family in Imperial Russia*, ed. David L. Ransel (Urbana, Chicago and London, 1978), pp. 60–74
Wroblewski, Viktor A., 'Lambsdorff über Deutschland und seine Zukunft',

Berliner Monatshefte 14, 5 (1936)

Yarmolinsky, Abraham (ed.), *The Memoirs of Count Witte*, English translation (Garden City, NY, 1921)

Zechlin, Egmont, *Krieg und Kriegsrisiko. Zur deutschen Politik im Ersten Weltkrieg. Aufsätze* (Düsseldorf, 1979)

Zedlitz-Trützschler, Robert Graf von, *Twelve Years at the Imperial German Court*, English translation (London, 1924)

Index

Aehrenthal, Alois Count Lexa von 43, 61
Alexander of Battenberg, Prince 75–6, 81
Alexandra Feodorovna, Tsarina (formerly
    Princess Alix of Hesse) 23, 156
Alexander III, Tsar 16, 17–20, 21, 22, 34, 70,
    71, 156
  and the Battenburg marriage 75–6
  and Wilhelm II's denunciations of Edward
    VII 81–2, 88
Alexander Mikhailovitch, Russian Grand
    Duke 45, 46
Alexandra, Queen (formerly Princess of Wales)
    55, 82–4, 104, 112, 144, 164, 190, 204
Alexei, Russian Grand Duke 26
Alexseev, Admiral 47
Algeciras conference (1906) 51, 125–6, 151,
    152, 187
Alphonso XIII, King of Spain 150–1, 170,
    171
Alvensleben, Friedrich Johann Count von 43,
    108
Anglo-French relations
  and Edward VII 13, 14, 106, 108, 109, 110,
    143–55, 211; visit to Paris (1903) 48, 105,
    106, 144–8, 170, 184, 209, 213
  entente 13, 14, 106, 108, 109, 110, 114, 127, 132,
    148, 185, 211
Anglo-German relations 12–14, 31, 73–140
  and naval armaments 73, 93, 94, 102, 107,
    122, 130, 131–2, 135, 154, 184–5, 187, 194,
    206–8, 209–10, 213
  and royal visits 13–14, 186–210, 213–14
  see also Edward VII, King (formerly Prince of
    Wales); Wilhelm II, Kaiser
Anglo-Japanese alliance 45–6, 127
Anglo-Russian relations 21, 53–4, 55, 61, 68,
    71, 108–9, 110–12, 125, 127, 155–69
Arthur of Connaught, Prince (son of Arthur,
    Duke of Connaught) 116, 123–4
Arthur, Duke of Connaught 87, 92
Asquith, H. H. 182, 192

Augusta, Kaiserin (grandmother of Wilhelm
    II) 75, 81, 82
Augusta Victoria, Kaiserin (Dona, wife of
    Wilhelm II) 23, 35, 77, 112, 117, 121
  dislike of the English 74–5, 83–4
Austria
  annexation of Bosnia–Herzegovina 57–8,
    59, 135, 167, 168
  and German–Russian relations 63, 64
  Three Emperors' League 25–6, 59, 67,
    70
  Triple Alliance (Germany, Austria and
    Italy) 19
Balfour, A. J. 102, 141–2, 144, 147–8
Balkans
  and the Battenburg marriage 75–6
  Bosnian crisis (1908/9) 12, 57–9, 64, 68, 69,
    71, 135, 167–8, 187
  crisis (1912) 191, 197
  and German–Russian relations 12, 15, 17,
    46, 57–9, 63, 64, 72, 212
  war with Turkey 65, 66–7
Ballin, Albert 130, 179–80
Baltic Port, meeting between Wilhelm II and
    Nicholas II at (1912) 65
Battenburg marriage controversy 75–6, 77, 81,
    82, 139
Beatrice, Princess (daughter of Queen
    Victoria) 76, 77
Beit, Alfred 89
Benckendorff, Count Alexander 55, 157, 158,
    162, 169, 178–9
Bentinck, Count Godard 74
Berchtold, Count 70
Berghahn, Volker 9
Berlin–Baghdad railway 63, 64, 200
Bertie, Sir Francis 134, 139, 149, 151, 177–8,
    184, 200, 202
Bethmann Hollweg, Theobald von 4, 5, 60,
    62, 63, 137, 173, 188

Bezobrazov, A. A.   46–7
Bigge, Sir Arthur (later Lord Stamfordham)
   181, 192
Bismarck, Herbert Count von   75, 77, 82, 84
Bismarck, Otto Prince von   5, 7, 17, 19, 74, 75
Björko, German–Russian treaty (1905)   50, 51,
   71
Boer (South African) War   93, 95–6, 143–4,
   156
Bogdanor, Vernon   11–12
Bosnian crisis (1908/9)   12, 57–9, 64, 68, 69, 71,
   135, 167–8, 187
Brandenburg, Erich   3
Breslau, Nicholas II's visit to (1896)   31, 32
Britain
   Anglo-Japanese alliance   45–6, 127
   and the Fashoda crisis (1898/9)   37, 146
   naval and military policy   13
   professional historians and the British
      monarchy   11–12
   and the War Scare (1904/5)   111–13
   see also Anglo-French relations;
      Anglo-German relations; Anglo-Russian
      relations; Edward VII, King; George V,
      King
British government
   Liberal   150, 151, 191
   and royal visits   195–6, 200–6
British press
   hostility towards Germany   104, 105, 114, 116
   on royal visits   186–7
Buchanan, Sir George   68, 201
Bülow, Adolf von   75
Bülow, Bernhard Prince von   9, 24, 25, 27–8,
   29, 34, 36, 38, 40–1, 42, 60, 188
   and the Anglo-French alliance   108, 110
   and Anglo-German relations   93, 94–5, 97,
      100, 101–2, 105, 119, 123, 124, 130
   and Edward VII's visit to Kiel (1904)   110
   and Lascelles   116–17
   and the meeting at Reval (1902)   43–4
   and the meeting at Wiesbaden (1903)   46
   and the Russian–German alliance   51, 52,
      58, 71
   and the Russo-Japanese War   48, 50
   and the War Scare (1904/5)   112, 113
   and Wilhelm II's relations with Edward
      VII   82
   and Wilhelm II's visit to Britain (1907)   204,
      205
'bureaucratic' school of international
   relations   2

Cambon, Paul   109–10, 149, 151, 153, 161,
   191–2

and the Anglo-French agreement   144, 148
   on the death of Edward VII   141
   and royal visits   202
Campbell-Bannerman, Sir Henry   150, 154,
   181, 182, 203
Cannadine, David   11
Caprivi, General Leo von   15, 19
Carlos, King of Portugal   146
Cartwright, Sir Fairfax   131
Cassel, Sir Ernest   89, 121, 129, 134, 166, 173,
   179–80, 208
Cecil, Lamar   9
Chamberlain, Joseph   99, 102, 143–4
Charles of Denmark, Prince   118
China
   Boxer Rebellion   39
   German seizure of Kiaochow (1897)   35, 38,
      69
Chirol, Valentine   133–4
Christian IX, King of Denmark   82, 83
Claparède, Alfred de   66
Clemenceau, Georges   131–2, 153–5, 154, 179,
   180, 183, 190, 208
Crewe, Lord   172
Crowe, Eyre   200
Crozier, M. (French ambassador in Vienna)
   62

Daisy, Princess of Pless   124, 135, 136
Danzig, meeting between Wilhelm II and
   Nicholas II at (1901)   40–1, 42, 44
Dardanelles
   Russia and the opening of the   67, 167
   and Wilhelm II   33
Darmstadt, meeting between Wilhelm II and
   Nicholas II at   32–3, 45
Delbrück, Hans   3
Delcassé, Théophile   67–8, 115, 144, 153, 155,
   170, 172, 183
   and Edward VII's visit to Paris   146, 147, 148
   and the first Moroccan crisis   148–98
Deym, Count   144
Dogger Bank incident (1904)   111–12, 160–1, 169
Dona *see* Augusta Victoria, Kaiserin
Dönhoff, Marie Countess von   75
Doumer, Paul (French politician)   64
Dual Alliance (Franco-Russian)   12, 19–20, 23,
   24, 25, 38, 42, 45, 46, 50–1, 64, 67–8, 211
   and German–Russian estrangement   69,
      70–1
Durnovo, P. N.   68

Eckardstein, Hermann Baron von   80, 106
Edward VII, King (formerly Prince of Wales)
   4, 13

accession of 96–7
and Anglo-French relations 13, 14, 106, 108,
109, 110, 143–55, 211; visit to Paris (1903)
48, 105, 106, 144–8, 170, 184, 209, 213
and Anglo-German relations 73–140;
attitudes to Germany 104–5, 106, 135–7,
184–5, 188; failure to visit Berlin 106–7,
127–8
and Anglo-Russian relations 13, 14, 53, 55,
56, 108–9, 110–11, 125, 127, 155–69, 213–14;
visit to Russia (1908) 55, 130, 165–7, 169,
182–3, 186, 209
and the Bosnian crisis 167–8
and British foreign policy 139, 141–3, 166–7,
170–3, 185
death 137–8, 141, 185
entourage 173–80; Germanophobes
139–40, 173–9; pro-Germans 179–80
and Gleichen 117–18
and Nicholas II 13, 125, 130, 155–6, 158–9,
160, 162, 163, 165–7, 168, 169, 182–3,
213–14
and the Norwegian crown 118
political role of 180–5
professional historians on 11
relations with his ministers 181–2
and royal visits 186–90, 194–7, 199, 200,
203–4
and the Tweedmouth letter controversy
(1908) 128–30
and the Vienna incident 85, 86
visits to Germany: Berlin (1909) 134–5, 194,
195, 199, 202, 204, 207; Friedrichshof
(1908) 126, 131, 153, 154, 172, 201, 207–8,
209; Kiel (1904) 109–10
and the War Scare (1904/5) 112, 113
and the wedding of the Crown Prince of
Prussia 115, 116
and Wilhelm II; *Daily Telegraph* interview
134; and the disposal of Osborne House
103; Hale interview 134; and the Kruger
telegram affair 89; refusal to visit on way
to Marienbad (1905) 119–21, 150; on
relations with Russia 39–40; relations
with 12–13, 73, 79–88, 96–140, 151–2,
188–90, 196–7, 208–9, 212; Tangier
escapade (1905) 113–15; visits to Britain
by 85–6, 87–8, 92–3, 95, 96–7, 101–2,
199, 200, 202, 203–4, 205
Wilhelm II's derogatory remarks about
103–4
Wilhelm II's moral condemnation of 82,
103, 118
Egypt 143
Fashoda crisis (1898/9) 37, 146

Eisendecher, Karl von 105
Eley, Geoffrey 7, 9
An Englishman's Home 174–5
Ernst Ludwig, Grand Duke of Hesse 23, 32,
35, 45, 56, 62, 83
Esher, Viscount 4, 111, 132, 135, 137, 139
and Anglo-French relations 154, 155
anti-German feelings 173–5, 179, 180
and the political role of Edward VII 141,
166–7, 180, 182, 183
and royal visits 200
and the Tweedmouth letter controversy
(1908) 128, 129, 130
Eulenburg-Hertefeld, Philipp Count (from
1900 Prince) zu 8, 26, 27, 30, 33, 68–9,
73, 77, 123

Fallières, Armand (President of France) 151,
202
Far East
Russian abandonment of interests in the
54, 72
Russian expansion in the 25, 26–7, 32, 38,
44, 45, 46–7
Russo-Japanese War 26, 47–50, 52, 69, 70,
111, 157, 158, 162, 169
Faure, François Félix 35
Ferdinand of Bulgaria, Prince 132
First World War
and Anglo-German relations 14, 140
and Edward VII 138, 184
German historians on the 3, 4–5
and German–Russian relations 12, 15, 16,
71–2
Wilhelm II's role in the 9
Fischer, Fritz 4–5
Fisher, Admiral Sir John 111–12, 135, 139, 150,
174
anti-German feelings 173, 175–6, 179, 180
and royal visits 200
and the Tweedmouth letter controversy
128–9, 130
France
Britain's *entente* with 13, 14, 106, 108, 109,
110, 114, 127, 132, 148, 185, 211
Edward VII and Anglo-French relations
13, 14, 106, 108, 109, 110, 143–55, 211
Edward VII's visit to Paris (1903) 48, 105,
106, 144–8, 170, 184, 209, 213
Fashoda crisis (1898/9) 37, 146
Franco-Russian alliance 12, 19–20, 23, 24,
25, 38, 42, 45, 46, 50–1, 64, 67–8, 211; and
German-Russian estrangement 69, 70–1
and Morocco 115, 148–9, 151, 152, 153, 198,
200

France (*cont.*)
　Nicholas II's visit to (1901)　41–2
　royal visits and Anglo-French relations
　　205–6
Franco-Prussian war　195
Franz Ferdinand, Archduke of Austria　12, 15,
　189, 197
Franz Joseph, Emperor of Austria　121, 132,
　153
Fredericksz, Count　50
French, General Sir John　206
Friedrich, Grand Duke of Baden　40
Friedrich III, Kaiser (formerly Crown Prince
　Friedrich Wilhelm of Prussia)　74, 75, 78,
　84
Friedrichshof, Edward VII's meeting with
　Wilhelm II at (1908)　126, 131, 153, 154,
　172, 201, 207–8, 209
Fürstenberg, Max Egon Prince zu　120

Gall, Lothar　6
GDR (German Democratic Republic)　6
Geoffray, M. (French chargé d'affaires in
　London)　124
George I, King of the Hellenes　144
George, Russian Grand Duke　37
George V, King (formerly Duke of York and
　Prince of Wales)　28, 90
　accession　192
　and Anglo-German relations　14, 190–3, 196
　as anti-German　104
　meetings with Wilhelm II　187
　state visit to Paris (1914)　203, 205, 206
　visits to Germany (1902)　99–100; (1913)
　　193, 197, 202
　and the wedding of the Crown Prince of
　　Prussia　115, 116
　Wilhelm II's view of　138, 198–9
　and Wilhelm II's visit to Britain (1911)　201
German historians　3–10
　'Fischer controversy'　4–5
　and *Gesellschaftsgeschichte* (history of society)
　　5–7
German–Russian relations　12, 14, 15–72,
　211–12
　and the Balkans　12, 15, 17, 46, 57–9, 63, 64,
　　65, 66–7, 72, 212
　reasons for German–Russian
　　estrangement　68–72
　and the Reinsurance Treaty　15, 19, 68–9
　see also Nicholas II, Tsar; Wilhelm II, Kaiser
Germany
　and the Algeciras conference (1906)　51,
　　125–6, 151, 152, 187
　and monarchical power　1

naval armaments　73, 93, 94, 102, 107, 122,
　130, 131–2, 135, 154, 184–5, 187, 194,
　206–8, 209–10, 213
　press reports on royal visits　194
　public opinion　12
　reasons for German–Russian
　　estrangement　68–72
　and the Russo-Japanese War　48–50
　Three Emperors' League　25–6, 59
　and the War Scare (1904/5)　112–13
　see also Anglo-German relations;
　　German–Russian relations; Wilhelm II,
　　Kaiser
Gesellschaftsgeschichte (history of society)　5–7
Giers, N.K.　19, 29
Gleichen, Lord Edward　117–18
Gorbachev, Mikhail　6
Goschen, Sir Edward　131, 178, 184, 196
Grey, Sir Edward　142, 150, 155, 162, 163, 169,
　170, 176
　Edward VII's relations with　182
　and George V　191, 192, 199
　and naval rearmament　208
　and royal visits　166, 171–3, 187, 195–6,
　　200–1, 201–4, 205–6

Haldane, R. B.　195, 196, 200, 204
Hale, Dr William B. (American journalist),
　interview with Wilhelm II　133–4
Hanotaux, Gabriel (French foreign minister)
　26, 32
'Hardinge Gang'　184
Hardinge, Sir Charles　55, 131, 132, 134, 135,
　136, 139, 182, 184
　and Anglo-French relations　151, 153, 154
　and Anglo-German relations　152, 154, 189;
　　naval rearmaments　207–8
　and Anglo-Russian relations　157, 158–60,
　　162, 163, 165, 166, 167, 169; Dogger Bank
　　incident　160, 161
　anti-German feelings　173, 176–7, 180
　presence in the royal entourage　171, 172,
　　173
　and royal visits　147, 183, 199, 200, 203
Hatzfeldt-Wildenburg, Paul Count von　31
Heinrich, Prince (brother of Wilhelm II)　36,
　42, 45, 61, 82
　and Anglo-Russian relations　156
　and George V　190–1, 198–9
　visit to London (1902)　104
Heligoland–Zanzibar Treaty　87
Henry of Battenburg, Prince　76, 77
Herbert, Sir Arthur　133
Hildebrand, Klaus　3, 7
Hintze, Captain Paul von　49, 56–7, 59, 60, 61,

62, 70
historiographical 'schools' of international
  relations 2
Hitler, Adolf 4
Hohenlohe-Schillingsfürst, Chlodwig Prince
  17, 25, 26–7, 29, 33, 34, 97
Holstein, Friedrich von 27, 30, 43–4, 109, 126,
  133–4, 152, 207
  and the War Scare (1904/5) 112, 113
Huguet, Lieutenant Colonel Auguste 155
Hull, Isabel 8, 9, 10

Isvolsky, Alexander
  and Anglo-German relations 23, 53, 54–5,
  59, 61, 62, 71
  and Anglo-Russian relations 157–8, 163,
  165, 167–9
  Edward VII's relations with 179, 183, 190
Italy, Triple Alliance (Germany, Austria and
  Italy) 19

Jameson Raid 88–9
Japan
  Anglo-Japanese alliance 45–6, 127
  and Russian expansion in the Far East 32,
  44, 45
  Russo-Japanese War 26, 47–50, 52, 69, 70,
  111, 157, 158

Kayser, Paul 89
Keppel, Alice 118
Kiderlen-Wächter, Alfred von 32, 63, 64, 135,
  198, 209
Kiel, Edward VII's state visit to (1904) 109–10
Knollys, Sir Francis (from 1902 Viscount) 47,
  95, 96, 99, 119, 120, 122, 123, 134, 176
  and Anglo-German relations 152, 172
  and Anglo-Russian relations 158, 162, 163,
  165, 167
  anti-German feelings 175, 179
  on Edward VII's attitude to Germany 137
  and Edward VII's visit to Paris 144
  and George V 192
  and the political role of Edward VII 180,
  181
  and royal visits 199, 203, 205
  and the Tweedmouth letter controversy 129
Kokovtsov, Count V. N. 51, 65
Kruger telegram affair (1896) 31, 78, 88–90,
  91, 93
Kuropatkin General A. N. (Russian minister of
  war) 46

Lambsdorff, Major General von 49
Lamsdorf, Count (Russian foreign minister)

23, 27, 41, 43–4, 158, 159, 160, 161, 162, 163,
  169
Lansdowne, Marquess of 40, 50, 99, 100, 123
  and Anglo-French relations 144
  and Anglo-Russian relations 155, 157, 159,
  168
  on Edward VII and British diplomacy
  141–2
  Edward VII's relations with 182
  and Edward VII's visit to Paris 145–6, 147,
  148
  and Wilhelm II's Tangiers escapade 114
Lascelles, Sir Frank 31, 92, 100, 106, 111,
  116–17, 119, 120, 121–2, 123
  Germanophile sympathies 177
  and royal visits 200, 204, 205
  and the War Scare (1904/5) 112, 113
Lecomte, Raymond 54, 127, 189
Lee, Arthur 189
Lee, Sir Sidney, biography of Edward VII 80
Leyds, Dr 95–6
Lieven, Dominic 10–11
Liman von Sanders, Colonel 67, 72
Lisbon, Edward VII's visit to (1903) 105,
  144–5, 146–7
Lobanov-Rostovsky, Prince 23, 25–6, 29, 31
Lonsdale, Earl of 124
Loubet, Emile 121, 144, 145, 147–8, 149, 151,
  155
Louis of Battenburg, Prince 76, 114–15, 117,
  119
  visit to Russia (1904) 159–60, 169
Louis, M. (French ambassador) 64
Luise, Grand Duchess of Baden 109, 197

Maria Pavlovna, Russian Grand Duchess 22
Marie Feodorovna, Dowager Empress of
  Russia
  and Anglo-German relations 20–1, 28–9,
  32, 33–4, 38, 53, 71, 82
  and Anglo-Russian relations 156, 158, 159,
  164, 168
Marschall von Biebersbein, Adolf Baron 89
Marx, Karl 6
Mary, Queen (wife of George V) 190, 202, 203
Mayer, Arno J. 2
Mensdorff, Albert Count von 136, 173, 178,
  179, 184
Metternich, Paul Count von Wolff (German
  ambassador in London) 100, 101, 102,
  105, 118, 119, 123, 124, 152
  on Edward VII's attitude to Germany 136
  and the Hale interview 134
  and Queen Victoria 181
  and royal visits 203, 204

Metternich, Paul (_cont._)
    and the Tweedmouth letter controversy   129
    and the War Scare (1904/5)   112, 113
Michael, Russian Grand Duke   42–3
modernization of European society   2–3
Moltke, Helmuth von   29–30, 196–7
Moltke, Kuno Count von   203–4
Mommsen, Wolfgang   9
monarchical power   1–2, 28, 213
    in Britain   13, 28
    in Russia   1, 27, 28, 36
    in Wilhelmine Germany   8–9, 27, 28
Monson, Sir Edward   144, 145, 147
Montebello, Marquis de   44
Morley, John   200
Morocco
    and the Algeciras conference   51, 125–6, 151,
        152, 187
    and Anglo-French relations   143, 144, 151,
        152, 153, 200
    first crisis (1905/6)   113–15, 119, 120, 148–9,
        152, 155, 186–7, 188
    second crisis (1911)   192, 198, 206
Moulin, General   111
Müller, Admiral Georg Alexander von   62, 93
Muraviev, M. A.   23, 33, 38

naval armaments, and Anglo-German
    relations   73, 93, 94, 102, 107, 122, 130,
        131–2, 135, 154, 184–5, 187, 194, 206–8,
        209–10, 213
'negative personal rule', in Wilhelmine
    Germany   8–9
newspapers
    attitudes to Anglo-German royal visits
        194–5
    British press hostility towards Germany
        104, 105, 114, 116
Nicholas II, Tsar
    accession of   16–17, 24
    and the Balkan–Turkey war (1912)   66, 67
    and the Bosnian crisis (1908/9)   12, 57–8, 71
    character   16–17, 28, 39
    criticisms of Wilhelm II   44, 69
    and Edward VII   13, 125, 130, 155–6, 158–9,
        160, 162, 163, 165–7, 168, 169, 182–3,
        213–14; meeting at Reval (1908)   55, 130,
        165–7, 169, 182–3, 186
    and the First World War   71–2
    and the Franco–Russian alliance   70–1
    and German–Russian relations   12, 14,
        15–72, 211–12; estrangement   69, 70–1
    historians' portrayal of   10–11
    influence of his mother (Dowager Empress
        Marie Feodorovna)   21, 28–9, 32, 33–4,

        38, 71, 164
    meetings with Wilhelm II: Baltic Port   65;
        Danzig   40–1, 42, 44; Darmstadt   32–3,
        45; Potsdam   37–8, 62–4; Reval   27,
        43–4, 71; Swinemünde   54; Wiesbaden
        32, 45–6
    murder of   16
    power of   1, 27–8, 57
    relations with George V   193
    and the revolution of 1905   52, 56
    and the Russian royal family   21–3
    and the Russo-Japanese War   47–50, 69
    secret correspondence with Wilhelm II
        24–5, 33
    visit to Breslau (1896)   31, 32
    weaknesses of rule   27–8, 36, 52
    and Wilhelm II's visit to St Petersburg
        (1897)   34–5
Nicolson, Sir Arthur   52, 55, 56, 163, 178, 184,
        196, 201
Northcliffe, Lord   174–5
Norway, candidates for the throne of   118

Oldenbourg, S. S.   10–11
Olga, Russian Grand Duchess   68
Osten-Sacken, Nikolai Dimitriovich Count von
        der   24
Ottoman empire, and German–Russian
    relations   65
Owen, Humphreys   103

Paulis (Russian naval attaché)   43
Pichon, S. (French foreign minister)   153, 196
Poincaré, Raymond   202
Ponsonby, Sir Frederick   121, 154, 181, 189
    and Edward VII's visit to Paris   145
Potsdam, meetings between Nicholas II and
    Wilhelm II at (1899)   37–8, (1910)   62–4
Pourtalès, Friedrich Count von   55–6, 60, 67
public opinion
    and Anglo-German relations   14, 90, 97, 98,
        104, 194, 195
    French   42
    German   12, 98, 194, 196, 211–12
    Russian   12, 23–4, 69–70, 211–12

Radolin, Hugo Prince von   30, 34, 35, 38, 106,
        126
Radziwill, Princess Marie   129, 197
railways
    across German–Russian frontiers   65
    Berlin–Baghdad   63, 64, 200
Rathenau, Walther   198
Reich, Emil, _Germany's Swelled Head_   176
Reinsurance Treaty (between Germany and

Russia) 15, 19, 68–9
Repington, Colonel Charles à Court 129, 130
Reval
  Edward VII's visit to Nicholas II at (1908)
    55, 130, 165–7, 169, 182–3, 186
  meeting between Wilhelm II and Nicholas II
    at 27, 43–4, 71
revisionist historians 5, 6
Rex, Count von 16–17
Roberts, Field-Marshal Earl 97
Röhl, John 4, 7, 8–9, 10
Rosebery, Earl of 87, 96, 150
Rothschild, Alfred de 165–6, 173, 179
Rouvier, M. (French minister in Lisbon) 146,
  147
Rouvier, Maurice (French foreign minister)
  150, 151
Royal Archives 11
royal biographers, and the British monarchy 11
royal visits, and Anglo-German relations
  13–14, 186–210, 213–14
Rudolf, Crown Prince of Austria 75, 82
Russia
  Anglo-Russian relations 21, 53–4, 55, 61,
    68, 71, 108–9, 110–12, 125, 127, 155–69, 185;
    and the Dogger Bank incident (1904)
    111–12, 160–1, 169
  Edward VII's visit to as Prince of Wales
    (1984) 156
  Far East expansion 25, 26–7, 32, 38
  foreign ministers 23
  Franco-Russian alliance 12, 19–20, 23, 24,
    25, 38, 42, 45, 46, 50–1, 64, 67–8, 211; and
    German–Russian estrangement 69, 70–1
  history 10–11
  public opinion in 12, 23–4, 69–70
  and revolutionary disturbances (1905/6)
    51–2, 55, 212
  royal family 21–3
  Three Emperors' League 25–6, 59
  and the War Scare (1904/5) 111–12
  see also Alexander III, Tsar;
    German–Russian relations; Nicholas II,
    Tsar
Russian nationalism 17
Russo-Japanese War 26, 47–50, 52, 69, 70,
  111, 157, 158, 162, 169

St Petersburg, Wilhelm II's visit (1897) 34–5
Salisbury, Marquess of 32, 41, 77, 78, 85, 87,
  88, 92, 100, 181
Samoan Islands dispute 91, 92, 94
Sazonov, Sergei D. 23, 62, 64, 67, 68, 191
Schebeko, Colonel 49, 111
Schoen, Wilhelm Baron von 206

Seckendorff, Götz Count von 104, 119, 120,
  199
Serbia
  and German–Russian relations 68
  and war with Turkey 55
Sergei, Russian Grand Duke 22, 33
Seven Years' War 37
Siberia, Russian expansion in 25, 31–2, 42
Sophie, Crown Princess of Greece 119
Soulange-Boudin, M. 34
South African (Boer) War 93, 95–6, 143–4,
  156
Soveral, Luis, Marquis de 104–5, 106, 139
  anti-German feelings 135, 136, 173, 178–9
  and Edward VII's visit to Paris 144–5, 146,
    147
Spain, and Anglo-French relations 150, 153
Spitzemberg, Hildegard Baroness von 58, 108
Spring-Rice, Cecil 56, 139, 177, 178
Stamfordham, Lord, see Bigge, Sir Arthur 192
Steinberg, Jonathan 204
Stolypin, Peter A. 166, 169, 190
Stone, Norman 2–3
Stumm, Wilhelm von 153, 172, 182
Sudan, Fashoda crisis (1898/9) 37
Swinemünde, meeting between Wilhelm II and
  Nicholas II at (1907) 54
Szögyény-Marich, Ladislaus Count von 117

Taft, William Howard 210
Tangiers, Wilhelm II's landing at (1905)
  113–15
Tattenbach, Christian Count von (German
  minister in Lisbon) 105–6, 108, 146–7
Three Emperors' League (Germany, Russia
  and Austria) 25–6, 59, 67, 70
Tirpitz, Admiral Alfred von 36, 82, 93, 137–8,
  187, 199, 207, 209
Tittoni (Italian foreign minister) 127, 170
Touchard, Admiral 52–3
Triple Alliance (Germany, Austria and Italy)
  19
Tschirschky und Bögendorff, Heinrich von
  36, 62, 120, 200
Turkey, war with the Balkan League 65, 66–7
Tweedmouth letter controversy (1908)
  128–30, 174

United States of America, and Wilhelm II
  116, 133–4

Versailles, Treaty of (1919) 3
Victor Emmanuel III, King of Italy 107
Victoria, Crown Princess of Prussia (Vicky) 17
  pro-British feelings 73–4, 91, 95

Victoria (*cont.*)
  relations with Wilhelm II   75–7, 78, 80–1,
    84, 139
Victoria of Hesse, Princess   159
Victoria, Queen   18, 33, 39, 114
  and the Coburg succession   91–2
  death and funeral   79, 96–7
  and Edward VII's political role   180–1
  and the Kruger telegram affair   89
  memorial to   201
  and Osborne House   103
  relations with Wilhelm II   77–80, 85–6,
    92
Viktoria Luise, Princess (daughter of Wilhelm
    II)   193, 197, 202, 206
Vladimir, Russian Grand Duke   22, 30, 33, 40
Vogel, Barbara   3

Waldersee, General Alfred Count von   18, 39,
    75
Wallace, Sir Donald Mackenzie   47, 52, 126,
    151, 163–4
  anti-German feelings   173, 176
Waterloo, Battle of   107–8
Waters, Colonel W. H.-H. (British military
    attaché in Berlin)   106
Weber, Max   5, 6, 170
Wehler, Hans-Ulrich   5–7
West German revisionist historians   5, 6
Wickham Steed, H.   154
Wiesbaden, meeting of Wilhelm II and
    Nicholas II at   32, 45–6
Wilhelm, Crown Prince (son of Wilhelm II)
    42–3
  invitation to visit England   120, 121–2, 123–4
  wedding   115–17
Wilhelm I, Kaiser   18, 74, 75, 76, 81, 82
Wilhelm II, Kaiser
  abdication and exile   138–9
  accession   17
  and Anglo-French relations   150
  and Anglo-German relations   12–13, 14, 31,
    73–140; and Admiral Fisher   176;
    anti-British remarks   107–8, 189; and the
    Battenburg marriage controversy   75–6,
    77, 81, 82, 139; and the British political
    system   197–9; and the British royal
    family   12–13, 17, 73–88; and the
    diplomatic corps in London   178–9;
    Edward VII's death   137–8; Edward
    VII's failure to visit Berlin   106–7, 127–8;
    Edward VII's refusal to visit on way to
    Marienbad (1905)   119–21; and George
    V   193; incident with Lascelles (1905)
    116–17; and Lord Esher   173–4, 175;

meeting with Edward VII at Friedrichshof
    (1908)   126, 131, 153, 154, 172, 201;
    relations with Edward VII   12–13, 73,
    79–88, 96–140, 151–2, 188–90, 196–7,
    208–9, 212; Tweedmouth letter
    controversy   128–30, 174
  and Anglo-Russian relations   55–6, 110–11
  attempts to win over the Americans   116,
    133–4
  and the Balkan–Turkey war (1912)   66, 67
  and the Boer War   95–6
  and the Bosnian crisis (1908/9)   12
  character   4
  and the Coburg succession   91–2
  and the Crown Prince's invitation to
    England   121–2, 123–4
  Daily Telegraph interview   133, 134, 170, 195
  and the disposal of Osborne House   103
  domestic policies   18–19
  and Edward VII's visit to Kiel (1904)
    109–10
  and Edward VII's visit to Paris   146–7
  and the First World War   71–2
  and the Franco-Russian alliance   45
  and German foreign policy   213
  and German historians   4
  and German–Russian relations   12, 14,
    15–72, 211–12; criticisms of Nicholas II
    16, 39, 40, 61–2; and Russian expansion in
    the Far East   26–7, 32, 45; and Russian
    foreign ministers   23; and the Russian
    royal family   21, 22–3; and the
    Russo-Japanese War   47–50, 52, 69;
    secret correspondence with Nicholas II
    24–5, 33; and Tsar Alexander III   17–18,
    25; visit to St Petersburg (1897)   34–5
  and *Gesellschaftsgeschichte* (history of society)
    5–6, 7
  and Gleichen   117–18
  and the Kruger telegram affair (1896)   31,
    78, 88–90, 91, 93
  meetings with Nicholas II; Baltic Port   65;
    Danzig   40–1, 42, 44; Darmstadt   32–3,
    45; Potsdam   37–8, 62–4; Reval   27,
    43–4, 71; Swinemünde   54; Wiesbaden
    32, 45–6
  and monarchical rule   1, 8–9, 27, 28
  and Morocco (Tangiers escapade)   113–15,
    148–9, 150
  and naval armaments   93, 94, 102, 107, 122,
    131–2, 135, 154, 184–5, 187, 194, 206–8,
    210
  relations with his mother   73–7, 75–7, 78,
    80–1, 84

relations with Queen Victoria 77–80, 85–6, 92, 139
visits to Britain 78–9, 81, 85–6; (1902) 101–2; (1907) 199, 200, 202, 203–4, 205; (1911) 196, 201; Cowes regatta 86, 87, 90; as Kaiser 87–8, 92–5; for Queen Victoria's funeral 96–7
and the War Scare (1904/5) 112–13

Witte, Sergei 16, 17, 38, 46, 68, 162
Wolff-Metternich, Count *see* Metternich, Count
Wortley, Colonel Stuart 144, 145

Zedlitz-Trützschler, Robert Count von 110, 125, 170, 183